The Masterworks of Literature Series

SYLVIA E. BOWMAN, *Editor*
Indiana University

Sut Lovingood's Yarns

Sut Lovingood's Yarns

by GEORGE WASHINGTON HARRIS

Edited for the Modern Reader by
M. Thomas Inge
MICHIGAN STATE UNIVERSITY

COLLEGE & UNIVERSITY PRESS · *Publishers*
NEW HAVEN, CONN.

Copyright © 1966 by
College and University Press Services, Inc.
All Rights Reserved

Library of Congress Catalog Card Number: 65-26678

New Material, Introduction and Notes
by M. Thomas Inge

MANUFACTURED IN THE UNITED STATES OF AMERICA BY
UNITED PRINTING SERVICES, INC.
NEW HAVEN, CONN.

Contents

	PAGE
Introduction	9
Preface	25
Dedicatory	29
Sut Lovingood's Daddy, Acting Horse	33
Sut's New-Fangled Shirt	39
The Widow McCloud's Mare	44
Parson John Bullen's Lizards	51
A Razor-Grinder in a Thunder-Storm	59
Old Skissim's Middle Boy	63
Blown Up With Soda	69
Sicily Burns's Wedding	76
Old Burns's Bull-Ride	84
Sut Lovingood's Chest Story	90
The Snake-Bit Irishman	97
Eaves-Dropping a Lodge of Free-Masons	101
Taurus in Lynchburg Market	107
Mrs. Yardley's Quilting	114
Sut Lovingood's Dog	123
Sut at a Negro Night-Meeting	128
Sut Lovingood's Sermon	138
Bart Davis's Dance	144
Tripetown: Twenty Minutes for Breakfast	152
Hen Baily's Reformation	155
Frustrating a Funeral	163
Rare Ripe Garden-Seed	174
Contempt of Court—Almost	186

	PAGE
Trapping a Sheriff	193
Dad's Dog-School	206
Sut Lovingood's Adventures in New York	221
Sut Lovingood at Bull's Gap	230
Sut Lovingood Travels With Old Abe as His Confidential Friend and Advisor	241
Sut Lovingood With Old Abe on His Journey	244
Sut Lovingood Lands Old Abe Safe at Last	248
Sut Lovingood's Hog Ride	253
Sut Lovingood's Big Dinner Story	260
The Rome Egg Affair	270
Sut Lovingood, on the Puritan Yankee	272
Sut Lovingood Reports What Bob Dawson Said, After Marrying a Substitute	276
Sut Lovingood's Big Music Box Story	282
Sut Lovingood, a Chapter from His Autobiography	287
The Forthcoming Early Life of Sut Lovingood, By His Dad	295
The Early Life of Sut Lovingood, Written by His Dad	298
The Early Life of Sut Lovingood (Continued)	303
The Early Life of Sut Lovingood (Concluded)	306
Bill Ainsworth's Quarter Race	307
Sut Lovingood's Allegory	315
"Well! Dad's Dead"	321
On Young Gals and Old Ones	326
Sut Lovingood Sets Up with a Gal—One Pop Baily	329
Glossary	333

Sut Lovingood's Yarns

Introduction

ONLY within the last three decades has the work of the humorists of the Old Southwest come to the serious attention of critics. This vigorous literature, based largely upon frontier oral tradition, not only gave Mark Twain his literary background and influenced much of his work, but was also an important influence on modern southern literature in general and, in particular, on the work of no less a writer than William Faulkner. Among the humorists of the Old Southwest, George Washington Harris was the most gifted and original; and his creation, Sut Lovingood, is one of the most genuine, robust comic figures in American literature.

I

The first scholar to accord Harris a position for the serious consideration of modern literary critics was Franklin J. Meine in his pioneer collection of humorous writings *Tall Tales of the Southwest* (1930). His importance was brought into sharper focus by four subsequent authoritative studies: Constance Rourke's *American Humor* (1931), Bernard De Voto's *Mark Twain's America* (1932), Walter Blair's *Native American Humor* (1937), and F. O. Matthiessen's *American Rennaissance* (1941). Harris was given his most complete biographical and critical appraisal by Donald Day in three admirable articles, the first published in *American Literature* for January, 1943, and the subsequent two in the *Tennessee Historical Quarterly* of December, 1945, and of March, 1947. Recent scholars who have actively contributed to an assessment of Harris's accomplishment include Edmund Wilson, Kenneth S. Lynn, Brom Weber, and Ben Harris McClary. A critical volume is forthcoming from Milton Rickels for Twayne's United States Authors Series.

The inclusion of examples of Harris's work in American literature text books and humor anthologies has followed as a matter of course—not that he was not well anthologized before. His sketches appeared contemporaneously in such popular collections of humorous stories—to mention a few—as *A Quarter Race in Kentucky*, edited by William T. Porter (1846); *Polly Peablossom's Wedding*, edited by T. A. Burke (1851); and *The Harp of a Thousand Strings*, edited by S. P. Avery (1858).

Yet, not since the last printing around the turn of the century of the original edition of Harris's one collection of stories, *Sut Lovingood. Yarns Spun by a "Nat'ral Born Durn'd Fool"* (New York: Dick and Fitzgerald 1867), has a new edition of this seminal work in American humor appeared. And besides that, a wealth of uncollected sketches and yarns by Harris are extant. Most of these appeared in print only in newspapers of the time, but many of them were undoubtedly destined for publication in a second collection of tales, the manuscript of which was lost after Harris's sudden death.

This edition contains the best of the Sut Lovingood sketches written by Harris between 1854 and 1869, the year of his death. It includes the complete text of *Sut Lovingood. Yarns Spun by a "Nat'ral Born Durn'd Fool"* and most of the other hitherto uncollected pieces which appeared in several Tennessee newspapers (as did most of his writings originally): the Nashville *Union and American* and *Press and Times*, the Chattanooga *Daily American Union*, and the Knoxville *Press and Messenger* and *Daily Press and Herald*.

With one exception, Harris's order of arrangement of the tales in the 1867 collection has been maintained (beginning with "Sut Lovingood's Daddy, Acting Horse," and concluding with "Dad's Dog-School"); the uncollected pieces follow immediately in chronological order according to date of publication. The one exception in this procedure is the insertion of the story "Sut Lovingood's Chest Story" into the text of the original collection following "Sicily Burns's Wedding." It is placed here because it completes the trilogy of tales concerning the Burns family which began with "Blown Up With Soda," and it brings to a conclusion Sut's revenge on Sicily for the love-soda prank she perpetrated on him in the beginning. Harris undoubtedly intended for the story to be included in his published collection, for he mentions a principal character, Dock

Fabin, in paragraph five of the Preface to the original edition; but for some reason it was omitted.

The stories collected for the first time are each followed by a note indicating the newspaper source from which the text was derived. No indication has been made of possible earlier printings or subsequent reprintings in other newspapers, but in many cases this was the first and only printing. Since none of Harris's manuscripts have survived, the first printing (or the nearest to the first now extant) of all material included has constituted the copy-text. The editorial procedure has been to correct the obvious typographical errors and to regularize the punctuation for the sake of consistency and readability. Also, in accordance with Harris's preferred spelling in the 1867 collection, Sut's surname has been changed in all cases to "Lovingood" from the original spelling of "Lovengood."

Several of Harris's political satires which involved Sut have been omitted because they depend too heavily upon a knowledge of local events and personalities for appreciation and because the space was not available to explain their historical relevance with introductory notes. Since most readers will be familiar enough with general Southern sentiment during the Civil War years and with such figures as Lincoln and Grant, sketches alluding to these have been included without additional comment.

Also not included are several fragments or incomplete texts of stories which have not survived in their entirety, as well as one decidedly spurious sketch, a poor attempt at imitating Harris. The second installment of "Sut Lovingood in New York" has been included (the first part is not extant) because it is complete enough to stand alone. We have evidence of several tales the texts of which have not yet been uncovered, such as the fragment cited at the conclusion of this introduction from the story of Sut's death. This loss is regrettable, especially since it alone would have been the suitable story with which to conclude the present collection.

II

Harris and his incorrigible creation, Sut, have elicited a variety of reactions across the years. Sut's escapades have a tendency to either completely repugnate the reader or decidedly capture his fancy and imagination. A typical reaction to Sut's indelicacy was that of Jennette Tandy, who wrote (*Crackerbox Philosophers,* 1925): "There is an extravagance about his stories which just passes discretion," and she added that she had "more than once been embarrassed" in her childhood by a Sut Lovingood yarn. Stark Young, in his novel *So Red the Rose* (1934), set in Tennessee before the Civil War, has a character react in a similar fashion at the mention of Sut and comment upon his stories as being "well known but generally considered rather broad." Recently, in the unpublished family memoirs of a retired Nashville business man, the fact was mentioned that one of the few books read by his father was the collection of Harris's yarns. When asked if he were familiar with the book himself, he replied no, with a waggish grin, and then said that he had always heard that Sut was a bit too bawdy.

The most vehement condemnation has come from Edmund Wilson, who wrote in an article for the *New Yorker* on May 7, 1955 (reprinted in *Patriotic Gore,* 1962), "One of the most striking things about 'Sut Lovingood' is that it is all offensive as possible. It takes a pretty strong stomach to get through it.... I should say that, as far as my experience goes, it is by far the most repellent book of any real literary merit in American literature."

But the positive comments have outnumbered the negative and have exceeded in spirited overstatement even Wilson's extreme reaction. During the writer's lifetime, Elbridge G. Eastman—the editor of the Nashville *Union and American* in which many of Harris's stories first appeared—enthusiastically wrote on June 30, 1858, that the Sut Lovingood sketches "have obtained a circulation and popularity, throughout the country, which no similar productions, in modern times have enjoyed. Sut is well known in the distant States of the Union, as he is at home; he is as great a favorite in the refined and educated circles of the Southern and Eastern Cities as he is among his native mountains of Tennessee. His stories are sought with avidity wherever genuine wit and humor are appreciated. ... He is regarded by the critic and the scholar as a compound of fun and folly blended by the power of genius into a character at once life-like, truthful and original. ... [We] venture to predict that Sut will live in the recollection of his acquaintances ... as long as there are lovers of good fun and mean whisky on earth."

Franklin J. Meine paid the high compliment in 1930 that, "for vivid imagination, comic plot, Rabelaisian touch, and sheer *fun,* the *Sut Lovingood Yarns* surpass anything else in American humor." And a host of scholars have agreed with Walter Blair's undeniable statement in 1937: "In *Sut Lovingood*, the antebellum humor of the South reaches its highest level of achievement before Mark Twain."

III

Oddly enough, the center of all this attention was not by profession or intention a humorous writer, a fact which is nearly common to all the humorists of the Old Southwestern school. They were all either professional men—doctors, lawyers, journalists, actors, politicians—or common farmers and business men; writing sketches was a hobby or sideline. They all shared, however, the same impulse—the desire to amuse. They did not write for a literary public. Their work appeared first in newspapers and periodicals directed to a male audience, as their ribaldry indicates; and that their work ever appeared between hard covers was due solely, as a matter of course, to their popularity.

Some were possessed with a desire to report and preserve the peculiarities of the local scene, and in their own fashion the Southwestern humorists were pioneer realists. But they should not be confused, as they frequently are, with the local-color writers of a generation later who consciously attempted to preserve the regional eccentricities passing away with the defeated Southern society. Both groups achieved an accurate use of dialect and a realistic portrayal of character—but for different reasons.

Sut is a realistic representative of the typical Tennessee mountaineer, a native born of the soil, and perhaps an early fulfillment of what Walt Whitman believed in *Democratic Vistas* in 1871: "Today, doubtless, the infant genius of American poetic expression ... lies sleeping far away, happily unrecognized and uninjured by the coteries, the art-writers, the talkers and the critics of the saloons, or the lecturers in the colleges—lies sleeping, aside, unrecking itself, in some western idiom, or native Michigan or Tennessee repartee, or stump speech. ... Rude and coarse nursing beds, these; but only from such beginnings and stocks, indigenous here, may happly arrive, be grafted, and sprout in time, flowers of genuine American aroma, and fruits truly and fully our own." Harris's writings were grounded in an acquaintance with many kinds of native stocks and occupational experiences, were phrased in "Tennessee repartee," and remained untouched in manner and style by contemporary literary "coteries."

The Tennessee dialect in which Harris couched the yarns of Sut Lovingood has been praised and condemned for obvious reasons. The language has been praised for its accurate and vivid recreation of the nineteenth-century local Southern idiom. Napier Wilt (*Some American Humorists*, 1929) found it "the nearest thing to the undiluted oral humor ... that has found its way into print." F. O. Matthiessen (*American Renaissance*, 1941) wrote that Harris "brings us closer than any other writer to the indigenous and undiluted resources of the American language ..." Donald Davidson (*The Tennessee*, Vol. I, 1946) has even been able to trace the language—so accurately did Harris preserve it—back to its European origins: "Sut's language was Devonshire, or Southwest England, with some mixture of Scots and brand-new American."

But most serious scholars of dialectal linguistics have placed Harris without the pales of those writers who have attempted to preserve with calculated accuracy the grammatical, lexical, and phonetic peculiarities of a particular region or people. He has been associated with such writers as Henry Wheeler Shaw (Josh Billings) and David Ross Locke (Petroleum V. Nasby), who exuberantly misspelled words as an indication of their characters' illiterateness as well as for the funny appearance they made on the printed page. One scholar, in fact, found the frequency of misspelled words without phonetic meaning in Harris "annoying" (Sumner Ives, "A Theory of Literary Dialect," *Tulane Studies in English*, II, 1950).

It is quite true that Harris did not approach his employment of dialect with any scientific or systematic accuracy.

However, anyone who is familiar with southern speech of the less-educated classes, and with the East Tennessee brand in particular, will find that, when read aloud, Harris has achieved in the main a fairly accurate transcription of the native vernacular. At the same time, Harris also felt free to indulge in frequent and varied misspellings, or "eye dialect," as it is called. (*Of* is spelled indiscriminately two ways, *ov* and *ove*, for example; but both preserve the actual manner of pronunciation.) If, as some have contended, the dialect is his least valuable achievement, it need not impede an appreciation of Harris's artistry which is so rich in other qualities.

But many have found Harris almost unreadable because of the dialect. To offset this difficulty when quoting from a tale, such scholars as Walter Blair and F. O. Matthiessen —following the lead of Bernard De Voto in *Mark Twain's America* (1932)—felt it necessary to transliterate the dialect. In 1954, Brom Weber published a selection of stories from the original Sut Lovingood collection, but he translated them into common American English. Although this may have presented Harris to many readers unwilling to surmount the slight difficulty of deciphering his dialect, it also brought down upon Weber the critical wrath of many scholars and textual purists—an unfair amount perhaps in view of his editorial purpose.

Another solution to the problem is offered in the present edition. Since extensive footnoting is untenable and might only impede the reader who has an occasional difficulty, a glossary has been added at the rear of the volume. It is not a complete lexicon to Harris's work, and only those words which might present difficulties are included. If a word seemed to be easily recognizable, despite a slight misspelling for phonetic or arbitrary reasons, it has been excluded. The standard English equivalent for the word in question is given; and, if the equivalent can be found in most abridged dictionaries, no further definition was attempted. Also excluded are Harris's ingenious word coinages (such as *cumbustifikashun* or *kerthrash*) which may be figured out in context.*

IV

Harris had ample opportunity to learn the Tennessee dialect for he had been brought at a very early age to Knoxville, Tennessee, by his half-brother, Samuel Bell, from Allegheny City, Pennsylvania, where he was born on March 20, 1814. From the time he was old enough to know the difference, he became a *Southerner* in the most zealous sense of the word. In all, he received no more than eighteen months of schooling; and, because of an expressed interest in mechanical skills, his half-brother, a worker in metals, apprenticed him in his jewelry shop.

At twenty-one, Harris left the trade of metal working to answer the call of adventure and the fulfillment of the dream of any southern boy then living in a river town (as Mark Twain tells us in *Life on the Mississippi*)—a dream promised by the steamboats running between Knoxville and Decatur, Alabama. He was appointed captain in 1835 of the steamboat *Knoxville*, a responsible position which he held for three years. Such competence, Donald Davidson has suggested, bespeaks a precociousness in river knowledge which could result only from earlier service on flatboats and keelboats. Those who knew Harris during these years have described him as small built, quiet and unassuming (but actively alert when challenged to defend a cause); public spirited in citizenship; personable; and, upon occasion, as full of jokes and tricks as his literary brainchild, Sut.

Farming next attracted Harris's interest, and in 1839 he contracted for a piece of land in the foothills of the Smokies. Continuing debts due to poor financial manage-

---

* The glossary makes no pretense of completeness, and the editor will welcome corrections and additions. The primary reference authorities in compiling the glossary have been *A Dictionary of Americanisms,* edited by Mitford M. Mathews (1951); *A Dictionary of Slang and Unconventional English* by Eric Partridge (1956); *The American Thesaurus of Slang* by Lester V. Berry and Melvin Van Den Bark (Second edition, 1952); and *Webster's Third New International Dictionary* (1961).

ment caused Harris to lose the farm in 1842. He then returned to metal working and operated a shop in Knoxville for seven years. During the 1850's, while Harris was doing his best writing, he drifted through a variety of jobs. He was associated with the Holston Glass Works and he established a sawmill; both business ventures were failures. In the political ferment of 1856, he allied his sympathies with the Democratic party. After surveying the Ducktown Copper Mines (lower East Tennessee was a prime prospecting area for copper then), he was appointed postmaster at Knoxville, a position which lasted only six months. Further unsuccessful political ventures were followed by a position with the Nashville and Chattanooga Railroad. When Nashville fell to Union forces in February, 1862, Harris probably joined the general exodus of southern sympathizers with his wife and children. The only places he was definitely known to have been during the war were Trenton, Georgia, and Decatur, Alabama. But after the war he returned to a position with the Wills Valley Railroad, in whose employ he remained for the rest of his life. His first wife died in 1866; in 1869, he married a widow from Decatur, Alabama.

Less than two months later, after fifty-five years of continuous defeat and failure in professional and political life (except for his popular but unprofitable sketches), including having to observe the fall of his beloved South, Harris died on December 11, 1869 from unknown causes after his return from a business trip to Lynchburg, Virginia. The mysterious circumstances of his death elicited the following appeal a few days later in the Knoxville *Press and Herald:* "In behalf of a community, who deeply deplore the death of Captain Harris, and who shudder to think of his horrible, lonely ride in a railway train, without one pitying glance or gentle hand to soothe his dying moments, we ask that whatever facts in the possession of any one, tending to explain this most mysterious death, be published, that the world may know, whether Capt. George W. Harris, died by the stroke of his God, or the poisoned chalice of a wicked man."

V

Despite the unfortunate circumstances of the life and death of this follower of dreams and unrealized goals, his wide experiences and his continually changing interests provided him with a vast storehouse of material from which to draw when he set pen to paper. Though he was not widely traveled, he had every opportunity to observe the manners and customs of the people of his home regions. Most of his jobs kept him in constant contact with people, and he undoubtedly heard many tales at the then popular social gatherings. These stories he later reshaped to his own purposes.

How Harris came to learn the craft of writing, especially in consideration of his brief education, we cannot tell. More than likely he learned to write by emulating other writers of his day (he was known to be an omnivorous reader), and perhaps by submitting his efforts for critical comment to Elbridge G. Eastman, a friend who was then editor of the Knoxville *Argus and Commercial Herald.* At any rate, it was while Harris was farming in 1840 that he began to write political sketches for the *Argus.* He next contributed to the New York *Spirit of the Times* (edited by William T. Porter) several "sporting epistles" which he occasionally enlivened with descriptions of local East Tennessee events and of the "odd specimens of humanity" he observed. Then he began to contribute both to the *Spirit* and to a Nashville paper—now edited by his friend Eastman—a series of stories based entirely on local customs and characters.

In one, "A Knob Dance—A Tennessee Frolic" (reprinted by Meine in *Tall Tales of the Southwest),* Harris began to turn the sights of his experience into the vivid action and colorful imagery which later flowed so easily from his pen. He also adopted the framework device, so important in the development of Sut Lovingood, that permits another person, Dick Harlan, to tell the tale. Typical also of his later coarse, earthy, but wildly extravagant style was "A Snake-Bit Irishman" (*Spirit of the Times,* January 17, 1840), which was purported to relate an occurrence Harris observed while on a hunting party in the mountains and which he later reshaped into a "Sut" yarn. For years,

Harris was known as "the author of the 'Snakebit Irishman'." The remainder of his early sketches were rather nostalgic in temper; and, though moderately humorous, they do not represent Harris at his best.

VI

Then in the November 4, 1854, issue of the *Spirit of the Times* appeared the tale "Sut Lovingood's Daddy 'Acting Horse,'" the debut of the inimitable Sut Lovingood. In this milestone in Harris's career, he attained a fortuitous combination of the elements of Southwestern humor, and he distinguished himself as a superior to his contemporaries in comic artistry. Harris had mastered by now the use of the tall tale and the depiction of local color and character, and he had already experimented with the device of allowing one character to tell the story. The use of a narrator as a framing device was a classic technique most prominently used by Boccaccio and Chaucer, and it became the standard pattern among the Southwestern yarnspinners.

Such humorists as Joseph Baldwin and Augustus Baldwin Longstreet had for the most part written their sketches with a certain degree of detachment. From a point of elevation, they viewed and moralized upon the odd habits of the strange characters presented in their essays. But Harris deserted the traditional gentlemanly style; he permitted a representative of the East Tennessee mountaineers to tell a story in his own vernacular and from his own point of view—just as Mark Twain did thirty years later with a southern teenage rebel in *Huckleberry Finn*. The detached gentleman, in the person of "George" Harris himself, remained a part of Harris's framework; but his only purpose was to provide a frame of reality by which the reader could make an immediate transitional step into and return from the wild and fanciful world of Sut Lovingood. And in some of the later yarns, "George" disappeared altogether; the name of Sut in the title of a yarn automatically prepared the reader for the fantastic tale or monologue to follow.

The remainder of Harris's writing career was devoted primarily to exploiting the fortunate creation of his imagination, Sut Lovingood. There may be significance in that strikingly incongruous selection of names. "Sut" is a common name among backwoods folk and farmers (perhaps an abbreviation of Sutpen, a name given by Faulkner to the central character in his novel *Absalom, Absalom!*); and the surname is composed of two meaningful words: "loving" and "good." Thus the combination of a common, earthy name with a surname of spiritual connotations may reflect an intent on Harris's part to suggest that Sut, like all humankind, is of a spiritual and physical nature, the one usually in conflict with the other.

Following a practice which was to become usual, the second Sut sketch was a political satire written in 1856 to express Harris's views on that year's presidential race between Buchanan, Fillmore, and Fremont. At least one-third of his total output now extant, for that matter, has, explicit or disguised political implications. A satirist of no mean order, he cannot be matched for pure invective in the series of satirical yarns attacking Abraham Lincoln, "Sut Lovingood Travels with Old Abe," published just after his inauguration as President. And Harris approached the brilliant but vicious irony of the master ironist himself, Jonathan Swift, when he has Sut suggest in a vituperative monologue on the Puritan Yankee that, when the *Mayflower* arrived, the Indians should have "carcumsized the head ove the las' durn'd one, burnt thar clos, pack'd thar carkuses heads-an-tails, herrin fashun, in thar old ship, sot the sails, an' pinted her snout the way Ward's ducks went...." Harris's series, "The Early Life of Sut Lovingood, Written by his Dad," is a direct parody of "The early life of Grant, by his father," which appeared in the New York *Ledger* in March, 1868.

In some of the satirical pieces, Sut is forced out of character as a political mouthpiece in that he expresses and understands things beyond his expected intellectual range. But in most cases, it is simply a matter of the same fun-loving, whiskey-guzzling Sut of the non-political pieces being unleashed and sicked by Harris on the designated objects of scorn, as in the Lincoln satires. For the most part, however, Sut is a credible and coherent creation; he was based, according to tradition and some evidence (uncovered by Ben Harris McClary), on a real person—William S. Miller, a corn farmer from the Ducktown mining area who may have assisted Harris while surveying that locale for the Hiwassee Mining Company. But Harris had no qualms when the name became attached to him and he was addressed as "Sut." In this acceptance he was quite unlike Southwestern humorist Johnson Jones Hooper, who became disagreeable when people called him Simon Suggs, the name of his picaresque creation.

VII

Sut Lovingood the character, in all his prejudice, brutality, cowardice, sensuality, coarseness, and vulgarity —coupled with his basic respect for veracity and freedom and hatred of hypocrisy—lies close to the basic nature of humanity. To see Sut as totally sadistic is to refuse to recognize within ourselves Conrad's "heart of darkness," our own tendency towards innate depravity. Sut is only doing what Hawthorne's Reverend Dimmesdale lacked the courage to do in *The Scarlet Letter:* Sut openly confesses to the world his "univarsal onregenerit human nater," and he proclaims "I'se a goner I 'speck, an' I jis don't keer a durn. I'm no count, no how. ...I feels like I'd be glad *tu be* dead, only I'se feared ove the dyin. I don't keer fur herearter, fur hits onpossibil fur me tu hev ara soul."

No doubt, Sut immensely enjoys "raising hell" and sowing pain and discomfort; but, at the same time, Sut attacks not morality but the perverters of moral principles. This is why Sut's pet victims are "groanin ole Hardshell" circuit riders, who present one face, stretched "long enuf tu fill the pius standurd," to their congregation; but on the side they make and sell poor quality moonshine whiskey, subsist upon invitations to dinner, rob corn fields, father illegitimate children, and hold night meetings which develop into bacchanalian orgies. And, since nearly all of the victims of Sut's pranks are either hypocritical, falsely self-righteous, sinful, or down-right criminal, Sut in effect may be considered an unintentional reformer or divine scourge—of sorts. Sut is never out to profit materially from human gullibility; he is unlike Hooper's Simon Suggs and Faulkner's Flem Snopes, who are the consummate sharpers of American literature.

VIII

The most frequently repeated phrase with which Sut describes himself is "nat'ral born durn'd fool." By designating him a fool, Harris, without conscious intent, placed Sut squarely within one of the most persistent European literary traditions used for the artistic criticism of contemporary societies and human nature. When the funny fellow in motley dress and cap and bells, who entertained kings with levity and license, passed out of existence and into a symbolical figure who inspired a great body of imaginative literature, tradition granted him in exchange for his lack of normal wit a divinely inspired higher wisdom. Hence, Shakespeare sprinkled courtly fools among his plays almost always as vehicles for his more perceptive and most profound philosophical reflections.

Among the finest contributions to the so-called "Fool-literature" of the fifteenth and sixteenth centuries which influenced Shakespere was Sebastian Brant's verse satire *Narrenschiff*, which more recently inspired the title and structural image of Katherine Anne Porter's novel, *Ship of Fools*. Sut is a whole ship of fools, compressed into one individual with his feet firmly planted on American soil. When Enid Welsford writes about the traditional fool in her book, *The Fool, His Social and Literary History* (1935), much of what she says is equally applicable to Sut:

> The Fool is an unabashed glutton and coward and knave, he is—as we say—a *natural*; we laugh at him and enjoy a pleasant sense of superiority; he looks at us oddly and we suspect that he is our *alter ego;* he winks at us and we are delighted at the discovery that we also are gluttons and cowards and knaves. The rogue has freed us from shame. More than that, he has persuaded us that wasted affection, thwarted ambition, latent guilt are mere delusions to be laughed away. For how can we feel spiritual pain, if we are only animals? But even the primitive joke about the human body has its complexity. We laugh to find that we are as natural as the Fool, but we laugh also because we are normal enough to know how very unnatural it is to be as natural as all that .... the Fool does not necessarily inhabit a

romantic or beautiful world; on the contrary his world may very well be adapted to his nature, which is often greedy, grasping, dirty and heartless .... The Fool is a creator not of beauty but of spiritual freedom.

Like the Fool he is, Sut cannily sees beneath appearances to the heart of reality and suffers no illusions about himself or the world. His joy of life and his spirit of freedom, in spite of adverse circumstances, ally him with the Wife of Bath, Falstaff, and all the great comic figures of literature.

IX

Besides the achievement of creating such a corporeal figure as Sut, there is much to be admired in Harris's artistry. He displays a remarkable and inventive talent in his wild and complex use of metaphors, similes, and other imagery. In his definitive study of Harris's imagery (*American Literature*, May, 1959), Milton Rickels notes:

> The first effect of [his] frequency of imagery is speed and intensity. The reader is whirled into the illusion of sheer delight in motion and wild action. Racy colloquialism, nonce words, corruptions of names and bookish terms, compression of detail, astonishing expansion of connotation, and controlled changes in the tensions of the action and of the language, shifting from litotes to the highest hyperbole, give a constant illusion of speed and movement. Images are expanded by piling detail upon detail until the reader is bewildered in a complexity of emotions and ideas.

This imagery accounts for the impression of fast-moving action in the reading of a Sut yarn, something F. O. Matthiessen described aptly as a "wonderful kinetic quality." The only writer who was able to approach Harris in this ability was William Faulkner, also a self-confessed admirer of Sut.

As an epitaph for both Harris and Sut, perhaps we can make no better choice than the brief funeral oration of Parson Bullen over Sut Lovingood's corpse at the grave (the full text of which story unfortunately has not been preserved; only these lines survive by quotation in Henry Watterson's *The Compromises of Life and Other Lectures*, 1906):

"We air met, my brethering, to bury this ornery cuss. He had hosses, an' he run 'em; he had chickens, an' he fit 'em; he had kiards, an' he played 'em. Let us try an' ricollect his virtues—ef he had any—an' forgit his vices —ef we can. *For of sich air the kingdom of heaven!*"

—M. Thomas Inge.

Michigan State University.

Preface

"You must have a preface, Sut; your book will then be ready. What shall I write?"

"Well, ef I must, I must; fur I s'pose the perducktion cud no more show hitsef in publick wifout hit, than a coffin-maker cud wif out black clothes, an' yet what's the use ove either ove em, in pint ove good sense? Smells tu me sorter like a durned humbug, the hole ove hit—a little like cuttin ove the Ten Cummandmints intu the rine ove a water-million; hits jist slashed open an' the inside et outen hit, the rine an' the cummandmints broke all tu pieces an' flung tu the hogs, an' never tho't ove onst—them, nur the 'tarnil fool what cut em thar. But ef a orthur *mus'* take off his shoes afore he goes intu the publick's parlor, I reckon I kin du hit wifout durtyin my feet, fur I hes socks on.

"Sumtimes, George, I wished I cud read an' write, jis' a littil; but then hits bes' es hit am, fur ove all the fools the worild hes tu contend wif, the edicated wuns am the worst; they breeds ni ontu all the devilment a-gwine on. But I wer a-thinkin, ef I cud write mysef, hit wud then *raley* been my book. I jis' tell yu now, I don't like the idear ove yu writin a perduckshun, an' me a-findin the brains. 'Taint the fust case tho' on record by a durned site. Usin uther men's brains is es lawful es usin thar plunder, an' jis' es common, so I don't keer much nohow. I dusn't 'speck this yere perduckshun will sit purfeckly quiet ontu the stumicks ove sum pussons—them hu hes a holesum fear ove the devil, an' orter hev hit, by geminey. Now, fur thar speshul well-bein herearter, I hes jis' this tu say: Ef yu ain't fond ove the smell ove cracklins, stay outen the kitchin; ef yu is fear'd ove smut, yu needn't climb the chimbley; an' ef the moon hurts yer eyes, don't yu ever look at a Dutch cheese. That's jis' all ove hit.

"Then thar's sum hu haint much faith in thar repertashun standin much ove a strain; they'll be powerful keerful how an' whar they reads my words. Now, tu them I haint wun word tu say: they hes been preached to, an' prayed fur, now ni ontu two thousand years an' I won't dart weeds whar thuty-two poun shot bounces back.

"Then thar's the book-butchers, orful on killin an' cuttin up, but cud no more perjuce a book, than a bull-butcher cud perjuce a bull. S'pose they takes a noshun tu stick, skin, an' cut up this yere one. Ef they is fond ove sicknin skeers, I advises em tu take holt tu onst; but fust I begs tu refer em respectively tu the fate ove three misfortinit pussons menshun'd inside yere—Passun Bullin, Dock Fabin, an Sheriff Dolton. Read keerfully what happened tu them afore yu takes eny ove my flesh ontu yer claws, ur my blood ontu yer bills, an' that I now is a durnder fool then I wer in them days, fur I now considers myself a orthur. I hes tuck my stan amung the nashuns ove the yeath, fur I, too, hes made me a book, so ef enybody wants dish rags, I thinks hit wud be more healthy fur em not tu tar em ofen my flag.

"Mos' book-weavers seem tu be skeery folks, fur giner'lly they cums up tu the slaughter pen, whinin an' waggin thar tails, a-sayin they 'knows they is imparfeck'—that 'yu'd scace 'speck one ove my age,' an' so forth, so on, so along. Now ef I *is* a-rowin in that boat, I ain't awar ove hit, I ain't, fur I knows the tremenjus gif I hes fur breedin skeers amung durned fools, an' then I hes a trustin reliance ontu the fidelity, injurance, an' speed ove these yere laigs ove mine to tote me an' my sins away beyant all human ritribushuns ur revenge. Now, 'zamin yer hans, ole ferrits an' weazels, an' ef yu don't hole *bof* bowers an' the ace, yu jis' 'pass' hit.

"Ef eny poor misfortinit devil hu's heart is onder a millstone, hu's raggid children am hungry, an' no bread in the dresser, hu is down in the mud, an' the lucky ones a-trippin him every time he struggils tu his all fours, hu hes fed the famishin an' is now hungry hissef, hu misfortins foller fas' an' foller faster, hu is so foot-sore an' weak that he wishes he wer at the ferry—ef sich a one kin fine a laugh, jis' one, sich a laugh as is remembered wif his keerless boyhood, atwixt these yere kivers—then, I'll thank God that I *hes* made a book, an' feel that I hev got my pay in full.

"Make me a Notey Beney, George. I wants tu put

sumwhar atween the eyebrows ove our book, in big winnin-lookin letters, the sarchin, meanin words, what sum pusson writ ontu a 'oman's garter onst, long ago——"

"Evil be to him that evil thinks."

"Them's em, by jingo! Hed em clost apas' yu, didn't yu? I want em fur a gineral skeer—speshully fur the wimen.

"Now, George, grease hit good, an' let hit slide down the hill hits own way."

Dedicatory

"WELL, Sut, your stories are all ready for the printer; to whom do you wish to dedicate the work?"

"I don't keer much, George; haint hit a kine ove lick-skillet bisness, enyhow—sorter like the waggin ove a dorg's tail, when he sees yu eatin ove sassengers? But yere goes: How wud Anner Dickinson du tu pack hit ontu?"

"Oh, Sut, that would never do. What! dedicate such nonsense as yours to a woman? How will this do?

DEDICATED TO

THE MEMORY OF

ELBRIDGE GERRY EASTMAN,

THE ABLE EDITOR, AND FINISHED GENTLEMAN, THE
FRIEND, WHOSE KINDLY VOICE FIRST INSPIRED
MY TIMID PEN WITH HOPE.

GRATEFUL MEMORY

DROPS A TEAR AMONG THE FLOWERS, AS AFFECTION
STREWS THEM O'ER HIS GRAVE."

"Won't begin tu du, George The idear ove enybody bein grateful, ur rememberin a dead friend now-a-days! Why, if that wer tu git out onto me, I'd never be able tu mix in decent s'ciety while I lived. Tare that up, George."

"Well, what do you say to this, Sut?

TO

WILLIAM CRUTCHFIELD, OF CHATTANOOGA,

MY FRIEND IN STORM AND SUNSHINE, BRAVE ENOUGH TO
BE TRUE, AND TRUE ENOUGH TO BE SINGULAR;
ONE WHO SAYS WHAT HE THINKS, AND VERY
OFTEN THINKS WHAT HE SAYS."

"That won't du either, hoss. 'Tis mos' es bad tu be grateful tu the livin es the dead. I tell yu hit ain't smart. Ef ever yu is grateful *at all*, show hit tu them what yu *expeck will* du a favor, *never* tu the 'tarnil fool what *hes dun hit*. Never es yu expeck tu git tu heaven, *never pay fur a ded hoss*. An' more, every fice ur houn dorg what either him ur me has wallop'd fur thar nastiness, wud open ontu our trail—ontu him fur buyin me, an' ontu me fur bein bought. No, George, I'll do ontill Bill gets poor ur dus sum devilmint. I'll tell yu what I'll du, I'll jis' dedercate this yere perduction *tu the durndest fool* in the United States, an' Massachusets too, he or she. An then, by golly, I'll jis' watch hu claims hit."

"Very well, Sut; how shall I write it? how designate the proper one?"

"Jis' this way; hits the easiest dun thing in the world:

DEDERCATED
WIF THE SYMPERTHYS OVE THE ORTHUR,
TU THE MAN UR 'OMAN, HUEVER THEY BE,
WHAT *DON'T* READ THIS YERE BOOK.

Don't *that* kiver the case tu a dot? Hu knows but what I'se dedercatin hit tu mysef at las'. Well, I don't keer a durn, I kin stan hit, ef the rest ove em kin."

Sut Lovingood's Yarns

Sut Lovingood's Daddy, Acting Horse

"HOLE that ar hoss down tu the yearth." "He's a fixin fur the heavings." "He's a spreadin his tail feathers tu fly. Look out, Laigs, if you aint ready tu go up'ards." "Wo, Shavetail." "Git a fiddil; he's tryin a jig." "Say, Long Laigs, rais'd a power ove co'n didn't yu?" "Taint co'n, hits redpepper."

These and like expressions were addressed to a queer looking, long legged, short bodied, small headed, white haired, hog eyed, funny sort of a genius, fresh from some bench-legged Jew's clothing store, mounted on "Tearpoke," a nick tailed, bow necked, long, poor, pale sorrel horse, half dandy, half devil, and enveloped in a perfect net-work of bridle, reins, crupper, martingales, straps, surcingles, and red ferreting, who reined up in front of Pat Nash's grocery, among a crowd of mountaineers full of fun, foolery, and mean whisky.

This was SUT LOVINGOOD.

"I say, you durn'd ash cats, jis' keep yer shuts on, will ye? You never seed a rale hoss till 1 rid up; you's p'raps stole ur owned shod rabbits ur sheep wif borrerd saddils on, but when you tuck the fus' begrudgin look jis' now at this critter, name Tearpoke, yu wer injoyin a sight ove nex' tu the bes' hoss what ever shell'd nubbins ur toted jugs, an' he's es ded es a still wum, poor ole Tickytail!

"Wo! wo! Tearpoke, yu cussed infunel fidgety hide full ove hell fire, can't yu stan' still an listen while I'se a polishin yer karacter off es a mortul hoss tu these yere durned fools?"

Sut's tongue or his spurs brought Tearpoke into something like passable quietude while he continued:

"Say yu, sum ove yu growin hogs made a re-mark jis' now 'bout redpepper. I jis' wish tu say in a gineral way that eny wurds cupplin redpepper an Tearpoke tugether am durn'd infurnal lies."

"What killed Tickeytail, Sut?" asked an anxious inquirer

after truth.

"Why nuffin, you cussed fool; he jis' died so, standin up et that. Warn't that rale casteel hoss pluck? Yu see, he froze stiff; no, not that adzactly, but starv'd fust, an' froze arterards, so stiff that when dad an' me went tu lay him out an' we push'd him over, he stuck out jis' so (spreading his arms and legs), like ontu a carpenter's bainch, an' we hed tu wait ni ontu seventeen days fur 'im tu thaw afore we cud skin 'im."

"Skin 'im?" interrupted a rat-faced youth, whittling on a corn stalk, "I thot yu wanted tu lay the hoss out."

"The hell yu did! Aint skinin the natral way ove layin out a hoss, I'd like tu no? See a yere, soney, yu tell yer mam tu hev yu sot back jis' bout two years, fur et the rate yu'se a climbin yu stan's a pow'ful chance tu die wif yer shoes on, an' git laid hoss way, yu dus."

The rat-faced youth shut up his knife and subsided.

"Well, thar we wer—dad, an' me (counting on his fingers), an' Sall, an' Jake (fool Jake we calls 'im fur short), an' Jim, an' Phineass, an' Callimy Jane, an' Sharlottyann, an' me, an' Zodiack, an' Cashus Clay, an' Noah Dan Webster, an' the twin gals (Castur and Pollox), an' me, an' Catherin Second, an' Cleopatry Antony, an' Jane Barnum Lind, an' me, an' Benton Bullion, an' the baby what haint nam'd yet, an' me, an' the Prospect, an' mam hersef, all lef in the woods alone, wifout ara hoss tu crup wif."

"Yu'se counted yersef five times, Mister Lovingood," said a tomato-nosed man in ragged overcoat.

"Yas, ole Still-tub, that's jis the perporshun I bears in the famerly fur dam fool, leavin out Dad in course. Yu jis let me alone, an' be a thinkin ove gittin more hoops ontu yu. Yus leakin now; see thar." Ha! ha! from the crowd, and "Still-tub" went into the doggery.

"Warnt that a devil's own mess ove broth fur a 'spectabil white famerly tu be sloshin about in? I be durned ef I didn't feel sorter like stealin a hoss sumtimes, an' I speck I'd a dun hit, but the stealin streak in the Lovingoods all run tu durned fool, an' the onvartus streak all run tu laigs. Jis look down the side ove this yere hoss mos' tu the groun'. Dus yu see em?

"Well we waited, an' wished, an' rested, an' plan'd, an'

wished, an' waited agin, ontil ni ontu strawberry time, hopin sum stray hoss mout cum along; but dorg my cats, ef eny sich good luck ever cums wifin reach ove whar dad is, he's so dod-dratted mean, an' lazy, an' ugly, an' savidge, an' durn fool tu kill.

"Well, one nite he lay awake till cock-crowin a-snortin, an' rollin, an' blowin, an' shufflin, an' scratchin hissef, an' a whisperin at mam a heap, an' at breckfus' I foun' out what hit ment. Says he, 'Sut, I'll tell yu what we'll du: I'll be hoss *mysef*, an' pull the plow whilst yu drives me, an' then the "Ole Quilt" (he ment that fur mam) an' the brats kin plant, an' tend, ur jis let hit alone, es they darn pleze; I aint a carein.'

"So out we went tu the pawpaw thicket, an' peel'd a rite smart chance ove bark, an' man an' me made geers fur dad, while he sot on the fence a-lookin at us, an' a studyin pow'rful. I arterards foun' out, he wer a-studyin how tu play the kar-acter ove a hoss puffectly.

"Well, the geers becum him mitily, an' nuffin wud du 'im but he mus hev a bridil, so I gits a umereller brace—hit's a litil forked piece ove squar wire bout a foot long, like a yung pitch-fork, yu no—an' twisted hit sorter intu a bridil bit snaffil shape. Dad wanted hit made kurb, es he hedn't work'd fur a good while, an' said he mout sorter feel his keepin, an' go tu ravin an' cavortin.

"When we got the bridil fix'd ontu dad, don't yu bleve he sot in tu chompin hit jis like a rale hoss, an' tried tu bite me on the arm (he allers wer a mos' complikated durned ole fool, an' mam sed so when he warnt about). I put on the geers, an' while mam wer a-tyin the belly ban', a-strainin hit pow'rful tite, he drapt ontu his hans, sed 'Whay-a-a' like a mad hoss wud, an' slung his hine laigs at mam's hed. She step'd back a littil an' wer standin wif her arms cross'd a-restin em on her stumick, an' his heel taps cum wifin a inch ove her nose. Sez she, 'Yu plays hoss better nur yu dus husban.' He jis' run backards on all fours, an' kick'd at her agin, an'——an' pawd the groun wif his fis.

" 'Lead him off tu the field, Sut, afore he kicks ur bites sumbody,' sez mam. I shoulder'd the gopher plow, an' tuck hole ove the bridil. Dad leaned back sulky, till I sed cluck, cluck, wif my tounge, then he started. When we cum

tu the fence I let down the gap, an' hit made dad mad; he
wanted tu jump hit on all fours hoss way. Oh geminy! what
a durn'd ole fool kin cum tu ef he gins up tu the complaint.

"I hitch'd 'im tu the gopher, a-watchin him pow'ful clost,
fur I'd see how quick he cud drap ontu his hans, an' kick,
an' away we went, dad leanin forard tu his pullin, an' we
made rite peart plowin, fur tu hev a green hoss, an' bark
gears; he went over the sprowts an' bushes same as a rale
hoss, only he traveled on two laigs. I wer mitily hope up bout
co'n; I cud a'mos' see hit a cumin up; but thar's a heap ove
whisky spilt twixt the counter an' the mouf, ef hit ain't got
but two foot tu travil. 'Bout the time he wer beginin tu break
sweat, we cum tu a sassafrack bush, an tu keep up his karacter es a hoss, he buljed squar intu an' thru hit, tarin down a
ball ho'nets nes' ni ontu es big es a hoss's hed, an' the hole
tribe kiver'd 'im es quick es yu cud kiver a sick pup wif a saddil blanket. He lit ontu his hans agin, an kick'd strait up onst,
then he rar'd, an' fotch a squeal wus nur ara stud hoss in the
State, an' sot in tu strait runnin away jis es natral es yu ever
seed any uther skeer'd hoss du. I let go the line an' holler'd,
Wo! dad, wo! but yu mout jis' es well say Woa! tu a locomotum, ur Suke cow tu a gal.

"Gewhillitins! how he run: when he cum tu bushes, he'd
clar the top ove em wif a squeal, gopher an' all. P'raps he
tho't thar mout be anuther settilment ove ball ho'nets thar,
an' hit wer safer tu go over than thru, an' quicker dun eny
how. Every now an' then he'd fan the side ove his hed, fust
wif wun fore laig an' then tuther, then he'd gin hissef a roun-
handed slap what soundid like a waggin whip ontu the place
whar the breechbands tetches a hoss, a-runnin all the time an'
a-kerrien that ar gopher jis 'bout as fas' an' es hi frum the
yeath es ever eny gopher wer kerried I'll swar. When he
cum tu the fence, he jis tore thru hit, bustin an' scatterin
ni ontu seven panils wif lots ove broken rails. Rite yere
he lef the gopher, geers, close, clevis, an' swingltress, all
mix'd up, an' not wuf a durn. Mos' ove his shut staid ontu
the aind ove a rail, an' ni ontu a pint ove ho'nets stop'd
thar a stingin all over; hits smell fool'd em. The balance
on em, ni ontu a gallun, kep' on wif dad. He seem'd tu run
jis adzactly es fas' es a hon'et cud fly; hit wer the titest race
I ever seed, fur wun hoss tu git all the whipin. Down thru
a saige field they all went, the ho'nets makin hit look like

thar wer smoke roun' dad's bald hed, an' he wif nuffin on the green yeath in the way ove close about im, but the bridil, an' ni ontu a yard ove plow line sailin behine, wif a tir'd out ho'net ridin on the pint ove hit. I seed that he wer aimin fur the swimin hole in the krick, whar the bluff am over twenty five foot pupendiculer tu the warter, an' hits ni ontu ten foot deep.

"Well, tu keep up his karacter es a hoss, plum thru, when he got tu the bluff he loped off, ur rather jis' kep on a runnin. Kerslunge intu the krick he went. I seed the warter fly plum abuv the bluff from whar I wer.

"Now rite thar, boys, he over-did the thing, ef actin hoss tu the scribe wer what he wer arter; fur thars nara hoss ever foaldid durned fool enuf tu lope over eny sich place; a cussed muel mout a dun hit, but dad warn't actin muel, tho' he orter tuck that karacter; hits adzactly sooted tu his dispersition, all but not breedin. I crept up tu the aidge, an' peep'd over. Thar wer dad's bald hed fur all the yeath like a peeled inyin, a bobbin up an' down an' aroun, an' the ho'nets sailin roun tuckey buzzard fashun, an' every onst in a while one, an' sum times ten, wud take a dip at dad's bald head. He kep' up a rite peart dodgin onder, sumtimes afore they hit im, an' sumtimes arterard, an' the warter wer kivered wif drownded ball ho'nets. Tu look at hit frum the top ove the bluff, hit wer pow'ful inturestin, an' sorter funny; I wer on the bluff myse'f, mine yu.

"Dad cudent see the funny part frum whar he wer, but hit seem'd tu be inturestin tu him frum the 'tenshun he wer payin tu the bisness ove divin an' cussin.

"Sez I, 'Dad, ef yu's dun washin yersef, an hes drunk enuff, less go back tu our plowin, hit will soon be powful hot.' 'Hot—hell!' sez dad; 'hit am hot rite now. Don't (an onder went his hed) yer see (dip) these cussed (dip) infun—(dip) varmints arter me?' (dip) 'What,' sez I, 'them ar hoss flies thar, that's nat'ral, dad; you aint raley fear'd ove them is yu?' 'Hoss flies! h—l an' (dip) durnation!' sez dad, 'theyse rale ginui—(dip) ball ho'nets, (dip) yu infunel ignurant cuss!' (dip) 'Kick em—bite em—paw em—switch em wif yure tail, dad,' sez I. 'Oh! soney, soney, (dip) how I'll sweeten yure—(dip) when these (dip) ho'nets leave yere.' 'Yu'd better du the levin yursef dad,' sez I. 'Leave yere! Sut yu d—n fool! How (dip) kin I, (dip) when they won't (dip) let me stay (dip) atop (dip) the warter even.' 'Well, dad, yu'l hev tu stay thar till nite, an' arter they goes tu roos' yu cum home. I'll hev yer feed in the troft redy; yu won't need eny curyin tu-nite will yu?' 'I wish (dip) I may never (dip) see to-morrer, ef I (dip) don't make (dip) hame strings (dip) outer yure hide (dip) when I dus (dip) git outen yere,' sez dad. 'Better say yu wish yu may never see anuther ball ho'net, ef yu ever play hoss agin,' sez I.

"Them words toch dad tu the hart, an' I felt they mus' be my las, knowin dad's onmollified nater. I broke frum them parts, an' sorter cum over yere tu the copper mines. When I got tu the hous', 'Whar's yer dad?' sez mam. 'Oh, he turn'd durn fool, an' run away, busted every thing all tu cussed smash, an's in the swimin hole a divin arter minners. Look out mam, he'll cum home wif a angel's temper; better sen' fur sum strong man body tu keep him frum huggin yu tu deth. 'Law sakes!' sez mam; 'I know'd he cudent act hoss fur ten minutes wifout actin infunel fool, tu save his life.'

"I staid hid out ontil nex' arternoon, an' I seed a feller a-travelin'. Sez I, 'How de do, mister? What wer agwine on at the cabin, this side the crick, when yu pass'd thar?' 'Oh, nuthin much, only a pow'ful fat man wer a lyin in the yard ontu his belly, wif no shut on, an' a 'oman wer a greasin ove his shoulders an' arms outen a gourd. A pow'ful curious, vishus, skeery lookin cuss he is tu b'shure. His head am as big es a wash pot, an' he hasent the fust durned sign ove an eye—jist two black slits. Is thar much small pox roun yere?' 'Small hell!' sez I, 'no sir.' 'Been much fightin in this neighborhood lately?' 'Nun wuf speakin ove,' sez I. He scratched his head—'Nur French measils?' 'Not jis clost,' sez I. 'Well, do yu know what ails that man back thar?' 'Jist gittin over a vilent attack ove dam fool,' sez I. 'Well, who is he eny how?' I ris tu my feet, an' straiched out my arm, an' sez I, 'Strainger, that man is my dad.' He looked at my laigs an' pussonel feeters a moment, an' sez he, 'Yas, dam ef he aint.'

"Now boys, I haint seed dad since, an' I dusent hev much appertite tu see im fur sum time tu cum. Less all drink! Yere's luck tu the durned old fool, an' the ho'nets too."

Sut's New-Fangled Shirt

I met Sut, one morning, weaving along in his usual rambling uncertain gait. His appearance satisfied me at once that something was wrong. He had been sick— whipped in a free fight, or was just getting on his legs again, from a "big drunk."
But upon this point I was soon enlightened.
"Why, Sut, what's wrong now? You look sick."
"Heaps wrong, durn my skin—no my haslets—ef I haint mos' ded, an' my looks don't lie when they hints that I'se sick. I is sick—I'se skin'd."
"Who skinned you—old Bullen?"
"No, hoss, a durnder fool nor Bullen did hit; I jis skin'd mysef."
"What in the name of common sense did you do it for?"
"Didn't du hit in the name ove common sense; did hit in the name, an' wif the sperit, ove plum nat'ral born durn fool.
"Lite ofen that ar hoss, an' take a ho'n; I wants two ove 'em (shaking his constant companion, a whisky flask, at me), an' plant yersef ontu thar ar log, an' I'll tell ef I kin, but hit's a'mos beyant tellin.
"I'se a durnder fool nor enybody outside a Assalum, ur Kongriss, 'sceptin ove my own dad, fur he actid hoss, an' I haint tried that yet. I'se allers intu sum trap what wudn't ketch a saidge-field sheep. I'll drownd mysef sum day, jis see ef I don't. I spects that wud stop the famerly dispersition tu act durn fool, so fur es Sut's consarn'd."
"Well, how is it Sut; have you been beat playing cards or drinking?"
"Nara wun, by geminy! Them jobs can't be did in these yere parts, es enybody no's on, but seein hits yu I'll tell hit. I'se sick-sham'd-sorry-sore-an'-mad tu kill, I is. Yu no I boards wif Bill Carr, at his cabin ontu the mountin, an' pays fur sich es I gits when I hes munny, an' when I hesent eny, why he takes wun third outer me in holesum

hot cussin; an' she, that's his wife Betts, takes tuther three thirds out wif the battlin stick, an' the intrus' wif her sharp tongue, an' she takes more intrus' nur principal. She's the cussedes' 'oman I ever seed eny how, fur jaw, breedin, an' pride. She kin scold a blister rite plum ontu a bull's curl in two minits. She outbreeds enything frum thar tu the river, takin in the minks—an' patterns arter all new fangl'd fashuns she hears tell on, frum bussils tu britches. Oh! she's wun ove em, an' sumtimes she's two ur three, she is.

"Well, yu see I'd got hole on sum homade cottin cloff, fur a shirt, an' coax'd Betts tu make hit, an' bout the time hit wer dun, yere cum a cussed stuck up lawyer, name Jonsin, an' ax'd fur brekfus'—rite yere I wishes the bread had been asnick, an' the meat strikenine, an' that he'd a staid an tuck dinner too, fur he hes ni ontu fotch about my aind, durn his sashararer mitimurs ole soul tu thunder!

"I wonder hit didn't work 'im pow'ful es hit wer; fur Betts cooks up sum tarifyin mixtrys ove vittils, when she tries hersef. I'se pizen proof my sef; fur thuty dullars, I jis' let a sluice ove aquafotis run thru me fur ha'f a day, an' then live tu spen' the las' durn cent, fur churnbrain whiskey; ef I warnt (holding up his flask and peeping through it), I'd dun been ded long ago.

"Well, while he wer eatin, she spied out that his shut wer mons'ous stiff, an' es slick es glass, so she never rested ontill she wurmed hit outen 'im that hit wer dun wif a flour preparashun. She went wif 'im a piece ove the way down the mountin, tu git the purticulers, an' when she cum back she sed she *had em*. I thot she had myse'f.

"She imejuntly sot in, an' biled a big pot ove paste, ni ontu a peck ove hit, an' tole me I wer gwine tu hev 'the gonest purty shut in that range.' Well, she wer sorter rite, fur when I las seed hit, hit wer purty—yas orful purty, tu a rat, ur a buzzard, ur eny uther varmint fon ove dirty, skary lookin things; but frum the time I staid inside ove hit, I can't say that es a human shut I'd gin a durn fur a dozin ove em. 'Gonest purty shut'—the cussed ole hen jay bird, I jis' wish she hed tu war it wif a redpepper linin' on till she gits a-pas' hatchin, an' that wud be ni ontu eleving year, ef she tells the truff.

"She soused my shut intu the pot, an' soaked hit thar,

ontil hit tuck up mos' ove the paste; then she tuck hit an' iron'd hit out flat, an' dry, an sot hit on hits aidge agin the cabin in the sun. Thar hit stood, like a dry hoss hide, an' hit rattiled like ontu a sheet ove iron, hit did, pasted tugether all over—'gonest purty shut!'—durn'd huzzy!

"When I cum tu dinner, nuffin wud du Betts, but I mus' put myse'f inside hit rite thar. She partid the tails a littil piece wif a case nife, an' arter I got my hed started up intu hit, she'd pull down, fus' at wun tail, an' then tuther, ontil I wer farly inside ove hit, an' button'd in. Durn the everlastin, infunel, new fangled sheet iron cuss ove a shut! I say. I felt like I'd crowded intu a ole bee-gum, an' hit all full ove pissants; but hit wer a 'born'd twin ove Lawyer Jonsin's,' Betts sed, an' I felt like standin es much pussonal discumfurt es he cud, jis tu git tu sampil arter sumbody human. I didn't know, tu, but what hit hed the vartu ove makin a lawyer outen me agin hit got limber.

"I sot in tu bildin ove a ash-hopper fur Betts, an' work'd pow'ful hard, sweat like a hoss, an' then the shut quit hits hurtin, an' tuck tu feelin slippery. Thinks I, that's sorter lawyer like enyhow, an' I wer hope up bout the shut, an' what mout cum outen hit.

"Arter I got dun work, I tuck me a four finger dost ove bumble-bee whisky, went up intu the lof' an' fell asleep a-think'n bout bein a rale sashararer lawyer, hoss, saddil bags, an' books; an' Betts went over the top tu see her mam.

"Well, arter a while I waked up; I'd jis' been dreamin that the judge ove the supreme cort had me sowed up in a raw hide, an' sot up agin a hot pottery kiln tu dry, an' the dryin woke me.

"I now thort I wer ded, an' hed died ove rhumaticks ove the hurtines' kind. All the jints I cud muve wer my ankils, knees, an' wrists; cudn't even move my hed, an' scarsely wink my eyes; the cussed shut wer pasted fas' ontu me all over, frum the ainds ove the tails tu the pints ove the broad-axe collar over my years. Hit sot tu me es clost es a poor cow dus tu her hide in March. I worm'd an' strain'd an' cuss'd an' grunted, till I got hit sorter broke at the shoulders an' elbows, an' then I dun the durndes' fool thing ever did in these yere mountins. I shuffl'd an' tore my britches off, an' skin'd loose frum my hide bout two inches ove the tail all roun in orful pain, an quick-stingin trebulashun. Oh! great golly grampus, how it hurt! Then I tuck up a plank outen the lof', an' hung my laigs down thru the hole, sot in an' nail'd the aidge ove the frunt tail tu the floor afore me, an' the hine tail I nail'd tu the plank what I sot on. I flung the hammer outen my reach, tu keep my hart frum failin me, onbutton'd the collar an' risbans, raised my hans way abuv my hed, shot up my eyes, sed a short grace, an' jump'd thru tu the groun' floor, jis' thuteen foot wun inch clear ove jists."

Here Sut remarked, sadly shaking his head, "George, I'se a durnder fool nor dad, hoss, ho'nets, an' gopher. I'll hev tu drown'd myself sum ove these days, see ef I don't."

"Well, go on Sut; did the shirt come off?"

"I—t-h-i-n-k—h-i-t——d-id.

"I hearn a nise like tarin a shingle ruff ofen a hous' at wun rake, an' felt like my bones wer all what lef the shut, an' reach'd the floor. I stagger'd tu my feet, an' tuck a moanful look up at my shut. The nails hed hilt thar holt, an' so hed the tail hem; thar hit wer hangin arms down, inside out, an' jis' es stiff es ever. Hit look'd like a map ove Mexico, arter one ove the wurst battils. A patch ove my skin 'bout the size ove a dullar, ur a dullar an' a 'alf bill yere, a bunch ove har bout like a bird's nes' thar, then sum more skin, then sum paste, then a littil more har, then a heap ove skin—har an' skin straight along all over that newfangl'd everlastin', infunel pasted cuss ove a durnd shut! Hit wer a picter tu look at, an' so wer I.

"The hide, har, an' paste wer about ekally devided atwix me an' hit. George, listen tu me: hit looked adzactly like the skin ove sum wile beas' tore off alive, ur a bag what hed toted a laig ove fresh beef frum a shootin match.

"Bill cum home wif Betts, an' wer the fust inter the cabin. He backed outen hit agin an' sez he, 'Marcyful payrint! thar's been murderin dun yere; hits been ole Bullen; he's skinn'd Sut, an' *thars his hide* hung up tu dry.' Betts walked roun hit a zaminin hit, till at las' she venter'd clost, an' know'd her sowin.

"Sez she, '*Yu* dad dratted ole pot-head, that's his Sunday shut. Hes hed a dreful fite tho' wif sumbody; *didn't* they go fur his har ofen?' 'An rine in 'bun dance,' sed Bill. 'Yas hoss,' sed Betts agine, 'an' ef I'd been him, *I'd a shed hit*; I wudnt a fit es nasty a fite es that wer, in my fines' shut, wu'd yu, Bill?"

"Now, George, I's boun tu put up Jonsin's meat fur im on site, wifout regardin good killin weather, an' ef *ever* a 'oman flattins out a shut fur me agin, durn my everlastin picter ef I dont flattin her out, es thin es a stepchile's bread an' butter. I'll du hit ef hit takes me a week.

"Hits a retribushun sartin, the biggest kine ove a preacher's regular retribushun, what am tu be foun' in the Holy Book.

"Dus yu mine my racin dad, wif sum ho'nets, an' so forth, intu the krick?

"Well, this am what cums ove hit. I'll drownd mysef, see ef I don't, that is ef I don't die frum that hellfired shut. Now George, ef a red-heded 'oman wif a reel foot axes yu tu marry her, yu *may* du hit; ef an 'oman wants yu tu kill her husbun, yu *may* do hit; ef a gal axes yu tu rob the bank, an' take her tu Californy, yu *may* du hit; ef wun on em wants yu tu quit whisky, yu *mout* even du that. But ef ever an 'oman, ole ur yung, purty es a sunflower ur ugly es a skin'd hoss, offers yu a shut aninted wif paste tu put on, jis' yu kill her in her tracks, an' burn the cussed pisnus shut rite thar. Take a ho'n?"

The Widow McCloud's Mare

"THAR cum tu this country, onst, a cussed sneakin lookin rep-tile, name Stilyards. He wer hatched in a crack—in the frosty rocks, whar nutmaigs am made outen maple, an' whar wimmin paints clock-faces an' pints shoe-paigs, an' the men invents rat-traps, mantraps, an' new fangled doctrins fur the aid ove the devil. In fac' hit am his gardin, whar he kin grow what won't sprout eny whar else.

"Well, this critter look't like a cross atween a black snake an' a fireman's ladder. He wer eighteen an' a 'alf hans high, an' modeled like ontu a shingle maker's shavin hoss, an' wer es yaller as a warter dorg wif the janders. His eyes wer like ontu a coon's, an' his foot wer the biggest chunk ove meat an' knotty bones I ever seed tu hev no guts intu hit. Now ef he hed wun gif what wud make yu take tu him, I never seed hit, an' ef he ever did a good ur a straight ahead thing, I never hearn ove hit. He cud praps be skar'd intu actin rite fur a minit ur two at a time, but hit wudn't las'. He cum amung us a ole field schoolmarster—soon shed that shell, an' cum out es oily, slippery a lawyer as ever tuck a fee. Why, he'd a hilt his own in a pond full ove eels, an' a swallerd the las durn one ove em, an' then sot the pond tu turnin a shoe-paig mill. Well, he practised on all the misfortinat devils roun that sarkit, till he got sassy, got niggers, got rich, got forty maulins fur his nastiness, an' tu put a cap sheaf ontu his stack ove raskallity, got religion, an' got tu Congress.

"The fust thing he did thar, wer to proffer tu tend the Capitol grouns in inyuns, an' beans, on the shears, an' tu sell the statoot ove Columbus tu a tenpin alley, fur a sign, an' the she injun wif him, tu send back the balls. He stole the Romun swoard ofen the stone picter ove War thar, an' fotch hit tu his wife fur a meat-chopper. He practised lor ontu yu fur eny thing yu hed, frum a hanful ove chesnuts tu a plantushun, an' tu tell hit all in a minit, when he dies, he'll make the fastes trip tu the senter ove soot, sorrer, an' smoke, on record, not even sceptin ole Iskariott's fas' time.

"Well, a misfortinit devil happen'd tu steal a hoss by accidint, got Stilyards tu 'fend him, got intu the penitensary, an' Stilyards got all he had—a half houn' dorg, an' a ole eight day Yankee clock, fur sendin him thar.

"He tuck a big young mar frum a widdar name McCloud, fur losin a land case. So he walked out intu that neighborhood tu gether up an' tote home his fees, an' I met up wif him. He hed the clock tied ontu his back pedler fashun, leadin the mar in wun han' an' the dorg by a rope wif tuther. The dorg wer interprisin an' led too fas'—the mar wer sulky an' led tu slow, an' the clock wer heavy, an' the day hot, an' he wer hevin ove a good time gineraly wif his fees, his sweat, an' his mean thoughts. So he cumenced tryin tu hire me tu help him tu town, fur a gill ove whisky.

"Now, whu the devil ever hearn tell ove a gill ove whisky, in these parts afore? Why hit soundid sorter like a inch ove cord-wood, ur a ounce ove cornshuks. Hit 'sulted me. So I sot in tu fix a way tu put a gill ur so ove pussonal discumfort onder his shut, an' I did hit. Sez I, 'Yu mout save that whisky ef yu dus' es I tells yu:

"'Jis' yu git atop, an' outside that she hoss thar, tie that ar dorg's rope roun her neck, set the time-mill up ontu her back, ahine yu, an' tie hit roun yersef; that makes her tote the furniture, tote yu, an' lead yer valerabil dorg, while yu governs the muvemint wif a good hickory, an' them bridil strings, don't yu see?'

"He pouched out his mouf, nodded his hed five ur six times, a-bendin but wun jint 'bout the midil ove that long yaller neck ove hisn, an' said, 'Yas, a good surgistshun, mister Lovingood,' an' I sot in tu help him fix things. I peeled lots ove good bark, sot the clock on aind, back tu back wif him ontu the mar's bar cupplin, an' I tied hit roun his cackus like I ment them tu stick es long es hit run, ur he lived, an' hit cum durnd ni doin hit. He sed he thot the thing wud work, *an so did I*. By golly, I seed the redish brown fire a playin in the mar's eyes, an' a quick twitchin in her flank, what I knowd, an' onderstood tu mean, that she'd make orful things happen purty durn'd soon. The sharp pint ove Stilyard's tail bone, an' the clock laigs wer a makin lively surgistshins tu a devil intu her es big as a yearlin.

"All wer redy fur the show tu begin. 'Yu git up, yu pesky critter,' sed he, a-makin his heels meet, an' crack onder her belly. Well she did 'git up,' rite then an' thar, an' staid up long enuf tu lite twenty foot further away, in a broad trimblin squat, her tail hid a-tween her thighs, an' her years a dancin a-pas' each uther, like scissors a-cuttin. The jolt ove the litin sot the clock tu strikin. Bang-zee-bang-zee whang-zee. She listined pow'ful 'tentive tu the three fus' licks, an' they seem'd tu go thru an' thru her as quick es quick-silver wud git thru a sifter. She waited fur no more, but jis' gin her hole soul up tu the wun job ove runnin frum onder that infunel Yankee, an' his hive ove bumble bees, ratil snakes, an' other orful hurtin things, es she tuck hit tu be. I knows how she felt; I'se been in the same 'bout five hundred times, an' durn my cackus ef she didn't kerry out my idears ove gittin outen trubil fus' rate.

"Every jump she made, she jerk't that misfortinat dorg six foot upard, an' thurty foot onward. Sumtimes he lit on his starn, sumtimes on his snout, then ontu bof ainds at wunst. He changed sides every uther lunge, clar over Stilyards, an' his hour-mill tu. He sed O! Outch! every time he lit, in houn talk loud enuff tu skeer the devil. An the road wer sprinkled worm fence fashun, like ontu a drunken man a-totin a leaky jug.

"The durn'd ole clock, hit got exhited too, an' los' control ove hits sef, an' furgot tu stop, but jis scizzed an' whang'd away strait along, an' the mar a hearin hit all, an' a b'levin the soun' tu be cumin nigher tu her inards every pop. She thort, too, that four hundred black an' tan houn' dorgs wer cumpassin her etarnal ruin.

"She seed em above her, below her—behine her—afore her—an' on bof sides ove her, eny whar, every whar, nuffin but houn' dorgs. An she jis' tried tu run outen her sorril hide. I seed her two hine shoes shinin way up in the a'r, like two new moons. I know'd she wer a-mixin in sum high pressure vishus kickin, wif a heap ove as yearnest, an' fas' runnin es hosses ever 'dulges in.

"'Wo yeow now!' I hearn this, sprinkled in now an' then wif the yowls ove the dorg, an' the whangin ove the clock, an' all hit out-dun wif the mity nise ove clatterin huffs, an' crashin brush.

"Stilyards sot humpt up, his puddin foots lock'd onder that skeerd critter's belly, an' his paws wove intu her mane, double twill'd. I speck she thot the devil wer a-huggin her, an' she wer durnd near right.

"Thinks I, ole feller, *if* yu gain *this* suit, yu may ax Satun, when yu sees him, fur a par ove lisence tu practice at his cort. He'll sign em, sure.

"I cut acrost the ridge, what the road woun roun', an' got whar I cud see em a cummin, sorter to'ards me agin. She wer stretched out strait as a string, an' so wer he—he wer roostin pow'ful low ontu her withers, his long arms locked roun her neck, his big feet a flyin about in the air, each side ove her tail, sorter limber like, an' the dorg mus' hev been nigh ontu killed dead, fur bof his hine laigs wer gone plumpt up tu his cuplin, an' a string ove inards cumin outen the hole his laigs hed lef, wer a flutterin arter him like a bolt ove grey ribbon, slappin agin the saplins, an' stumps, an' gettin longer every slap. His paunch wer a bobbin up an' down about a foot ahine whar the pint ove his tail used tu be. Ef he yowld any now, I didn't hear hit.

"That clock, the cussed mischeaf-makin mercheen, the cause ove all this onyeathly nise, trubbil, an' vexashun ove sperit, wer still ontu ole Stilyards's back, an' a maulin away as ef hit wer in the strait line ove a houshole juty, an the bark wer a holdin hits holt powful well, considerin the strain. They met a ole bald-heded, thick-sot feller a-cummin frum mill, a-ridin ontu a grist ove meal, an' hit on a blaze-face hoss, wif burs in his tail. He wer totin a kaig ove strain'd honey in his lap, an' a 'oman behine him, wif a spinnin wheel ontu her hip. The mar run squar intu the millin experdishun. Jis' es she did hit, Stilyards holler'd, 'Yeow, cut the bar'——He never addid the K tu that word, fur sumthin happen'd, jis' then an' tharabouts."

Sut scratched his head, and seem'd to be in deep thought.

"Well, Sut, go on."

"I wer jis' a-studyin how tu gin yu a sorter idear ove how things look'd arter them two hoss beastes mixed. Spose yu take a comon size frame doggery, sortar old an' rotten, wif all the truck generly inside them nesesary instertushuns; sit hit down squar ontu a railroad track, jis' *so*— an' du hit jis' in time fur the kerrs a-cummin forty miles a hour, an' thar whistil string broke. How du yu say things wud look bout a minit arterards?"

"Very much injured, I'd say, Sut."

"An' pow'fuly mixt?"

"Yes."

"An' tremenjusly scattered?"

"Yes."

"An' orfully changed in shape?"

"Yes."

"An' in nater?"

"Yes."

"An' in valuer?"

"Yes."

"An' a heap more pieces?"

"Yes."

"An' smaller wuns?"

"Yes."

"Splinters, an' scraps perdominant?"

"Yes."

"An' not wuf a durn, by a duller an' a 'alf?"

"Yes."

"Well, yu kin sorter take in the tremenjus idear ove that spot ove sandy road, whar Stilyards met the bald-heded man. That onlucky ole cuss lit twenty foot out in the woods, never look'd back, but sot his trampers tu work, an' distributed hissef sumwhar toward the Black Oak Ridge. The 'oman hung by wun foot in the fork ove a black-jack, an' a-holdin tu a dogwood lim' wif her hans, an' she hollerin, surter spiteful like—'Split the black-jack, ur fetch a quilt!" Nuffin ove the sort wer dun whilest I wer thar, es I knows on. Stilyards wer ni tuther side ove the road, flat ontu his back, fainted cumfortabil, an' quiet as a sick sow in a snowstorm, his arms an' laigs stretched till he look'd like a big letter X. His hat wer sumwhar, an' a boot sumwhar else. His clothes wer in strings, like he'd been shot thru a thorn thicket, outen a canyun. His nose wer a bleedin jis' about rite tu bring 'im too sumtime to'ards the middil ove the arternoon. His eyes wer shot up, an' his face wer pucker'd like a wet sheep-skin afore a hot fire, an' he look'd sorter like he'd been studyin a deep plan tu cheat sumbody, an' hed miss'd. The dorg—that is what wer lef ove 'im—wer a-lyin bent over the top ove a saplin stump, an' the tuther aind ove his inards wer tangled up amung the mar's hine laigs, an' she wer stretched out in runnin shape, not hurt a bit, only her naik wer broke, an' a spinin-wheel spoke a-stickin atween her ribs a foot ur so deep. Ole Ball-face wer ontu his side, now an' then liftin his head an' takin a look at the surroundin deserlashun an' sorrer. The ole time counter wer a-leanin up agin a tree, sum bark still roun hit, the door gone, the face smashed, but still true tu what hit thort hits juty, jis bangin away es reguler es ef hit wer at home; an' I reckon hits at hit yet. Thar wer honey-kaig hoops, heads, an' staves, an' spinnin-wheel spokes, permiskusly scattered all about, an' meal sprinkiled over everybody, an' everything.

"Jis' then a feller what look't like he mout be a tract sower, ur a map agent, rid up an' tuck a *big* look all roun. Sez he, 'Mister, did the litenin hurt *yu?*' Sez I, 'Wus nur litenin; a powder mill busted.' The 'oman in the black-jack holler'd at him jis' then, savidge as a cat, 'Look tuther way, yu cussed imperdint houn!' He hed tu turn his hed tu see whar the vise cum frum; he jis' look't one squint, an' sed, 'Great hevings!' an' gin his hoss a orful dost ove whip an' spurs, an' lef' a-flyin, an' he tolt at town what he'd seed. The feller wer orful skeer'd, an' no wonder; he'd seed enuf tu skeer a saw-mill plum ofen the krik.

"I now tuck the meal-bag, put in the remnant ove the dorg, an' sich ove the honey es I cud scoop up, an' draw'd hit over Stilyards's head, tied hit tite roun his naik, in hopes hit mout help fetch him tu sooner; split the black-jack, an' lef' in a lope. I hearn the 'oman squall arter me, 'Never mind, laigs, *I'll pay yu!*' She haint dun hit *yet.*

"I tuck the road Stilyards, an' the mar, an' his tuther geer, hed cum over so fur, an' pass'd a cabin whar a ole 'oman dress'd in a pipe an' a stripid aprun wer a-standin on the ash-hopper lookin up the road like she wer 'spectin tu see sumthin soon. Sez she, talkin 'bout es fas' es a flutter-mill: 'Say yu mister, did yu meet enything onkimon up thar?' I shook my head. 'Well,' sez she, jumpin ofen the hopper an' a-shakin the ashes outen her coteail, an' settin her specks back, 'Mister, I'se plum outdun. Thar's sumthin pow'ful wickid gwine on. A crazy organ-grinder cum a-pas' yere jis' a small scrimpshun slower nur chain litenin, on a hoss wif no tail. His organ wer tied ontu his back, an' wer a-playin that good tchune, 'Sugar in the Gourd,' ur 'Barbary Allin,' I dunno which, an' his monkey wer a-dancin Hail Columby all over the road, an' *hits* tail wer es long es my clothes-line, an' purfeckly bar ove har. He hed no hat on, an' wun ove his boots flew off as he passed yere, an' lit on the smoke-'ous. Thar hit is; he mus' been a pow'ful big man, fur hits like ontu a indigo ceroon.'

"All this wer sed wifout takin one breff.

"I tole her hit wer the advance gard ove a big sarkis purclaimin hits cummin, ur the merlennium, an' durn'd ef I know'd which.

"She 'lowed hit cudent be the merlennium, fur hit warnt a playin hyme-tchunes; nur a sarkis either, fur the hoss warn't spotted. But hit mout be the Devil arter a tax collector, ur a missionary on his way tu China; hit look'd ugly enuf tu be one, an' fool enuf tu be tuther. She wer pow'fully exersised; she sweat an' snorted onder hit.

"Now don't yu b'leve, es soon es Stilyards cum tu, an' got outen the bag, he sot in an' burried the mar' so es tu hide her, an' then, at nex' cort, *indited me fur stealin her*, an' durn'd ni provin hit; now haint that the Devil?"

"What ever become of Stilyards, Sut, anyhow?"

"I dono; ef he haint in Congriss he's gone tu h—l."

Parson John Bullen's Lizards

AIT ($8) DULLARS REW-ARD.

'TENSHUN BELEVERS AND KONSTABLES! KETCH 'IM!
KETCH 'IM!

THIS kash wil be pade in korn, ur uther projuce, tu be kolected at ur about nex camp-meetin, *ur thararter*, by eny wun what ketches him, fur the karkus ove a sartin wun SUT LOVINGOOD, dead ur alive, ur ailin, an' safely giv over tu the purtectin care ove Parson John Bullin, ur lef' well tied, at Squire Mackjunkins, fur the raisin ove the devil pussonely, an' permiskusly discumfurtin the wimen very powerful, an' skeerin ove folks generly a heap, an' bustin up a promisin, big warm meetin, an' a makin the wickid larf, an' wus, an' wus, insultin ove the passun orful.
Test,   JEHU WETHERO.
                    Sined by me,
         JOHN BULLEN, the passun.

I found written copies of the above highly intelligible and vindictive proclamation, stuck up on every blacksmith shop, doggery, and store door, in the Frog Mountain Range. Its blood-thirsty spirit, its style, and above all, its chirography, interested me to the extent of taking one down from a tree for preservation.

In a few days I found Sut in a good crowd in front of Capehart's Doggery, and as he seemed to be about in good tune, I read it to him.

"Yas, George, that ar dockymint am in dead yearnist sartin. Them hard shells over thar dus want me the wus kine, powerful bad. *But*, I spect ait dullers won't fetch me, nither wud ait hundred, bekase thar's nun ove 'em fas' enuf tu ketch me, nither is thar hosses by the livin jingo! Say, George, much talk 'bout this fuss up whar yu're been?"

For the sake of a joke I said yes, a great deal.

"Jis' es I 'spected, durn 'em, all git drunk, an' skeer thar fool sefs ni ontu deth, an' then lay hit ontu me, a poor innersent youf, an' es soun' a belever es they is. Lite, lite, ole feller an' let that roan ove yourn blow a litil, an' I'll 'splain this cussed misfortnit affar: hit hes ruinated my karacter es a pius pusson in the s'ciety roun' yere, an' is a spreadin faster nur meazils. When ever yu hear eny on 'em a spreadin hit, gin hit the dam lie squar, will yu? I haint dun nuffin tu one ove 'em. Hits true, I did sorter frustrate a few lizzards a littil, but they haint members, es I knows on.

"You see, las' year I went tu the big meetin at Rattlesnake Springs, an' wer a sittin in a nice shady place convarsin wif a frien' ove mine, intu the huckil berry thickit, jis' duin nuffin tu nobody an' makin no fuss, when, the fust thing I remembers, I woke up frum a trance what I hed been knocked inter by a four year old hickory-stick, hilt in the paw ove ole Passun Bullin, durn his alligater hide; an' he wer standin a striddil ove me, a foamin at the mouf, a-chompin his teeth—gesterin wif the hickory club— an' a-preachin tu me so you cud a-hearn him a mile, about a sartin sin gineraly, an' my wickedness pussonely; an' mensunin the name ove my frien' loud enuf tu be hearn tu the meetin 'ous. My poor innersent frien' wer dun gone an' I wer glad ove hit, fur I tho't he ment tu kill me rite whar I lay, an' I didn't want her tu see me die."

"Who was she, the friend you speak of Sut?" Sut opened his eyes wide.

"Hu the devil, an' durnashun tole *yu* that hit wer a she?"

"Why, you did, Sut"———

"I *didn't*, durn ef I did. Ole Bullin dun hit, an' I'll hev tu kill him yet, the cussed, infernel ole talebarer!"———

"Well, well, Sut, who was she?"

"Nun ove y-u-r-e b-i-s-n-i-s-s, durn yure littil ankshus picter! I *sees yu* a lickin ove yure lips. I *will* tell you one thing, George; that night, a neighbor gal got a all fired, overhandid stroppin frum her mam, wif a stirrup leather, an' ole Passun Bullin, hed et supper thar, an' what's wus nur all, that poor, innersent, skeer'd gal hed dun her levil bes' a cookin hit fur 'im. She begged him, a trimblin, an' a-cryin not tu tell on her. He et her cookin, he promised her he'd keep dark—an' then went strait an' tole her mam. Warnt that rale low down, wolf mean? The durnd infunel, hiperkritikal, pot-bellied, scaley-hided, whisky-wastin, stinkin ole groun'-hog. He'd a heap better a stole sum *man's* hoss; I'd a tho't more ove 'im. But I paid him plum up fur hit, an' I means tu keep a payin him, ontil one ur tuther, ove our toes pints up tu the roots ove the grass.

"Well, yere's the way I lifted that note ove han'. At the nex big meetin at Rattilsnaik—las' week hit wer—I wer on han' es solemn es a ole hat kivver on collection day. I hed my face draw'd out intu the shape an' perporshun ove a tayler's sleeve-board, pint down. I hed put on the convicted sinner so pufeckly that an'ole observin she pillar ove the church sed tu a ole he pillar, es I walked up to my bainch:

" 'Law sakes alive, ef thar ain't that *orful* sinner, Sut Lovingood, pearced plum thru; hu's nex?'

"Yu see, by golly, George, I *hed* tu promis the ole tub ove soap-greas tu cum an' hev myself convarted, jis' tu keep him frum killin me. An' es I know'd hit wudn't interfare wif the relashun I bore tu the still housis roun' thar, I didn't keer a durn. I jis' wanted tu git *ni* ole Bullin, onst onsuspected, an' this wer the bes' way tu du hit. I tuk a seat on the side steps ove the pulpit, an' kivvered es much ove my straitch'd face es I could wif my han's, tu prove I wer in yearnis. Hit tuck powerful—fur I hearn a sorter thankful kine ove buzzin all over the congregashun. Ole Bullin hissef looked down at me, over his ole copper specks, an' hit sed jis' es plain es a look cud say hit: 'Yu am thar, ar you—durn yu, hits well fur yu that yu cum.' I tho't sorter diffrent frum that. I tho't hit wud a been well fur *yu,* ef I hadent a-cum, but I didn't say hit jis then. Thar wer a monstrus crowd in that grove, fur the weather wer fine, an' b'levers wer plenty roun' about Rattilsnaik Springs. Ole Bullin gin out, an' they sung that hyme, yu know:

> "Thar will be mournin, mournin yere, an' mournin thar,
> On that dredful day tu cum."

"Thinks I, ole hoss, kin hit be possibil enybody hes tole yu what's a gwine tu happin; an' then I tho't that nobody know'd hit but me, and I wer cumforted. He nex tuck hisself a tex pow'fly mixed wif brimstone, an' trim'd wif

blue flames, an' then he open'd. He cummenced ontu the
sinners; he threaten'd 'em orful, tried tu skeer 'em wif all
the wust varmints he cud think ove, an' arter a while he
got ontu the idear ove Hell-sarpints, and he dwelt on it sum.
He tole 'em how the ole Hell-sarpints wud sarve em if they
didn't repent; how cold they'd crawl over thar nakid bodys,
an' how like ontu pitch they'd stick tu 'em as they crawled;
how they'd rap thar tails roun' thar naiks chokin clost,
poke thar tungs up thar noses, an' hiss intu thar years.
This wer the way they wer tu sarve men folks. Then he
turned ontu the wimmen: tole 'em how they'd quile intu
thar buzzims, an' how they *wud* crawl down onder thar
frock-strings, no odds how tite they tied 'em, an' how sum
ove the oldes' an' wus ones wud crawl up thar laigs, an'
travil *onder* thar garters, no odds how tight they tied *them*,
an' when the two armys ove Hell-sarpents met, then——
That las' remark *fotch 'em*. Ove all the screamin, an'
hollerin, an' loud cryin, I ever hearn, begun all at onst, all
over the hole groun' jis' es he hollered out that word 'then.'
He kep on a bellerin, but I got so busy jis' then, that I
didn't listen tu him much, fur I saw that my time fur
ackshun hed cum. Now yu see, George, I'd cotch seven
ur eight big pot-bellied lizzards, an' hed 'em in a littil
narrer bag, what I had made a-purpus. Thar tails all at
the bottim, an' so crowdid fur room that they cudent turn
roun'. So when he wer a-ravin ontu his tip-toes, an'
a-poundin the pulpit wif his fis'—onbenowenst tu enybody, I ontied my bag ove reptiles, put the mouf ove hit
onder the bottim ove his britches-laig, an' sot intu pinchin
thar tails. Quick es gunpowder they all tuck up his bar
laig, makin a nise like squirrils a-climbin a shell-bark
hickory. He stop't preachin rite in the middil ove the word
'damnation,' an' looked fur a moment like he wer a listenin
fur sumthin—sorter like a ole sow dus, when she hears yu
a whistlin fur the dorgs. The tarifick shape ove his feeters
stopp't the shoutin an' screamin; instuntly yu cud hear a
cricket chirp. I gin a long groan, an' hilt my head a-twixt
my knees. He gin hisself sum orful open-handed slaps wif
fust one han' an' then tuther, about the place whar yu cut
the bes' steak outen a beef. Then he'd fetch a vigrus ruff
rub whar a hosses tail sprouts; then he'd stomp one foot,
then tuther, then bof at onst. Then he run his han' ateen

his waisbun an' his shut an' reach'd way down, an' roun' wif hit; then he spread his big laigs, an' gin his back a good rattlin rub agin the pulpit, like a hog scratches hisself agin a stump, leanin tu hit pow'ful, an' twitchin, an' squirmin all over, es ef he'd slept in a dorg bed, ur ontu a pisant hill. About this time, one ove my lizzards scared an' hurt by all this poundin' an' feelin, an' scratchin, popp'd out his head frum the passun's shut collar, an' his ole brown naik, an' wer a-surveyin the crowd, when ole Bullin struck at 'im, jis' too late, fur he'd dodged back agin. The hell desarvin ole raskil's speech now cum tu 'im, an' sez he, 'Pray fur me brethren an' sisteren, fur I is a-rastilin wif the great inimy rite now!' an' his voice wer the mos' pitiful, trimblin thing I ever hearn. Sum ove the wimmen fotch a painter yell, an' a young docter, wif ramrod laigs, lean'd toward me monstrus knowin like, an' sez he, 'Clar case ove Delishus Tremenjus.' I nodded my head an' sez I, 'Yas, spechuly the tremenjus part, an' Ise feard hit haint at hits worst.' Ole Bullin's eyes wer a-stickin out like ontu two buckeyes flung agin a mud wall, an' he wer a-cuttin up more shines nor a cockroach in a hot skillet. Off went the clawhammer coat, an' he flung hit ahine 'im like he wer a-gwine intu a fight; he hed no jackid tu take off, so he unbuttond his galluses, an' vigrusly flung the ainds back over his head. He fotch his shut over-handed a durnd site faster nor I got outen my pasted one, an' then flung hit strait up in the air, like he jis' wanted hit tu keep on up furever; but hit lodged ontu a black-jack, an' I seed one ove my lizzards wif his tail up, a-racin about all over the ole dirty shut, skared too bad tu jump. Then he gin a sorter shake, an' a stompin kine ove twis', an' he cum outer his britches. He tuck 'em by the bottim ove the laigs, an' swung 'em roun' his head a time ur two, an' then fotch 'em down cherall-up over the frunt ove the pulpit. You cud a hearn the smash a quarter ove a mile! Ni ontu fifteen shorten'd biskits, a boiled chicken, wif hits laigs crossed, a big dubbil-bladed knife, a hunk ove terbacker, a cob-pipe, sum copper ore, lots ove broken glass, a cork, a sprinkil ove whisky, a squirt, an' three lizzards flew permiskusly all over that meetin-groun', outen the upper aind ove them big flax britches. One ove the smartes' ove my lizzards lit head-fust intu the buzzim ove a fat 'oman, es big es a skin'd hoss, an' ni ontu es ugly, who sot thuty yards off, a fannin hersef wif a tucky-tail. Smart tu the las', by golly, he imejuntly commenced runnin down the centre ove her breas'-bone, an' kep on, I speck. She wer jis' boun' tu faint; an' she did hit fust rate—flung the tucky-tail up in the air, grabbed the lap ove her gown, gin hit a big histin an' fallin shake, rolled down the hill, tangled her laigs an' garters in the top ove a huckilberry bush, wif her head in the branch an' jis' lay still. She wer interestin, she wer, ontil a serious-lookin, pale-faced 'oman hung a nankeen ridin skirt over the huckilberry bush. That wer all that wer dun to'ards bringin her too, that I seed. Now ole Bullin hed nuffin left ontu 'im but a par ove heavy, low quarter'd shoes, short woolen socks, an' eel-skin garters tu keep off the cramp. His skeer hed druv him plum crazy, fur he felt roun' in the air, abuv his head, like he wer huntin sumthin in the dark, an' he beller'd out, 'Brethren, brethren, take keer ove yerselves, the Hell-sarpints *hes got me!*' When this cum out, yu cud a-hearn the screams tu Halifax. He jis' spit in his han's, an' loped over the frunt ove the pulpid *kerdiff!* He lit on top ove, an' rite amung the mos' pius part ove the congregashun. Ole Misses Chaneyberry sot wif her back tu the pulpit, sorter stoopin forrid. He lit a-stradil ove her long naik, a shuttin her up wif a snap, her head atwix her knees, like shuttin up a jack-knife, an' he sot intu gittin away his levil durndest; he went in a heavy lumberin gallop, like a ole fat waggon hoss, skared at a locomotive. When he jumpt a bainch he shook the yeath. The bonnets, an' fans clar'd the way an' jerked most ove the children wif em, an' the rest he scrunched. He open'd a purfeckly clar track tu the woods, ove every livin thing. He weighed ni ontu three hundred, hed a black stripe down his back, like ontu a ole bridil rein, an' his belly wer 'bout the size, an' color ove a beef paunch, an' hit a-swingin out frum side tu side; he leand back frum hit, like a littil feller a-totin a big drum, at a muster, an' I hearn hit plum tu whar I wer. Thar wer cramp-knots on his laigs es big es walnuts, an' mottled splotches on his shins; an' takin him all over, he minded ove a durnd crazy ole elephant, pussessed ove the devil, rared up on hits hind aind, an' jis' *gittin* frum sum imijut danger ur tribulashun. He did the loudest, an' skariest, an' fussiest runnin I ever seed, tu be no faster nur hit wer, since dad tried tu outrun the ho'nets.

"Well, he disapear'd in the thicket jis' bustin—an' ove all the noises yu ever hearn, wer made thar on that camp groun': sum wimen screamin—they wer the skeery ones; sum larfin—they wer the wicked ones; sum cryin—they wer the fool ones (sorter my stripe yu know); sum tryin tu git away wif thar faces red—they wer the modest ones; sum lookin arter ole Bullin—they wer the curious ones; sum hangin clost tu thar sweethearts—they wer the sweet ones; sum on thar knees wif thar eyes shot, but facin the way the ole mud turtil wer a-runnin—they wer the 'saitful ones; sum duin nuthin—they wer the waitin ones; an' the mos' dangerus ove all ove em by a durnd long site.

"I tuck a big skeer mysef arter a few rocks, an' sich like fruit, spattered ontu the pulpit ni ontu my head; an' es the Lovingoods, durn em! knows nuffin but tu run, when they gits skeerd, I jis' out fur the swamp on the krick. As I started, a black bottil ove bald-face smashed agin a tree furninst me, arter missin the top ove my head 'bout a inch. Sum durn'd fool professor dun this, who hed more zeal nor sence; fur I say that eny man who wud waste a quart ove even mean sperrits, fur the chance ove knockin a poor ornary devil like me down wif the bottil, is a bigger fool nor ole Squire Mackmullen, an' he tried tu shoot hissef wif a onloaded hoe-handle."

"Did they catch you Sut?"

"Ketch thunder! *No sir!* jis' look at these yere laigs! Skeer me, hoss, jis' skeer me, an' then watch me while I stay in site, an' yu'll never ax that fool question agin. Why, durn it, man that's what the ait dullers am fur.

"Ole Barbelly Bullin, es they calls 'im now, never preached ontil yesterday, an' he hadn't the fust durn'd 'oman tu hear 'im; *they hev seed too much ove 'im.* Passuns ginerly hev a pow'ful strong holt on wimen; but, hoss, I tell yu thar ain't meny ove em kin run stark nakid over an' thru a crowd ove three hundred wimen an' not injure thar karacters *sum.* Enyhow, hits a kind ove show they'd ruther see one at a time, an' pick the passun at that. His tex' wer, 'Nakid I cum intu the world, an' nakid I'm a gwine outen hit, ef I'm spard ontil then.' He sed nakidness warnt much ove a sin, purtickerly ove dark nights. That he wer a weak, frail wum ove the dus', an' a heap more sich truck.

Then he totch ontu me; sed I wer a livin proof ove the hell-desarvin nater ove man, an' that thar warnt grace enuf in the whole 'sociation tu saften my outside rind; that I wer 'a lost ball' forty years afore I wer born'd, an' the bes' thing they cud du fur the church, wer tu turn out, an' still hunt fur me ontil I wer shot. An' he never said Hell-sarpints onst in the hole preach. I b'leve, George, the durnd fools am at hit.

"Now, I wants yu tu tell ole Barbelly this fur me, ef he'll let me an' Sall alone, I'll let him alone—a-while; an' ef he don't, ef I don't lizzard him agin, I jis' wish I may be dod durnd! *Skeer him if yu ken.*

"Let's go tu the spring an' take a ho'n.

"Say George, didn't that ar Hell-sarpint sermon ove his'n, hev sumthin like a Hell-sarpint aplicashun? Hit looks sorter so tu me."

A Razor-Grinder in a Thunder-Storm

"FRUM the orful faces yu's a-makin at that ar scrap ove lookin-glass, yu wants tu skeer yure picter, ur yu's et sumthin what hes cuttin aidges; which is hit, George?"

"Neither" said I.

"Well, p'raps sumbody hes been a-cuttin shoe-strings outen a sandy deer-skin wif yur rayshure; yu wants hit ground, don't yu? Bake Boyd's man cud a dun hit."

"Who was Bake Boyd's man? Was he a negro?"

"Wus nor that; he wer a mighty mean Yankee rayshure grinder, what wunst cum tu Knoxville a footback, wif a mercheen strapt ontu his shoulders like ontu a patent corn-sheller, an' he narated hit about, that he would grind raysures, scissors, ur pint needils, mons'ous cheap. He soon got tu grindin away fus' rate. He wer a pow'ful slow-speakin, dignerfied sorter varmint, an' thort that hissef an' mercheen cummanded the respeck an' submishun ove the poperlashun, wharever he went. That idear wus chased outen his skull *thru* his years, mons'ous quick, at Knoxville. He cudn't hev cum tu a better place than hit wer in them days, fur sweepin out the inside ove stuft up fellers' skulls clean ove all ole rusty, cob-web, bigited idears, an' then a fillin hit up fresh wif sumthin new an' activ; an' in the 'sort-mint wer allers wun king idear sure, an' hit wer in words sorter so: '*If* I gits away alive, durn ef ever I cum *yere* agin.' I speck ni ontu a thousin fellers, off an' on, cum tu that ole town sufferin pow'ful wif a onintemitant attack ove swell head, an' every durn'd wun ove em lef thar wif the words I spoke jis now, a-drapin ofen thar limber onder lips, sorter like a ole heart-broken hoss slobbers.

"Bake Boyd (Bake wer the short fur Bacon, an' Bacon wer his nickname yu know) wer ni ontu es clever a feller es ever wer born'd. Thar wer durn'd littil weevil in his wheat, mity small chance ove warter in his whisky, an' not a drap ove streakid blood in his veins. But he *hed* a besettin sin: he wer pow'fully pursessed wif the devil; he wer so chock full ove hit that his har wudn't lie still. He watched fur *openins* tu work off sum kind ove devilment, jist es clost es a ole 'oman what wer wunst onsanctified hersef, watches her darters when a suckus ur a camp meetin am in heat.

"Well, Bake thort he seed a openin in that ar raysuregrindin establishmint, so he sot in tu make the durnd fool bleve that lecterin ontu the skyance ove raysure-sharpenin wer his speshul gif, an' that rite *thar* wer the place tu try that sock on. Bake dwelt long ontu the crop ove dimes tu be gethered frum that field; that he'd make more than thar wer spots ontu forty fawns in July, not tu speak ove the big gobs ove repertashun he'd tote away, a shinin all over his close, like litnin bugs ontu a dorg fennil top. The argymint fotch him, particularly the spotted fawn part ove hit. But he wer a Yankee, an' wanted tu know, afore he begun, how many spots thar wur ontu *wun* fawn: so he went tu the stabil, an' axed ole Dick, Bake's hossler.

"The ole niggar scratched his hed, an' tole him, 'Marster, I'se never counted em, but I specks thar am a gallun, suah an' sartin.'

"He got Bake tu git sum 'vartisments printed, an' stuck up all over town. Bake show'd that he onderstood the 'vartisment bisness, fur he put the picter ove a rarin stud hoss at the top, a runaway buck niggar wif a bundil each side, while two barrils marked whisky, a wool-cardin mersheen, an' a cider mill top't off the bottum.

"While Bake wer a-doin ove this, ole Grinder wer a-ritin out the lecter. Hit wer a complikated sort ove dockymint —talked sorter like a feller wud tu a Konstable, tu take his mind ofen the warrant he know'd he hed fur him, ontill he seed a chance tu run. Hit spoke in purtickeler ove the commit, Niagray Falls, the merlennium, hatchin chickins, fallin frum grace, an' makin mush outen sawdust, an' generally ove everything on the A'mitey's green yeath, sceptin raysure-grindin, an' the depravity ove man, when he am a boy. He ortent tu hev lef that pint out, fur hit wer boys what he wer dealin wif jis' then, an' a rite tight preacher mout hev call'd them deprav'd or onsanctified at leas'.

"Well, that nite the Court Hous wer plum full; everybody

wer thar, sceptin Lum Jones, an' he wer hid out frum the Free Masons. Bake sot ahine the lecterin-mersheen, tu read frum the paper tu him when he furgot what wer in hit. Thar wer fotch intu the yard, clost tu the winder whar they wer a-standin, a ole brass canyun full tu the muzzle, wif powder an' red clay. Up in the lof by a trap door, an' plum over the feller's hed, sot Joe Jacksin, a-holdin ontu a half barril full ove warter outen a puddil, whar a misfortinat dead sow hed been floatin fur ten days.

"Well, the lecter begun, an' promised tu las' till daybreak, fur the mersheen soon stall'd, an' Bake's juty wer tu gin hit ile by readin frum the paper; but he red so low that the man cudn't make out what he sed, so he twistid roun his hed an' whisper'd, 'louder an' plainer.' Bake, instid ove duin better, got wus—sot intu readin in sum furrin tung, sorter like Cherokee, wif a sprinkil ove Irish. Hit wer loud enuf; so fur so good; but hit lacked a durn'd site ove bein plainer. The raysure renovatur stood wif his hed high an' squar tu the congregashun, his eyes takin a site jis' abuv thar heds, an' a-gittin rounder an' bigger at every word; you cud see the whites all roun them; an' he wer a pursin up his mouf like ontu a tied bag. I wer listnin fur him tu whistil nex thing.

"'Tshish! tshish!' sorter low like, now begun tu cum outen the wimin an' boys, all over the house. The ole men's specks begun tu shine, an' thar mouf ainds hed started towar'd thar years. The feller hissef begun tu twist sorter like pisants wer surveyin a railroad route up his laigs; eyes still spreadin, an' the infunel Cherokee gittin louder—not a durnd word in Inglish—when 'bo-lang' went the canyun, litin up all the town, smashin in the winders, an' shakin down the plasterin. Imejuntly Joe Jacksin up-sot the kaig, kerswish-selush cum the warter ontu Mr. Grinder's hed, every drap ove hit.

"Fur a momint he look'd like a iron statoot ove a durn'd fool in a playin fountin.

"He were dresst in a linnin bob-tail coat, an' trowsis, an' no drawers; the warter made them hug him pow'ful clost, an' look a heap thinner; yu cud see the adjact laingth ove his shut-tail, the width ove the hem, an' even tu the moles on his laigs, an' the har on his shins.

"He cum tu hissef like he wer used tu bein duck't, shook

the warter ofen hissef like ontu a dorg, an' sez he: 'Ladies an' gentlemen, when I seed the litenin, an' hearn the thunder, I 'spected a pow'ful rain-storm, an' hit am here.' (Here he tuck a smell ove fust wun coat sleeve, an' then tuther, an' turn'd up the pint ove his nose.) 'So, owin tu the inclemuncy ove the nite, I dismissis this yere congregashun, *siner diar*,' (here he tuck anuther smell at his sleeve) 'an' ef yu hesn't been vaxinashun'd fur the yaller fever, cholery, an' the black-tung, yu'd better leave this yere town, fur they's *all* a-cummin if thar's enything in the smell ove a rain.' Nobody claim'd back thar dime, an' Bake can't fur the soul ove him fix that case up tu this day, hu got the bes' of hit, the raysure-grinder ur tuther side; sumtimes he thinks wun, sumtimes tuther."

While Sut was telling this story, a fat-headed young man listened throughout without moving a muscle of his face; when it was finished he raised his expressionless eyes and asked: "Did anybody laugh at the unfortunate man that night Mr. Lovingood?"

Sut eye'd him for a moment, from head to foot and back again, with an expression of supreme contempt, and shambling off, looking back over his shoulder, said: "Yu mus' be a dam fool."

Old Skissim's Middle Boy

WHEN I war a littil over half grown, hed sprouted my tail feathers, an' wer beginnin tu crow, thar wer a livin in the neighborhood a dredful fat, mean, lazy boy, 'bout my age. He wer the middil son ove a ole lark, name Skissim. He tinkered ontu ole clocks, an' spinin wheels, et lye hominy, an' exhortid at meetin fur a livin, while this middil boy ove hisen, did the sleepin fur the hole famurly. He cud beat a hog an' a hungry dorg eatin, an' then beat his eatin wif his sleepin, es bad es his eatin beat the eatin ove a rat, arter bein shut in a church, ur a snake in a jug wif no mouf tu hit. They waked him tu eat, an' then hed tu wake him agin tu make him quit eatin; waked him tu go tu the spring, an' waked him tu start back agin; waked him tu say his prayers, an' waked him tu stop sayin 'em. In fac they wer allers a-wakin him, an' he wer allers a-goin tu sleep agin. Ole Skissim waked 'im wif a waggin whip, an' a buckshot in the cracker, what he toted apupus. His mam waked him wif the tea-kittil an' scaldin warter. Bof the buck-shot cracker an' the warter los thar vartu et las, an' they jis' gin him over tu onaindin sleepin, an' onmitigated hardness ove hed. Charley Dickins's son, the fat boy, mout been es ni kin tu him es a secund cuzzin, ef his mam wer a pow'ful wakeful 'oman.

I hedn't foun' out then, sartinly, that I wer a natr'l born durnd fool. I sorter suspishiond hit, but still hed hopes. So I wer fool enuf tu think I wer smart enuff tu break him frum snoozin *all* the time, so I lay wake ove nites fur a week, fixin the way tu du hit; an' that minds me tu tell yu what I thinks ove plannin an' studdyin: hit am ginerly no count. All pends, et las' on what yu dus an' how yu kerries yursef *at the moment ove ackshun*. Sarcumstances turn about pow'ful fas', an' all yu kin du is tu think jis' es fas es they kin turn, an' jis' es they turn, an' ef yu du this, I'm durnd ef yu don't git out sumhow. Long studyin am like preparin a supply ove warter intu a wum hole barril, tu put out fire: when the fire dus cum, durn'd ef yu don't hev tu hustil roun pow'ful fas', an' git more warter, fur thar's nun in the barril. But es I wer a-tellin yu, I studied out at las' a plan what I thort wud wake the devil; an' I sot in tu kerrin hit out.

The ole man Skissim an' his wife went tu a nite meetin, an' tuck the ballance ove his ur rather *her* brats—a feller shu'd allers be pow'ful keerful in speakin on that pint. I'se allers hearn that hit tuck a mons'us wise brat tu know hits daddy, an' I thinks hit takes a wiser daddy tu know his own brats. Dad never wud speak sartin bout eny ove our famerly but *me*, an' he counted fur that by sayin I wer by a long shot tu cussed a fool tu belong tu enybody else, so I *am* a Lovingood. My long laigs sumtimes sorter bothers me, but then mam tuck a pow'ful skeer et a san-hill crane a-sittin on a peel'd well-pole, an she out-run her shadder thuty yards in cumin half a mile. I speck I owes my laigs an' speed tu that sarcumstance an' not tu eny fraud on mam's part.

Well, they went tu nite meetin an' lef him in the kitchin fas' asleep, belevin tu fine him right thar when they cum back; but they wer mistaken'd that pop, fur when they cum they foun the widest awake boy ever born'd in that ur eny uther house, ur outen doors either, an' es tu bein rite thar he warn't by a durn'd site; he wer here, thar, an' every whar, et the same time, an' ef he hed any apertite fur vittils jis' then, he didn't hang out his sign, that I cud see.

They lef him sittin ontu a split-bottom cheer, plum asleep all over, even tu his ole hat. I tuck about thuty foot ove clothes line, an' tied him tu the cheer by his neck, body, an' arms, levin his laigs loose. He looked sorter like the Lion in the spellin-book, when the rat wer a-cuttin a fish net off ove him. That wern't a skeer'd rat, wer he? I hed him safe now tu practize on, an' I sot in tu duin hit, sorter this way: I painted his face the culler ove a nigger coal-burner, scept a white ring roun his eyes; an' frum the corners ove his mouf, sorter downards, slouch-wise, I lef a white strip. Hit made his mouf look sorter like ontu a hoss track an' ni ontu es big. He wer a fine picter tu study, ef your mind wer fond ove skeery things. He look't savidge es a sot steel trap, baited wif asnick, an wer jis' fit fur tresun, straterjim, an' tu spile things. Tu this day, when I dreams ove the devil, dad, Passun Bullin, an' uther orful oppressive things, that infunel boy, es he look't that nite, am durnd intermitly mix't wif the hole ove em. I speck he's dead is the reason ove hit.

I screw'd ontu each ove his years a par ove iron hanvices, what his dad squeezed ole clocks, an' crac't warnuts wif, an' they hung down like over-grow'd year-rings; I tied a gridiron tu wun ankil, an' a par ove fire-tongs tu tuther; I pour'd a bottil ove groun red-pepper down his back, onder his shut; I turn'd loose a pint ove June-bugs, what I kotch apupus, intu his buzzum, an' buttoned em up; I tied a baskit full ove fire crakers tu the cheer back, tu his har, an' tu his wrists; I button'd up a big grey-whisker'd aggravated ole rat, tied wif a string intu the slack ove his britches; tuther aind ove the string wer fas' ontu his gallus button, an the rat, like all the res' ove that tribe, imejuntly sot in cuttin his way out; but owin tu his parvarse nater ur the darkness ove the place, he sot in tu cuttin the wrong way; he wer a workin towards the back-bone, an' furder frum the britches, every cut. I learnt this fac' frum the cheer risin frum the flure, an' fallin agin jis' tu rise imejuntly a littil higher, an' sum souns, a mixtry ove snort, snore, grunt, an' groan, which he wer beginin tu isoo tolabil fas', an' gettin louder every bounce ove the cheer, an' becumin more like ontu a howl every pop. In the beginin ove his oneasines he dream'd ove wagin whip, nex' he dream'd ove a tea-kittil es big es a still, an' lots ove bilin warter, an' nex he drempt ove bof ove 'em; an' now he wer a dreamin that the tea-kittil wer a steam ingine, a drivin the waggin whip, an' a cottin gin wif red hot saws fifteen hundred licks a minit, an' that *he wer in the cottin hopper*.

I now thot hit ni ontu the proper time tu tetch the crackers, so es tu hev everything bar hits shar in the kontemplated cummin waknin. An' I did hit. The fust handful ur so gwine off help'd, wif the industry ove that energetic ole rat, the sarchin ove the red pepper, an' the permiskus scratchin roun ove the bugs, tu begin tu wake him sorter gradually, a littil faster nor light bread rises, an' a littil slower then a yeathquake wakes weazels. A few hundred more gwine off, still hevin the rat, pepper, an' insex tu back em, got him wide enuf awake tu bleve that he wer threatened wif sum orful pussonal calamerty, what wanted pow'ful quick work on his part tu dodge. He wer awake now all over, even tu his durnd ole hat, an' he show'd hit in es meny ways es a cat dus, lock'd up in a empty room wif a strange an' interprisin big dorg.

He grabbed the fire shovil, an' bounc'd half bent (the cheer kep him frum straitin up) all over that kitchen, a strikin over-handed, onder-handed, up-handed, down-handed, an' lef-handed, at every 'spishus shadder he seed. He fit by the light ove ten million sparks; he wer es active as a smut-mercheen in full blast, an' every grain ove wheat a spark. An' he wer a hollerin everything anybody ever did holler in dredful tribulashun ove spirit, even tu, "Now I lay me down tu sleep," an' "Gloree."

When I'se in trubbil, skeer, ur tormint, I dus but wun thing, an' that's onresistabil, onekeled, an' durn'd fas' runnin, an' I jis' keeps at hit till I gits cumfort. Now his big idear onder nise an' varigated hurtin wer tu fite, an' keep on a-fitin, ontil peace ove mine cum. I never seed sich keryins on in all my born'd days. He made more fuss, hit more licks at more things, wer in more places, an' in more shapes, in a shorter time, then eny mortal auctioneer cud tell ef he hed es meny tungs es a baskit full ove buckils. Every now an' then he'd gin his head a vishus, vigrus shake, an' the han-vices wud hit him fore an' arter, till his skull rattiled like ontu a ole gourd.

The ole Skissim an' his tribe cum home frum meetin, an' hearin the onyeathly riot, thort sumbody hed opened a dorggery in thar kitchen, an' that a neighborhood fite wer gwine on, an' every feller's dorg along. They rushed in tu drive out the crowd, an' capter the whisky, an' a durnder more misfortinit mistake never wer made by a man, 'oman, an' a string ove fifteen brats, since ole Bill Shivers went fur a runnin threshin-meesheen tu smash hit, thinkin hit wer a big musick-box.

The ole hoss hisse'f imejuntly cum in contack wif a holesum knock down, what calm'd him intu sumthin mons'us like sleep, fur about a minit. Now a heap ove things ken happen in a minit, purtickerly ef thar's sumbody who hes sot his hole soul tu the bisiness ove makin em happen. Hit wer so in that kitchen. Agin the ole feller cum tu, the ole 'oman wer knocked hed fust intu the meal-barril, whar she wer breathin more meal nur air, an' she wer snortin hit up over the aidges ove the barril like hit wer a fountin playin corn meal. The ol'est gal wer sturn fus' in a soap-kittil, an' she wor a-makin suds outen sum ove hit. The nex' wun wer laingthwise belly down in the pot corner. The biggest boy wer whar the back-log orter been, ontu his all fours a-scratchin up all the embers an' ashes, a-tryin tu cum out frum thar. Anuther cub, in a jackid wif a wun inch tail, wer knocked plum thru the tin intu the safe amung the cold vitils an' things. A littil gal, doll baby an' all, wer on the top shelf ove cup-board, amung the delf, a-screamin like a littil steam whistil.

The neighbors wer a-getherin in roun the nise an' rumpus, an' not a durn'd wun hed the least idear ove what wer wrong, sceptin ove me. I onderstood hit all, durn'd fool es I is. Tu 'scape frum bein 'spishioned, I sot in tu cuttin the cheer loose es I got chances, an' a-keepin outen the range ove that flyin fire shovil, fur hit wer still spreadin hurtin an' mischief on a perpetul moshun plan. Everybody hit totch fell, an' everything hit cum agin got grief. The tin buckits look'd like drunk men's hats. Pails hed lef' thar hoops, an' the delf war was in scrimpshuns. When he got divorced frum the cheer, I tho't he'd sorter simmer down. But no sir! He got wus, an' did his work faster an' better; he wer as crazy as a bed-bug, an' as savidge as a mad-dorg.

I seed a-cummin, a ole widder, what wer a pow'ful pius turn'd pusson, in the same church wif ole Skissim, an' she wer the news-kerrier gineral ove the neighborhood. Folks sed that they hed a religus feelin fur each uther, what led tu meny love-feas, wif nobody at em but tharsefs, an' wer bof doin mouns'ous well, considerin the thorn in the flesh. Sez she—

"Oh, my soul! Du tell me what *hes* happened! Oh, lordy massy!" sed I, "hits a-happenin yet!" a-lookin orful solemn in the moonshine. Sez I, "I'll tell yu, es I knows yu won't speak ove hit; fur ef hit gits out, hit mout make the pepil sorter think hard ove Mister Skissim. He cum home frum meetin plum crazy, talkin about the seventh cumandment, an' he's sot intu murderin hes folks wif a crowbar. He hes dun got his wife an' six ove the brats; thar a-lyin in thar es cold es krout; an' he's hot arter the rest ove em;

sez he's in a hurry tu git thru, es he hes *yu* tu kill an' salt down afore day. Now I know by that he's turn'd durned fool."

She never sed a word, but put out fur Squir Haley's, an' swore her life agin ole Skissim, an' tuck out a warrint fur him a-chargin murder, arson, blasfemy, fleabottomry an' rape. Hit skeer'd ole Skissim ontil he run away.

By the time I got dun inlitenin the widder, that ar onquinchable boy hed the kitchen all tu hissef. Everybody wer feard tu go ni the door. Now yu cudent guess in ten year what he then went an' did. He jis' made a piller outen the cheer, an' sot intu sleepin agin. Ef ever I'se call'd on tu stop his sleepin eny more agin, I'll try a muskit an' sixteen buckshot, at jis' about ten steps.

Blown Up With Soda

Sut's hide is healed—the wounds received in his sudden separation from his new shirt have ceased to pain, and, true to his instincts, or rather "a famerly dispersition," es he calls it, he "pitches in," and gets awfully blown up by a wild mountain girl. Hear him, poor fellow!

"George, did yu ever see Sicily Burns? Her dad lives at the Rattil-snake Spring, clost ontu the Georgia line."

"Yes, a very handsome girl."

"Handsome! that ar word don't kiver the case; hit souns sorter like callin good whiskey strong water, when yu ar ten mile frum a still-hous, hit a rainin, an' yer flask only haf full. She shows amung wimen like a sunflower amung dorg fennil, ur a hollyhawk in a patch ove smartweed. Sich a buzzim! Jis' think ove two snow balls wif a strawberry stuck but-ainded intu bof on em. She takes adzactly fifteen inches ove garter clar ove the knot, stans sixteen an' a 'alf hans hi, an' weighs one hundred an' twenty-six in her petticoatail afore brekfus'. She cudent crawl thru a whisky barrel wif bof heads stove out, nur sit in a common arm-cheer, while yu cud lock the top hoop ove a chun, ur a big dorg collar, roun the huggin place."

"The *what*, Sut?"

"The *wais*' yu durn oninishiated gourd, yu! Her har's es black es a crow's wing et midnite, ur a nigger hanlin charcoal when he's hed no brekfus'; hit am es slick es this yere bottil, an' es long es a hoss's tail. I've seed her jump over a split-bottim cheer wifout showin her ankils, ur ketchin her dress ontu the knobs. She cud cry an' larf et the same time, an' either lov'd ur hated yu all over. Ef her hate fell ontu yu, yu'd feel like yu'd been whipp'd wif a pizen vine, ur a broom made outen nettils when yer breeches an' shut wer bof in the wash-tub. She kerried enuf devil about her tu run crazy a big settlment ove Job's children; her skin wer es white es the inside ove a frogstool, an' her cheeks an' lips es rosey es a pearch's gills in dorgwood blossum time—an' sich a smile! Why, when hit struck yu far an' squar hit felt jis' like a big ho'n ove onrectified ole Munongahaley, arter yu'd been sober fur a month, a tendin ove a ten hoss prayer-meetin twist a day, an' mos' ove the nites.

"Three ove her smiles when she wer a tryin ove hersef, taken keerfully ten minutes apart, wud make the gran' captin ove a temprunce s'iety so durn'd drunk, he wudn't no his britches frum a par ove bellowses, ur a pledge frum a—a—warter-pot. Oh! I be durned ef hits eny use talkin, that ar gal cud make me murder ole Bishop Soul, hissef, ur kill mam, not tu speak ove dad, ef she jis' hinted she wanted sich a thing dun. Sich an 'oman cud du more devilmint nur a loose stud hoss et a muster ground', ef she only know'd what tools she totes, an' I'se sorter beginin tu think she no's the use ove the las' durnd wun, tu a dot. Her ankils wer es roun', an' not much bigger nur the wrist ove a rifle-gun, an' when she wer a-dancin, ur makin up a bed, ur gittin over a fence—— Oh durn sich wimen! Why aint they all made on the hempbreak plan, like mam, ur Betts Carr, ur Suke Miller, so they wudn't bother a feller's thinker et all.

"George, this worl am all 'rong enyhow, more temtashun than preventitive; ef hit wer ekal, I'd stand hit. What kin the ole prechurs an' the ugly wimen 'spect ove us, 'sposed es we ar tu sich invenshuns es she am? Oh, hits jis' no use in thar talkin, an' groanin, an' sweatin tharsefs about hit; they mus' jis' upset nater ontu her head, an' keep her thar, ur shet up. Less taste this yere whisky."

Sut continued, wiping his mouth on his shirt-sleeve:

"I'se hearn in the mountins a fust rate fourth proof smash ove thunder cum onexpected, an' shake the yeath, bringin along a string ove litenin es long es a quarter track, an' es bright es a weldin heat, a-racin down a big pine tree, tarin hit intu broom splits, an' toof pickers, an' raisin a cloud ove dus', an' bark, an' a army ove lim's wif a smell sorter like the devil wer about, an' the long darnin needil leaves fallin roun wif a tif—tif—quiet sorter soun, an' then a quiverin on the yeath es littil snakes die; an' I felt quar in my in'ards, sorter ha'f cumfurt, wif a littil glad an' rite smart ove sorry mix'd wif hit.

"I'se seed the rattil-snake squar hissef tu cum at me, a

sayin z-e-e-e-e, wif that nisey tail ove his'n, an' I felt quar agin—mons'rous quar. I've seed the Oconee River jumpin mad frum rock tu rock wif hits clear, cool warter, white foam, an' music"——

"What, Sut?"

"Music; the rushin warter dus make music; so dus the wind, an' the fire in the mountin, an' hit gin me an oneasy queerness agin; but every time I look'd at that gal Sicily Burns, I hed all the feelins mix'd up, ove the litenin, the river, an' the snake, wif a totch ove the quicksilver sensashun a huntin thru all my veins fur my ticklish place.

"Tu gether hit all in a bunch, an' tie hit, she wer gal all over, frum the pint ove her toe-nails tu the aind ove the longes' har on the highis knob on her head—gal all the time, everywhar, an' wun ove the exhitenis kine. Ove corse I lean'd up tu her, es clost es I dar tu, an' in spite ove these yere yaigs, an' my appertite fur whisky, that ar shut-skinin bisness an' dad's actin hoss, she sorter lean'd tu me, jis' a scrimpshun, sorter like a keerful man salts uther pepil's cattil in the mountin, barly enuf tu bring em back tu the lick-bog sum day—that's the way she salted me, an' I 'tended the lick-log es reg'lar es the old bell cow; *an'* I wer jis' beginin tu think I wer ontu the rite trail tu es much cumfurt, an' stayin awake a-purpus, es ole Brigham Young wif all his saddil-culler'd wimen, an' the papers tu fetch more, ef he wants em.

"Well, wun day a cussed, palaverin, inyun-eatin Yankee pedlar, all jack-nife an' jaw, cum tu ole man Burns wif a carryall full ove appil-parin-mersheens, jewsharps, calliker, ribbons, sody-powder, an' uther durn'd truck.

"Now mine, I'd never hearn tell ove sody-powder in *my* born'd days; I didn't know hit frum Beltashazur's off ox; but I no's now that hit am wus nur gunpowder fur hurtin, an' durn'd ni es smart tu go off.

"That ar Yankee pedlar hes my piusest prayer, an' I jis wish I hed a kaig ove the truck intu his cussed paunch, wif a slow match cumin out at his mouf, an' I hed a chunk ove fire. The feller what foun a mossel ove 'im big enuf tu feed a cockroach, orter be turn'd loose tu pastur amung seventy-five purty wimen, an' foun in whisky fur life, becase ove his good eyes in huntin los' things. George, a Yankee pedlar's soul wud hev more room in a turnip-seed tu fly roun in than a leather-wing bat hes in a meetin-hous; that's jis' so.

"Sicily hed bot a tin box ove the cold bilin truck an' hid hit till I cum tu the lick-log agin, yu know. Well, I jis' happen'd tu pass nex' day, an' ove corse stopp'd tu injoy a look at the temtashun, an' she wer mity luvin tu me. I never felt the like—put wun arm roun my naik, an' tuther whar the susingil goes roun a hoss, tuck the inturn ontu me wif her lef' foot, an' gin me a kiss. Sez she——

"Sutty, luv, I'se got sumthin fur yu, *a new sensashun*"——

"An' I b'leve in hit strong, fur I begun tu feel hit pow'ful. My toes felt like I wer in a warm krick wif minners a-nibblin at em; a cole streak wer a racin up an' down my back like a lizzard wif a tucky hen arter 'im; my hans tuck the ager, an' my hart felt hot an' on-satisfied like. Then hit wer that I'd a-cut ole Soul's froat wif a hansaw, an' never batted my eye, ef she'd a-hinted the needsesity.

"Then she pour'd 'bout ten blue papers ove the fizilin powder intu a great big tumbler, an' es meny white papers intu anuther, an' put ni ontu a pint ove warter intu bof on em, stir'd em up wif a case-nife, an' gritted a morsel ove nutmaig on top, the 'saitful she torment lookin es solemn es a jasack in a snow storm, when the fodder gin out. She hilt wun, an' tole me tu drink tuther. I swaller'd hit at wun run; tasted sorter salty like, but I tho't hit wer part ove the sensashun. But I wer slitely mistaken'd; hit wer yet tu cum, an' warn't long 'bout hit, hoss, better b'leve. Ternally durn all sensashuns ove every spot an' stripe! I say. Then she gin me tuther, an' I sent hit a chasin the fus' instalmint tu the sag ove my paunch, race-hoss way. Yu see I'd got the idear onder my har that hit wer *luv-powders,* an' I'd swaller'd the devil red hot frum home, a-thinkin that. Luv-powders *frum her!* Jis' think ove hit yerse'f solemnly a minit, an' sit still ef yu kin.

"Jis' 'bout the time I wer ketchin my breff, I tho't I'd swaller'd a thrashin-meersheen in full blast, wif a cuppil ove bull-dorgs, an' they hed sot intu fitin; an' I felt sumthin cumin up my swaller, monstrus like a hi pressur steamboat. I cud hear hit a-snortin, and scizzin. *Kotch agin, by the great golly!* tho't I; same famerly dispersishun tu make a durn'd fool ove myse'f jis' es ofen es the sun sets, an' fifteen times ofener ef thar's a half a chance. Durn dad evermore, amen! I say.

"I happen'd tu think ove my hoss, an' I broke fur him. I stole a hang-dorg look back, an' thar lay Sicily, flat ove her back in the porch, clapin her hans, screamin wif laughin, her feet up in the air, a-kickin em a-pas' each uther like she wer tryin tu kick her slippers off. I'se pow'ful sorry I wer too bizzy tu look at em. Thar wer a road ove foam frum the hous' tu the hoss two foot wide, an' shoe mouf deep—looked like hit hed been snowin—a poppin, an' a-hissin, an' a-bilin like a tub ove soap-suds wif a red hot mole-board in hit. I gethered a cherry tree lim' es I run, an' I lit a-straddil ove ole Blackey, a-thrashin his hide like the devil beatin tan-bark, an' a-hissin wus nur four thousin mad ganders outen my mouf, eyes, nose, an' years. All this waked the ole hoss, an' he fotch one rar, one kick, an' then he went—he jis' mizzel'd, skar'd. Oh lordy! how the foam rolled, an' the hoss flew! Es we turned the corner ove the gardin lot, I hearn Sicily call, es clar es a bugle:

"'Hole hit down, Mister Lovingood! Hole hit down! Hits a cure fur puppy luv; hole hit *down!*'

"Hole hit down! Hu ever hearn sich a onpossibil—— Why, *rite then* I wer a-feelin the bottim ove my paunch cumin up arter hit, inside out, jis' like the bottim ove a green champain bottil. I wer spectin tu see hit every blast. That, wif what Sicily sed, wer a-hurtin my thinker pow'ful bad, an' then the ise-warter idear, that hit warn't a luv-powder arter all that hurtin—takin all tugether, I wer sorter wishin hit mout keep on till I wer all biled tu foam, plum tu my heel-strings.

"I wer aimin fur Dr. Goodman's, at the Hiwasee Copper Mine, tu git sumthin tu simmer hit down wif, when I met ole Clapshaw, the suckit-rider, a-travelin to'ards sumbody's hot biskit an' fried chicken. As I cum tarin along, he hilt up his hans like he wanted tu pray fur me; but es I wanted sumthin tu reach furder, an' take a ranker holt nur his prars cud, I jis' rambled ahead. I wer hot arter a ten-hoss dubbil-actin steam paunch-pump, wif wun aind sock'd deep intu my soda lake, an' a strong manbody doctur at tuther; hit wer my *big want* jis' then. *He* tuck a skeer, es I wer cumin strait fur him; his faith gin out, an' he dodged, flat hat, hoss, an' saddil-bags, intu the thicket. I seed his hoss's tail fly up over his back, es he disappear'd intu the bushes; thar mus' a-been spurrin gwine on 'bout thar. I liked his moshuns onder a skeer rite well; he made that dodge jis' like a mud-turkil draps ofen a log when a big steamboat cums tarin a-pas'. Es he pass'd ole man Burns's, Sicily hailed 'im tu ax ef he met enybody gwine up the road in a sorter hurry. The poor devil tho't that p'raps he mout; warnt sure, but he hed seed a dreadful forewarnin, ur a ghos', ur ole Belzebub, ur the Tariff. Takin all things tugether, however, in the litil time spar'd tu 'im fur 'flection, hit mus' a-been a crazy, long-laiged shakin Quaker, fleein frum the rath tu cum, on a black an' white spotted hoss, a-whipin 'im wif a big brush; an' he hed a white beard what cum frum jis onder his eyes down tu the pumil ove the saddil, an' then forked an' went tu his knees, an' frum thar drapp'd in bunches es big es a crow's nes', tu the groun; an' he hearn a soun like ontu the rushin ove mitey warters, an' he wer pow'fully exersized 'bout hit enyhow. Well, I guess he wer, an' so wer his fat hoss, an' so wer ole Blackey, an' more so by a durn'd site wer me mysef. Arter he cumpos'd hissef he rit out his fool noshuns fur Sicily, that hit wer a new steam invenshun tu spread the Catholic doctrin, an' tote the Pope's bulls tu pastur in distunt lans, made outen sheet iron, ingin rubber, tann'd leather, ise cream, an' fat pine, an' that the hoss's tail wer made outen iron wire, red hot at the pint, an' a stream ove sparks es long es the steerin-oar ove a flatboat foller'd thararter; an' takin hit all tugether hit warnt a safe thing tu meet in a lane ove a dark nite; an' he tho't he hed a call over the mountin tu anuther sarkit; that chickens warnt es plenty over thar, but then he wer a self-denyin man.

"Now, George, all this beard, an' spotted hoss, an' steam, an' fire, an' snow, an' wire tails, wer durn'd skeer'd suckit rider's humbug; hit all cum outen my paunch, wifout eny vomitin ur coaxin, an' ef hit hedn't, I'd a dun been busted intu more scraps nur thar's aigs in a big catfish.

" 'Hole hit down, Mister Lovingood! Hole hit down!' Now warnt that jis' the durndes' onreasonabil reques' ever an o'man made ove man? She mout jis es well ax'd me tu swaller my hoss, an' then skin the cat on a cob-web. She's pow'ful on docterin tho', I'll swar tu that."

"Why, Sut?"

"Kase she cur'd my puppy-luv wif wun dost, durn her! George, am sody *pizen?*"

"No; why?"

"I sorter 'spected hit wer, an' I sot in, an' et yarbs, an' grass, an' roots, till I'se pounch'd out like ontu a ole cow; my hole swaller an' paunch am tann'd hard es sole leather. I axes rot-gut no odds now. Yere's a drink tu the durndes' fool in the worl'—jis' me!"

And the bottom of Sut's flask flashed in the sun light.

Sicily Burns's Wedding

"HEY GE-ORGE!" rang among the mountain slopes; and looking up to my left, I saw "Sut," tearing along down a steep point, heading me off, in a long kangaroo lope, holding his flask high above his head, and hat in hand. He brought up near me, banteringly shaking the half-full "tickler," within an inch of my face.

"Whar am yu gwine? Take a suck hoss? This yere truck's *ole*. I kotch hit myse'f, hot this mornin frum the still wum. Nara durn'd bit ove strike-nine in hit—I put that ar piece ove burnt dried peach in myse'f tu gin hit color—better nur ole Bullen's plan: he puts in tan ooze, in what he sells, an' when that haint handy, he uses the red warter outen a pon' jis' below his barn;—makes a pow'ful natral color, but don't help the taste much. Then he correcks that wif red pepper; hits an orful mixtry, that whisky ole Bullen makes; no wonder he seed 'Hell-sarpints.' He's pisent ni ontu three quarters ove the b'levin parts ove his congregashun wif hit, an' tuther quarter he's sot intu ruff stealin an' cussin. Ef his still-'ous don't burn down, ur he peg out hisse'f, the neighborhood am ruinated a-pas' salvashun. Haint he the durndes sampil ove a passun yu ever seed enyhow?

"Say George, du yu see these yere well-poles what I uses fur laigs? Yu sez yu sees em, dus yu?"

"Yes."

"Very well; I passed 'em a-pas' each uther tuther day, right peart. I put one out a-head jis' so, an' then tuther 'bout nine feet a-head ove hit agin jis' so, an' then kep on a-duin hit. I'll jis gin yu leave tu go tu the devil ha'f hamon, ef I didn't make fewer tracks tu the mile, an' more tu the minit, than wer ever made by eny human man body, since Bark Wilson beat the sawlog frum the top ove the Frog Mountin intu the Oconee River, an' dove, an' dodged hit at las'. I hes allers look'd ontu that performince ove Bark's as onekel'd in histery, allers givin way tu dad's ho'net race, however.

"George, every livin thing hes hits pint, a pint ove sum sort. Ole Bullen's pint is a durn'ed fust rate, three bladed, dubbil barril'd, warter-proof, hypockracy, an' a never-tirein appertite fur bal'-face. Sicily Burns's pint am tu drive men folks plum crazy, an' then bring em to agin. Gin em a rale Orleans fever in five minits, an' then in five minits more, gin them a Floridy ager. Durn her, she's down on her heels flat-footed now. Dad's pint is tu be king ove all durn'd fools, ever since the day ove that feller what cribb'd up so much co'n down in Yegipt, long time ago (he run outen his coat yu minds). The Bibil tells us hu wer the stronges' man—hu wer the bes' man—hu wer the meekis' man, an' hu the wises' man, but leaves yu tu guess hu wer the bigges' fool.

"Well, eny man what cudent guess arter readin that ar scrimmage wif an 'oman 'bout that coat, haint sense enuf tu run intu the hous', ef hit wer rainin ded cats, that's all. Mam's pint am in kitchen insex, bakin hoecake, bilin greens, an' runnin bar laiged. My pint am in takin aboard big skeers, an' then beatin enybody's hoss, ur skared dorg, a-runnin frum onder em agin. I used tu think my pint an' dad's wer jis' the same, sulky, unmix'd king durn'd fool; but when he acted hoss, an' mistook hossflies fur ho'nets, I los' heart. Never mine, when I gits his 'sperence, I may be king fool, but yet great golly, he gets frum bad tu wus, monstrus fas'.

"Now ef a feller happens tu know what his pint am, he kin allers git along, sumhow, purvided he don't swar away his liberty tu a temprins s'ciety, live tu fur frum a still-'ous, an' too ni a chu'ch ur a jail. Them's my sentimints on 'pints,'—an' yere's my sentimints ontu folks: Men wer made a-purpus jis' tu eat, drink, an' fur stayin awake in the yearly part ove the nites; an' wimen wer made tu cook the vittils, mix the sperits, an' help the men du the stayin awake. That's all, an' nuthin more, onless hits fur the wimen tu raise the devil atwix meals, an' knit socks atwix drams, an' the men tu play short kerds, swap hosses wif fools, an' fite fur exersise, at odd spells.

"George, yu don't onderstan life yet scarcely at all, got a heap tu larn, a heap. But 'bout my swappin my laigs so fas'—these yere very par ove laigs. I hed got about a fox squirril skin full ove biled co'n juice packed onder my shut, an' onder my hide too, I mout es well add, an' wer aimin fur Bill Carr's on foot. When I got in sight ove ole man Burns's, I seed ni ontu fifty hosses an' muels hitch'd tu the fence. Durnashun! I jis' then tho't ove hit, 'twer Sicily's wedding day. She married ole Clapshaw, the suckit rider. The very feller hu's faith gin out when he met me sendin sody all over creashun. Suckit-riders am surjestif things tu me. They preaches agin me, an' I hes no chance tu preach back at them. Ef I cud I'd make the institushun behave hitsef better nur hit dus. They hes sum wunderful pints, George. Thar am two things nobody never seed: wun am a dead muel, an' tuther is a suckit-rider's grave. Kaze why, the he muels all turn intu old field schoolmasters, an' the she ones intu strong minded wimen, an' then when thar time cums, they dies sorter like uther folks. An' the suckit-riders ride ontil they marry; ef they marrys money, they turns intu store-keepers, swaps hosses, an' stays away ove colleckshun Sundays. Them what marrys, an' by sum orful mistake *misses the money*, jis' turns intu polertishuns, sells 'ile well stock,' and dies sorter in the human way too.

"But 'bout the wedding. Ole Burns hed a big black an' white bull, wif a ring in his snout, an' the rope tied up roun his ho'ns. They rid 'im tu mill, an' sich like wif a saddil made outen two dorgwood forks, an' two clapboards, kivered wif a ole piece ove carpet, rope girth, an' rope stirrups wif a loop in hit fur the foot. Ole 'Sock,' es they call'd the bull, hed jis' got back frum mill, an' wer turn'd intu the yard, saddil an' all, tu solace hissef a-pickin grass. I wer slungin roun the outside ove the hous', fur they hedn't hed the manners tu ax me in, when they sot down tu dinner. I wer pow'fully hurt 'bout hit, an' happen'd tu think— SODY. So I sot in a-watchin fur a chance tu du sumthin. I fus' tho't I'd shave ole Clapshaw's hoss's tail, go tu the stabil an' shave Sicily's mare's tail, an' ketch ole Burns out, an' shave his tail too. While I wer a-studyin 'bout this, ole Sock wer a-nosin 'roun, an' cum up ontu a big baskit what hilt a littil shattered co'n; he dipp'd in his head tu git hit, an' I slipp'd up an' jerked the handil over his ho'ns.

"Now, George, ef yu knows the nater ove a cow brute,

they is the durndes' fools amung all the beastes ('scept the Lovingoods); when they gits intu tribulashun, they knows nuffin but tu shot thar eyes, beller, an' back, an' keep a-backin. Well, when ole Sock raised his head an' foun hissef in darkness, he jis' twisted up his tail, snorted the shatter'd co'n outen the baskit, an' made a tremenjus lunge agin the hous'. I hearn the picters a-hangin agin the wall on the inside a-fallin. He fotch a deep loud rusty beller, mout been hearn a mile, an' then sot intu a onendin sistem ove backin. A big craw-fish wif a hungry coon a-reachin fur him, wer jis' nowhar. Fust agin one thing, then over anuther, an' at las' agin the bee-bainch, knockin hit an' a dozen stan ove bees heads over heels, an' then stompin back'ards thru the mess. Hit haint much wuf while tu tell what the bees did, ur how soon they sot intu duin hit. They am pow'ful quick-tempered littil critters, enyhow. The air wer dark wif 'em, an' Sock wer kivered all over, frum snout tu tail, so clost yu cudent a-sot down a grain ove wheat fur bees, an' they wer a-fitin one anuther in the air, fur a place on the bull. The hous' stood on sidelin groun, an' the back door wer even wif hit. So Sock happen tu hit hit plum, jis' backed intu the hous' onder 'bout two hundred an' fifty pouns ove steam, bawlin orful, an' every snort he fotch he snorted away a quart over bees ofen his sweaty snout. He wer the leader ove the bigges' an' the madest army ove bees in the world. Thar wer at leas' five solid bushels ove 'em. They hed filled the baskit, an' hed lodged ontu his tail, ten deep, ontil hit wer es thick es a waggin tung. He hed stuck strait up in the air, an' hit looked adzackly like a dead pine kivered wif ivey. I think he wer the hottes' and wus hurtin bull then livin; his temper, too, seemed tu be pow'fully flustrated. Ove *all* the durn'd times an' kerryins on yu *ever* hearn tell on wer thar an' thar abouts. He cum tail fust agin the ole two story Dutch clock, an' fotch hit, bustin hits runnin geer outen hit, the littil wheels a-trundlin over the floor, an' the bees even chasin them. Nex pass, he fotch up agin the foot ove a big dubbil injine bedstead, rarin hit on aind, an' punchin one ove the posts thru a glass winder. The nex tail fus' experdishun wer made aginst the caticorner'd cupboard, outen which he made a perfeck momox. Fus' he upsot hit, smashin in the glass doors, an' then jis' sot in an' stomp'd everything on the shelves intu giblits, a-tryin tu back furder in that direckshun, an' tu git the bees ofen his laigs.

"Pickil crocks, perserves jars, vinegar jugs, seed bags, yarb bunches, paragorick bottils, aig baskits, an' delf war —all mix'd dam permiskusly, an' not worth the sortin, by a duller an' a 'alf. Nex he got a far back acrost the room agin the board pertishun; he went thru hit like hit hed been paper, takin wif him 'bout six foot squar ove hit in splinters, an' broken boards, intu the nex room, whar they wer eatin dinner, an' rite yere the fitin becum gineral, an' the dancin, squawkin, cussin, an' dodgin begun.

"Clapshaw's ole mam wer es deaf es a dogiron, an sot at the aind ove the tabil, nex tu whar ole Sock busted thru the wall; tail fus' he cum agin her cheer, a-histin her an' hit ontu the tabil. Now, the smashin ove delf, an' the mixin ove vittils begun. They hed sot severil tabils tugether tu make hit long enuf. So he jis' rolled 'em up a-top ove one anuther, an' thar sot ole Missis Clapshaw, a-straddil ove the top ove the pile, a-fitin bees like a mad wind-mill, wif her calliker cap in one han, fur a wepun, an' a cract frame in tuther, an' a-kickin, an' a-spurrin like she wer ridin a lazy hoss arter the doctor, an' a-screamin rape, fire, an' murder, es fas' es she cud name 'em over.

"Taters, cabbige, meat, soup, beans, sop, dumplins, an' the truck what yu wallers 'em in; milk, plates, pies, puddins, an' every durn fixin yu cud think ove in a week, wer thar, mix'd an' mashed, like hit had been thru a thrashin-meesheen. Ole Sock still kep a-backin, an' backed the hole pile, ole 'oman an' all, also sum cheers, outen the frunt door, an' down seven steps intu the lane, an' then by golly, turn'd a fifteen hundred poun summerset hissef arter em, lit a-top ove the mix'd up mess, flat ove his back, an' then kicked hissef ontu his feet agin. About the time he ris, ole man Burns—yu know how fat, an' stumpy, an' cross-grained he is, enyhow—made a vigrus mad snatch at the baskit, an' got a savin holt ontu hit, but cudent *let go quick enuf;* fur ole Sock jis' snorted, bawled an' histed the ole cuss heels fust up intu the air, an' he lit on the bull's back, an' hed the baskit in his han.

"Jis' es soon es ole Blackey got the use ove his eyes, he tore off down the lane tu out-run the bees, so durn'd fas' that ole Burns wer feard tu try tu git off. So he jis' socked his feet intu the rope loops, an' then cummenc'd the durndes' bull-ride ever mortal man onder-tuck. Sock run atwix the hitched critters an' the railfence, ole Burns fust fitin him over the head wif the baskit tu stop him, an' then fitin the bees wif hit. I'll jis' be durn'd ef I didn't think he hed four ur five baskits, hit wer in so meny places at onst. Well, Burns, baskit, an' bull, an' bees, skared every durn'd hoss an' muel loose frum that fence—bees ontu all ove 'em, bees, by golly, everywhar. Mos' on 'em, too, tuck a fence rail along, fas' tu the bridil reins. Now I'll jis' gin yu leave tu kiss my sister Sal till she squalls, ef ever sich a sight wer seed ur sich nises hearn, es filled up that long lane. A heavy cloud ove dus', like a harycane hed been blowin, hid all the hosses, an' away abuv hit yu cud see tails, an' ainds ove fence-rails a-flyin about; now an' then a par ove bright hine shoes wud flash in the sun like two sparks, an' away ahead wer the baskit a-sirklin roun an' about at random. Brayin, nickerin, the bellerin ove the bull, clatterin ove runnin hoofs, an' a mons'ous rushin soun, made up the noise. Lively times in that lane jis' then, warnt thar?

"I swar ole Burns kin beat eny man on top ove the yeath a-fitin bees wif a baskit. Jis' set 'im a-straddil ove a mad bull, an' let thar be bees enuf tu exhite the ole man, an' the man what beats him kin break me. Hosses an' muels wer tuck up all over the county, an' sum wer forever los'. Yu cudent go eny course, in a cirkil ove a mile, an' not find buckils, stirrups, straps, saddil blankits, ur sumthin belongin tu a saddil hoss. Now don't forgit that about that hous' thar wer a good time bein had ginerally. Fellers an' gals loped outen windows, they rolled outen the doors in bunches, they clomb the chimleys, they darted onder the house jis' tu dart out agin, they tuck tu the thicket, they rolled in the wheat field, lay down in the krick, did everything but stan still. Sum made a strait run *fur* home, an' sum es strait a run *frum* home; livelyest folks I ever did see. Clapshaw crawled onder a straw pile in the barn, an' sot intu prayin—yu cud a-hearn him a mile—sumthin 'bout the plagues ove Yegipt, an' the pains ove the secon death. I tell yu now he lumbered.

"Sicily, she squatted in the cold spring, up tu her years,

an' turn'd a milk crock over her head, while she wer a drownin a mess ove bees onder her coats. I went tu her, an' sez I, 'Yu hes got anuther new sensashun haint yu?' Sez she—

"'Shet yer mouth, yu cussed fool!'

"Sez I, 'Power'ful sarchin feelin bees gins a body, don't they?'

"'Oh, lordy, lordy, Sut, these yere 'bominabil insex is jis' burnin me up!'

"'Gin 'em a mess ove SODY,' sez I, 'that'll cool 'em off, an' skeer the las' durn'd one ofen the place.'

"She lifted the crock, so she cud flash her eyes at me, an' sed, 'Yu go tu hell!' *jis es plain*. I thought, takin all things tugether, that p'raps I mout es well put the mountin atwix me an' that plantashun; an' I did hit.

"Thar warnt an' 'oman, ur a gal at that weddin, but what thar frocks, an' stockins wer too tite fur a week. Bees am wus on wimen than men, enyhow. They hev a farer chance at 'em. Nex day I passed ole Hawley's, an' his gal Betts wer sittin in the porch, wif a white hankerchef tied roun her jaws; her face wer es red es a beet, an' her eyebrows hung 'way over heavy. Sez I, 'Hed a fine time at the weddin, didn't yu?' 'Yu mus' be a durn'd fool,' wer every word she sed. I hadent gone a hundred yards, ontil I met Missis Brady, her hans fat, an' her ankils swelled ontil they shined. Sez she,—

"'Whar yu gwine, Sut?'

"'Bee huntin,' sez I.

"'Yu jis' say bees agin, yu infunel gallinipper, an' I'll scab yer head wif a rock.'

"Now haint hit strange how tetchus they am, on the subjick ove bees?

"Ove all the durn'd misfortinit weddins ever since ole Adam married that heifer, what wer so fon' ove talkin tu snaix, an' eatin appils, down ontil now, that one ove Sicily's an' Clapshaw's wer the worst one fur noise, disappintment, skeer, breakin things, hurtin, trubbil, vexashun ove spirrit, an' gineral swellin. Why, George, her an' him cudent sleep tugether fur ni ontu a week, on account ove the doins ove them ar hot-footed, 'vengeful, 'bominabil littil insex. They never will gee tugether; got tu bad a start, mine what I tell yu. Yu haint time now tu hear how ole Burns finished his bull-ride, an' how I cum tu du that lofty, topliftical speciment ove fas' runnin. I'll tell yu all that sum uther time. Ef eny ove 'em axes after me, tell 'em that I'm over in Fannin, on my way tu Dahlonega. They is huntin me tu kill me, I is fear'd.

"Hit am an orful thing, George, tu be a natral born durn'd fool. Yu'se never 'sperienced hit pussonally, hev yu? Hits made pow'fully agin our famerly, an all owin tu dad. I orter bust my head open agin a bluff ove rocks, an' jis' wud du hit, ef I warnt a cussed coward. All my yeathly 'pendence is in these yere laigs—d'ye see 'em? Ef they don't fail, I may turn human, sum day, that is sorter human, enuf tu be a Squire ur school cummisiner. Ef I wer jis' es smart es I am mean, an' ornary, I'd be President ove a Wild Cat Bank in less nor a week. Is sperrits plenty over wif yu?"

Old Burns's Bull-Ride

Well, now, George, while yu am waitin' fur yer chain-kerriers, I'll tell yu how old Burns finish'd that onspeakable Bull-ride, an' how I won my race agin all his sons, thar houns, an the neighborhood ginirally. Well, arter he got outen the lane, they struck a piece ove timber lan', an' thar he los' his baskit. Then he betuck hissef tu onwindin the rope ofen the bull's ho'ns, an' wrapp'd hit roun his lef han.

Now es hit happens, Squire Mills hes a bull too—a mons'rous fitin, cross ole cuss, what hes the Frog Mountain fur his surkit this year. He jis' goes whar he durn'd please, an' thinks he is the bes' man in the range. He happen'd tu be browsin about in this piece ove woods, an' hearin ole Sock a-bellerin, tuck hit fur a challenge; so he raked up sum dirt wif his huff, an' sprinkild hit over his back; then he dug sum outen a bank wif his ho'ns, an' smelt ove hit; then he tuck a twis' ur two intu his tail, an' histed hit, an' felt hissef then ready fur activ sarvice.

Ole Sock an' his rider cum in site a-tarin, an' they smelt each uther. Both wer dead game an' mad, so a big fite wer morrily durn'd certin. Es soon es old Burns seed tuther bull, he onderstood adzackly what wer a-cumin, an' when; so he leaned hissef back ontu the rope pow'ful, till he pull'd the stirrup loops tight ontu his feet, an' hauled ole Sock's nose an' lip 'way up atween his eyes by the ring, sorter like bustin a rawhide outen a rat wif a ho'n hook. His face look'd like hit wer skin'd, ur dead beef's head on a live bull's body. He wer the wust lookin cow brute, in the face, yu ever seed, an' hit made his bellerin soun like he hed the rattils. But in spite ove all this, he steamed strait ahead fur the inemy. He didn't keer a durn fur enything, since his intercourse wif the bees, an' his mistification in the baskit.

Ole Burns cumenced snatchin brush frum the trees, fust one side an' then tuther, es he pass'd, an' then warin ove em out over the inside ove ole Sock's histed lip, squar down atwix his ho'ns. Es fas' es he wore em out, he wud snatch fur more; he's jis' the bes' man fur usin baskits ur brush in an emargincy I ever seed. How he'd thrive in a bad 'skeeter country! They'd never git in suckin distance ove him. But hit wer all hard thrashin wasted. The bellerin-mersheans associated, an' they sot thar heads tugether like two drunk locomotives wud. When they hit, down cum thar tails, but they histed em agin in a moment, an' a-shakin em at the pints, like they wanted tu git the dust outen the har. The shock fotch ole Burns outen the dorg wood saddil, an' ontu the naik; but he craw-fish'd back durn'd quick, an' never stopt his thrashin ove em over thar heads an' eyes fur one momunt. The nex time they mix'd, they cum by guess wif thar eyes shot, fur fear ove that perpetul-motion brush. Hit jis' rain'd brush, well mix'd wif sum orful off-han' cussin.

The Mills bull's a mity smart critter, tu be only a cow beas', an' he preshiated adzactly ole Burns's power wif a hanful ove brush. So while old Sock wer a gwine thru a gran' charge blind, he tuck a circumbendibus roun, an' gin him Marcy's game on ole Fuss an' Feathers—a-bustin hot fire in the rar. He jis' cum in atween his hine laigs, an' burried his head an' ho'ns thar onder a full run, a histin Sock's starn two foot clar ove the yeath, an' rite then down cum his tail wif a swish, an' he wer tuck along wheelbarrow fashun, ontu his fore laigs, pow'ful agin his will an' cumfort, wif the smellin aind ove his head draw'd higher nor ever to'ards his curl, the brush-mershean in full blast, an' gittin faster an' harder, an' ole Burns a-snatchin ove more. The bellerin an' cussin wer mix'd now ni ontu es ekal es a keerful man mixes whisky an' wartar, an' the mixtry made a mos' doleful soun. Ef you'd a hearn hit at half a mile, yu wud a know'd thar wer a heap ove hurtin an' rath a-gwine on whar hit cum frum.

Ole Sock wer hurried on in this onnaterel an' onmanerly manner over a fell pine tree, an' thar old Mills stopt, I spose tu see the effeck ove his new plan ove fitein, an' thar he did a durn'd fool thing; fur if he hed a-kept that ar head ove hisn in clost communion wif old Sock's sturn, he wud been boun' tu spoke the word afore long. But es hit wer, hit gin him time tu turn roun' wif 'cumulated rath, the natrel bull fitein way.

Ole Mills hed a holesum fear ove the steam brushmill, what Sock toted on his upper deck. So he cum it bline agin, an,' the nex time they met they miss'd, an' the ho'n run onder old Burns's laig, an' atwix the rope girth an' ole Sock's hide. He gin a twis an' busted the girth, swung that misfortinat ole man an' the saddil roun, an' then lent em a big hist. Up they went, saddil fust, an' hit hung ontu the snag lim over a ded pine, jis' high enuf tu let ole Burns's hans sorter tetch groun'. Thar he hung by the heels.

He sot in now, an' cussed in rale yearnis. He mixed in a littil prayin wif hit now an' then, fur thar wer a streak ove skeer in his mad, es he foun' hissef hung hog-fashun, an' a par ove bulls a-fitein roun him. His voice wer changed so yu wudent a-know'd 'im by hit; hit sounded like he wer down in a well, ur hed a locus' in his throat. He bemoan'd his condishun pow'ful, cuss'd Sicily awhile as the fus' cause, an' Clapshaw as the secon' cause, an' then went way back twenty-five years an' cussed hissef fur ever marryin at all, as that wer the beginnin ove hit; talked dredful tu hear 'bout shot-guns, hickory clubs, an' the devil's brimstone works, a-mensunin my name often in these las' remarks.

I tell yu hit wer tremenjusly orful tu listen tu, cumin frum a man ove famerly an' property, hung up by the heels whar two dredful ole bulls wer at war. Wun got a-runnin go ontu tuther, an' backed in agin the old man pow'ful fas'; they pushed him es fur es the rope let em, an' tu make hit wus, a durn'd ole fool, grabb'd a death holt ontu the tail, an' hilt on as long as he cud stan' hit fur his ankils. At las' he let go an' away he swung—tick, tick, like a durn'd ole clock, what wer behine time, an' wer a-tryin tu ketch up agin; an' him a-snatchin at the weeds, an' grass, a fetchin handsful every swing—the prayin an' cussin never slackin off fur enything. I tell yu he hes lots ove san' in his gizzard; he is the bes' pluck I ever seed.

Well thar they fit, roun an' roun, tarin up the yeath an' roots, an' bull meat; he a-watchin em es well es he cud wif his head down. Torreckly they cum agin frum ahine, slather agin the ole feller, an' kerried 'im forrid this time, an' not clock-fashun, sidewise. Jis' es soon es the sturn ove the Mills bull totch 'im, he went fur tail holt agin, an' by golly, he hilt hit this time ontil his shoes cum off, an' he fell smack atop ove Mills, face tu the tail. He tuck hissef good han' holt intu each ove the flanks, an' locked his laigs roun the critter's naik. Oh! durn 'im! He is jis' es redy an' quick es a cat; his 'rangemints wer made tu stay thar all nite, an' fur fear ove acksidents he tuck a good bill holt on the tail wif his teeth.

Ole Mills now dident begin tu onderstan' what wer atop ove 'im; hit wer sumthin sartin what hed bof claws an' teeth, an'——*painter,* flash'd ontu his mine wif all the force the bill holt ontu his tail cud give hit. Dredful, dredful tho't! His pluck wilted, an' he jis' turn'd tail tu the battil groun, an' went aimin fur North Caliney, ole Sock a-trottin arter 'im, sorter keerless like.

Now the ticklin intu his flanks, the chokin roun' his naik, an' the steel trap sprung ontu his tail, did discumfort 'im pow'ful. He jis' mizzild. Every few jumps, he'd giv a hurried hurtin short beller, an' kick bof heels es hi es he cud; but ole Burns wer thar, still thar. By golly, golly, he wer *grow'd* thar. He struck the river at a pint whar the bluff wer sixty feet high, abuv warter thuty foot deep. Durn'd ef ever he tho't even ove measurin hit, but jis' loped over head down, an' ove course the ole man wer gwine tail down. Jis' es soon es he seed the warter onder 'im, quick es a cat agin, *he sot in tu climbin the tail,* overhandid; but hit warn't eny use, George, fur they bof went outen site, jis' bustin the river plum open. The las' part gwine onder wer one ove Burns's hans *a-huntin roun' fur more tail tu climb.* I never seed sich waves in the Oconee afore ur since, an' the bluff wer wet tu the top, an' draps ove warter wer fallin off the cedars on hits brow.

Thinks I, great Jeminy! Will they never cum up? Arter a long time, up popp'd the ole man, already a-headin fur this shore, an' away yander, the bull ris ho'ns fus, an' he aim'd fur tuther bank. They bof crawl'd out, lay down in the san' an' eyed each uther acrost the ruver. If either ove em ho'nd up a mossel ove dirt, I dident see em du hit; but jis' took hit out in restin, watchin each uther, an' 'vengeful tho'ts. That man an' that bull wer mortul inemys fur life.

His sons foun' ole Burns, an' haul'd 'im home ontu a sled, kivered wif straw an' a bed-quilt. Mills's bull sought hissef anuther suckit, an' becum es morril es a draft-steer. Ole

Sock becum more depraved, an' run wile in the mountins, an' I is jis' about es I wer, the durndes' fool in the mess.

I jis' hearn frum ole Burns yesterday. He am powerful bad off; made his will, a-cuttin off old Sock wif a shillin, leavin Sicily an' me his maladickshuns (what am they eny how?), an' fifty dullurs in trus' in ole Bullen's hans fur the cumpasmint ove my death. To ole Clapshaw, he's lef fifteen feet ove new hemp rope, an' tu his wife, an' ole Missis Clapshaw, a dullar tu buy asnick.

Then thinkin the bissines ove this world dun, he jis' went plum crazy—crazy es a bed-bug in July; talks nuffin but nonsince; sez the house is upside down; hears bees a humin ove nights, an' sees hole droves ove bulls a-fitein all day; an' that I is a-standin atop ove the bureau, wif a baskit ove bees, a flingin hanfuls at his hed every time he looks tuther way—jis' turn'd dam fool, that's all.

All the old quilts ove wimen, an' the old soggy men roun thar' visits 'im. The wimen fans 'im, fixes the bed close, an' biles yarbs fur 'im; an' the men iles his bruses, an' poltusis his body. Ole Missis Burns is mad as a ho'net bout that asnick claws in his will, an' won't cum a-nigh him; sez she hes plenty ove swellins ove her own tu swage, an' haint time tu waste on no durn'd old ongrateful murderin fool. An' strange tu tell, George, she sticks tu me; sez I am the bes' ove the lot; sez, too, that I haint one half es durn'd a fool es ole Burns, an' ten times more ove a Cristshun than Clapshaw. Wonder ef hit kin be possabil that 'oman is right? One thing am sartin, she am my frien'.

Well, the vardick ove the neighborhood wer, that I wer the cause ove all the hole thing. Greater injestice wer never dun; fur all that I did in the worild, wer jist tu help ole Sock git a few grains ove shatter'd co'n, by liftin the baskit over his ho'ns; an' when I did hit, the fuss warn't begun at all. Arter'ards, I did nuffin but stan clar ove danger, an' watch things happen. When they tuck the vote on hu wer the cause, every durn'd one ove em voted "Sut," 'scept Sicily an' her mam. Sicily voted "bull an' bees"; her mam voted *"Clapshaw."*

Well, they all got together, headed by Burns's two big fox-huntin sons, an' tuck my case in han'. The fust thing I know'd, they wer ontu my trail, hosses, houns, ho'ns, muskits, shot-guns, cur dorgs, an' all. Now my superfine runnin begun.

Arter a long time, I seed frum a high pint that one ove the houns, down the mountin below me, wer a great way ahead ove everything else, an' wud soon cum up wif slack ove my britches, so I waited fur 'im; when he bulged fur my throat, I reached fur hisn', flung 'im down, slit a hole in each year, an' run his hine laigs thro 'em over the hock, gin 'im sum cumfortin advice wif a keen hickory, an' laid 'im down ontu my trail—he did look powerful sorry fur what he had dun—an' then I went tu travelin agin. When the ballunce ove the dorgs cum up (human like), they all pitched into the poor helpless devil, an' when the two-laiged dorgs cum up, wer a-pas' prayin fur, at leas' ha'f a mile. I beat em so bad, my trail got too cold tu foller. That's what *I calls* runnin. I feels, tho', George, like my time mos' cum. Fifty dullars am a heap ove money, an' the mos' ove the wimen am agin me; that's the danjerus part ove hit.

I'se a goner I 'speck, an' I jis don't keer a durn. I'm no count, no how. Jis' look at me! Did yu ever see sich a sampil ove a human afore? I feels like I'd be glad *tu be* dead, only I'se feard ove the dyin. I don't keer fur hereafter, fur hits onpossibil fur me tu hev ara soul. Who ever seed a soul in jis' sich a rack heap ove bones an' rags es this? I's nuffin but sum newfangil'd sort ove beas', a sorter cross atween a crazy ole monkey an' a durn'd wore-out hominy-mill. I is one ove dad's explites at makin cussed fool invenshuns, an' cum afore my time. I blames him fur all ove hit, allers a-tryin tu be king fool. He hes a heap tu count fur, George—a heap.

Sut Lovingood's Chest Story

I *told you*, George, that Sicily an her hoss, ole Clapshaw, warn't agwine ter pull well in the same yoke, as soon as I seed the orful misfortinate start they got. No man an oman could ever get as clost as man and wife should, arter sich a h——l ove a fuss an hurtin as tuck place at ole Burns' that day.

Theyse all got a spite at me yet about that ar trubil, an I swar I warnt tu blame for hit. "Ole Sock" orter be made beef outen: he did hit all; an yet the cussed fools dont blame him a bit. He orter have his durned haslet cut outen him, an I'll do hit fur him ef ever I ketches him, fur gittin me inter trubil, arter he did all the devilment, while I has to bar the blame. Now aint hit hard that being a natural born d——d fool es I owns I is, I has to bar the blame of the doins of a infunel stumpy hon'd, curly faced hole fool bull; an that, too, arter I'd dun him a kindness, puttin the baskit handil over his hons, so he could eat the corn while he war a travelin; fur I swar they'd a mauled him good ef they had kotch him a eatin ove hit. He's an ongrateful beast, an I'll do him wus than the bees an ole Mills bull did. I'll wheel barrer him into Eternity, an ole Burns tu, mine ef I dont.

Es fur Sicily, ef I haint even with her, you may jist nail my tung to a tree an then skeer me till I reels my hole carcuss inter about a mile of tung, an thar'll be nothin left but my bones on tu the toe nails, an perhaps a scrimpshun of laigs, an a pile ove rags an har at the end of hit. *She dont owe me nuffin now;* an I'll tell you how I paid up—it wer about layin by corn time when she married that hard faced, meaty fisted, groanin ole cuss. At nex aignog time I begin to see that he wernt her "affinity" es a school teachin oman called hit, when she wanted to circumvent me so as tu get her wood cut an her mar curried. George, did you ever hev a strong minded oman git arter you—a rale he oman? "No" Well, ef ever wun does—jist you fight her like she wore whiskers or run like h——l; ef you dont, ef she dont turn you inter a kidney worm'd hog what cant raise his bristles in less nor a month, you ar more or less ove a man than I takes you to be. Ove all the varmints I ever seed Ise feardest of them. They aint human; theyse an ekal mixtry ove stud hoss, black snake, goose, peacock britches—an d——d raskil. They wants tu be a man; an es they cant, they fixes up thar case by bein devils. Take keer ove em; you'd better cum in contact with a comit ur a coal porter than wun ove em any time. They'll ondermine your constitution sure.

Well, matters rocked along, all hands doin es they pleased, an I a watchin ov em—fur I wur arter revenge—ontil about the time hosses begin tu squeal an tuckys tu gobble I discivered her "affinity." She wur runnin an oppersishun line to the ole chicken eater, in cahoote with a man powfull with pills an squts—Doctor Gus Fabin—an they wer makin fast time, all conections, an the male wer kerried purfectly fust rate. An I don't much wonder; she never did feel warm tu old Clapshaw; hit wus the suckit rider's charm what foch her agin her will. George, youse got a *heap* tu larn yit. There am three varmits what kin charm wimmin an birds—the suckit rider, the cat, an the black snake. They kin du hit, an nun ove em ever misses a chance. Ef I hed a pet mockinbird an a darter, I'd make war on all cats an suckit riders—I'd fill the beryin groun with wun, an the big sink hole with tuther; an I'd hev a barrel ful ove hyme books an claws es medals ove my skill in clost shootin. I seed a loaded shot gun once lyin broadside ontu the counter ove Congdon's store, and thar wer a cat washin ove her face a top ove a hat box, an a suckit rider wer a tryin tu git Congdon tu gin sumthin tu pay fur "overcoats fur the pious Sepoys," at tuther aind ove the room; an durn'd ef hit didn't cock hitself, an then swung round like the needle of a compus, fust towards one an then tuther. I duno *how often,* an at last went off—killed the cat es ded es be d——d, an tuther barrell tore off four squar yards ove the suckit rider's overcoat tail. Thar's an instink in shot guns about this thing, sartin; fur you never seed a suckit rider with one in his han, nur a cat what loved the smell ove gunpowder.

Well, arter I larnt what road they run thar line over,

an all the pints ove the case, I went tu work tu gin both a skeer, an him a little hurtin. Doct. Gus Fabin wer wun ove em; the boys call'd him Gut Fatty fur short, an he call'd em "imperdent onedicated d——d jackasses" fur long. He wur jist four foot fourteen inches high, an wer taller a lyin down than when he wer standin up. His eyes wer like ontu two huckelberrys es tu color an size, stuck deep inter a big ball ove red putty. Ef he'd been killed an biled in a hogshead ove lye, he'd a made soap enuf tu a washed away the sins ove a whole know-nothin Congressional deestrict—Congressman, lawyers, wimmen an all. He dress'd hissef *tu kill,* an rid a monsous big black hoss, seventeen hans high, an ni ontu seventeen feet long. When I got done with him his perporshuns wer changed—he wurnt over ten hans high, an es long as one ove ole Bullin's sarmints. I hed gethered an hid a fust rate lot ove fox fire, all reddy tu use. Well, one night I found this black king hoss hitched tu a swingin limb, in a "sink hole" not fur ahind ole Clapshaw's house, *an he wer over the mountin a collectin store debts*; so I tuck off the Doctor's squar bodied saddil bags an sarched em, an tuck all the docterin truck outen the vials an boxes, an poured hit inter his half-full big bottil ove whisky, shuck hit up good, an jist drenched the durned big dromedary hoss with the last spoonful. Hit wer the biggest mixtry ove a dost ever tuck by man ur beaste, septin ove my soda. I stole a set ove plow geers outen the stable, an put on the ole black "patient," now laborin onder my perskripshun (warnt hit beyant common docterin?); then I tied lumps ove fox fire all over the harness, inter his mane, an onter his years. He looked—the ole black devil did—like onter a star lite night, ur a convention ove big litenin bugs mixed with a scattered camp fire. But his looks warn't nuthin tu his feelins afore he got dun with hit, ef I em eny judge ove medicine mixed with an orful skeer an a powful site ove good hoss hurtin. Then I spliced on tu the onder side ove his tail a big jint ove case, pack full ove wet powder, with the open aind towards—his—his hed. Now, I meant tu lite hit, an start him on his travels with a tree top fast in the swingletree; but I thot I'd fust sneak up tu the house an see what wer a gwine on, an what I saw altered my plans mitely. I speck I must a made a nise; fur when I peeped through the crack in the door, that wur Sicily a flingin out bed quilts outen a big chist, but she left in her skeer a baskit with two hundred aigs an a paper ove lamp black onder the till. In jumped Gut Fatty in his shut tail. She slam'd the lid, turned the key, an flung on her dress terrectly. I knocked a staggerin sorter onsartin lick an wur so drunk I cud scasely stand. I managed tu ax Sicily fur sum supper, an she wer mity willin an pleasin an broke out tu the kitchen tu git hit in the hopes that when I'd stuffd my carcuss I'd go tu sleep. When she lef, *so did I*, arter the ole thrashin mersheen kivered with hoss hide an fox fire. I foch him up clost tu the door, an tied a stout rope tu the handil ove the chist an tu the swingle tree. That wer a new conection fur Mister Doctor Gut Fatty's line. Now mind, he'd never seed me in all his bornd days, an praps never hearn ove me, so while I wer makin the hoss pufectly fast ontu the chist, he whispered, "Sicily, love, is *he* gone?" Sez I, "yes, but du yu keep still; sumthin orfuls agwine tu happen imedjutly; thar's signs an wunders in the ar; ni ontu twenty full moons am a hangin in the ar abov the comb of the mountin, an they all has eyes an noses like mister Clapshaw's, an they's a makin dredfull mouths et me, an thar's a 'thousand laig' wum ontu the fence es long es a close line, hits body is red an streaks ove sheet litenin is a playin amung hits scales, an hit hev two imiges ove peple in hits mouf, like ontu you an me. I kin see my har a hangin most tu the yeath, an now an then hit gins them a shake an great big drops ove fat comes outen you, an afore they draps tu the groun they ketches fire an burns like tupentine. Oh Lordy! Gus, love? We hev ruinated our sefs. You begin rite in the middle ove the biggest six hoss prayer you know—nun ove yer little 'now I lay me down tu sleeps,' but rale strong devil skurin prayr, an keep on at hit, fur thars vexashun ove sperit an bodily tribulashun ahead fur us bof." I hearn him groan an he trimbled till he shuck the chist, but he sot in tu prayin fur the heathen, an spread ove the gospil, like a hoss. I know'd that I hed planted a big skeer an that hit would bar fruit afore moon down, so I jist snatched up a chunk ove fire ofen the hath an toch off the powder onder the tail ove the ole hoss. Now I'll jist be continentally an espesially durnd ef that chist didn't go outen the door breast high, and the fus time hit struck the yeath wer forty feet down the hill; rite thar the fust ove the aigs got thur sefs busted; the nex time hit toch the yeath wer on tuther aind (an thar the ballance of Sicily's aigs gin up thar shells) away below the stable; now the mixtry begun: aigs, lamp black, an ole Gut Fatty. The chist tuck down the mountin; I seed hit's course by the lite ove the cane squib an the fox fire, an every now an then the hoss fotch a yell—hit won't a squeal, ur a bray, but sorter between the two: a orful sound. I've never hearn eny live thing make jist that nise afore or sence, an I swar I don't want tu.

I thort I'd foller an see what went with the chist. Arter I'd went a mile ur so I hearn a voice up in the ar, say, "mister, you'd better not travel much furder that course. H—l's busted plumb open, an this yere mountain's full ove the devels. I wish I wer back in ole Noth Calina, whar onest people ken sleep ove nites." I looked up sorter skeer'd, an thar sot astraddle ove a limb ove a big red Oak, a long bony speciment ove a regular herrin mercheen, in his shut-tail; his eyes shined like a mink's an the bottoms ove his feet looked sorter like a tater patch in the weeds. Sez I, "hev yer got any liquor lef, or is yer drunk et all, ur only a durn'd fool?" "I ain't neither (gin us a chaw terbacker). I jist camped round the pint over thar with the ole oman on her litter, when we wus woke up by an arful yell, an here cum the devil a tarin es big es a corn crib, an he had hellfire harness on, an a knot on the aind ove his tail es big es a turpentine still, an he run over my hosses an upsot the waggin, en tuck thru my camp fire, makin the chunks, an sparks, an ashes fly es high es the trees, an out ove site in a minit. The ole hen an the chickens am scattered an I tuck this yere tree, as I'm gwine tu keep hit till mornin. (Gin us a chaw terbacker.) I'll tell you, mister, this yere Tennessee don't suit me. Sich sites ove nites, an sich mountains ove a day, will break down arry man ever foal'd, an no herrin, nor tar; dam the place. I'm gwine back, do you hear my horn?" Sez I, "I speck you had best go back, and travel in the woods et that, for that warnt the devil you seed, but the fool killer fur Polk county, an ef ever he sees you, you'll never see ole Noth Calina, nur yer tar kiln either, so you had better mind."

I went on tu his camp, an thar sot Gut Fatty, squatted

onter his hunkers, all alone, an jist sich a site were never hilt up tu mortal eyes. He wer orfully swell'd, he'd a rolled wun way es well es tuther, an he wer every color ever invented. His shut wer stuck es tite tu him es my pasted one, an he wer peppered all over with broken aig shells, nara piece es big es a grain ove corn.

Here were a black streak aidged with yaller, thar a yaller one aidged with black, then a mixed splotch ove all cullurs, then a little blood oozing thru a sunflour calliker pattern on his belly ur his laigs, an his har looked like hit had been dipped in thunder an litenin an sky blue; he was no more like human than dad wer like a hoss when he acted hit, an he out stunk a buzzard's nest, fur sum ove the aigs were sorter spiled like an sum were almost ready to chirp. To look at him an smell ove him you couldn't think he ever thought of an oman or that wun would let him cum inter the lot. I think his appertite fur them kind ove vittals are all gone. Sez I, "What ar you?" "Do no." "Ar you sum invenshun to skare wimmin an hosses?" "Do no." "Whar do you live." Now his senses seemed sorter to cum tu him, and he axed how fur hit wer to the Hiwassee copper mine. Sez I, "I never hearn tell ove hit." "Well, hit's in Polk county, Tennessee." "You am jist about one hundred an fifty miles frum thar, on the noth side of the Tennessee river, in Jackson county, Alabama." "Is that a fac, mister?" "Sartin," sez I. He fetched a big breath, "Well, I've made the fastest time ever made by mortal man atween them pints. I'se jest been about four minutes a doin hit, but hit has ni onto killed me." "Now," sez I, "mister ef that is so, don't you tell hit here, fur they'll take you fur the tellegraph what they've been watchin fur with guns fur a long time, an they'll hev your scalp a durned site quicker nor you made your fast trip; they dont believe in you ur the devil what invented you; so dont waste time in puttin another hundred miles ur so atween you en this yere place." I follered the hoss about seven miles by the Doctor's truck what I'd giv him, but I couldent ketch up. I never seed him nor the chest nor Gut Fatty arter that nite, an *I dont care a durn ef I never do.* Wonder ef Sicily misses him much! Ole Clapshaw believes in "witches, an warlocks, an long nebbed things" more than he does in Sicily, an his "growin" skeer ove ghostes keeps him at home on nights; I really think he's gettin to be a pious man. Poor Sicily, she's warin thin, her eyes am growin bigger, an she has no roses on her cheeks. She *cant* laugh, an she *wont* cry. Haint hit orful to think ove? Say, George, dont sum feller up your way make whisky outen corn an not strike nine? If thar is, send me wurd by the fust chance.

Nashville *Union and American,* June 30, 1858.

The Snake-Bit Irishman

"WHAT have you got there, Sut?"

"Nuffin but a rattil-tail snake; he's got livin rattils. I kill'd him a-cumin tu camp on the spur thar. He made me mind what happened tu a durn'd tater-eatin Irishman las' fall in these yere mountins, an' I wanted tu tell hit tu yu. So I fotch him along, tu keep me frum forgittin hit. Now ef I wer that ar durn'd Paddy, yu mout jis' bet that hoss ove yur'n, I wudent hev tu tote a snake tu keep that ar scrape in mind. He's in Irishdum now ef he kep his oath, whar thar's no snakes, an' yet I'll swar he dreams ove em an' prays agin em ove nights, an's watchin fur em an' a-cussin ove em ove days, an' will keep up that habit till the devil sends a supener fur him, even ef the ole feller waits seventy-five years fust.

"If yu cud see that shovel-totin, pipe-smokin, raskil's gizzard, yu'd fine the picter ove a big snake branded intu hit es deep es we brands muels.

"Sum three ur four clever fellers frum Knoxville fix'd tharselves up fur a camp hunt ove a cupple ove weeks out yere, an' they met up wif me, an' pinted out two kaigs tied across a muel's back, an' told me tu smell at the bunghole. I follered em wifout ara halter. We camp't jist tuther side that high pint yu see yander, an wer gittin on fust rate, killin lots ove deer an' sich like, when wun nite here cum that cussed Irishman, wif a bundil ontu the aind ove a stick, an' jis' tuck up boardin wif us, never so much es even *lookin* tu see ef he wer welcum. He et, an' drunk, an' slep't thar, es cumfortabil es ef he own'd this country, an' wer the sassyest, meddelsumest, mos' imperdint son ove a diggin-mersheen I ever seed, allers 'sceptin a young suckit rider, ur a duck-laig'd Jew. Sez Jedge Alexander tu me:

---

* This story was originally prepared for, and published in the *New York Spirit of the Times*, when that splendid paper was under the control of the lamented William T. Porter. Having lost the original draft, it has been re-written from memory and adapted to the genius of "Sut." [Harris's note.]

" 'Sut, ef yu'll manage tu run that raskil off frum yere I'll gin ye a par ove boots.'

"Sez I, jumpin tu my feet, 'I'll du hit, durn'd ef I don't! Jis' wait till nite.'

" 'Now,' sez the kind-hearted Jedge, 'Sut, yu musn't hurt the poor feller, mine that; but I want him skared away frum this camp.'

"Sez I, 'All the hurtin he'll git will cum frum skeer. *I* won't hurt him, but I specks the skeer *may* du hit; my sperience (an' hits sum on the nater an' workin ove skeers) is, Jedge, that the hurtin cumin outen a big ripe skeer, jis' can't be beat on *top* ove this yeath, enyhow. Hoss-whips, yaller jackits, an' fire, haint nowhar. Yu wants him skeer'd clean away frum this camp. Now s'pose I happens tu put in a leetle too much powder, an' skeer him plum outen the United States—what then?'

"Sed he, larfin, 'I won't indite yu; jis' go ahead, Sut.'

"I fix'd things.

"Well, nite cum, an' arter we hed lay down, Irish stole hissef anuther suck outen the barlm ove life kaig, an' cum an' jis' rooted his way in atween me an' Jim, an' fix'd hissef fur a big sleep, went at hit imejuntly, an' sot up a systim ove the infunelest snorin yu ever hearn; hit wer the dolefulest, skeeriest soun ever blown outen a human nose. The cussed allfired ole poshole digger *snored in Irish!*

"Now I hed cut off ni outu about nine foot ove gut, frum the offal ove a big buck what wer kill'd that day, an' I tied the ainds wif twine, tu keep in the truck what wer intu hit, an' sunk hit in the krick, so es tu hev hit good cold. I ris up rite keerful, put on the Jedge's spurs, got me a long black-thorn, an' greazed hit wif hog's fat outen the skillet. I fotch the gut up frum the krick, an' wer ready tu begin the sponsibil work I hed on han. The tater-eater hed a hole inter the sittin down part ove his britches, an' his shut tail hed cum outen hit tu git sum fresh ar. I tied wun aind ove thar orful gut tite an' fas' tu the ole coarse shut-tail, an' quiled up the gut nice an' snake-like, clost tu him es he lay. I lay'd down agin, an' reached down my han wif the black-thorn in hit till I got in stickin distunce ove his starn. I felt fur a saft place, an' jis' socked in the thorn about a inch, four ur five times, 'bout es fas' es a ho'net ken sting when he hesn't much time tu spar, an' a big job ove stingin tu du sumwhar else. Every time I socked in that thorn, I raked him up an' down the shins wif them Mexican spurs. I hearn them rattilin ontu his shin-bones like buckshot in a bottil, an' I wer a-hollerin—yu cud hearn me a mile—'Snake! Snake! Big snake! Oh, lordy! Oh, lordee! A big copperheaded black rattil-snake is crawlin up my britches, up bof laigs, an' is a-tyin hissef intu a double bow-knot roun my body. Help! Lordee, oh!'

"The rest on 'em hed the hint, an' all wer shoutin 'Snake! Snake! Big snake!' es I did. Now hits not onreasonabil tu tell that this hurtin an' noise woke Paddy purty eshenshully all over, an' all et onst tu.

"He slaped down his hans each side ove hissef tu help 'im tu rise, an' laid one ove 'em flat ontu the nice cold quile ove gut. He went ofen that pallet an' outen that camp jis' like a sparrer-hawk starts tu fly frum the soun ove a shot-gun, an' he lit twenty foot out in the dark, a-straitnin out that gut ontil the string on the hinmos' aind snapped like ontu a 'cussion cap. Es he went, his words wer—'Howly mither ove Jayzus!' an' he sot inter runnin in a sirkil ove about fifty yards thru the brush, room an' aroun the camp, a-makin meny surjestshuns, an prayers, an' uther dierbolical souns. 'Shute the long divil! Shute all ove yees, but don't aim et his head! Och Shint Patherick! Oh, Howly Vargin! Can't nun ove yees ketch 'im? Stop him! Och howly wather! How swate he's a-bitin! I *tell* yees he's got me by me bottum, *an' he's a-mendin his hoult!* Praist, praist, pope, praist! Howly wather! praist, och, och! Fitch me a cross—a big cross! Bring me me bades, me bades! The divil's own son is a-aitin in strait fur me kednays.'

"In one ove his sarkits, he run thru the embers ove the camp-fire, an' the string at the aind ove the gut hed kotch, an' wer a-burnin like a slow match. Paddy hed ventered tu peep over his shoulder, an' seed hit a-bobbin about arter him; he got a bran new idear onder his har. 'Och! Howly Jayzus! He'll ait now as he plazes; *he's a-totin a lite tu see how tu bite by.*'

"The very thought ove hit made him ni ontu dubbil his speed. He tore thru that brush thicket like a bull wif honey-bees arter him, an' made more nise than a hoss a-doin the same work at the same speed, an' onder a like skeer. I wer up ontu a stump, a-hollerin 'Snake! Snake! Snake!'

es regular es a steamboat snorts, an' in a orful voice, like I hed a Jew's-harp in my froat.

"Arter he'd run ni ontu a mile in that sirkil, an' hed broke a good sweat, an' when his back wer to'ards the camp, I bellered out:

" 'Fling away yer spade; hit makes agin yu.'

"I wish I may be dodrabbited ef he didn't go thru the moshuns ove flingin a spade back'ards over his head. *He* thought he hed his spade, sure es yu ar born'd. See what a skeer kin du in mixin up the idears ove a critter what sorter leans to'ards bein a dam fool, enyhow. Then I hollered, 'Go in a strait line an' out-run yer snake, yu infunelly durn'd fool!' That idear happened tu go strait tu his brains afore hit tangled, an' Pat tuck me at my word, an' wer outen site in the shake ove a lamb's tail. In about a half minit, way over ontu the nex ridge, I hearn 'Howly Jay'——an' hit wer so far off I cudent hear the aind ove the word.

"Nex day he wer makin a bee line thru town, to'ards the East, in a stiff, short, dorg-trot, an' lookin like he'd been thru a smut-mersheen. A feller hail'd 'im:

" 'Hollo, Pat, which way!'

"He looked slowly roun wifout stoppin, wif a hang-dorg sorter face, an' a-feelin a-hine him wif one han, he growl'd out a word fur every step he tuck—

" 'Strate tu swate Ireland, wher ther's no snakes.'

"An dam ef I don't b'leve he kep his word. I got *two* par ove boots, an' ole tangle-foot whisky enuf tu fill 'em.''

Eaves-Dropping a Lodge of Free-Masons

"SUT, when you were telling the razor-grinder's story, what did you mean by saying that Lum Jones hid out from the mason's?"

"Now durn your littil sancterfied face, yu knows mity well why he hid out. Yu an' Lum wer the fellers what *did hit*, an' this crowd orter make yu tell ur treat. I think yu orter du bof."

"The crowd" insisted on the story, so I commenced in my way to tell it somewhat thus:

"Those who remember Knoxville thirty-five years ago, must still almost see 'the old stone Court-house,' with its steep gable front to the street; its disproportionately small brick chimney, roosting on the roof at the rear; its well-whittled door-jambs, its dusty windows, its gloomy walls and ghostly echoes. Then its history, crime unveiled, the ingenious defence, the powerful prosecution, the eloquent 'charge,' the tears of sorrow, the flashes of wit; but like the sturdy old Court-house itself, they belong to the past. But even now, and here in the thickening twilight, I see gliding past in misty ranks, the forms of Jackson, Hu Lawson White, the Williamses, the Dunlaps, Haywood, Peck, Powell, McKinny, Pleasant Miller, the Andersons, Carrick White and Mynott Scott. In my boyish eyes they seemed giants, and manhood's more discriminating gaze sees them undiminished. The quiet grave has long ago claimed the last of the band, but memory preserves their fame, and deeds of well-doing. There too, is 'College Hill,' with its clear cool spring at the foot. The 'Bluff,' with its triple echo, the 'Flag Pond,' and its sunny-sided inhabitants, 'Old Aunt Edy's cakes' and beer, the white mill and its dripping dam, Scuffletown Crick, and its walnut-trees, 'the Dardis lot, and its forbidden grapes,' 'Witt's old field, and its forbidden black-berries,' the 'old church,' and its graveyard.

'Tis strange how faithfully memory paints the paths and places belonging to our boyhood—happy, ragged, thoughtless boyhood. The march of improvement first, then the march and crash of armies, have nearly swept away those, to me, almost sacred places. But they and those who 'were boys then,' still have a place in memory that time nor distance can take, nor the pressing, crowding, bloody events of now dim, nor sorrow obliterate with its tears''——

"Oh, komplikated durnashun! That haint hit," said Sut. "Yu's drunk, ur yure sham'd tu tell hit, an' so yu tries tu put us all asleep wif a mess ove durn'd nonsince, 'bout echo's, an' grapes, an' warnit trees; oh, yu be durn'd! Boys, jis' gin me a hoult ove that ar willer baskit, wif a cob in hits mouf, an' that ar tin cup, an' arter I'se spunged my froat, I'll talk hit all off in English, an' yu jis' watch an' see ef I say 'echo,' ur 'grapes', ur 'graveyard' onst."

So Sut told it *his* way.

"Ahem! I takes fur my tex, the fac' that eavesdrappin am a durn'd mean sorter way tu make a livin. Hits es bad es stealin frum blind folks, ur tellin lies on widders; an' hit hes hits retribushun, a orful wun, an' yu'd all (not scept George thar) say so when I'se dun.

"The upstars ove that Court-hous' wer one big rume, plastered over-head wif three quarter plank, an' no floor ontu the jists in the loft abuv. The masons hed fenced off a lodge in wun corner. The trap-door intu the lof wer jis' outside hit, an' a ladder cum down clost by hits side, an' landed jis' a littil short ove the door intu the lodge. So yu got tu the lof frum what wer lef ove the big rume, an' jis' outside the mason den.

"Well, Lum an' George, thar, wer pow'fully exercised 'bout hit—wanted tu know the secret pow'ful bad—hit pester'd 'em ni ontu es bad es the eatch. So they konkluded arter much fastin an' prayin, in thar way, that they'd evedrop 'em.

"Now they wer about, say thuteen years ole, an' jis' two ove the durndest littil back-slidin devils outen jail. Warn't much alike either. Lum, allers *afore* he did eny devilmint, studied out keerfully what mout happen ef he did hit. George studied too, but hit wer allers *arter* the deed wer dun, an' the orful consekences clost arter him.

"Well, wun day 'bout sundown, they crawl'd up onbenowen tu enybody inter the lof, an' clar tu the tuther aind furthest frum the lodge room, an' trap-door, an' lay pow'ful low, waitin fur night an' the masons. Lots ove pidgeons cum in tu roost, an' as hit got dark, their 'boo coo ah! coo-ooin!' sorter made the littil devils think ove thar trundil beds and the light at home. In fac' a big onmitigated skeer wer a-settilin like ontu a fog all over 'em, an' *onder* thar shuts at that; but they didn't own hit tu each uther yet a-while. Well, arter hit got good dark outside, hit wer es black inter that durn'd ole hanted loft, es hit wud be tu a bline flea on a black catskin, onder the fur, an' hit onder forty bushil ove wet charcoal dust.

"The ole Socks ove the cumpus an' squar persuashun begun tu gether in, an' sartin nises cummenced tu soak up thru the ceilin—sich nises! Oh, lordy!—groanin nises, chokin nises, crunchin nises, ugly nises, orful nises mix'd wif sum discumfurtin souns, not much loud, but dredful plain, an' sure skeer-gitters, the las' one eve em.

"Torrectly they hearn sumthin like twenty foot ove trace chain drap, aind fust on the floor, cherrash! Their skeer now broke out good all over em in splotches es big es a craddil quilt, an' *git outen this loft* wer the only idear lef in thar head. 'Let's go home,' sed wun; 'Oh, lordy yas!' sed tuther; an' they started fur the trap-door, a-steppin frum jise tu jise, quiet an' quick es cats.

"The ole ruff wer leakin fur a long time, an' the drip hed rotted the ceilin about in spots, an' wun ove these spots wer rite plum over the middil ove the lodge; when they got thar, Lum he happen'd tu step jis' a *littil* too short, an' he lit ontu the doated ceilin insted ove the jise. Did yu ever hear a cart-load ove brickbats dumpt'd ontu a pile ove clapboards frum the top ove a high bank? Ef yu did, yu then hearn sumthin ni ontu the soun he made gwine thru that ceilin. Hit jis' rain'd rotten wood, nails, mud-daubers' nests, chips, spiders, an' thar webs, black bugs, was' nests, an' ole dust all over that lodge ove barheaded masons.

"Now they keeps thar secrets pow'ful well, fur most on 'em tu be married men, yet hit sorter leak'd out that they unanamusly an' individully thort that hit wer the anti-masons, ole Morgin, ur the devil, a-cumin down ontu 'em frum way abuve the roof, an' a-bringin wif 'em all the trash frum Kenneday's saw-mill. They huddled tugether intu wun corner, an' star'd up et the forkid fernomonon, what wer a-hangin in the hole, fur Lum hed cotch wif his arms over the two nighes' jise, an' wer a-reachin an' a-feelin all roun in the air, es far es he cud, wif his laigs spred out like a par ove cooper's cumpuses, fur sumthin *tangerbil,* sumthin like ontu a foot-holt, ur sich.

"Great Beltashashur! [and Sut stretched his legs to their utmost extent, knocking his feet together, and affectionately surveying them from hip to toe] spose this yere par ove litnin-rods hed been hung thru that hole, an' es big a skeer at the top ove em es wer a-restin on Lum! Why, I'll jis' be durn'd rite yere afore I kin swaller this ho'n, ef I hadn't a swept the las' cockroach outen the corners ove that room, broke all the winders, haf the masons' necks, put out the candils, disparsed the jewils, los' the mallits an' call'd that ar lodge frum labor tu refreshmint furever more. I'd a-made em reach everywhar, afore a quick-spoken 'oman cud say 'kiss,' *wudn't* I?

"Well, es it wer, Lum's fat latter aind looked like ontu a yearlin's paunch a-swingin about, what hed died pow'ful full ove grass an' wheat bran. His britches wer draw'd so tite that the hems ove em wer six inches abuv his knees. His short socks an' low-quarter'd shoes made his red laigs look like two bedpostes sock'd intu the pipe hole ove a par ove cookin-stoves, an' a skeer'd divil intu the oven ove each stove, they husteled roun *so* fas'.

"Ole Stack seed the true nater ove the fernomonon afore eny ove the res' ove em. So he snatched a long strip ove the broken ceilin plank, es broad es a canew paddil at wun aind, in bof hans', an' jis busted hit intu seventeen an' a 'alf pieces at wun swollopin lick ontu the part ove Lum, what fits a saddil. Hit crack'd sorter like a muskit a-bustin, an' the tetchin sensashun shot Lum up thru the hole like a rocket."

Here Sut raised himself slightly from the log on which he was sitting, by the aid of his hands each side, and rubbing himself sidewise quickly, a few times on rough bark, said, with an air of startled surprise, "Boys, I'm durn'd ef *I* can't feel Lum's sensashun frum that orful lick *rite now,*" and he rubbed himself again.

"Well, him an' George bulged down that ar ladder like rats wif a tarrier clost tu thar tails, an' at the foot ove hit they *met a sight*—oh, sweet Jinny! How glad I is I warn't thar! Thar sot a littil tabil wif a lit candil ontu hit, an' thar stood, bolt up on aind, a grim, grey-haired man, wif a glitterin drawn swoard in his han, es big an' as long es a mowin blade; ontu his breas' wer a par ove littil silver crooked bowie-knives cross'd, an' he wore a aprun like he wer gwine tu butcher ur cook supper. They look'd at this, jis' 'bout es long es a weazel looks at a cumin rock, an' they went a-scizzin pas', George hinmos'.

"The ole man made a wicked cirklin lick at him wif his orful nakid wepun. 'Voop,' hit went, an' cut the flat crown outen his cap, smoof es yu cud onkiver a huckleberry pie wif a case-knife."

"That part's not true, Mr. Sut," said I.

"Yes hit am, fur yu see he dun hit so slick that the crown whirl'd roun like a tin plate in the ar, six foot abuv yer hed, went faster nur yu did, an' lit afore yu, es yu flew down stars fas' es yu wer gwine. Oh, littil hoss, *he did du hit,* an 'ef he'd lower'd his sites jis' a scrimpshun he'd a-saved a pow'ful site ove meat an' bread frum bein wasted, an' curius pepil wud a-been now a-readin ove yur vartu's frum a lyin stone newspaper stuck in the yeath ove the graveyard yu wer a-blatherin about jis' now.

"An I haint told all, fur in yer skeer a-gwine away frum that orful place, yu run over the spot whar a fancy hous' 'bout five foot squar hed been upsot, slunged in up to yur eyebrows, amungst the slush in the hole, broke fur the krick, lunged in, onbuttoned yer shut collar, dove plum thru that ar crownless cap—hit cum ofen yer heels like a hoop—swum outen yer clothes, an' jis' let every durn'd rag float away, an' then went home es nakid es a well-scraped hog, but not half es clean. The pepil what yu passed on yer way tu the krick tho't yu wer the cholery a-cumin, an' burn't tar in thar yards an' stuff'd ole rags onder thar doors, an' intu the keyholes; an' es yu sneaked back nakid frum the krick, they tho't yu wer the ghost ove a skin'd bull-frog, ur a forewarnin ove cumin famin.

"Yu see hit wer Lum what foun the saft soap mine an' went tu the krick tu see what sorter suds hit wud make. Now jis' let enybody ax Lum an' see ef he don't say hit wer yu, afore they'se dun axin him, an' offer tu prove hit by Frank Dudley—try hit.

"Lum narrates hit that the masons' secret konsists in a piece ove dry plank wif a strong, willin man at wun aind, an' about thuty pounds ove live, tender, thin-skin'd meat ni ontu tuther; while yu sez hit am nuthin but a hole in the groun, what orter be kivered up ove nights; yu bof orter know.

"Now I hes jis' wun remark tu make afore I drinks, an' hit am this: neither ove em hes ever tried tu watch enything in the dark since, an' jis' let wun ove em, even tu this night, see a cumpus ur a squar, ef hits even a-lyin ontu a carpenter's bainch, an' I'm durn'd ef they don't hist thar noses an' take a sniff ove the air all roun wif thar bristils sot. They s'pishions danger. I don't blame em, du yu? Thar's no muny nur credit either, in evedroppin; they'se bof sot agin hit, an' they haint fear'd tu say so."

Taurus in Lynchburg Market

"Daddy kill'd the blind bull,
 Human nater, human nater!
Mammy fried a pan full,
 Sop an' tater, sop an' tater."

"STOP that noise Sut, I can't sleep."
"Nize? Well, I be durn'd! Calls superfine singin ove a hart-breakin luv song, what's purtier by a gallun an' a 'alf, than that cussed fool thing *yu* wer a-readin, jis arter supper 'bout the youf what toted a flag up a mountin by hissef ove a nite, wif 'Exelcider' writ ontu hit, nize! Why, I speck yu'd call the singin ove the cherrybeans, howlin. *Yu* be durn'd."
"That was no love song, you jackass, that you were bawling just now."
"The devil hit warn't! I hedn't got tu the luv part. Eatin allers goes jis' afore luv. 'Less a feller hes his belly stretched wif vittils, he can't luv tu much pupus, that's so. Vittils, whisky, an' the spring ove the year, is what *makes* luv; an' yu jis' bring em all tu bar tugether, an' yu'll see luv tu sum pupus, I'm durn'd if yu don't. Did yu ever try hit, wif a purty gal sot on steel springs wif injun rubber heels, an cinamint ile smell tu help yu?"
"No; shut up!"
"Oh, yas, hit am onplesant tu yu, es the ole maid sed when a gal kiss'd her; hits sorter like smellin ole Burbon thru a jail winder—aint jist the thing.
"Now yu's a cussin at my luv song, I wants tu say a word about that 'Excelcider' youf ove your'n, what sum Longfeller writ. *I* say, an' I'll swar tu hit, that eny feller, I don't keer hu the devil he is, what starts up a mountin, kiver'd wif snow an' ise, arter sundown, wif nuffin but a flag, an' no whisky, arter a purty gal hed offer'd her bussum fur a pillar, in a rume wif a big hath, kiver'd wif hot coals, an' vittils, [here Sut rose to his tip-toes, and elevated his clenched fists high above his head] am a dod durn'd, com-

plikated, fullblooded, plum nat'ral born durn'd fool; he warn't smart enuf tu fine his mouf wifout a leadin string; he orter froze es stiff es a crow-bar, an' then been thaw'd out by the devil; dod durn him! An' there's Lum Jack yu tole about, darin the litenin."

"Ajax, I suppose you mean."

"Yas, ove cours; didn't I say so? An' he wer a jack, ove the longes' year'd kine, fus', because eny fool mout know the litenin wudn't mine him no more nur a locomotum wud mine a tumble-bug. An' then, spose hit hed met his dar, why durn me ef thar'd been a scrimshun ove 'im lef big enuf tu bait a minner hook wif.

"Now I sets *him* down es wun ove the fore-daddys ove the Lovingoods, sure. Our famerly am an' ole wun. Dad used tu trace hit back tu Joseph in Yegipt, an' he sed hit wer pufeckly useless tu hunt furder fur better fool blood. I'se furgot what that feller's name wer, hu's wife got his coat! Hits no odds, *he* wer no count, nohow. I sorter sumtimes thinks he mout been the fust ove the unicks— poor 'oman!

"Singin that song 'bout the bline bull, minds me ove what happen'd tu me at Lynchburg, in ole Firginny. Hits a town chock full ove clever fellers, an' jis' es few nat'ral born durn'd fools as ever yu seed in any town. A ole Dutchman bilt hit, an' sot hit up on hits aidge tu dry. The Injuns chased him clean away, an' the town stans on hits aidge tu this day. Sumtimes the boys gits ontu a 'tare' ove nites, an' tries tu upset hit ontu hits side, but haint never got hit turn'd down yet.

"A drovyer tuck sum hogs thar wunst frum Tennessee, an' I foller'd his dorg the hole way. When I got thar, I wer mon'sous shy an' keerful, fur thar aint much good groun bout thar tu run on, ef a feller happen'd tu take a runnin skeer.

"Wun mornin I wer standin ni ontu the top ove the hill, lookin roun stonish'd till I wer benum'd all over at the sites. I seed, rite in the middil ove the street, a hous' what mout been bilt fur a depot when railroads wer jis' a-tasselin; they warn't es fur on es roasin-ear time nohow, an' they foun hit too small at that; an' hit sorter look't like women hed lived thar, an' the boys hed stove in the sides an' ainds wif rocks, jis' leavin the corners tu hole up the ruff. I larnt frum a nigger, that hit wer a market hous, whar they sells oncook'd vittils ove every kine, frum a rabbit tu a cow's laig, an gardin truck tu kill. Hit wer plum full.

"I wer wonderin my levil bes', keepin a skin'd eye an' a open year fur trubbil ur a skeer, when I hearn a tarin big fuss on tuther side, squawkin, cussin, hollerin, an' a gineral soun ove things a-smashin, an' seed people a-mixin tharsefs pow'ful, sorter like bees a-fixin tu swarm. Thinks I, Look out Sut, hit am cumin; hits mos' time; yu haint hed a skeer fur ni ontu three days—when yere cum roun the corner ove the market house, jis' a-tarin, a thuteen hunder' poun' black an' white bull, wif his tail es strait up in the air es a telegraf pole, an' a chesnut fence rail tied acrost his ho'ns wif hickory withs. He wer a-totin his hed low, an' every lick he made at eny pusson ur thing, he'd blow whoff, outen his snout. He wer a citizen ove Amherst County, an' ove the Devonshear persuashun, an' mout a-hed good standin at home fur all I knows, but he wer actin like a durn'd blackgard in Lynchburg, an' I b'leves he wer one.

"I'se sorter fear'd tu try tu tell yu, George, the devilment that cussed infunel fool cow beaste wer a-doin. He wer a-killin, smashin, ur spilin everything he toch wif ho'ns, huffs, ur fence rail. He look'd like he wer mad—'sulted an' plum crazy, an' gittin wus fas.' He'd say whoff! an' a hunder' an' sixty poun' nigger wud fly up in the air like ontu a grasshopper, an' cum back spread like a frog. Whoff! an' a fat she nigger wud dart hanketcher aind fus' thru sumbody's glass winder. Whoff! agin, an' a boy wud turn ten sumersets towards the river. Whoff! an' a Amherst 'oman lit a-straddil ove a ole fat feller's neck, wif a jolt what jumped his terbacker outen his mouf an' scrunched *him,* while she went on down hill on all fours in a fox trot. Whoff! an' a set ove hoops, an' a par ove black stockins wif white garters, lit atop ove a kiver'd waggin an' slid down feet fus' on tuther side.

"A littil bal'-heded man, dress'd in gole specks an' a gole-heded walkin stick, wer a-passin, an' duin nuffin tu nobody; he look'd like he wer a-cyferin out a sum in the Qbrute, in his hed. Whoff! an' the specks lit on the ruff ove the market hous', an' the stick, gole aind fus', sot in a milk can sixty foot off. As tu ball head hissef, I los' site ove 'im while the specks wer in the air; he jis' disappear'd frum mortul vishun sumhow, sorter like breff frum a lookin-glass. I wunders ef he lef a widder. Smack! an' the sides ove a milk can cum tugether, an' a squt ove milk shot up, an' trickl'd ofen the house eaves. Crash! an' a baskit went way up yander, an' then hit wud rain aigs, an' bats ove cottin. Anuther baskit wud start up, an' torreckly we'd hev a thunder shower ove cherrys; the bull furnish'd the thunder, plenty ove hit.

"The air wer full ove things; stockins wif laigs in em, showin tu mos' 'vantage; hats wif heds in em wer cumin down like they wer hir'd tu ram the pavemint that way. Truck ove all kind wer flyin ur lyin about jis durn'd permiscusly. The street wer white wif milk an' aigshells; hit wer red wif cherrys; hit wer black wif blackberrys, an' hit wer green wif gardin truck. Cherrys roll'd down hill in the cracks atween the stones, in litil rivers ove milk. The dead chickens lay whar they fell, an' the live ones lit on the ruffs. Oh! gemeny Jerusalem! I never seed sich a mixtry ove oncook'd vittils in all my born'd days! Blowin up a powder-hous', while a harycane am ragin, mixes things mon'sous' well I reckon, but I gins my vote tu that Amherst bull.

"I wer a-standin ni ontu what I tuck tu be the upper aind ove the steepil ove a chu'ch, what they hed buried onder groun', not likin the perswashun ur the passun, an' hed lef the pint ove the steepil stickin out, fur a grave stone, an' a warnin tu the uther chu'ches how tu kery tharsefs; but on 'zaminin hit clost, I foun' hit wer a lam'-postez, made outen iron, whar they burns sum greasy kine ove air, tu lite fellers home what stay out late ove nites. They'se mity good things, too, fur a feller tu straiten up on, fur a fresh start, when he's layin off the wum ove a fence, onder a deck-load ove tangle-laig whisky. I observed also that they'se jis' the thing tu freeze fas' ontu when the watch man's got yu, an' yu don't want tu go, an' yu'll say, afore I'se dun, they can't be beat at stoppin bulls frum actin durn'd fool. Lam'-postez tharfore am good things, when they keeps outen your way. A cushion roun em about es hi es a comon man's nose frum the ground', an' a cock what wud run sweetened whisky, wud make em a public invenshun.

"Well, that ar insashate bull, in flyin roun, got his sturn clos tu me, an I, like a durn'd fool as I is, tuck sides in the fite agin the critter; I reached up fur the tassil on his tail, an' run twist roun the lam'-postez wif hit, my fingers fas' wove intu the har, bonnit plat fashun, sot my foots agin the iron, an' tuck a leanin pull. A feller, a-lookin outen a small crack ove a door, gin me a cumfortin word. Sez he: 'That's a *good* holt, laigs; ef raw-hide don't tar, yu've got im till the devil freezes.'

"Sez I, 'Hes these postez got deep roots?'

"'Seventeen foot,' sez he.

"'Then,' sez I, 'this yere bull's tail will dry wif two kinks in hit; what's beef wuf?'

"The bull sed whoff! an' sot in tu pull his tail outen his sturn by the root; but hit wer well sot, an' he didn't du hit. He swung hissef frum side tu side, an' pull'd pow'ful. Oh! he wer in yearnest bout that matter ove tarin out his tail. At las' he beller'd, an' I obsarv'd that the lam'-postez an' my footses warn't es clean as a dinner plate. Thinks I, that's a sign ove givin in, an' I hearn my frien' holler, 'Two tu one on laigs.'

"My han's begun tu cramp orful, an' I felt my big skeer a cumin on. I look'd roun', an' thar warn't a soul in site but my frien', an' I know'd I cudent count on him only fur kind words, *by the way he hilt the door*. Everybody gone glimerin, even the huxters, an' Amherst wimen.

"Thar I wer, froze tu a savidge bull's tail, no frien's, an' hed begun hit mysef. My skeer wer now ripe, redy tu bust, an' knowin but wun thing fit tu du in such cases, I look'd which way I'd run. I hearn the durn'd raskil what hed been my frien' say, 'Ha! ha! two tu one *on the bull!*' That las' remark broke my hart. I made up my mine tu go home tu the tavrin, on the river, as hit wer down hill, an' I know'd 'Owens' wer my frien'.

"The bull wer showin white mix'd wif bloody veins all roun his eyes, while the midil wer green as a bottil. I hed mistaken'd the givin-in signs; he wer madder nor ever. I watched fur him tu wink his eyes, an' while he wer duin hit I hearn the cussed cole-harted devil a-hine the door now offer *four* tu one on the bull. He wink'd at las', an' while his eyes wer shot, I let go the bes' holt ever mortul man hed on a bull. Ef hit hadn't been fur the cramp, skeer, an' that feller's bettin agin me, I'd been thar yet, a monument ove enjurance, parasvarance, an' dam fool, still holdin a dry bull's hide by the tail.

"As I let go, I sot these yere laigs a-gwine onder three hunder' pound preshure ove pure skeer. Long es they is, they went apast each uther as fas' as the spokes ove two spinnin wheels a runnin contrary ways. That hell-cat ahine the door parsecuted me tu the las', fur he now cum out an' farly yell'd: *'Ten* tu one on the bull, an' iseters fur the wun what takes the bet.'

"I look'd roun, an' seed one aind ove the fence rail wif the yaller ove aigs on hit, an' a lettuce leaf stickin on a splinter, jist one good jump ahine that part ove me what wud git all the kickin if ole Burns ever cotch me. Well, all I kin say is, I didn't go any slower fur that orful glimpse. I cud hear fust one aind an' then tuther ove that dry chesnut fence rail strike the rocks, as he wud try tu hist me with a whoff! every lunge. Owens, the lanlord, wer a-gwine up on the pavement, an' know'd me. Clever tu the las', even ef I wer onder par, he holler'd—

"'Number ten, Sut, the key's in the door; ha! ha!'

"Them wer cumfortin words, an' I put on a scrimshun more steam, 'bout all I had. I never 'spected tu see number ten agin.

"A feller wif a face like a dry sheep-skin, what hed laid in a cellar till hit got moulded, holler'd frum a upper winder: 'Go hit, dubbil laigs! He's *lost his rail.*'

"Now this wer kine ove him, but hit warn't any use. I wer at the top ove my speed aready, an' at las' hit proved tu be a durn'd lie.

"When I got tu whar a warter rail-road fur boats, an' ducks, runs onder the street, I begun tu try tu bar tu the lef, so as tu hit the tavrin door, but I wer a gwine so fas', I cudn't sheer a bit, but struck the flat-form about the midil, cross'd hit like a shot, busted thru the railin an' a bainch, carryin away bout six foot ove each, an' a sleepin nigger. Down, down—ker-lunge, twenty-five foot intu the river. I lit a-swimin, fur I spected every moment tu hev tail, rail, an' ho'ns, wif thuteen hundr' poun's ove bull meat, atop ove me. I swum out tu a rock pile, an' hearn him lumberin thru the bridge like he weighed four tons. I seed him run outen tuther aind, rail an' all, an' his tail es strait up in the air as hit wer when he wer histin aig-baskits an' wimin, scept hit hed two kinks in hit, put thar by the lam'-postez. He disappeared amung the Amherst hills, a smarter bull by a durn'd site, ef 'sperience am wuth a durn. I'll bet he often counts the valuer ove a tail in fly-time, agin the bother ove one in fitin, an' envys stump-tail bulls 'cordinly. That's the las' muss I hes tuck sides in, whar I din't keer a cuss which whipp'd, an' I hed tu du a marster fool thing while hit wer gwine on."

"What do you allude to, Sut?"

"Why, instead ove freezin tu that bull's tail, what didn't pay, I orter saved them gole specks, an' stick tu what wud pay.

"They telegrafed tu Stantun fur a committee ove doctors, tu 'zamine me fur the honors ove the lunatic asslum. When they got thar, they foun' nuffin tu 'zamine, but the karacter I hed fur bein a nat'ral born durn'd fool, an' a crack'd whisky flask. They wer sittin on *hit,* when I hearn frum em las', an' hed sent fur the bull tu take *his* testimony. I bet he don't cum, by thunder!"

Mrs. Yardley's Quilting

"THAR'S one durn'd nasty muddy job, an' I is jis' glad enuf tu take a ho'n ur two, on the straingth ove hit."

"What have you been doing, Sut?"

"Helpin tu salt ole Missis Yardley down."

"What do you mean by that?"

"Fixin her fur rotten cumfurtably, kiverin her up wif sile, tu keep the buzzards frum cheatin the wurms."

"Oh, you have been helping to bury a woman."

"That's hit, by golly! Now why the devil can't I 'splain myself like yu? I ladles out my words at randum, like a calf kickin at yaller-jackids; yu jis' rolls em out tu the pint, like a feller a-layin bricks—every one fits. How is it that bricks fits so clost enyhow? Rocks won't ni du hit."

"Becaze they'se all ove a size," ventured a man with a wen over his eye.

"The devil yu say, hon'ey-head! Haint reapin-mersheens ove a size? I'd like tu see two ove em fit clost. Yu wait ontil yu sprouts tuther ho'n, afore yu venters tu 'splain mix'd questions. George, did yu know ole Missis Yardley?"

"No."

"Well, she wer a curious 'oman in her way, an' she wore shiney specks. Now jis' listen: Whenever yu see a ole 'oman ahine a par ove *shiney* specks, yu keep yer eye skinn'd; they am dang'rus in the extreme. Thar is jis' no knowin what they ken du. I hed one a-stradil ove me onst, fur kissin her gal. She went fur my har, an' she went fur my skin, ontil I tho't she ment tu kill me, an' wud a-dun hit, ef my hollerin hadent fotch ole Dave Jordan, a *bacheler*, tu my aid. He, like a durn'd fool, cotch her by the laig, an' drug her back'ards ofen me. She jis' kivered him, an' I run, by golly! The nex time I seed him he wer bald headed, an' his face looked like he'd been a-fitin wildcats.

"Ole Missis Yardley wer a great noticer ove littil things, that nobody else ever seed. She'd say right in the middil ove sumbody's serious talk: 'Law sakes! thar goes that yaller slut ove a hen, a-flingin straws over her shoulder; she's arter settin now, an' haint laid but seven aigs. I'll disapint *her,* see ef I don't; I'll put a punkin in her ne's, an' a feather in her nose. An' bless my soul! Jis' look at that cow wif the wilted ho'n, a-flingin up dirt an' a-smellin the place whar hit cum frum, wif the rale ginuine still-wurim twis' in her tail, too; what upon the face ove the yeath kin she be arter now, the ole fool? Watch her, Sally. An' sakes alive, jis' look at that ole sow; she's a-gwine in a fas' trot, wif her empty bag a-floppin agin her sides. Thar, she hes stop't an's a-listenin! Massy on us! What a long yearnis grunt she gin; hit cum frum way back ove her kidneys. Thar she goes agin; she's arter no good, sich kerryin on means no good.'

"An' so she wud gabble, no odds who wer a-listenin. She looked like she mout been made at fust 'bout four foot long, an' the common thickness ove wimen when they's at tharsefs, an' then had her har tied tu a stump, a par ove steers hitched to her heels, an' then straiched out a-mos' two foot more—mos' ove the straichin cumin outen her laigs an' naik. Her stockins, a-hangin on the clothes-line tu dry, looked like a par ove sabre scabbards, an' her naik looked like a dry beef shank smoked, an' mout been ni ontu es tough. I never felt hit mysef, I didn't; I jis' jedges by looks. Her darter Sal wer bilt at fust 'bout the laingth ove her mam, but wer never straiched eny by a par ove steers, an' she wer fat enuf tu kill; she wer taller lyin down than she wer a-standin up. Hit wer her who gin me the 'hump shoulder.' Jis' look at me; haint I'se got a tech ove the dromedary back thar bad? Haint I humpy? Well, a-stoopin tu kiss that squatty lard-stan ove a gal is what dun hit tu me. She wer the fairest-lookin gal I ever seed. She allers wore thick woolin stockins 'bout six inches too long fur her laig; they rolled down over her garters, lookin like a par ove life-presarvers up thar. I tell yu she wer a tarin gal enyhow. Luved kissin, wrastlin, an' biled cabbige, an' hated tite clothes, hot weather, an' suckit-riders. B'leved strong in married folk's ways, cradles, an' the remishun ove sins, an' didn't b'leve in corsets, fleas, peaners, nur the fashun plates."

"What caused the death of Mrs. Yardley, Sut?"

"Nuffin, only her heart stop't beatin 'bout losin a nine dimunt quilt. True, she got a skeer'd hoss tu run over her, but she'd a-got over that ef a quilt hadn't been mix'd up in the catastrophy. Yu see quilts wer wun ove her speshul gifts; she run strong on the bed-kiver question. Irish chain, star ove Texas, sun-flower, nine dimunt, saw teeth, checker board, an' shell quilts; blue, an' white, an' yaller an' black coverlids, an' callickercumfurts reigned triumphan' 'bout her hous'. They wer packed in drawers, layin in shelfs full, wer hung four dubbil on lines in the lof, packed in chists, piled on cheers, an' wer everywhar, even ontu the beds, an' wer changed every bed-makin. She told everybody she cud git tu listen tu hit that she ment tu give every durn'd one ove them tu Sal when she got married. Oh, lordy! What es fat a gal es Sal Yardley cud ever du wif half ove em, an' sleepin wif a husbun at that, is more nor I ever cud see through. Jis' think ove her onder twenty layer ove quilts in July, an' yu in thar too. Gewhillikins! George, look how I is sweatin' now, an' this is December. I'd 'bout es lief be shet up in a steam biler wif a three hundred pound bag ove lard, es tu make a bisiness ove sleepin wif that gal—'twould kill a glass-blower.

"Well, tu cum tu the serious part ove this conversashun, that is how the old quilt-mersheen an' coverlidloom cum tu stop operashuns on this yeath. She hed narrated hit thru the neighborhood that nex Saterday she'd gin a quiltin—three quilts an' one cumfurt tu tie. 'Goblers, fiddils, gals, an' whisky,' wer the words she sent tu the men-folk, an' more tetchin ur wakenin words never drap't ofen an 'oman's tongue. She sed tu the gals, 'Sweet toddy, huggin, dancin, an' huggers in 'bundunce.' Them words struck the gals rite in the pit ove the stumick, an' spread a ticklin sensashun bof ways, ontil they scratched thar heads wif one han, an' thar heels wif tuther.

"Everybody, he an' she, what wer baptized b'levers in the righteousnes ove quiltins wer thar, an' hit jis' so happen'd that everybody in them parts, frum fifteen summers tu fifty winters, wer unannamus b'levers. Strange, warn't hit? Hit wer the bigges' quiltin ever Missis Yardley hilt, an' she hed hilt hundreds; everybody wer thar, 'scept the constibil an' suckit-rider, two dam easily-spared pussons; the numbers ni ontu even too; jis' a few more boys nur gals; that made hit more exhitin, fur hit gin the gals a chance tu kick an' squeal a littil, wifout runnin eny risk ove not gittin kissed at all, an' hit gin reasonabil grouns fur a few scrimmages amung the he's. Now es kissin an' fitin am the pepper an' salt ove all soshul getherins, so hit wer more espishully wif this ove ours. Es I swung my eyes over the crowd, George, I thought quiltins, managed in a morril an' sensibil way, truly am good things—good fur free drinkin, good fur free eatin, good fur free huggin, good fur free dancin, good fur free fitin, an' goodest ove all fur poperlatin a country fas'.

"Thar am a fur-seein wisdum in quiltins, ef they hes proper trimmins: 'vittils, fiddils, an' sperrits in 'bundunce.' One holesum quiltin am wuf three old pray'r meetins on the poperlashun pint, purtickerly ef hits hilt in the dark ove the moon, an' runs intu the night a few hours, an' April ur May am the time chosen. The moon don't suit quiltins whar everybody is well acquainted an' already fur along in courtin. She dus help pow'ful tu begin a courtin match onder, but when hit draws ni ontu a head, nobody wants a moon but the ole mammys.

"The mornin cum, still, saft, sunshiney; cocks crowin, hens singin, birds chirpin, tuckeys gobblin—jis' the day tu sun quilts, kick, kiss, squeal, an' make love.

"All the plow-lines an' clothes-lines wer straiched tu every post an' tree. Quilts purvailed. Durn my gizzard ef two acres roun that ar house warn't jis' one solid quilt, all out a-sunnin, an' tu be seed. They dazzled the eyes, skeered the hosses, gin wimen the heart-burn, an' per-dominated.

"To'ards sundown the he's begun tu drap in. Year-nis' needil-drivin cummenced tu lose groun; threads broke ofen, thimbils got los', an' quilts needed anuther roll. Gigglin, winkin, whisperin, smoofin ove har, an' gals a-ticklin one anuther, wer a-gainin every inch ove groun what the needils los'. Did yu ever notis, George, at all soshul getherins, when the he's begin tu gather, that the young she's begin tu tickil one anuther an' the ole maids swell thar tails, roach up thar backs, an' sharpen thar nails ontu the bed-posts an' door jams, an' spit an' groan sorter like cats a-courtin? Dus hit mean *rale* rath, ur is hit a dare tu the he's sorter kivered up wif the outside signs ove danger? I honestly b'leve that the young shes' ticklin means, 'Cum an' take this job ofen our hans.' But that swellin I jis' don't onderstan; dus yu? Hit looks skeery, an' I never tetch one ove em when they am in the swellin way. I may be mistaken'd 'bout the ticklin bisiness too; hit may be dun like a feller chaws poplar bark when he haint got eny terbacker, a-sorter better nur nun make-shif. I dus know one thing tu a certainty: that is, when the he's take hold the ticklin quits, an' ef yu gits one ove the ole maids out tu hersef, then she subsides an' is the smoofes, sleekes, saft thing yu ever seed, an' dam ef yu can't hear her purr, jis' es plain!

"But then, George, gals an' ole maids haint the things tu fool time away on. Hits widders, by golly, what am the rale sensibil, steady-goin, never-skeerin, never-kickin, willin, sperrited, smoof pacers. They cum clost up tu the hoss-block, standin still wif thar purty silky years playin, an' the naik-veins a-throbbin, an' waits fur the word, which ove course yu gives, arter yu finds yer feet well in the stirrup, an' away they moves like a cradil on cushioned rockers, ur a spring buggy runnin in damp san'. A tetch ove the bridil, an' they knows yu wants em tu turn, an' they dus hit es willin es ef the idear wer thar own. I be dod rabbited ef a man can't 'propriate happiness by the skinful ef he is in contack wif sumbody's widder, an' is smart. Gin me a willin widder, the yeath over: what they don't know, haint worth larnin. They hes all been tu Jamakey an' larnt how sugar's made, an' knows how tu sweeten wif hit; an' by golly, they is always ready tu use hit. All yu hes tu du is tu find the spoon, an' then drink cumfort till yer blind. Nex tu good sperrits an' my laigs, I likes a twenty-five year ole widder, wif roun ankils, an' bright eyes, honestly an' squarly lookin intu yurn, an' sayin es plainly es a partrige sez 'Bob White,' 'Don't be afraid ove me; I hes been thar; yu know hit ef yu hes eny sense, an' thar's no use in eny humbug, ole feller—cum ahead!'

"Ef yu onderstans widder nater, they ken save yu a power ove troubil, onsartinty, an' time, an' ef yu is inter- prisin yu gits mons'rous well paid fur hit. The very soun ove thar littil shoe-heels speak full trainin, an' hes a knowin click as they tap the floor; an' the rustil ove thar dress sez,

'I dar yu tu ax me.'

"When yu hes made up yer mind tu court one, jis' go at hit like hit wer a job ove rail-maulin. Ware yer workin close, use yer common, every-day moshuns an' words, an' abuv all, fling away yer cinamint ile vial an' burn all yer love songs. No use in tryin tu fool em, fur they sees plum thru yu, a durn'd sight plainer than they dus thru thar veils. No use in a pasted shut; she's been thar. No use in borrowin a cavortin fat hoss; she's been thar. No use in har-dye; she's been thar. No use in cloves, tu kill whisky breff; she's been thar. No use in buyin clost curtains fur yer bed, fur she has been thar. Widders am a speshul means, George, fur ripenin green men, killin off weak ones, an makin 'ternally happy the soun ones.

"Well, es I sed afore, I flew the track an' got ontu the widders. The fellers begun tu ride up an' walk up, sorter slow, like they warn't in a hurry, the durn'd 'saitful raskils, hitchin thar critters tu enything they cud find. One red-comb'd, long-spurr'd, dominecker feller, frum town, in a red an' white grid-iron jackid an' patent leather gaiters, hitched his hoss, a wild, skeery, wall-eyed devil, inside the yard palins, tu a cherry tree lim'. Thinks I, that hoss hes a skeer intu him big enuf tu run intu town, an' perhaps beyant hit, ef I kin only tetch hit off; so I sot intu thinkin.

"One aind ove a long clothes-line, wif nine dimunt quilts ontu hit, wer tied tu the same cherry tree that the hoss wer. I tuck my knife and socked hit thru every quilt, 'bout the middil, an' jis' below the rope, an' tied them thar wif bark, so they cudent slip. Then I went tu the back aind, an' ontied hit frum the pos,' knottin in a hoe-handil, by the middle, tu keep the quilts frum slippin off ef my bark strings failed, an' laid hit on the groun. Then I went tu the tuther aind: thar wer 'bout ten foot tu spar, a-lyin on the groun arter tyin tu the tree. I tuck hit atwix Wall-eye's hine laigs, an' tied hit fas' tu bof stirrups, an' then cut the cherry tree lim' betwix his bridil an' the tree, almos' off. Now, mine yu thar wer two ur three uther ropes full ove quilts atween me an' the hous', so I wer purty well hid frum thar. I jis' tore off a palin frum the fence, an' tuck hit in bof hans, an' arter raisin hit 'way up yander, I fotch hit down, es hard es I cud, flatsided to'ards the groun, an' hit acksidentally happen'd tu hit Wall-eye, 'bout nine inches ahead ove the root ove his tail. Hit landed so hard that hit made my hans tingle, an' then busted intu splinters. The first thing I did, wer tu feel ove mysef, on the same spot whar hit hed hit the hoss. I cudent help duin hit tu save my life, an' I swar I felt sum ove Wall-eye's sensashun, jis' es plain. The fust thing he did, wer tu tare down the lim' wif a twenty foot jump, his head to'ards the hous'. Thinks I, now yu hev dun hit, yu durn'd wall-eyed fool! Tarin down that lim' wer the beginin ove all the troubil, an' the hoss did hit hissef; my conshuns felt clar es a mountin spring, an' I wer in a frame ove mine tu obsarve things es they happen'd, an' they soon begun tu happen purty clost arter one anuther rite then, an' thar, an' tharabouts, clean ontu town, thru hit, an' still wer a-happenin, in the woods beyant thar ni ontu eleven mile frum ole man Yardley's gate, an' four beyant town.

"The fust line ove quilts he tried tu jump, but broke hit down; the nex one he ran onder; the rope cotch ontu the ho'n ove the saddil, broke at bof ainds, an' went along wif the hoss, the cherry tree lim' an' the fust line ove quilts, what I hed proverdensally tied fas' tu the rope. That's what I calls foresight, George. Right furnint the frunt door he cum in contack wif ole Missis Yardley hersef, an' anuther ole 'oman; they wer a-holdin a nine dimunt quilt spread out, a-'zaminin hit, an' a-praisin hits purfeckshuns. The durn'd onmanerly, wall eyed fool run plum over Missis Yardley, frum ahine, stompt one hine foot through the quilt, takin hit along, a-kickin ontil he made hits corners snap like a whip. The gals screamed, the men hollered wo! an' the ole 'oman wer toted intu the hous' limber es a wet string, an' every word she sed wer, 'Oh, my preshus nine dimunt quilt!'

"Wall-eye busted thru the palins, an' Dominicker seed 'em, made a mortal rush fur his bitts, wer too late fur them, but in good time fur the strings ove flyin quilts, got tangled amung em, an' the gridiron jackid patren wer los' tu my sight amung star an' Irish chain quilts; he went frum that quiltin at the rate ove thuty miles tu the hour. Nuffin lef on the lot ove the hole consarn, but a nine biler hat, a par ove gloves, an' the jack ove hearts.

"What a onmanerly, suddin way ove leavin places sum folks hev got, enyhow.

"Thinks I, well, that fool hoss, tarin down that cherry tree lim', hes dun sum good, enyhow; hit hes put the ole 'oman outen the way fur the balance ove the quiltin, an' tuck Dominicker outen the way an' outen danger, fur that gridiron jackid wud a-bred a scab on his nose afore midnite; hit wer morrily boun tu du hit.

"Two months arterwards, I tracked the route that hoss tuck in his kalamatus skeer, by quilt rags, tufts ove cotton, bunches ove har (human an' hoss), an' scraps ove a gridiron jackid stickin ontu the bushes, an' plum at the aind ove hit, whar all signs gin out, I foun a piece ove watch chain an' a hosses head. The places what know'd Dominicker, know'd 'im no more.

"Well, arter they'd tuck the ole 'oman up stairs an' camfired her tu sleep, things begun tu work agin. The widders broke the ice, an' arter a littil gigilin, goblin, an' gabblin, the kissin begun. *Smack!*—'Thar, now,' a widder sed that. *Pop!*—'Oh, don't!' *Pfip!*—'Oh, yu quit!' *Plosh!*—'Go *way* yu awkerd critter, yu kissed me in the eye!' anuther widder sed that. *Bop!* 'Now yu ar satisfied, I recon, big mouf!' *Vip!*—'That haint fair!' *Spat!*—'Oh, lordy! May, cum pull Bill away; he's a-tanglin my har.' *Thut!*— 'I jis' d-a-r-e yu tu du that agin!' a widder sed that, too. Hit sounded all 'roun that room like poppin co'n in a hot skillet, an' wer pow'ful sujestif.

"Hit kep on ontil I be durn'd ef *my* bristils didn't begin tu rise, an' sumthin like a cold buckshot wud run down the marrow in my back-bone 'bout every ten secons, an' then run up agin, tolerabil hot. I kep a swallerin wif nuthin tu swaller, an' my face felt swell'd; an' yet I wer fear'd tu make a bulge. Thinks I, I'll ketch one out tu hersef torreckly, an' then I guess we'll rastil. Purty soon Sal Yardley started fur the smoke-'ous, so I jis' gin my head a few short shakes, let down one ove my wings a-trailin, an' sirkiled roun her wif a side twis' in my naik, steppin sidewise, an' a-fetchin up my hinmos' foot wif a sorter jerkin slide at every step. Sez I, 'Too coo-took a-too.' She onderstood hit, an stopt, sorter spreadin her shoulders. An' jis' es I hed pouch'd out my mouf, an' wer a-reachin forrid wif hit, fur the article hitsef, sunthin interfared wif me, hit did. George, wer yu ever ontu yer hans an' knees, an' let a helltarin big, mad ram, wif a ten-yard run, but yu yearnis'ly, jis' onst, right squar ontu the pint ove yer back-bone?"

"No, you fool; why do you ask?"

"Kaze I wanted tu know ef yu cud hev a realizin' noshun ove my shock. Hits scarcely worth while tu try tu make yu onderstan the case by words only, on-less yu hev been tetched in that way. Gr-eat golly! The fust thing I felt, I tuck hit tu be a back-ackshun yeathquake; an' the fust thing I seed wer my chaw'r terbacker a-flyin over Sal's head like a skeer'd bat. My mouf wer pouch'd out, ready fur the article hitsef, yu know, an' hit went outen the roun hole like the wad outen a pop-gun—thug! An' the fust thing I know'd, I wer a flying over Sal's head too, an' a-gainin on the chaw'r terbacker fast. I wer straitened out strait, toes hinemos', middil finger-nails foremos', an' the fust thing I hearn wer, 'Yu dam Shanghi!' Great Jerus-a-lam! I lit ontu my all fours jis' in time tu but the yard gate ofen hits hinges, an' skeer loose sum more hosses—kep on in a four-footed gallop, clean acrost the lane afore I cud straiten up, an' yere I cotch up wif my chaw'r terbacker, stickin flat agin a fence-rail. I hed got so good a start that I thot hit a pity tu spile hit, so I jis' jump'd the fence an' tuck thru the orchurd. I tell yu I dusted these yere close, fur I tho't hit wer arter me.

"Arter runnin a spell, I ventered tu feel roun back thar, fur sum signs ove what hed happened tu me. George, arter two pow'ful hardtugs, I pull'd out the vamp an' sole ove one ove ole man Yardley's big brogans, what he hed los' amung my coat-tails. Dre'ful! dre'ful! Arter I got hit away frum thar, my flesh went fas' asleep, frum abuv my kidneys tu my knees; about now, fur the fust time, the idear struck me, what hit wer that hed interfar'd wif me, an' los' me the kiss. Hit wer ole Yardley hed kicked me. I walked fur a month like I wer straddlin a thorn hedge. Sich a shock, at sich a time, an' on sich a place—jis' think ove hit! Hit am tremenjus, haint hit? The place feels num, right now."

"Well, Sut, how did the quilting come out?"

"How the hell du yu 'speck me tu know? I warn't thar eny more."

Sut Lovingood's Dog

"BOYS, I never told eny on ye ove my dog scrape, did I?"

"No, Sut, not as we knows on; you've mixed up dog so in all yer doins, that we can't tell adzactly what dog scrape ye mean."

"Well, I mean ole 'Stuff-gut.' Did eny on ye ever see 'im "

"No."

"Well, ye missed a site. He wur a powerful dog, an' sometimes ye'd think that he wur two ur three dogs, ef ye seed him eat; not a-countin ove his tail, fur he hedn't eny. When he wur a pup, dad, durn *him,* tuck 'im tu a straw-cutter, jamed his starn clost up tu the frame ove the cussed gullotine, an' foch down the knife, an' thar lay the hole tail in the troft, like a letter S, an' here run the pup a youlin like a hound, an' his starn looked like you'd busted a ripe tomatis onto hit. Well, it changed his looks mitely, an' his nater more. Now as to his looks, rite ontu the spot whar his tail orter staid, thar grow'd a bunch ove stiff, ash-cullured bristles, what pinted every way, like onto a split broom with the rappin cut loose, an' rite in the middil ove all this fuzzy lookin patch ove har, the pint ove his back-bone, kivered with a gristil, stuck out like onto a pidgin's aig, caze he sot ontu hit so much. Well, the afar looked mity sassy and fite like, eny how, purticulerly when he wur a struttin up to a big strange dog tu smell ove 'im. It made his sturn look hier than his sholders, pupendiculer and squar; an' he hed a way ove walkin slow an' solemn like I've seed yung fellers do at camp-meetin when approachin ove a gal at the spring with thar stud-hoss close on, agwine sorter side ways an' mity keerful. I've seed little hogs go through the same motions, wun in a peach orchard, an' tuther in the lane, when they *thot* they wanted tu fite, an' wud a dun hit but fur the fence what wur atween em. I never found out that he wur good fur enything but tu keep bred frum mouldin, an' meat frum spilin; an' when he wanted tu show glad, es he hed no tale tu wag, he wagged his hole sturn, an' his hine feet slipped about on the groun, sorter like a fashunabil gal walks when she thinks sum he feller is lookin at 'er. He wur cullured adzackly like a mildewed saddil skirt, an' he kerried his years on a nowin sort of cock, like ontu a muel's when he is skeered. He'd whiskers round his eyes, an' on his hine laigs, an' must had a pow'ful activ consince, fur he wur the meanest countinenced dog I ever seed in my life. Now as tu his nater, yu cud never set 'im ontu enything yu wanted tu, an' cudn't call 'im ofen enything he got arter on his own accord. He wur skeered all the time, an' stud redy tu run ur tu steal, as the chances mout be; an' takin 'im altogether, he wur jis' the rite sort ove a dog tu belong tu me—not wurth a durn, an' orter been killed afore his eyes got open.

"Well, Stuff-gut he follered me tu town wun day jis' caze I didn't want 'im tu; an' while I wur gittin on a hed ove steam at the doggery, he started roun town on a stealin experdition ove his own, an' like his cussed fool owner, got hissef inter a fust rate scrape an' skeer, without half tryin, an' in less nor no time at that.

"I hed gin myself a shake in the doggery, an' hear the whisky in me slosh, I know'd I hed my load aboard, so I cum out intu the street, *an'*—the— fust thing I seed he cum a tarin down the street fifteen times faster nor I thot he cud run, jis' a bowin ove hissef, his years sot flat ontu his neck, an' his bristles all sot like a black pearch's top fin, his eyes shot up fast an' tite, and he hed on a sort ove haness made outer strings, sorter like the set dad wore when he acted hoss, an' he wer haulin ove an' old stage lantern and hit filled with wet powder, an' sot afire.

"Now the sparks, an' the scizlin, an' the dust, an' the ratlin, an' the youlin, an' growlin, an' barkin, an' the eighty-nine ur ninety dogs ove all kinds what wur a chasin ove him, made sum sensashun. Well—hit—did. Wheww-w! When I seed him pass without nowin me I thot ove Dad's ho'net tribulashun, an' felt that thar wur such a thing as a tribulashun at las'; an' then I got mad an' looked roun fur sum wun tu vent rath on, an' seed a long-legged cuss, sorter ove the Lovingood stripe, with his hat cocked before, sittin a straddil ove a hoss-rack, a swingin his legs an' a-singin—

> "Rack, back Davy, rarin up behine,
> You show me your foot, an' I'll show you mine."

"Thinks I, yu'll do, ef yu *didn't* start my dog on that hellward experdition ove his'n; yu'll do tu put it on enyhow, so here goes. Sez I: 'Mister-what-hed-my-dog-dun-tu-yu?' He pade no tention, but kep on a-singin—

> "Rack, back Davy, daddy shot a bar,
> Shot 'em in the eye, an' never toch a har."

"I seed it wur no use tryin tu breed a quarrel; so that I mout be able tu breed a fite, an' I jist lent him a slatharin calamity, rite whar his nose commenced a sproutin from atween his eyes, wif a ruff rock about the size ove a goose aig. Hit fotch 'im! He drapped ofen the hoss-rack, but hilt a squirrel-holt ontu the pole wif his paws an' hine feet, an' hung back down. I jumped hed fust through, atween his belly an' the pole; my heft broke his holt, an' we cum tu the ground a-fitin—me ondermost, an' turn'd heads an' tails. So the fust thing I did, was tu shut my jaws ontu a mouthful ove his steak, ni ontu the place wher yer foot itches to go when yu ar in kickin distance ove a fop. He fit mitily fur the chance he had, but I soon seed he had a cross ove bar in 'im, fur he cudn't stand ticklin behind, ef it mout be called ticklin at all; fur every time he got his hine legs onder him, he tried his durndest tu jump loose; but my holt hilt, an' we would take our fust persition agin. I thot ove a box ove matches what I hed in my pocket, so I foch the whole boxful a rake ontu the gravil, an' stuffed em all a-blazin inter one ove the pockets in his coat-tail. Now, mind, he now'd nuthin ove these perseedins, fur his mind wur exercized powful about the hurtin I wur a helpin 'im tu behine. I no'd he'd soon show strong signs ove wantin tu go. So the fust big rare he fotch arter the fire reached his hide, I jist let my mouth fly open—so—an' he *went!* his hole tail in a blaze!

"Rite here, boys, I must tell yu sumthin I didn't no mysef, ur durn me, ef I hedn't let him beat me inter a poultis, afore I'd a-sot him on fire—I'd a-seed him durn'd fust. The thot on it skeers me yet. He had two pounds ove gunpowder in tother pocket, a-takin home to a shootin match.

"Well, he aimed tu run past a tin peddlin waggin' what

was a-standin in the street, with a fust-rate set ove old live hoss bones atween the shafts, while the Yankee wus in the doggery, a-firin up tu leave town. Jist as he got clost tu the carryall, the powder cotch fire' an' soon arterwards *went off,* an' *so did he,* head fust, frog fashion, rite thru the top load ove tin war. He lit a runnin ten foot tuther side; his coat-tails wur blowed off tu his shoulders, the hine aind ove his galluses wus raped round his neck, the tale ove his shut wus loose, an, up in the air thirty feet, still a-risin an' blazin like a komit; his britches hung loose on the frunt side, like ontu a forked aprun, while the sittin part ove em wus blowed tu kingdom cum, and so wur everything else belongin tu that regin, while his back wus as black as a side ove upper lether. It rained tin buckets, an' strainers, an' tin cups, an' pepper boxes, an' pans, an' stage ho'ns, all over that street, fur two minits an' a 'alf.

"Now that explosion, an' the tin war ratlin an' a rainin, made a rite peart noise, specially ove a still day in fac, enuf tu wake up the ole hoss bones an' gin him the idear that he'd best leave town quick; so he laid *his* years back an' straitened out his tail an' shot. He made kindlin-wood outen the waggin agin a sine-post, an' betuck hissef tu the woods, stretched out about twenty feet long, an' not mor'n three feet high on the withers, with jis about enuf harness stickin tu him tu make a cullar for a bell cow.

"Thar wus wun cussed nutmeg-makin Yankee broke plum up, an' I'm durn'd glad ove it. Old Rack Back Davy, the hoss-rack man, made fur the river, an' I follered tu the bank tu see ef he hedn't drownded hissef; but no *sir!* Thar he wur, about the middil ove the river, a-swimin fur tuther bank, jist a splitin the warter wide open, an' his busted britches legs a-floatin arter him. He looked over his shoulder every uther lick like he spected tu see the devil; his face wur as black as a pot, sept a white ring roun his eyes, an' the smoke wur still risin frum amung the stumps ove his burnt har. His hed, boys, in that river, wus the ugliest, scuriest, an' savidgest site I ever seed or spec tu see in *this* wurld, eny how. I dreams ove it yet o'nights, an' it skares the swet outen me. I seed a lot ove fellers a fishin onder the bank, so I thot I'd help him on a leetle faster, an' I hollered, 'ketch the murderer, five hundred dullars an' a big hoss reward. He's kill'd an 'oman an' nine children, an' I speck a dog, an' like tu whipped anuther plum tu *deth*.' They jumped intur thar cunoes an' tuck arter him, openin on his trail like a pack ove houns. The last I ever seed ove him, he wur a rackin up the tother bank, on his all-fours, an' looked like an ole bar what hed jist cum outen a harycane.

"He still kept up his lookin back, an' I speck wus the wust scared man in the wurld, an' ef he aint ded, he's runnin yet. The idear now begin tu soak thru my har that owin to the fuss Stuff-gut an' me hed raised, that perhaps *I'd* better scoot, lest they mout want *me*. So I left in a peart trot, an' soon got on ole Stuff's trail. It wur like a waggin hed been drug upside down by a par ove runaway muels, an' the dry grass an' leaves, an' in sum places the fences wer sot afire. He tuck to the mountins, an' turn'd wolf, an' tuck up the trade ove sheep-killin fur a livin, an' the hole settlement is now out arter his skalp. That trip tu town, like the cuttin-box, hes changed his dispersition agin, all showin the pow'ful changes that kin be made in even a dog. I cum outen that scrape purty well, yet I hed tu show the family dispersition tu make d——d fools ove tharsefs."

"How, Sut?"

"Why, I ought to a-toted off a lode ove that permiscus tin war. Oughtent I? say!"

Sut at a Negro Night-Meeting

"QUIT yer kerd playin an' ritin, an' listen tu me; I'se swell'd up wif a tale, an' I'll bust rite yere in this camp ef I don't git hit outen me. I 'sisted wunst at a nigger meetin at Log Chapil camp-groun, tu more pupus an' wif more pint than folks ginerly 'sists on sich cashuns."

"You assisted? When?"

"Yas, yu may whistil, but durn ef I didn't. Aint the word rite? Ef a feller stands up when anuther's a-gittin tied tu an 'oman, don't the noospapers say he 'sisted? Ef a wun-hoss preacher sits intu the pulpit while a two-hoss one preaches, don't they print hit that he 'sisted? An' if a big-bug's wife's dorg wer tu hold a cow's tail in his teef while she milk'd, they'd say he 'sisted. Well, ef 'sistance is what the noospapers makes hit out tu be, I 'sisted sum, durn'd ef I didn't!

"Well, wun Sat'd'y nite, all the he, an' mos' ove the she niggers fur ten miles roun, started tu hold a big meetin. They cum a-foot, on hoss's, on muels, on oxes, on bulls, on sleds, in carts, waggins an' buggys. The meetin wer wuf ni ontu five hundred thousin dullars in flush times, an' yu cud a-smelt hit a mile, *afore* I begun tu 'sist, an' fifteen mile *arter* I 'sisted. An' the nise—well, when I larns tu spell an' pernounce the flavor ove a ded hoss, play the shape ove a yeathen war-jug ontu a fiddil, ur paint the swifness ove these yere laigs ontu a clap-board, then I'll 'scribe the nise ove that meetin, particulerly arter I 'sisted awhile. 'Sumthin mus be lef tu the 'maginashun,' ole Bullen sed, when he wer givin in his lizzerd 'sperience, an' hit am es true es sayin yas, when a man axes yu ur me ef we want a ho'n ove skin-gut when hits rainin, an' sich kerryins on hesn't been seed since ole Tam Shadrick wer a-seein the witches a-dansin thru the ole chu'ch winders what yu narrated tuther nite. I b'leves intu witches, ghostez, an' all long-nebbed things mysef, an' so dus mos' folks, but they's tu cowardly tu say so.

"I wer in the setilment runnin a daily line, wif no failures, atween Wheeler's hill-hous' an' Kidd's grocery, leavin a mail at ole Missis Cruze's wif the gals, an' a-shufflin roun' ginerally twixt trips ove a nite. I hearn hit narrated that the meetin wer a-goin tu be so I sot in an' fix'd mysef fur hit, so es tu be abil tu 'sist 'em sum.

"I purvided about a dozen ho'nets' nestes, big soun' wuns, an' stopped em up full ove disapinted, bewild'red, 'vengeful, savidge, oncircumsized ball ho'nets, sharpnin thar stings redy, an' jis' waitin hot an' willin fur the holes tu be open'd, tu spread pizin an' sweet hurtin an' swellin onder the skin ove everybody. They own'd tu no non-cumbitants outside them ar nestes.

"Then I got Doctur Stone, hu wer fond uv seein fun, tu fill a big passel ove beef-bladders wif sum kind ove a'r ur gas—he call'd hit ox-gin, ur steer-gin, ur sum kind ove cattil drink, an' I hes furgot plum hits cristen name."

"Perhaps it was carbureted hydrogen."

"Durn my ole galluses, an' buttuns tu, ef that warn't adzackly hit. *Hu* tole yu? say George? *Did* yu smell hit?"

"Oh, often."

"Well, by golly, that counts fur that shriveled up nose ove yourn, an' yer cussed ill temper. George, I furgives yu fur every cussin yu's ever sprinkled ontu me. No man shu'd be hilt sponsibil fur his acts arter a sniff at that ar devil's own parfume; hit am the superlatif ove the yeath; yu kin see, feel, an' taste hit six weeks arter hit hes et up yure power ove smellin altugether. I hilt a bladder uv hit, tu a bull's nose, tu see ef he wer a jedge ove perfumery. He jis' histed his tail, like tu hev snorted his brains out at wun snort, an jis' kill'd hissef a-runnin, a-pawin at his snout wif his fore-laigs like he wer a-tryin tu scrape off a bull tarrier. Twer the bes thing he cud do, wer tu die jis' then.

"I fix't my 'sortment ove stink skins onder the long seat ove the pulpit in the chu'ch, wif slip nots ontu the necks, so that pullin wun string ontied all ove em, an' let down a big slab tu squeese em flat. I planted my ball ho'nets colonys onder the bainches amung the straw onder the big shed what jined the chu'ch, an wun peculuer an' chosen nestes I laid away onder the exhortin box, ur shed pulpit. All on em hed strings so I cud open em at wunst frum the thickets, when I thort hit time tu take sich a sponsabil step. They hed hawl'd straw untill hit cum up ni ontu levil wif the tops ove the bainches, tu git happy in, an' du thar huggin an' wallerin on; hit hid the inemy what I hed ambush'd thar fus'rate, an' arterwards wer put tu a diffrent use than gittin happy on, I'll swar tu that fac'.

"Well, nite cum, an' fotch wif hit the mos pufick 'sortment ove niggers yu ever seed outen Orleans ur Tophett, a big pine torch-lite an ni ontu every uther tree roun the shed, an' taller candils intu the chu'ch hous whar they cumenc'd thar wurk; but I'm sistimatikally durn'd if they finished hit thar; not by a sirkil ove five mile.

"A pimpil-face, greasy-collar'd, limber-mouf'd suckit rider drap't ofen a fat hoss, an' sot in tu sorter startin the nigger brethrin in the rite track. He warn't fur frum bein a nat'ral born durn'd fool hissef, fur I seed him peep onder the seat es he sot down in the pulpit, whar he seed the bulge ove wun ove the bladders, stickin out frum onder the slab a littil. He licked his lips, then smak't em, an' wink'd a oily sort ove wink at a Baptis' nigger preacher, what sot by him, an' *he* show'd all ove his teef arter he'd tuck a peep, an' swaller'd like he wer gittin down a ho'n. They wer bof on em showin thar instinks: the suckit rider tuck hit tu be the breast ove a fat roas hen, an' the Baptis' thot hit wer the bulge ove a jug. *Shapes,* George, can't be 'pended upon; *taste* am the thing.

"Well, the pot-gutted, ball-heded Baptis' bull nigger, what wer fool'd on the jug question, sot his specks an' tuck a tex; hit wer:

"*Yu shall smell sweet-smellin yarbs, an' eat honey vittils dar, fur thars no stink, nur bitter, whar you's gwine, in Caneyan.*

"He wer jis' in the middil ove the sweet-smellin yarb part, a-citin ove poseys, sinamint draps, fried bacon, an' the scent ove the cupboard, as good yeathly smells, a-gittin hot, an' a-breakin a holesum sweat, when a ole she shouted—

"'Oh, bress hebin! I smell him now.'

"As she smack't her han's, I pull'd the string. The stinkabus begun tu roll an' rise, an' spread. Oh my lordy! lordy! Pimple-face wall'd up his eyes, coff'd, blow'd his nose in his hankecher, an' sorter looked behind the preacher, like he 'spected tu see a buzzard, or an' onbelever, or sich like, atween him an' the wall.

"The nigger stop't as short as ef he'd been shot, rite in the middil ove the wurd 'Caneyan,' histed the pint ove his snout up atween his eyes, turn'd his upper lip inside out, throw'd his head back, an' scented slowly all roun. I hes seed ole steers du hit adzackly the same way. He shook his hed till his years slapt like a hog's when he's a-gittin mad, an' his specks lit in the straw; then he scented roun' agin.

"By this time bout two hundred miserlanus niggers wer a-sayin *Hu-uu* thru thar snouts, wif thar moufs shot; 'bout half es meny a-coffin, a few sickly wuns tryin not tu vomit, an' wun skaley heel'd he wer a-stuffin two corn-cob pints intu his nose, an' a saft wool hat intu his mouf. Sum ten ur fifteen said 'Oh, lor a massy! what dat?' Wun ole feller wif meal on his wool, 'lowed sum fat brudder dun bust hissef, an' am leakin out the cabbage. Better 'tire tu de woods, git sow' up, an' den stay dar.' One ventered 'pole-cat'; anuther, 'twenty pole-cat'; 'an' a dorg a-stirrin em,' added anuther; 'ded hoss,' sed a big he, wif a hoarse cold; 'spild crout,' squeak't a she; 'buzzard's nes', frum a back bainch; 'rotten aigs an' a heap on em,' grunted a ole mammy wif a belly like a dinner-pot, an' a wool mitten in her mouf; 'wus nur dat, by golly,' snorted a dandy nigger, a-holdin his snout; 'burnt leder,' frum a fool gal; 'burnt brimstone,' frum a boy; 'maggoty soap grease,' guess'd two or three; 'all dem tings mix an' a-bilin, *dat's hit,*' said a knowin-lookin bow-laiged buck; 'de cumin ob de debil,' surjisted a ole she, a-pullin her aprun over her hed. 'Redy, heah, mum?' answered her darter. 'Meetin dun busted,' said one; 'hope I neber smell nuder bust,' said anuther. 'Less git outen heah,' said ten, while swarms ove em wer aready at hit.

"The passun nigger now holler'd, 'Sea heah, brudren an' sistren; sum fool niggah cum trou de back ob de gardin, an' sile he foot, on he way heah; let 'im make hesef scase, an' take he shoe wid 'im, fur he 'noxshus tu dis chosen congregashun, he am.' 'Sh-u-u-u tree hunder git sile in dat gardin on bof foot, shuah yu born,' added a chicken stealin yung he, wif feathers then in his wool.

"Here the passun's feelins overcum him, an' he cummenced a-yerkin like he'd swaller'd a hame string, an' the knot hed stuck in his froat.

" 'Preachin frum that fool tex what done hit,' growl'd a ole daddy wif wun toof, as he hobbled apas the passon a-rubbin his sleeve onder his nose like he wer sawin wood, an' a snortin like a hoss atween every rub.

" 'Missus kill me shuah yu lib, ef I totes *dis* stink home wid me. Hu got eny sinamint draps?' said a trim-lookin cook.

" 'Sum ob de sistren am dun faint, holler'd a bowlaiged, bladder-lipped he, a-rushin thru the crowd wif a gourd ove warter.

" 'Bress de Lord, dey'se rite tu faint, dey no smell him now,' said a knowin ole darky.

" 'This am more disagreabil than whisky an' inyuns,' said Pimple-face, tu me.

" 'Yas, perticulerly the inyuns,' sez I.

"He looked at me like he wer sorry fur me, an' wud es leve pray fur me es not, an' went an' dipt his hed in the branch.

"By this time the chu'ch wer empty, 'sceptin the stink, an' hit wer everywhar, oozin thru the shingles like smoke. The candils burnt dim like thar wer a fog in the hous', an' hit wer onhelthy tu preach in till fros', an' thar aint a nigger in that settlement what kin tell the smell ove a scent bottil frum a barril ove rotten fish tu this day. They'd be pow'ful good stock tu wurk in a soap factory. Don't yu speck they wud? The soggy an' muddy heded wuns hilt a pow-wow, an' narrated hit that in spite 'ob de ole sarpint de debil an' he stink in he hous,' they ment tu tote on the meetin tu a shoutin aind, onder the shed. So they shot up the door an' winder shutters ove the chu'ch, an' as the wind hed sorter ris, the outside smells warn't much wus nor yu ginerally smell et pork-killin houses, ur camp meetins. This wur the wust 'clusion ever a mess ove niggers did cum tu, since ole Shadwick's darkys ondertuck tu make white folks outen tharsefs by paintin thar cackuses wif onslack't lime. Ole Shadwick gethered enuff *wool* tu pay thar doctur's bills.

"Well, they blow'd a ho'n, an' 'Pimple face' tuck the crank ove the 'make happy cum' mersheen, es all the preachin an' grace hed been plum stunk outen his culler'd bruther. The sistren mos on em got ni ontu the pulpit, whar the straw wer deepest wif sich ove the he's es hed a appertite tu help du the huggin an' wallerin. 'Pimpil-face,' blow'd his nose, flung his hanketcher across the pulpit, an' sed 'hit wer all fur the bes' that they wer druv frum the hous'; grace allers spread hitsef better an' smoofer, outen doors then hit did in the hous'. Tu git happy *good,* yu mus hev elbow-room an' straw; these cundishuns wer fill'd, an' he'd be disapinted ef that wurn't a warm activ meetin.' Thinks I, wif me to ' 'sist,' ef hit aint all yu's sed, an' more tu, I'se no jedge ove the nater ove ball ho'nets, an' the power ove stimiluses.

"He sed, arter he'd dun preachin, he ment tu pass roun' a small hat, tu git sum means tu buy flannin petticoats wif, fur the freezin sistren in Africa. Ef ever *he* 'pass'd a hat' hit warn't at Log Chappil, 'sceptin what loose wuns he pass'd a runnin outen thar; I 'sisted in spilin wun coleckshun, I'm durn'd ef I didn't.

"He tuck a tex: *Thar shall be weepin an' railin an' chompin ove teef, bad, an' them wif no teef, shall smash thar gums tugether like ontu wolf traps.* Sez I tu mysef, that's hit, that *is* hit, dorg on me ef yu haint draw'd the rite kerd this pop, fur I know'd I wer 'sistin' ove him.

"He sot in in yeanest, ontied his choke-string, then shucked his coat, nex his jackid. He play'd pow'ful bad, didn't he? fur me tu hole the 'sisten han', fur shuckin hissef didn't fortify again my ho'nets much, hit didn't. About the time he drapt his jackid, an' wer a-tryin tu jump outen his trowsis wifout onbuttunin em, the niggers wer a-mixin, he an' she, hollerin an' beginin tu hug, an' rar, an' waller, rite peart, an' nat'ral like, the dus, an' the same ole stink, wif the sweat variashun a-risin agin. Wun ole she fotch her fat han's a slap like killin flies, an' she squall'd 'gloree,' an' her mouf look't like the muzzil ove a boot, wif red linin.

"Thinks I, jis' now is es good a time es eny; the patrollers mite cum in an' spile hit wif thar durn'd foolishness; so I jis' draw'd the strings keerfully. The fust fruit ove that ac', what I notised, wer ontu Pimple-face hissef. I seed him fotch hissef a lick a-side the hed what stagger'd him, then he hit hissef wif bof han's ontu the place whar they brands Freemasons an' mustangs, an' he shot his belly forwards an' his shoulders back'ards, like ontu a 'oman shettin the nex' tu the top drawer ove a beauro; an' he cum outen that pulpit back'ards a-tarin, his hans a-flyin roun his hed like a par ove windin blades. I thort he hed eitey fingers an twenty thumbs. He embraced a bruther, back-holts, what wer a-tryin tu roll off the hurtin in the straw, an' they jis' kick'd an' roll'd on in cahoote.

"Thar wer lots ove niggers, mix'd heads an' tails in that orful straw-pile—heds, laigs, arms, feet, ainds ove bainches, bunches ove straw an' strings ove dartin ho'nets a-showin tharsefs a-top fur a moment; then sum uther things wud cum upermos'. Hit looked like forty-eight cords ove black cats a-fitin, wif tupentine a soakin in roun the roots ove all thar tails.

"Sich nises—screechin like painters, cryin, hollerin, a few a-cussin, an' more a-jinin em, beggin, prayin, groanin, gruntin, nickerin, an' wun or two fool wuns singin. Ho'nets don't keer a durn fur music, when they's a-fitin, while abuv em a-flyin in the ar, jis' like they weighed nuthin, wer a desirabil 'sortmint ove hyme books, fans, hanketchers, hats, caps, umerellers, walkin-sticks, biskits, chicken-laigs, strings ove beads, Gouber peas, year-rings, ginger-cakes, collars, garters, babies, terbacker-pipes, ridicules, littil baskits, popco'n, scent bottils, ribbons, hollyhawk bokays, pint ticklers, bits ove straw, an' wun shiff—how she got outen hit wifout takin off her frock, I be durn'd ef I ken tell; but thar hit wer a-sailin roun wif a deck-load ove ho'nets ontu hit what wer the resarve I reckon. All this wer set off tu advantige by dus', an' millions ove insex, jis' a-hoverin over the sufferers an' then divin down fur a sting.

"Now, while this wer gwine on onder the shed, niggers wer a-shootin intu the woods in all direckshuns, like ontu arrers shot frum orful bows, an' every durn'd nigger hed a brigade ove insex roun his hed, tellin him tu hurry an' makin him du hit too, fur they went crash-in outen site intu the brush like canyun shots.

"Now, I thinks the ho'nets hed boun tharsefs wif a oath, while they wer shot up in thar nestes, tu fite furever every livin thing they met, frum the way they actid. Fur them what follered the niggers intu the woods foun' the hosses, muels, an' oxes, tied out thar, an' part ove em fastened ontu the beastes, an' they immejuntly sot in tu imitatin the niggers in actin dam fool; they jis' broke loose, rar'd, kick'd, fell down, roll'd over, run away, bawl'd, beller'd, nicker'd, screem'd, an' bray'd, till they farly shuck the leaves ontu the trees.

"Wun yoke ove steers wif a big sled cum tarin heds down, an' tails strait up, rite thru the shed, an' I think they mus hev swep' out ni ontu thuty niggers, big an' littil, an' a few bainches, intu the woods wif em, a-stickin ontu thar ho'ns, ontu the yoke, on thar backs, an' on the stakes ove the sled. Yere cum a big gray hoss, like a streak, draggin a buggy ontu hits side wif the top up. His eyes wer red, an' his years laid back; he scoop'd up his buggy plum full, an' jis' kep on. I observed Pimpil-face tangled up in the runnin gear, an' true tu the suckit rider's instink, he wer climbin powful fur a inside seat. He run a-pas' a postes what hed a ole tin pan atop ove hit full ove rich pine knots a burnin: he scoop'd that in amung his cargo ove niggers tu warm em on thar thorny way, an' then he jis' run by the lite ove hit. Thar went a big grizly muel, wif a side saddil way back ontu his rump, an' half a peach tree fas' tu his bridil; he gobbled up two ur three littil niggers in the tree-top, an' tuck em outen the trubbil.

"Wun long laiged nigger busted outen the bunch what wer down in the straw, hollerin 'whoosh! Oh goramity! Hit hurts till he feel sorter good,' an' tuck a rush skull fus' agin a weatherboarded camp, busted thru hit like hit wer a aig shell, an' out at tuther side thru a winder, a-totin the sash wif him roun his neck like a collar, an' his wool full ove plank splinters, broken glass, an' tangled ball ho'nets. I likes that nigger: he's the only feller I ever seed what tuck in the rale pure Lovingood idear ove what orter be dun onder strong hurtin an' a big skeer. Jis run over ur thru everthing yure durndest, till yu gits cumfort, that's hit.

"A hames-laiged spur-heel'd wun tuck up a white oak, sayin 'whoosh!' outen his nose every yerk he made, an' findin no pease ove mine up thar, tuck down agin her fus', squirrel fashion, an' run onder the chu'ch ontu his all fours, sum ho'nets makin the same trip on the same skedule.

"Wun big she run her hed onder a lean gal's coat-tail tu save her years, but a few activ ball ho'nets what wer a scoutin in her rar, made her git up blinefol' wif the gal 'stradil her neck, her long black snake laigs stickin strait out ahead, an' she a-holdin on tu the fat wun's wool thru the dress wif wun han, an' a fitin ho'nets wif a hat in tuther, her hed throw'd back, an' a yowlin like a scalded houn. 'Fatty' run her derndest, not seein ur keerin whar she went, down hill kerslunge intu the branch, an' like tu drownded bof ove em, an' sum ho'nets too.

"Wun slim buck nigger shot rat-like intu a littil jug closet, onder the pulpit, swell'd up in thar ontil they hed tu tar up the floor nex day tu git him out. He tuck in wif him about forty ho'nets, an' they helpt him tu be cumfortabil in thar; I knows they did frum thar nater an' what he sed in his hole.

"Jis' bout this time I foun' out how that gal got outen her shiff, fur I seed sumthin dispersin hitssef intu the woods, an' frum the glimpse I got hit look'd sorter like a black munkey shaved wif white hine laigs; hit wer that tormented gal in white stockins. The thing wer pufeckly plain; she hed jis' run outen her dress an' shiff at the same time. That's what cums ove bein a plum natral born'd durn fool; *yu'd* hev onderstood how she got outen hit, without eny studyin at all.

"Now I'se only narrated the main pints, an' hits tuck me a good spell. But in three minits an' a 'alf arter I finish'd my 'sistin ove em by pullin them ar strings, hit wer all over, scept the swellin, hurtin, an' gittin home. Thar warn't even a dorg lef on that camp-groun', an' yu cud hear nuffin but the humin ove the huntin ho'nets, an' the distunt nise ove scatterin niggers, ur uther beastez still gwine furder frum that place ove torment, an' general discumfort.

"People wer huntin thar niggers thru the county fur a week, an' sumtimes when they foun em, didn't know em, they'd fatten'd so. Dreadful! warn't hit? Thar haint been a nigger nite meetin hilt in the county since, an' they's mos' on em becum pius, an' morril.

"Jis' pullin a string wer my hole sheer in all that ar cumbustifikashun, hurtin, an' trubbil; yet as usual every body sez I'se tu blame fur the hole ove hit. Yu know that every time a ho'net shoots a nigger, hit makes a white spot that's the center ove the imejut hurtin, an' ove corse mos' ove em looked like ontu secon' mournin calliker, an' the durn'd fool white folks roun' thar, thot hit wer the small pox, an' that I hed gin hit tu the niggers, so they sot in tu huntin fur *me*, wif shot guns an' dorgs, but *du* yu see these yere laigs? They toted me outen thar safe an' soun.

"I can't git jestis nowhar, fur nuthin I du. I'l turn buzzard, an' eat ded hosses fur a livin; I b'leve theyse not blam'd fur enything much, only thar stink, an' as I hes got that aready es good es the oldest buzzard ontu the roos', that makes no differ."

"Well, Sut," said I, "I think I understand fully now what *'assisting'* at a meetin means."

Sut eyed me for a moment suspiciously, and said dryly—

"I speck yu dus."

Sut Lovingood's Sermon

TOUCHING YE CAT-FISHE TAVERN.

"I SAY, George, every critter what hes ever seed me, ef they hes sence enuff tu hide frum a cummin kalamity, ur run frum a muskit, jis' known five great facks in my case es well es they knows the road tu thar moufs. *Fustly,* that I haint got nara a soul, nuffin but a whisky proof gizzard, sorter like the wust half ove a ole par ove saddil bags. *Secondly,* that I'se too durn'd a fool tu cum even under millertary lor. *Thurdly,* that I hes the longes' par ove laigs ever hung tu eny cackus, 'sceptin only ove a grandaddy spider, an' kin beat *him* a usen ove em jis' es bad es a skeer'd dorg kin beat a crippled mud turkil. *Foufly,* that I kin chamber more cork-screw, kill-devil whisky, an' stay on aind, than enything 'sceptin only a broad bottum'd chun. *Fivety,* an' las'ly, kin git intu more durn'd misfortnit skeery scrapes, than enybody, an' then run outen them faster, by golly, nor enybody.

"Well now, ef these five pow'ful strong pints ove karactar don't gin me the right tu preach ef I wants tu, I wud like tu know whar sum preachers got *thar* papers frum. I means tu wade intu the bisiness es deep es wun sermon, on the free will plan enyhow, leavin out the singin an' totin roun the hat. Listen tu me, fur I'se in yearnis 'bout this thing. Ef yu hes a par ove burnin-glass specks, an' hit am a clar day, yu may fine my texis jis' inside, ur jis' outside (I'se furgot which), ove Longfeller's injun tale, an' hit reads 'bout so:

"*Stop not tu res' whar thar am a sign, fur thar aint res' onder hits shadder. Neither eat wif a lan'lord fur he's yer foe. But gird up yer coteail, an' marvil furder, leas' yu lose yer soul a-cussin, an' hev yer paunch et intu a partridge net wif pisen. Keep the dus' ove the dining room ofen yer foot, an' the smell ove the bed-room ofen yer close, that yer days may be longer in the lan' what yer daddy's tuck frum the Injuns.*"

"Feller suffrers, he an' she: The shakin an' jumblin ove this yere war ove ourn, hes fotch up tu the top ove the groun a new kine ove pisonus-reptile, which fur durty ways, an' short turns, kin jis' beat the bes' cross atwix' a buzzard an' a wolf yu ever seed, es soon es he bores his way outen the yeath what hatch'd im, an' whar he orter be yet. He gits him a long house, prints ontu the frunt ove hit sum ketchin name, tu tote in the hongry an' onwary, an' the dam fools ginerally, calls hissef the 'Perpryiter,' an' yu mustn't call 'im enything else, fur *ef* yu dus, yu'd better gird up yer coteails an' marvil furder, an' marvil faster, fur his boot hes a powful strong swing, a pow'ful long swing, an' a pow'ful quick swing. He is now perpar'd tu starve, 'sult, swindil, be-dirty, be-devil, an' turn inside out the puss, pockid an' stumick ove every misfortnit hungry tired devil, what am wayfarin on fun, bisness, ur frum a skeer. He an' she, ole an' young citerzen, ur soger, he sucks em all out es dry es a spider dus a hoss-fly, an' turns em out tu thar wayfarin agin, while he looks 'zaminly arter em wif his fis' full ove thar shinplasters, then he wipes his horny bill ontu the door jam like ontu a hen arter she hes swaller'd a toad, an' waits fur the nex' hoss-fly. Oh! Keep the dus' ove his dinin-room ofen yer foot, an' the smell ove his bed-room ofen yer close, that yer days may be longer in the lan' what yer daddy's tuck frum the Injuns.

"The Perpryiter's suckshun am strong: he cud suck a anvil (if hit wer gold) down his froat, frum wun aind ove Cumberland tunnil tu tuther, an' thar's no lor ove anybody's make, nur the squire's make, nur the ginerals' make, what kin weakin that suckshun a mossel, ur make a mark ontu his shell; lor jis' rolls ofen his back like draps ove warter ofen a duck or mallard, an' suffrin rolls ofen his casiron conshuns still a littil faster. I seed a thread-bar, faded, cryin sojer's widder, wif a skiliton dogratipe ove hits graveless father in her arms, a-tuggin at a dry bladder, what hed onst been a 'oman's breast, a-reachin pow'ful arter his conshuns wif a argymint es long es a fishin pole, an' pinted wif a lancit. Hit wer in few words, but every one ove em wer red, sparklin hot frum a burnin heart. 'Fur the sake of this fatherless infant, don't turn me away! Here's the last dollar ove the last eleven my husband lived to draw; yu are most welcome to it. Give me but a cold mouthful, *we* are starving, and oh! look, sir, the rain has turned to sleet. Her blue lips quiver'd, an' the rain draps ofen her bunnit, an' the tear draps outen her modes', hopeless eyes, splashed tugether ofen the littil dogratipe's cheek, hot an' cold tugether, an' hit hedn't life enuf lef tu skringe. He looked down at her es cold es the no'th side ove Lookout Mountin in January, an' tole her wifout payin a full bill in advance, she couldn't stay; an' he read a rule ofen the wall, 'pussons travelin wifout eny baggage, mus' pay thar bills in advance. Now my yearers, yu know I haint got nara a soul, an' dam ef the 'Perpryiter' aint in the same boat.

"Hint tu him that yer bill's bigger nor yer dinner, an' he'll smile like he luved yu, an' tell yu that he's jis' ruinatin hissef an' his famerly clean out, es fur es his wife's cuzzin's dorg (an' a durn'd inturestin famerly hit ginerly is to dorg in) by chargin yu es low es he hes. My 'sperience amung this sort ove taverins an' grub factorys hes been orful—tremenjusly orful. I knows, bein a plum natral born durn'd fool makes agin me everywhar; but ef thar's wun place wus tu me fur menyfeld tribulashuns nur anuther this side the place whar murd'rs, 'dult'rs, hook-nose Jews, suckit-riders, tavrin folk, an' sich like cattil go tu arter they's swep frum the face ove yeath by death's broom, tu cumfort tharsefs drinkin bilin tar, an' eatin red-hot casiron sassengers, hit is durn'd infunel single slay'd, pewter spoon, fly-blown, one hoss, half stock'd, single trigger, smoof bore tavrins, an' railroad feed troffs. They's shorten'd my days, they's lainthen'd my nights, they's poperlated the hole territory ove my cackus, clear'd lan' an' wood lan', wif all breeds ove dredful insex, they's gutted my pockid, they's disturb'd my dreams, they's 'stonish'd my stumick, they's skeer'd my appertite, they'se spilt my smellin tools, they's deafen'd my years, they's 'sulted my eyes, an' they's lef a marster stink all over ontu me furever an' ever more, an' more so too ay—men. Oh, my dear yearers, 'keep the dus' ove thar dinin-room ofen yer foot, an' the smell ove thar bed-room ofen yer close, that yer days may be longer in the lan' what yer daddy's tuck frum the Injuns.'

"I seed a well appearin man onst, ax one ove em what lived ahine a las' year's crap ove red hot brass wire whiskers run tu seed, an' shingled wif har like ontu mildew'd flax, wet wif saffron warter, an' laid smoof wif a hot flat-iron, ef he cud spar him a scrimpshun ove soap? The 'perpryiter' anser'd in soun's es sof an' sweet es a poplar dulcimore, tchuned by a good nater'd she angel in butterfly wings an' cobweb shiff, that he never wer jis' so sorry in all his born'd days tu say no, but the fac' wer the soljers had stole hit; 'a towil then'; 'the soljers hed stole hit'; 'a tumbler,' 'the soljers hed stole hit'; 'a lookin-glass,' 'the soljers hed stole hit'; 'a pitcher ove warter,' 'the soljers hed stole hit'; 'then please give me a cleaner room.' Quick es light cum the same dam lie, 'the soljers hed stole hit too.' They buys scalded butter, caze hit crumbles an' yu can't tote much et a load on yer knife; they keeps hit four months so yu won't want tu go arter a secon load. They stops up the figgers an' flowers in the woffil irons fur hit takes butter tu fill the holes in the woffils. They makes soup outen dirty towils, an' jimson burrs; coffee outen niggers' ole wool socks, roasted; tea frum dorg fennil, an' toas' frum ole brogan insoles. They keeps bugs in yer bed tu make yu rise in time fur them tu get the sheet fur a table-cloth. They gins yu a inch ove candil tu go tu bed by, an' a littil nigger tu fetch back the stump tu make gravy in the mornin, fur the hunk ove bull naik yu will swaller fur brekfus, an' they puts the top sheaf ontu thar orful merlignerty when they menshuns the size ove yer bill, an' lasly, while yu're gwine thru yer close wif a sarch warrun arter fodder enuf tu pay hit, they refreshes yer memory ove other places, an' other times, by tellin yu ove the orful high price ove tuckys, aigs, an' milk. When the devil takes a likin tu a feller, an' wants tu make a sure thing ove gittin him, he jis' puts hit intu his hed to open a cat-fish tavern, with a gran' rat attachmint, gong 'cumpanimint, bull's neck variashun, cockroach corus an' bed-bug refrain, an' dam ef he don't git him es sure es he rattils the fust gong. An' durn thar onary souls, they looks like they expected yu tu b'leve that thy am pius, decent, an' fit tu be 'sociated wif, by lookin down on yu like yu belonged tu the onregenerit, an' keepin a cussed ole spindel-shank, rattlin crazy, peaner, wif mud daubers nestes onder the soundin board, a-bummin out 'Days ove Absins,' ur 'The Devil's Dream,' bein druv thar too, by thar long-waisted, greasey har'd darter, an' listen'd to by jis' sich durn'd fools es I is. Thar am anuther feeter in the cat-fish tavrin, what hit haint pufeck wifout. Hit is tu these sweet scented instertushuns what the twis' is tu the pig's tail, an' am in the shape ove a ole hairy lipp'd 'oman: Sumtimes she is a motherinlor, sumtimes she is a she uncle, sumtimes a ole maid sister, wifout the fust four letters, an' allers a durn'd nuisans ginerally, an' a match fur the Scotch eatch pussonally. She am feater'd like ontu a white face muley cow, what hed been pisen'd wif pizen oak vine. She hes a par ove san'-bag ankils, her body looks like hit mout a been moulded in a barril wif a big bulge; she's fond ove biled taters, an' bad news; she wars roun' shiney specks, a bunch ove keys, a callicker redicule, an' a seed-bag cap, wun full ove quilt scraps an' pipes, an' tother es full ove deviltry, short cuts tu mean tricks an' plans tu discumfort folks. She watches the wimmen custumers' rooms ove nights, an' tells nex day what she seed, ur hoped tu see. She knows tu a crumb how much yu hev et, an ' begrudges hit tu half a crumb. She makes her garters outen the hems ove ole shuttails, an' is so savin, she wars but one et a time; she b'leves in low quarter'd shoes, fallin frum grace ofen, an' in dippin es the cure; she cou'dent live a minit enywhar, but in a cat-fish tavrin, an' I'm durn'd glad she can't.

"Now breatherin an' sistren, outen all this I hes gether'd the follerin orful facks, what orter be known tu all passuns, priests, an' pussons who preach. Fustly, the 'purpryiters' ove cat-fish tavrins, an' rail-road feed troffs, am hell's recruitin ossifers. *He* goes thar hissef, in course, afore his toe-nails git cold, an' mos' ove the misfortnit devils, what hes stopp'd wif 'im, goes thar too, fur cussin an' 'vengeful thinkin, fotch about by dirt, sloth, swindle, sufferin, stealin, an' starvashun. Secon'ly hit am a orful 'sponsabil ondertakin tu keep a cat-fish tavrin, fur hit hes a brimstone retribushun es big es a car shed, a-follerin clost arter hit, an' finerly, I'd jis' ruther du wifout the instertushun intirely; the plain one-bottil doggery fur my drinkin, the kitchens fur my vittils, an' the barns fur my bed, whar the bugs cease tu bite, an' the tired kin rest.

"Wharfore, 'stop not tu res' whar thar am a sign, fur thar aint res' onder hits shadder, neither sup wif a lanlord, fur he's yer foe, but gird up yer coteail an' marvil furder, leas' yu lose yer soul a-cussin, an' hev yer paunch et intu a partridge net wif pisen. Keep the dus ove the dinin-room ofen yer foot, an' the smell ove the bed-room ofen yer close, that yer days may be longer in the lan' what yer daddy's tuck frum the Injuns.'"

Bart Davis's Dance

"DU yu know that bow-laiged boy on the fence thar?" said Sut.

"No; who is he?"

"That's Bart Davis's yungest son, name Obed. Jis' obsarve how his snout's skin'd an' his year slit an' so forth."

"Yes, I see; how did it happen?"

"Happen? Hit didn't happen et all, hit wer dun a-pupos, permeditated a-pupos. Ther wer a dance et his dad's, las' Sat'day nite wer two weeks ago, what hed like tu bred a berryin ur two; the corpses wer mos' redy, an' nuffin but acksidint kep em frum bein finished. I wer thar mysef, an' kin say an' swar that the chances run mity even, a-tween mirth an' mournin. Fur a spell hit wer the exhitenest time I ever seed on sich a ocashun, not tu hev no more whisky nur we hed. Thar warn't but 'bout half a barril when we begun, an' when we quit, we burnt the hoops an' staves tu dance the las' reel by.

"Everybody knows Bart is a durn'd no-count, jug-kerryin, slow-thinkin, flea-hurtin, herrin-eatin, Noth Calinian, plays a three-string fiddil wif a grasshopper jirk, while his wife totes the wood. He hes but two gifs wuf a durn: wun is, he'll vide his whisky wif yu down tu the las' half pint; thar he stops, fur that's jis' a horn yu know; an' tuther is, he ain't feard ove enything a-livin, sept ole Peg. I don't wunder et that, fur hit mus' take a man wif a onnatrally big melt, not tu be fear'd ove his wife, onless she's blind ur hes a sweethart. Peg (she's his ole quilt, yu know) is a regular steel-trap ove an 'oman; she goes wif wun side ove her frock tucked up at the hips, her har down her back, an' a roasted hickory onder her arm tu scold the brats wif, an' tu skeer Bart. They's bof great on dancin ove Sat'day nites et home, an' sumwhar else on tuther nites. Ef thar's a frolic enywhar in five mile, Bart is sure tu be thar, an' Peg, too, ef she's in travilin fix, which ain't more nur five months in the year. She goes fur two reasons: wun is, tu eat an' dance, an' tuther tu watch Bart. He hes two reasons also: wun is tu suck in all the whisky floatin roun, an' tu du a heap ove things what needs watchin. They giner'lly hes a dermestic discussun arter they gets home, in which, teeth, claws, an' beggin am the argymints, an' 'I won't du so no more,' the aind ove hit. They am a lively an' even yok'd par. Nobody else on the green yeath orter be tied tu either ove em.

"Well they mounted that par ove hames yu see on the fence thar, the boy name Obed ontu a muel, an' sent him tu the still-hous, tu narrate hit that thar wud be a dance et home the nex nite, an' fur every feller what warn't married tu fetch a gal, an' them what wer married tu fetch two. Now this rangement show'd Bart's good sence, fur he know'd that hit takes more gals tu du married fellers then single wuns. Caze people what hes but one kind ove vittils et home, hit allers takes more tu du em abroad.

"When the nite cum they wer all thar, a hous' plum full, an' amung em a lot ove counter-hoppers wif strip'd sugar candy in ther pockets, an' young lawyers wif cinamint ile ontu ther har; all on em frum town, an' jis' ole enuf tu begin tu strut an' gobble. Thunder and litnin, an' sunflower pattrin calliker, mixed wif check an' stripe, homspun swept all about thar, wif one, jis' one black silk. They laid off two reels, wun call'd the leather shoe reel, an' tuther, the barfoot reel. I danced in the wun I nam'd las'."

"Why did they divide that way, Sut?"

"Why, durn hit, don't yu know that the dancin wud turn intu fitin afore the fust set got ofen the flure, ef they mix'd em? The shoes wud scronch the bar toes in dancin, and rite then an' thar they'd mix fur a fite. A hard-shell preacher wif his mouf mortised intu his face in shape like a muel's shoe, heels down, fotch hissef thar soon arter dark, an' made moshuns like he ment tu stay all nite. He got intu a corner, an' commenced a-tchunin up his sighin an' groanin aperatus, a-shakin ove his head, an' lookin like he hed the bellyake. He cudn't hev look'd more solemcoly, ef his mam hed died that mornin a-owin him two dullars an' a 'alf. All these wimin an' luvely souns an' moshuns wer made on count ove the dancin, an' p'raps the cussin an' kissin. The whisky part ove that inturtainment he'd nuffin against. I *know'd* that, fur every time he roll'd his eyes to'ards the barril, he'd lick his lips sorter sloppy like, jis' es ef he'd been dippin his bill intu a crock ove chicken gray, an' wer tryin tu save the stray draps, what hung outside his face. Oh! he wer jis' a-honin arter that ball-face whisky; he'd a jis' kiss'd hit es sweet, an' es long, es ef hit hed been a willin gal. I sorter aidged up a-side him, an' sez I—

"'Mister, will yu hev a few draps ove camfire, ur laudamy? Yu seems tu be pow'ful ailin in yer innards. Yu hesent swallered a live rat, ur a mole, hes yu?'

"He shook his head, an' fotch a sigh, what ainded in a groan. Sez I—

"'Rats ur moles am onhelthy things tu swaller afore they'se departed this life.'

"He blow'd out a orful sigh, part outen his nose, but mos' ove hit out whar the toe ove the muel-shoe wer, an' sez he—

"'This am a wicked an' a parvarse generashun ove vipurs, yung man.'

"'An' gin up tu hardness over hart, an' deviltry, an' belevin thunderin lies,' said I; an' I puff'd out a big sigh, wif a little groan fur a tail. Sez he—

"'Thar am no-o-o-o dancin in hell,' an sot intu shakin ove his head, till I thot he'd keep on fur everlastin, an' ever more. Sez I—

"'Haint yu *slitely* mistaken'd in that las' re-mark ove yourn? Ef thar's es much hot truck, an' brimstone, an' cinders, an' hickory smoke, an' big hurtin, in hell es yu folks sez thar am, thar mus be *sum* dancin, purtickelerly jigs an' quick-steps; they don't lack fur music, I reckon, fur I'se allers hearn hell wer full ove fiddlers, an' thar's Yankees enuf thar tu invent fireproof fiddils fur em, so they don't want fur tchunes. All on yeath that bothers me is the rosim.'

"'Ah, yung onregenerit man,' sez he, 'thar's more rosim in hell than thar's in all Noth Caliny.'

"'But hit ain't quite hard enuf tu rub ontu fiddil bows, is hit?' sez I.

"He groan'd an' shook his head, an' sent wun ove his eyes to'ards the whisky corner. I went an' fotch 'im a big slug intu a gourd. That shovel-shaped onder lip ove his'n jis' fell out'ards like ontu the fallin door ove a stone coal stove, an' he upsot the gourd inside ove his teef. I seed the mark ove the truck gwine down his froat jis' like a snake travelin thru a wet sassidge gut. He smelt intu the gourd a good long smell, turned up his eyes, an' sed 'Barlm ove life.'

"Thinks I, ole Sock, I know what fotch yu tu this frolic besides yu're hoss an' our whisky. Bart now cum up, an' Hardshell tole him he'd cum tu stay all nite, ef he suited all roun.

"'Sartinly, oh yas, an' welcum,' sed Bart.

"The ole Sock, never alterin the shape ove the hole tore in his face, sed, mity sneerin like, 'Yu is hosspitabil.' I seed Bart sorter start, an' look at him, an' go off a-winkin at me tu foller him. We went outside the hous', intu a chimbly corner, an' thar wer two fellers, wun ove em a she, a-whisperin. We went tu tuther corner, an' thar wer two more; then we went tu the stabil, an' hearn whisperin thar; hit mout been rats a-runnin in straw. So Bart cud hold in no longer. Sez he—

"'Never mine, I don't keer a durn who hears me. I b'leve I'se been 'sulted in my own hous'; didn't that durn'd preachin mersheen call me a hoss?'

"'That's jis' what he sed. He call'd yu a hoss-pitabil,' sez I.

"'Pitabil, pitabil,' sez Bart, 'dam ef I don't b'leve that's wus nur the hoss.'

"'Sartinly,' sez I, 'pitabil is a sorter Latin tail stuck tu hit so yu moutn't onderstand; hit means pitiful hoss in Inglish, an' ef I wer yu, I'd see that his stumack wer spiled fur Peg's fried chicken an' biskit. I'd go rite in an' show him how a hoss ken kick an' sich like.' He jis' gritted his teef, like he wer a-chompin aigshells, ur paragorick phials, an' put fur the hous', a-rollin up his shut-sleeves es he went, plum up tu his arm-pit.

"The durn'd, hiperkritikil, groanin ole Hardshell raskil hed dun got the dancin stop't; he'd tuck the fiddil away frum the nigger, an' wer a-holdin hit by the naik in wun han, an' a-makin gesters wif the bow in tuther. He wer mounted ontu a cheer, clost by the meal barril, an' wer exortin em orfully 'bout thar sins ove omishun an' cummishun, purtickerly the cummishun wuns, wif the dancin sins at the head, warin sunflower caliker wuns nex'; an' then cum thar smaller sins, sich es ridin a-hine fellers on the same hoss, whisperin outen doors, an' a-winkin a-hine fans, tuckey-tails an' hankechers, an' sed that black silk wer plenty in hell, that hit wer used fur mournin thar, an' not tu dance in. The *he* sins, ove the small sort, wer cumin frum town ove nites, a-warin store clothes, smellin ove cinamint ile, an' a-totin striped sugar candy in thar pockets, tu turn the minds ove the weak gals, instead ove a flask ove that good holesum ole truck, what they'se got in towns, name 'coniack.'

"The wimmen folks wer backed up in bunches, in the corners, an' agin the beds, wif thar fingers in thar moufs, an' wun ur two ove the saftest ove em wer gettin up a quiet sort ove dry cryin.

"The he fellers all looked like they'd mos' es leave fite es not, ef they knew how tu start the thing, when in bounced Bart; he looked like a catamount; wun jump an' he stood a-top ove the meal barril, squar in frunt ove Hardshell, his har a-swayin about wif pure mad, like a patch ove ripe rye in a wind, an' his eyes wer es roun an' es red as a bull's when he's a-jinin in battil wif anuther bull frum Bashan. He struck wun fistes away out a-hine, an' wif tuther reachin at arm's laingth, he cummenc'd borin, like he hed a gimblit in his shot fis', rite onder the snout ove the thunderin Hardshell, like he wer tryin tu bore his mouf inter a better shape, an' a-narratin thru his teef these facs, in words what sounded like grittin hard co'n.

"'*Yu* durn'd infunel, incumpassabil warter-dorg! *Yu* cuss'd hiperkritikal, ongrateful ole mus-rat! *Yu* h—ll fir'd, divin, splatterin, pond-makin, iron-jacket'd ole son ove a mud-turtil; yu hes 'sulted me in my own hous', *an' in Latin et that*, an' then yu've tuck the imperdent liberty tu skare these yere children outen thar innersent mucement (still borin away frum left tu right, wif that horny fis' ove his'n, an' the Hardshell's head gwine furder back every twist). Call'd me a hoss—Git ofen that cheer!'

"Es he sed 'git,' he loaned the passun a mos' tremenjus contushun, rite in the bull curl. I seed his shoe-soles a-gwine up each side ove Bart's fis' afore he hed time tu muve hit, arter he struck. Hit wer a lick, George, that hed hit been a kick, a four year ole muel wud hev been pow'ful proud ove. I seed ni ontu a gallon ove sparks ove fire fly outen the passun's eyes mysef (he mus hev seed a bushel) when hit reached his curl. He let the fiddil go when he wer in the highes part ove his backward summerset, an' the nigger what hed been watchin up at hit all this time, wis'ful like, es a dorg watches a meat-skin when yu holds hit too high fur him tu grab, cotch his fiddil in bof hans afore hit toch the yeath.

" 'Dar by golly, you no git tu smash dis fiddil, wid yu durn fool fitin an' preachin.'

"An' holdin it wavingly abuv his head, he dodged outen the surkil ove imejut danger. The old Shell lit ontu his all fours, hit bein that much more nur a full summerset, an' *the* black silk lit a-stradil ove him. I know'd hit wer the black silk, bekase I seed the white stockins an' grey garters. Hev I mention'd that thar wer one hundred an' twenty-five pouns ove live, black-eyed gal in under that black silk?"

"No, Sut."

"Well, thar wer, an' that she wer bof live an' willin, ole Dipper wer soon redy tu swar. 'Black silk in hell is thar,' scream'd she, a-hissin like ontu a cat, an' cummenced a-pullin up by the roots his long har, like hit wer flax, wif bof hans, an' a-shakin the bunches ofen her fingers, an' then gwine fur more, the hissin gittin a littil louder every pull. George, that wer the fust spessamin ove a smokin mad gal I've seed in a hen's age; she kerried out my idear ove a fust-rate flax-puller, pullin agin two, fur a bet. I think she gin the ole Shell the idear that sum strong man body wer a-holden his head ni ontu the saws ove a activ cotton gin.

"Now the boy name Obed, with the hame laigs, hevin a sorter jestis' ove the peace turn ove mine, run in tu pull her off, an' cudn't du hit afore she made a rake fur his har, an' got hit. She jis' mixed the handful wif the pile on the flure, an' gin hersef back tu the job ove preparin the passun fur a wig. A hawk-billed, weazel-eyed, rat-mouthed feller, what hed been a-struttin roun Black Silk all nite, a-trailin wun wing, an' a-lickin his lips, seed the fool boy name Obed, a-tryin tu git her tu lite ofen the ole Sock, so he jis' growl'd low, an' barked once, an' kiver'd him, an' afore his mam Peg, an' me, an' five uther gals, cud git him loose, he hed made her cub the speckterkil yu sees roostin on that ar fence, an' he's hed ni ontu three weeks tu mend his looks in, by Jew David's plarster, sweet ile, an' the keer ove his mam.

"The fitin now got tu be gineral on mos' parts ove the field, an' es the cuppils cum in frum outen doors, lookin sorter sneakin, an' pale (frum the nise ove the rumpus, I speck), wun at leas', outen every par, got jump't on by sumbody. P'raps a gal wud kiver a cumin in gal, anuther gal wud go fur the har an' skin ove a cumin in he feller; then, agin, the fis' ove a he wud meet anuther cumin in he, right atween the eyes, an' so on till the thing got tu be durn'dably mix'd up an' lively. Peg boun up the boy name Obed's wouns, bruises, an' petrifyin sores, an' then went on wif supper cookin, like all wer quiet on the Pertomack.

"Es soon es ole Shell begun tu cum to, frum Bart's dubbil distill'd thunder-bolt, the hurtin all over his head begun tu attrack his 'tenshun, an' soaked thru his skull, an' in thar tuck the shape ove an idear; the idear shaped hitsef intu spoken wurds, an' they wer, 'Gird up yer loins an' *git*.' I seed the wurkin ove his mind, so I jis' shouted es loud es I cud beller, 'The Pherlistshuns be upon yu Sampsin.' He hearn hit, an' wer struck wif the force ove the remark, an' started fur the back door, still on his all fours, in a single foot rack. Es soon es Black Silk felt him movin, she cummenced spurrin him wif her heels; while she hilt tu his har wif wun han, she tuck a pin outen her collar wif tuther, an' made a cushion fur hit in the hill, ontu the north side ove the pint ove his back-bone; he kicked up an' snorted, an' changed the single foot rack intu a tarin pace, loped outen the door intu outer darkness, an' his heel-tops wer the last I seed ove him. He stumbled an' fell down the log-steps, an' flung Black Silk like ontu a full balloon over his head (I seed a heap ove white shinin es she went). He felt his way in the dark, thru the woods, fur more pleasant places, an' she cum in larfin, 'Black silk in hell, hey?' wer every word she sed."

"Go on, Sut."

"That's all. I ain't like ole Glabbergab; when I'se spoke off what I knows, I stops talkin."

"Well, what became of Hardshell?"

"Oh! es tu that, he made his 'pearance las' Sunday, in the

pulpit, es bald es a jug, wif a black spot aidged wif green an' yaller, 'bout the size ove a priskly par, on his forehead, an' preach't 'bout the orful konsekenses ove Absalom's hevin long har, human depravity, an' the Salt Lake; sed he wer gwine thar right off, an' *he'll du hit.*"

Tripetown: Twenty Minutes for Breakfast

"I WER onst a-ridin ontu the kers ove a raleroad, an' hed been livin on nuffin but sum bites ove whisky fur a hole day an' nite, an' felt like a congrigashun ove rats wer a-bildin thar nestes outen sifter wire in my stumick, an' a hive ove bees wer a-fixin tu swarm in my head, when the conducter run his foreaind intu the door, up tu the butt ove his watch-chain, an' holler'd—

" 'Tripetown—twenty minutes fur breakfus'.'

" 'That's me,' sez I, an' I went over. I jis' tell yu this case tu show yu that the sarmint I hev been preachin, wif Catfishe Tavrins fur a tex, wer pervok'd outen me.

"I sot down, an' oh, lordy! Sich a breakfus! My talk, bad es yu sez hit wer, about the Catfishe peopil, don't begin tu du jestice tu this mess ove truck. A hungry dorg wudn't hev smelt, nur a sperienced buzzard even lit ontu hit, ef thar wer a ded hoss in a hundred mile. I tried a bite, an' hit flew outen my mouf like ther'd been a steel mattrass spring quiled in my froat; so ove course I wer the fust wun outen thar. Thar he wer, the everlastin 'perpryiter,' a-standin in the door, wif his paw full ove notes, a-lickin the ball ove his tuther thumb, like he wer hungry tu begin, that bein the chief aind ove (the Catfishe) man.

" 'Two dullars an' a 'alf; *yu* mus' make the change,' sed he, all in wun breff.

"I thor't I'd see ef *all* his feelins wer seared wif a red hot iron, an' so I sed—lookin mity serus an' pius like, rite squar intu the middil ove the glass ove his specks, what kivered a par ove es mean an' muny-luvin eyes es ever star'd at the eagle ontu a dime ontil that ar bird shot his'n up wif shame—

" 'Yu keep a all-fired good hous', Mister—good biskit,

an' coffee tu match; hit gins a man a appertite tu jis' look et yu; hit gins him a appertite an' a stumick tu look et yur wife, an' hit sets em bof a-rarin an' a-squealin tu smell yer tabil. This am a holesum place. An' es I hes far'd so well, about yu, I wants tu tell yu a valerabil secret; how tu make yer coffee, good es hit is, still better, an' not cos' a cent more.'

"'Much obleged, indeed,' sez he, an' lookin es sweet roun the mouf es ef he'd been a-tastin good brandy an' white sugar, an' wer wantin ove more.

"Now the travelers wer cumin out, ni ontu eighty ove em, an' wantin me outen the way, so they cud pay fur what nastiness an' pizen they'd swaller'd, an' git outen the smell ove hit es soon es possibil. I jis' kep on talkin 'bout my 'provement ontu coffee till I tho't mos' ove em wer in year shot, when I rais'd my soun, an' sed—

"'Ef yu want tu make that good coffee ove yourn better, jis' yu, instead ove makin hit all outen ole boot-laigs, put in about half ove a ole wool hat, chopp'd fine, finer nur yu chops yer hash say, intu pieces a inch squar; hit will help the taste pow'ful, an' not set the smell back a bit.' I flung down my munny an' put fur the train. I swar, es I went, I cud feel the fokis ove them specks a-burnin intu the back ove my head, an' I smelt my har singein. I know'd that he wer tryin tu look thru me, an' the peopil, men an' wimmen, wer screamin a-larfin et sumthin. Tu help his mad to a head, wun feller hed sot down ontu the step, wif a segar clamp't atween his knees, a biskit intu each han, whetin away, tryin tu strike fire outen them ontu hit. Anuther hed fired wun ove the biggest an hardes' biskit at the smoke-hous', an' hit went thru the wether boardin like a grape shot. Anuther perlite, bowin, smilin feller cum wif the drum-stick aind ove the hine laig ove a ole gander 'twixt his finger an' thumb, an' narrated hit that hit wer ole Powhattan's war club, an' he wer gwine tu start hissef a museum; while out in the yard, lay a long feller flat ontu his belly, wif his laigs wide apart, an' his paws locked roun a par-biled beef rib, an' he wer gnawin at tuther aind ove hit fust in wun side ove his mouf, an' then tuther, growlin like a dorg, an' a-eyein sidewise the picter sot in the door-frame all the while. A long-necked passenger, top'd off wif a sealskin cap, cum rushin out in a shanghi trot, wif a stripe ove tuff tripe es long es a sirsingle. He hed hit by the middil in his mouf, an' wer a-slashin an' a-slapin the aind agin everybody what he pass'd by, vigrusly shakin his head, jis like a dorg dus when he's a-killin snakes, ur a sow playin wif rags afore a storm. All these shines didn't stop the larfin a bit, ef I noticed right.

"Well, when I'd got off about thuty yards, I venter'd tu look back. Thar he stood, the mos' orful picter ove onregenerated rath, mortal man ever seed. He looked like he'd weigh five hundred pounds; he wer swell'd all over, ni ontu bustin, an' the door wer chock full ove him, all in a strut. His arms stuck out like a settin hen's wings, his hat cocked before, his feet wide apart, an' he *wer* a-lookin at me sure enuf. Them specks blazin like two red lamps, his lips a-flutterin es he blow'd out the hot breff an' foam ove his onbearabil pent up rath, what my onekeled an' on-hearn ove imperdence tu *him, the perpryiter,* hed sot a-bilin in his in'ards, ontil he wer ni ontu burnt out, thru tu the har, an' waiscoat. The smoke ove his torment wer a-cumin out in whiffs frum his breeches pockets, an' button holes.

"My lookin back toch the trigger; an idear, an' speech now cum tu him fur the fust time, an' he exploded. He jis' bellered like a bull bawlin in a tunnel, a-flingin big splotches ove foam an' spittil way ofen the step et every word.

" 'Spose—yu—go—tu—h—ll—yu—dam—raskill.'

"He wer ontu his tip-toes when he sed this, an' as he ainded the word 'raskill,' he cum down ontu his heels, till he made the winders chatter, an' his big watch-seals dance agin.

"I jis' kep ontu the kers, an' didn't du what he tole me tu. Arter we'd run two miles, I looked back, an we wer so fur that the door look'd like a black spot on the hous', an' I wish I may be tetotally durn'd, cordin tu law, ef I didn't still see them hot specks, rite in the middil ove hit, blazin away like two leetle red stars. Sum orful calamity tuck place at that rail road troff tu sumbody, afore *he* simmered down."

Hen Baily's Reformation

[This truthful narrative is particularly recommended to the careful consideration of the Rev. Mr. Stiggins, and his disciples, of the Brick Lane Branch of the Grand Junction Ebenezer Temperance Association. This mode of treatment can be fully relied upon.]

WE were resting by a fine cool spring, at noon, with an invitingly clean gourd hanging on a bush over the water. Sut, as usual, was at full length on the grass, intently looking at the gourd.

"Say fellers, that ar long-handil'd gourd thar, mout cum the temprince dodge over sum ove yu fellers afore yu wer quite ready fur the oaf. I looks on em all es dangrus, an' that's a mons'us 'spishus lookin wun, hit hes sich a durn'd long handil. Allers 'zamin the inside ove a gourd-handil wif a sharp pinted swich, afore yu drinks; hits a holesum foresight. Hen Baily—did eny ove yu know Hen?—he wer a peach wif a wurm intu hit, enyhow—a durn'd no-count, good, easy, good-fur-nuthin vagerbone, big es a hoss, an' lazy es a shingle-maker, but a pow'ful b'lever, not a sarcumsised b'lever, but a lie b'lever ove the straites seck, swallered everything he hearn, an' mos' everything he seed. That ar swallerin gif ove his'n cum wifin a eighth ove a inch, onst, ove sendin him tu kingdum cum, an' did send him head fust intu a life-everlastin temprince s'ciety. I'd a-liked pow'ful well fur tu hearn him gin in his 'sperince, even ef he tole one half. He lov'd biled drinks orful, never wer a hour's walk frum a still-hous' ur a doggery since he tuck tu warin breeches.

"Well, yu see the ole man Rogers up on Los' Creek wer a-paintin his hous' a-new, an' Hen wer suckilatin roun thar, jis' prospectin fur sperits, an' seed a bottil wif clar truck in hit what he tuck tu be new sperrits, so when the painter's back wer turned, he jis' run hits naik down his froat. He fotch hit out wif a onderhandid jerk, flung hit ahine him an' put, sputterin an' yerkin, fur the spring, a-swabbin out his mouf wif his ole wool hat rolled up. Now, boys, hit *wer* sperrits, but orful tu think ove, hit wer sperrits ove tupentine, fresh frum the rosinny part ove Noth Caliney.

"Me an' a few uther durn'd fools wer at the spring, sorter es we is now, a-mixin a few draps ove hit wif sum limber laig-whisky, an' gabblin, when we seed him a-cumin jis' a-flutterin. Es he run a-pas' the wash place, he flung the hat swab away, an' snatched the wash gourd, so es tu save time. The durn'd lazy cuss wer in a rale tarin hurry; fust time I ever seed him run ur cum ni runnin in all my born'd days. His mouf wer es red es a split beef, an' the light big bubbil kine ove slobber wer a-flyin like snow frum a-runnin hosses heels. Thinks I, *sody,* by the great golly! Oh, yu dam fool, sum gal's cum the luv-powder game over yu purfeckly. He *wer* trubbil'd in mine, fur at the landin part ove every jump, he'd say, in souns like he hed a gob ove scaldin mush stuck tu the ruff ove his mouf, the words 'Hell-fire,' nuffin else; them wer pow'ful suitabil words tu his case. I didn't think he wer so good at pickin out talk; they 'splained his ailmint better nur a doctor cud. He soused the ole soap suds gourd intu the spring, an' then filled his mouf over mos' half ove the aidge, quicker nor flea ketchin. Es he turn'd hit up, I seed a stripid eight inch lizard cum tarin outen the handil, whar he'd been hid es *he* thought. He sot his fore paws ontu the aidge ove the gourd an' peeped over. Seein us, gin him a turnin skeer, an' he jis' darted down Hen's froat. I seed his tail fly up agin Hen's snout, es he started down hill. The reptile tuck his mouf tu be a proverdenshul hole in the groun, an' I dusn't wunder, fur hit wud a-fool'd a kingfisher enytime. He drap't the empty gourd, an' holdin his belly in his lock't hans, sed—

" 'Warter makes hit wus, boys.'

"Sez I, 'Hen, hits the lizard.'

"He wall'd roun his sweaty stuck out eyes at me, an' sez he—

" 'What lizard?'

" 'Why that big striped he lizard what yu let run down yer froat jis' now, outen the gourd-handil. I speck I wer the las' pusson what seed him outside ove yu, fur I seed the pint ove his tail arter hit passed the gap whar that ar frunt tooth cum out.'

"He look't a-sorter listenin look, down at the groun, fur a second, an' sot intu hoppin up an' down ontu wun laig, an' then ontu tuther, a-shakin in the air the laig what warn't imejuntly engaged in hoppin, an' mentionin 'Hellfire,' every time he changed laigs, an' that wer every two hops. Then he fell down an' sot intu rollin, wus nur a yung dorg what hes ignurently yamped a pole-cat. He kep a-tuckin his head sorter onder, like he wer tryin tu make hit roll faster nor his body. Sez he—

"'Great fathers, boys, he's a-gallopin roun, he is by grashus!'

"Sez I, 'Hen, he's a-'zaminin yer whisky bag fur a good spot tu bild his nestes in; he means tu stay!

"'Oh, lordy!' yell'd Hen; 'he's dun foun hit, an's a-tarin up the linin ove my paunch tu bild hit wif,' an' he roll'd on faster nur ever. 'Sut, ef yu please, run fur a doctor; yu hes the laigs.'

"'Yas,' sez I; 'but hits dun gone fur apas' common doctorin.'

"When he hearn that vardic, he flounced tu his feet, fotch a yell what ef et hed went thru a three-foot tin ho'n wud a-busted hit plum open frum aind tu aind, an' sot intu flingin the bes' kine ove show actor summersets amung the roun rocks in the spring branch back'ards twice, forids onst, then sidewise, now a full turn an' a 'alf that wud fetch him ontu his head, now a 'alf turn, an' that wud lan' him ontu his sturn. Durnation, how he'd spatter warter when he made the three quarter turns, then clean over ontu his feet he'd cum, jis' tu yell an' fling sum more. I counted till hit got tu thuty-one, an' got outen heart, an' quit; a suckis agent wud a-gin him big wages jis' then, but he'd been the wust fool'd man ever born'd, onless he ment tu dose Hen wif tupentine an' lizards, an' I doubts hits movin him a secon time. Durn'd ef his kerryins on didn't mine me ove my sody misery in a minnit; hit struck me so pow'ful that I hed a vilent sarchin blow ove bellyache rite thar. Sez I—

"'That's hit Hen, jis' yu keep on, an' yu'll soon make that ar lizard b'leve he's tuck up lodgins in the cylinder ove a four hoss thrashin-mersheen, an' that harves time am cum. He's boun tu vacate yu; jis' rastil on, hoss; that's hit; no mortal lizard kin stan that sort ove churnin amung sich a mixin es yu ginerly totes intu yer paunch.'

"'Oh, lordy, Sut, yu'se right, fur I raley du b'leve he's cuttin his way out now. Can't yu (an' over he'd go agin) *du* sumthin?' (over onst more).

"'Yu dam fool,' sez I, 'I don't know; but ef yu means tu keep on at that rate, I wud surjis' that yu swaller a few ove these yere roun rocks, 'bout es big es goose aigs, an' dam ef he ain't a groun up rep-tile sooner nor ef he wer in a hungry goose's gizzard. He made a moshun ur two like he wer grabbin fur rocks es he lit, but jis' then he changed his mine, an' sot in tu runnin roun the spring-hous', a-leanin to'ards hit an' jis' a-missin the corners. He went so fas' he looked like three ur four fellers arter each uther, groanin, hollerin, an' remarkin 'Hell-fire,' all roun thar. He's a pow'ful activ injurin man, when onder stimuluses, that's a fac'. I tuck a stan ni ontu wun corner, an' es he cum roun, I cummenced in time, an' sed—

"'Hen, did yer take yer sody seperit?'

"Nex time he cum, sez he, 'Sody seperit—h—I!' an' nex roun sez he, 'Aka-fortis,' an' the nex arter that he addid the words 'Fourth-proof at that.' He wer gwine so fas' that his talkin seemed oninterrupted. The las' time he cum roun, he hollered in dispar, 'I haint a-gainin on hit a dam bit,' an' tuck hissef up a red elm. He went up by fas' jerks, jis' adzackly like a cat climbs a appil tree frum a clost cumin dorg. He locked his footsis roun the lowis lim's, an' hung hed down, swingin about, an' smackin his hans like he wer ni the shoutin pint ove happiness at a ravin camp meetin. Sez I—

"'*That* won't du; that's a wus idear nur sircklin the spring-hous' wer, an' don't cumpar wif yer suckis speri-mint, fur the lizard went pow'fully *down hill* a-gwine intu that sloppy hole he's intu now, an' he's too smart tu start *down* hill eny more fur fear hit'll git wus; he won't cum, Hen.'

"He answered me mons'ous cross an' spiteful—

"'Let him go up hill then, dam 'im; so he keeps gwine's all I ax.'

"The lizard wer a-tarin roun right peart, I speck, wadin an' swimin as he wer in a dark pon' ove whisky, an' tupentine, thickened wif a breakfus' ove blackberries an' mush, stirred intu a purfeck hurrycane by Hen's kerryins on. Hit warn't jis' adzackly the right place fur even a varmint tu go tu sleep in, enyhow.

"Hen soon foun that hit wud nither go up hill nur down hill, but kep a-tarin roun et randum wif hits long toe-nails, so he los' all hope, let foot holts loose, an' sunk his nose up tu his years in the branch bank mud, an' by golly, lay still. I begun tu think the show wer about tu close, an' I hed rights tu think so; thuty-one counted summersets, an' lots ove oncounted ones, averidgin a full turn each, a mile an' a quarter roun a spring-hous', an' nine hundred yards in rollin, not countin the small moshuns, in 'bout five minutes wer ni ontu enuf tu fetch eny man body tu lie still—an' then the lizard an' turpentine—hit wer a job ove' no common kine, an' speshfully fur Hen hit wer mos' wunderful. Thinks I, ole feller, yu're gwine tu make a die ove hit, an' sez I—

"'Hen, ole feller, while yu'se a-restin thar, jis' feel ni yer trousis an' git me that half duller yu borrowed frum me las' Chrismus; feel easy fur hit an' don't skeer yer lizard.'

"He never let on like he hearn me. Sez I, 'Yere, Hen, try a littil ove this yere *whisky*. I menshun whisky loud; dam ef even that moved the *pints* ove his fingers. Sez I, 'Boys, he's 'bout dun wif yeathly matters, he won't notis whisky, an' his hereafter's wifin ten steps ove him rite now.'

"Ole Missis Rogers hearn the fuss, an' seed the crowd roun her spring-hous', an' the safety ove her milk an' butter struck her pow'ful. So yere she cum, wif her ole brass specks ridin a-straddil ove the highes pint ove her calliker cap crown; thar laigs wer a-usin two locks ove her red roan har fur stirrups, away below her years. She hed a biled roasin ear mos' ove the time acrost her mouf, wif silks an' smashed grains plenty, stickin tu her ole moley chin, an' her nose. Sez she—

"'What upon yeath yu all duin yere—not holdin meetin, sure? Ah! Yu am thar, am yu, laigs, yu daddratted draggild san-hill crane? Sum devilment on han, rite now. Clar yersefs, yu nasty, stinkin, low-lived, sheep-killin dorgs. S-n-e-a-k off, afore yu steals sumthin. Yere Rove, yere Rove, yere, yere!'

"'Sez I, mouns'us solimn, straitenin mysef up wif foldid

arms, 'Missis Rogers, afore yer dorg Rove cums, take a look at sum ove yu're work. That ar a-dyin feller bein; let jis' a few ove yer bowils melt, an' pour out rite yere in pity an' rey-morse.'

"She tuck a short look at Hen. 'What ails *him?*'

"Sez I, wif my arms straiched strait out, 'Cholick, vilent cork-screw cholick, one ove the cholery perswashun; he jis' tast'd yer buttermilk in thar, an' by granny, hits dun kill'd 'im, that's all, Missis Rogers.' Yu see she wer noted fur feedin the work-hans on buttermilk so sour that hit wud eat hits way outen a yeathen crock in wun nite. Sez she, wif her hans ontu her hips, an' standin wide an' strait up, 'Yu're a liar, Mister Lovingood!' I hes allers notis'd nobody ever calls me Mister Lovingood (ef they knows me), onless they's mad at me. 'Very well,' sez I, 'we am gwine tu strip him now, an' yu kin see fur yersef; hits et hits way outen him by this time; jis' stay an' 'zamin his belly. I'll bet yu my shut agin that ar momoxed up roas'in ear, that hits chawed intu dish rags, frum his waisbun clean down tu——' She flung down the roas'in ear, an' put fur the hous', a-totin her frock-tail high hilt up wif bof her hans, wifout waitin fur me tu add 'his fork.' I wer gittin sorter skeer'd, an' sorry bof, fur Hen, the ornary devil, an' wer a-lookin at the groun studyin ef hit warn't bes' tu knock him on the head wif a rock, an' put him outen his misery, when I seed the break an' bulge ove a mole a-plowin. A idear, the bes' idear I ever own'd, struck plum thru my head, an' I dug out the mole. Sez I—

"'Boys, listen tu me: that ar feller's mons'us ni ded; desprit cases wants desprit docterin; let's tie his galluses roun his waisbun tight, an' start this yere bline, fury scramblin littil cuss up his breeches laig. When he feels the scramblin sensashun on the outside, he'll think the lizard hes got out sumwhar, an' the idear will make him feel good, enyhow, live ur ded; thar's no harm in a mole, nohow; les' try hit.'

"We turned Hen ontu his stomick, an' made the top ove his britches mole tight, an' I sot the mole a-straddil ove his heel-string, an' sunk my thumb-nail intu hits tail. Away hit went up his bar laig pow'ful fas', rootin like a hog; he wanted tu go tu his trade ove diggin agin, yu know, an' wer sarchin fur a saft place. He warn't outen site very long, when Hen sorter started forrid on his stomick; that wer the fust sign ove life he'd showd'd since he buried his nose in the blue mud. Sez I, wif a heap ove hope, 'Boys, things am workin; ef he wudn't notis speerits, he's a-notisin that ar mole.' He hed a par ove foot-holts agin a root, an' he shot hissef forrid ten foot intu the branch at one lunge wifout risin four inches frum the groun. I tho't I hearn 'Hell-fire,' agin in a sorter sick whisper. He ris tu his all fours, an' shook the warter outen his years pearingly as strong es ever, an' tuck down the branch in a rale fas' cavalry lope. He made the mud an' warter fly, 'speshully when he'd kick, an' that wer every two ur three jumps. He used his hine laigs jis' like a hoss a-fightin, an' as he'd fling up his shoes he'd menshun the kine ove fire I'se been tellin yu about, an' he'd wall a mons'us sarchin oneasy eye over his shoulder every time he'd kick. Sez I, 'Boys, the show ain't over yet; les' see the aind, an' git the wuf ove our munny.' One ur two ove the crowd dodged intu the bushes sorter des'arted; they wer fear'd tu see eny more. The res' ove us foller'd Hen. When he'd cum tu a deep hole, he'd squat intu hit up tu his years, a-sorter workin hissef roun like a hen a-fixin her nestes, gruntin orful, an' a-cussin everybody, an' everything in a lump; then he'd rar forrid ontu his all fours agin, an' jis' travil. I can't fur the life ove me think what kep him down tu his all fours. Ef hit hed been my case, yu'd a seed sum ove the durn'des straites up an' down runnin ever did by eny livin mortal. P'raps the kerryins on in his in'ards warn't es sarchin in that position. At las' he gallop'd out ontu a san bank, an' sunk spread out, wif his head in a short twis', ni clean gone.

"Sez I, 'Boys, the durn'd fool hes drowndid my mole atwixt his breeches an' his hide, a-squattin in them holes, an' I hes no hopes ove him now; les' kill 'im. Jis' then I seed him yerk, sorter vomitin way, so I straddiled him, an' cotch him by the har, an' pull'd up his head tu straiten his swaller, when imejuntly yere cum the lizard tarin outen his mouf, the wust skeer'd varmint I ever seed in all my born'd days. His eyes wer es big es fox graps, an' mos' all ove em outside ove his head, an' dam ef he didn't hev enuf tu skeer a lion, fur the mole hed 'im fas' by the tail, an' wer mendin his holt, an' that ar interprisin littil yeath-borer hadn't a durn'd mossel ove fur left ontu his hide; hit wer all *lime'd* off; he looked rite down slick an' funny, wif a lizard a-haulin 'im fru the san, I swar he did. Wunder what *they* thought hed been happenin.

"Well, we toted Hen home, an' when he got sorter well, he jined a ole well-sot temprince s'ciety, an' puts hit up that the hole thing, tupentine, lizards an' mole, wer interpersishun tu save him frum turnin intu a drunkard. The cussed hippercrit! He warn't never enything else. I oughtent tu speak hard ove the misfortnit critter tho', fur he hes got the dispepsy, the wust kine."

Frustrating a Funeral

"HIT mus' be a sorter vexin kine ove thing tu be buried alive, tu the feller what am in the box, don't yu think hit am, George?"

"Yes, horrible, Sut; what set you thinking about such a subject, with as much whisky as you have access to?"

"Oh, durn hit, I thinks at randum, jis' es I talk an' dus. I can't help hit; I'se got no steerin oar tu my brains. 'Sides that I thinks they'se *loose* 'bout the middil."

"How do you mean?"

"Well, I thinks peopil's brains what hev souls, am like ontu a chain made outen gristil, forkid at wun aind; wun fork goes tu the eyes, an' tuther tu the years, an' tuther aind am welded tu the marrer in the backbone, an' hit works sorter so. Thar stans a hoss. Well, the eyes ketches his shape, jis' a shape, an' gins that idear tu the fust link ove the chain. He nickers, an' the years gins that tu tuther fork ove the chain, a soun, nuffin but a soun. Well, the two ruff idears start along the chain, an' every link is smarter nur the wun ahine hit, an' dergests em sorter like a paunch dus co'n, ur mash'd feed, an' by the time they gits tu the back-bone, hit am a hoss an' yu *knows* hit. Now, in my case, thar's a hook in the chain, an' hits mos' ove the time onhook'd, an' then my idears stop thar half made. Rite thar's whar dad failed in his 'speriment; puttin in that durn'd fool hook's what made me a natral born fool. The breed wer bad too, on dad's side; they all run tu durn'd fool an' laigs powerful strong."

"But what about burying alive, Sut?"

"Oh, yas; I wer a-thinkin ove a case what happen'd on Hiwassee, what like tu started a new breed ove durn'd fools, an' did skare plum away a hole neighborhood ove ole breed.

"Ole Hunicutt hed a niggar name Cesar, they call'd 'im Seize fur short, an' he got sock full ove Wright's kill-devil whisky, an' tuck a noshun he'd spite ole Hunicutt by dyin, an' durned ef he didn't du hit. His marster got a coffin wif a hinge in the led acrost the breas', fur tuther niggers tu take farwell ove Seize thru, an' see the orful consekenses ove drinkin kill-devil by the gallun, at the same time. He ment tu gin em a temprance lecter when they went tu start tu the bone-yard, but durn me ef he staid thar hissef till funeral time. The niggers got Seize sot in the box mity nice, an' the led on. He wer in a empty room, 'sceptin a bed in wun aind ove a dubbil log nigger cabin, an' the niggers what sot up wif the corpse did hit in the tuther room. Thar wer lots ove em an' singin an' groanin wer plenty. Way in the night a nigger name 'Major' cum tu help du the sittin up, an' he wer drunk plum thru an' thru; so they fotch 'im intu whar Seize wer, an' laid him in the bed, whar he soon fell tu snorin, an' dreamin ove snakes, sky blue lizards, an' red hot reptiles.

"Now, a yung doctor what hed help'd Seize over the fence, twixt this an' kingdum cum, wanted his cackus tu chop up, an' bile, so he gits me tu git hit fur 'im arter hit wer onder the groun, an' I findin out how the land lay by slungin roun, fixed up a short-cut tu git hit wifout diggin. I slip't intu the room twixt midnite an' day, an' foun Maje sorter grumblin in his sleep, so I shuck him awake enuf tu *smell whisky,* an' hilt a tin cupful ove heart-burn, till the las' durn'd drap run down his froat, an' he sot intu sleepin agin, an' then I *swap't niggers.*

"Arter I got Maje intu the coffin, an' hed cut sum air-holes, I sot in an' painted red an' white stripes, time about, runnin out frum his eyes like ontu the spokes ove a wheel, an' cross-bar'd his upper lip wif white, ontil hit looked like boars' tushes, an' I fastened a cuppil ove yearlin's ho'ns ontu his head, an' platted a ded black-snake roun the roots ove em, an' durn my laigs ef I didn't cum ni ontu takin a runnin skeer myself, fur he wer a purfeck dogratype ove the devil, tuck while he wer smokin mad 'bout sum raskil what hed been sellin shanghis, an' a-pedlin matchless sanative all his life, then jinin meetin on his death-bed, an' 'scapin.

"I now turn my 'tenshun tu Mister Seize. I'd got 'bout a tin cup full ove litnin bugs, an' cut off the lantern ove the las' durn'd one; I smear'd em all over his face, har an' years, an' ontu the prongs ove a pitch-fork; I sot him

up in the corner on aind, an' gin him the fork, prong aind
up in his crossed arms. I then pried open his mouf, an'
let his teef shet ontu the back ove a live bull-frog, an' I
smeared hits paws an' belly wif sum ove my bug-mixtry,
an' pinned a littil live garter-snake by hits middil crosswise
in his mouf, smeared like the frog plum tu the pint ove his
tail. The pin kep him pow'ful bizzy makin suckils an'
uther crooked shapes in the air. Now, rite thar boys, in
that corner, stood the dolefulest skeer makin mersheen,
mortal man ever seed outen a ghost camp. I tell yu now,
I b'leves strong in ghosts, an' in forewarnins too.

"I hear sum one a-cumin, an' I backed on my all fours
onder the bed. Hit wer 'Simon,' the ole preachin an'
exhortin nigger ove the neighborhood. He hilt a lite made
outen a rag an' sum fat, in a ole sasser, an' he cum sighin
an' groanin wif his mouf pouched out, up tu the coffin
wifout seein Seize in the corner at all, an' histed the led—
drap't the sasser, an' los' the lite, an' sed 'Oh! Goramity
massy on dis soul; de debil hesef on top ob brudder Seize!'
As he straitened tu run, he seed Seize in the corner. Jis'
then I moaned out in a orful doleful vise, *'Hiperkrit, cum
tu hell; I hes a claim ontu yu fur holdin the bag while
Seize stole co'n.'* (I seed em a-doin that job not long
afore.) He jis' rar'd backwards, an' fell outen the door
wif his hans locked, an' sed he in a weak, fever-ager sort
ove vise, 'Please marster,' an' jis' fainted, he soon cum to
a-runnin, fur I hearn the co'n crashin thru the big field
like a in-gine wer runnin express thru hit. I haint seed
'Simon,' tu this day.

"Now, ole Hunicutt hed been pow'fully agrawated 'bout
the co'n stealin business gwine on; in fact he fell frum
grace about hit bad. So whenever he hearn eny soun outen
doors ove a spishus kine, up he'd jump wif a shot-gun, an'
take a scout roun the barn an' co'n-crib.

"Well, es soon es Simon cummenced runnin wif the feebil
hope ove beatin the devil, I shoulder'd Seize, an' toted him
out tu the crib, an' sot him up agin the door, as hit wer
thar the doctor wer tu fine him, 'cordin tu 'greemint. Yu
see I wanted tu break him frum suckin aigs. I thot when
he tuck a good 'zamine ove Seize, an' his pitch-fork, an'
bull-frog, an' fire-bugs' tails, hit wud take away his
appertite fur grave-yards an' bil'd bones, till he got ole

enuf tu practice wifout sich dirty doins, an' mout even make him jine meetins. I cudn't tell how much good hit mout du the onb'lever. I'd scarcely got Seize balanced so he'd stan good, when I hearn ole Hunicutt cummin; I hearn his gun cock, so I jis' betuck mysef onder the co'n-crib, wif my head clost tu Seize's laigs, an' hid ahine his windin-sheet, onbenowenst tu him, an' his durn'd ole shot-gun too. The ole thief-hunter sneak'd mons'ous kerful roun the corner in his shutail—cum wifin three feet ove the dead nigger, *an' then seed him*.

"In the same doleful souns I used ontu Simon, I sed: 'Hunicutt, yu'se fell frum grace; I'll take yu down home *now*, leas' yu mout git good, *an' die afore yu fell agin*.' Durn my picter ef I didn't cum mons'ous ni helpin the devil tu wun orful sinner, onexpected rite thar, in yearnist.

"He drap't in a pile like ontu a wet bed quilt; as he struck, he sed, 'I haint fell frum gr——' Rite then an' thar, I reached out an' grabbed his shut, a savin holt wif bof hans, sot my cold sandy foot agin his bare back, an' leaned intu pullin pow'ful strong. Sez I, '*Yes yu am* fell frum grace; don't yu lie tu *me;* du yu know Missis Loftin? *Cum wif me.*' When I menshun'd Missis Loftin, he fotch a marster lunge. I hearn his collar-buttons snap, an' he went outen that shut like a dorg outen a badger-barril, an' he run; yas, by the great golly! He flew. I trumpeted arter him, 'Stop; I means tu take Missis Loftin *wif yu*.' He wer a-runnin squar an' low till he hearn that, an' durn dad, ef he didn't rise now six foot in the air every lunge, an' he'd make two ur three runin moshuns afore he'd lite. I sent what wer in bof barrils ove his shot-gun arter him, but the shot never cotch up. I got a shot-gun and a shut fur mysef.

"I know'd the pill-roller wudn't venter clost now arter all the fuss, an' shootin; he'd lose his mess ove bil'd bones fus'. So I shouldered Seize, an' put over the hill tu his shop, takin a circumbendibus roun, so es not tu cum up wif him on the path. He warn't in; he sure enuf hed started, but the shot-gun hed made him hide hissef fus', an arterwards go home.

"I ainded Seize up in his bed, back agin the wall, an' facin the door. Torrectly I hearn his tin pill-boxes, his squ't an' his pullicans rattlin in his pockets; he wer a-cumin. I jis' slid onder the bed, an' stuck my head up atween hit an' the wall, an' ahine Seize. He step't intu the dark room, an' by the help ove the fire-bug plaster he seed a heap, in fact more nur wer cumfortabil by about sixty-two an' a 'alf cents. Thar wer a 'luminated snake a-wavin roun, thar wer the shiny frog movin his laigs an' paws like he wer a-swimmin, then he'd gester wif his arms like he wer makin a stump-speech; thar wer the pitch-fork wif hits hot prongs (the doctor hearn them sciz), an' more nur all thar wer the orful corpse, wif hits face an' har all a-fire. Too much hell-sign on that bed even fur a bone-biler's narves. He jis' stop't short, froze tu the heart. I felt his shiverin cum tu me in the floor-planks.

"I tuck the same ole vise what hed sich a muvin effect ontu Simon an' Hunicutt, an' sed: 'Yu wants sum bones tu bile, dus yu? Didn't raise eny tu-night, did yu? I'se in that bisness mysef—follered hit ni ontu thuty thousand years. I'se a-bilin Ike Green's, an' Polly Weaver's, an' ole Seize's what yu pizen'd fur me, *an' they sent me arter yu;* les's go, my bilin hous' is warm—yu's cold—cum, sonny.'

"When I spoke ove ole Seize, he know'd I wer that orful ole king ove sorrer, an' that he wer gwine tu ride ontu the prongs ove that ar pitch-fork, dripin now wif the burnin taller ofen Seize's ribs, strait tu whar all quacks go. Sez he, 'W-w-wait, sir, till I gits my phissick-box; I'se onwell, please.' An' outen the door he bulged. I hollered arter him, 'Bring yer diplomer; I wants tu 'zamin *hit*.' 'Oh, yes sir.' I hearn this away back ove the field. In thuty-one days frum that date, he wer tendin a grist-mill in Californy. Ef he tends hit on the plan he tended folks yere, he's got *hits* bones a-bilin afore now.

"I wish, George, sum smart man-body wud bile the bones ove a grist-mill, an' find the cause, an' p'raps the cure fur 'mill-sick.' "

"What in the name of the Prophet is 'mill-sick,' Sut?"

"Why, hits a ailin what mills giner'lly hes; hits mity hurtin too, fur the peopil in the hole neighborhood kin *feel* the sufferin ove the misfortinit mill."

"How does it affect the mills?"

"Why, orfully; *they don't pass all they chaws*. Yu sumtimes sees sign ove hit on the miller an' his hogs; they looks like they hes the dropsy.

"Now durn jis' sich luck; yere I wer wif Seize's corpse on han, an' hit ni ontu daylite, no box, no spade, no hole, an' wus nur all, no whisky. Durn fools don't allers hev sich luck es this wer; ef they did, how wud peopil ever git rich, ur tu Congriss. I made the bes' I cud outen a bad fix. I jis' toted the ole skare out intu the woods, an' hid him onder a log, an' went over tu Hunicutt's agin. I wer boun tu go, fur my whisky wer hid thar.

"The niggers wer all in a huddle in the kitchin, an' the white folks all a-cryin, an' a-snufflin. Missis Hunicutt wer out, a-top the bars, a-callin ove him. 'Oh, Hunicuttee,' like callin cows, an' he warn't answerin. In fac' everybody wer skar'd durn ni outen thar wits. I tole em the bes' thing they cud du, wer tu git the dirt a-top ove that nigger Seize es quick es spades an' hoes cud du hit; that I know'd sumfin wer wrong wif Seize; must hev been a orful hiperkrit afore he died. Passun Simon hed been spirited off wif a burnin sasser ove fat in his han; Maje warn't in the bed, an wer too drunk tu git away hissef, an' es I cum yere jis' afore day, I met Mr. Hunicutt way up in the air, ridin a-straddil ove a burnin ladder wif Missis Loftin ahine him, her petticoatail a-blazin, an' she a-singin, 'Farwell vain worl; I'se gwine home.'

"Hunicutt's ole cook rolled up her eyes an' sed, smackin her hands: 'Dar, dats hit; I'se know dis tree munf Missis Loftin fotch de debil heah afore she dun; goramity bress de worl, she dun du hit now!'

"Missis Hunicutt look't at me keenly, an' axed me ef I wer shure hit wer Missis Loftin I seed on the ladder. I tole her 'Yas; I'd swar hit; I know'd her kalliker.'

"Sez she: 'Now I kin bar my brevement.' An' she sot intu comin her har.

"Well, the niggers geard a par ove hosses tu a waggin, an' put the coffin in wifout scarcely sayin a word, ur even venterin tu take a farwell look ove the corpse; they wanted hit away frum thar, sure es yu are born. Jis' s'pose they hed open'd that led an' seed Maje dressed up es he wer. Oh, lordy! Enuf niggers wud hev jis' turned inside out, an' then mortified, tu manured a forty-acre saige-field.

"Suckey—that's Seize's wife—sot on the head ove the coffin, an the balance ove hit wer soon kivered wif she niggers; they jis' swarmed ontu the waggin, an' all roun hit, an' started. When they got intu the aidge ove town, ni ontu Wright's doggery, Maje begun tu wake frum the joltin, an' sot intu buttin the led wif his hed, his ho'ns a-rattlin agin hit. Suckey felt sumthin onder her she didn't like. 'Butt, rattil,' cum up Maje's head an' ho'ns harder nur before. Her eyes swelled tu the size an' looks ove hard-biled aigs, an' she ris hersef ofen the coffin a littil wif her hans. 'Butt, whosh!' sed Maje, an' the coffin-led cum up tu Suckey's starn like hit hed been a loadstone spat.

"'Pete, yu Pete; jis' wo dem hosses, rite heah, an' leff me off ob dis wagun.' Maje gin anuther suvigrus butt, an' sed, a-chokin like, 'Dis am the debil!' Suckey lit in the road. 'I'se gwine tu my missus, I is,' sed Suckey, an' back she put, shakin her petticoats, an' pullin em roun so she cud see the hineparts whar the led hed actid loadstone. 'De debil hesef in dat box wif Seize, shuah, fur he say so. *I* tole yu dis Seize; I hes more time nor I hes har; now yu's gone an' dun hit, yu hes,' an' she struck a cow gallop fur home.

"'Butt,' cum Maje's head agin, an' thar bein no Suckey wif her hundred an' fifty poun ove soap grease tu hole hit down, over cum the led slap. Maje rared up on aind. 'Whosh! dis am de debil;' he sed. Thuty screams mixed in one, clatterin ove shoes, an' scrachin ove toe-nails, an' thar warn't a nigger lef in site afore a stutterin man cud whistil.

"Now Maje know'd nuffin about how he look't, but he seed the coffin, an' the waggin. Sez he: 'Well, by golly! dis am a go; gwine tu burry dis chile, an' neber ax 'im. Whar de mourners? Whar de passun? An' whar de corpsis? Dats what I wants tu know. Sumfin wrong heah,' an' he bit his arm savidge es a dorg. 'Outch! I isn't ded, an' I'se a-cummin outen heah. Dus yu hear my h'on? I is dat. Datdurn 'saitful preachin Simon dun dis; he want Sally; I kill em bof, de coffin am redy. Mus' want tu bury sumbody pow'ful bad. Whar wer de white folks.' Yere he cummenced a mons'ous scufflin tu git out. The hosses look'd roun an seed 'im; ove course they instantly sot intu run away strong—hit a postes, an' pitched the black box up in the air whar hit look'd like a big grasshopper a-jumpin. Hit lit on aind, an' busted the led off; out bounced Maje, an' shakin hissef he tuck a drunk staggerin look at hit, an' sez he, a-moshunin the coffin away frum him wif bof hans, 'Sea heah; yu jis go long tu de bone-yard, yu black debbil, whar yu b'longs; I'se not gwine wid yu; I sends Simon tu yu dis arternoon.' An' he started fur the doggery.

"Wright hed cum tu the door, an' wer a-lookin an' a-wonderin at the upraised coffin, when Maje faced him an' started at him in a trot; he wanted a ho'n bad. His head, ho'ns an' snake penertrated Wright's mind wif the idear that hit wer the *devil*, an' knowin that the ole sootmaker hilt several notes ove han agin him, 'bout due, he fix'd it up that he wer gwine tu levy ontu him, an' he fotch a coffin tu tote him home in. So he jis' tried tu *dodge the lor*. He jump't the counter—out at the back door, an' cummenced a-litnin line fur the mountin.

"I wer ahine the doggery in the thicket, an' I bellered out, 'Stop, Wright; I owes yu fur a heap ove sinners; yu sent me Seize, yesterday, an' I'se cum tu settil fur em.'

"He wer the fust man I ever seed run frum a feller when he wanted tu pay a debt. Durn ole Hark, ef he warn't jis' openin a waggin road thru the pine thicket, thuty mile tu the hour. Yu cud see the limbs an' littil rocks a-flyin abuv the trees es he went, an' he sounded like a hurrycane, an' wer a-movin as fast.

"When I spoke them words, the limbs an' littil rocks farly darkened the air, an' the soun got louder ef hit wer a heap furder off. He wer es yearnist a man es ever run. I think he did the mos' onresistabil runnin I ever seed. Nuffin wer in his way; he jis' mow'd hit all down es he fled frum es jest a ritribushun as ever follered eny durn'd raskil since ole Shockly chased Passun Bumpas wif a shotgun ritribushun, fur onsanctifyin his wife."

"Did Shockly catch Bumpas, Sut?"

"I dunno; He mus' a-run 'im pow'ful clost, fur he fotch back his hoss, hat, an' hyme book, an' bof caps on his gun wer busted, an' nobody name Bumpas hes been seed 'bout thar since, 'sceptin sum littil flax-headed fellers scattered thru the sarkit, wif no daddys, an' not much mammys tu speak ove. Ef I'd a-seed the devil es plain es Wright did, the day they tried tu bury Seize, an' didn't, I'd a-ax'd him; *he* knows whether Shockly cotch Bumpas, ur not.

"Well, Maje cum blowin mad intu the doggery, an seein

nobody, he jis' grabbed a bottil, an' tuck hissef a buckload ove popskull, an' slip't the bottil intu his pocket. Es he raised his orful head frum duin this, he seed hissef fur the fust time in a big lookin-glass. He took hit tu be a winder, an' tho't what he seed wer in tuther room, a-watchin him. 'Yu—yu jis' lef me lone; I'se not yourn; *I b'longs tu meetin,*' sed Maje, as he back'd hissef to'ards the door. As he back'd, so did the taryfyin picter. Maje seed that. 'Gwine tu take a runnin butt, is yu,' sed Maje, as he fell a back summerset intu the street; as he lit, I groaned out at him: 'Major, my son, I'se cum fur the toll outen ole Hunicutt's co'n.' 'Simon dun got dat toll,' sed Maje, sorter sham'd like.

"He riz, showin a far sampil ove skared nigger runnin. 'Ho'ns an' buttin go tugether, an' dat am de debil in dar,' sed Maje tu hissef. I holler'd, 'Leave Wright's bottil; yu don't want hit, *I'll gin yu hotter truck nur hit is;* I'se farly arter yu now.' I seed the bottil fly over Maje's shoulder, an' lite in the san. I got hit, I did.

"He made down street fur the river, an' clear'd the road ove every livin thing. Wimen went head-fust intu the houses, doors slam'd, sash fell, cats' tails swell'd es they treed onder stabils, Maje jis' a-tarin along, his ho'ny head throw'd back, an' his elbows a-workin like a par ove skeer'd saw-mills runnin empty. I seed him fling sumthin over his head. I tho't hit wer anuther bottil, an' went fur hit, but hit wer nuffin but a greasy testemint.

"Ole Dozier, the sheriff, what hed hung a nigger name Pomp, 'bout ten days afore, cum outen a cross street, jis' ahead ove Maje, a-totin his big belly, hanful ove papers, an' a quill in his mouf, in a deep study. He hearn the soun ove Maje's huffs, an' look'd roun. As he did, I shouted, 'Run, sheriff, that's Pomp, an' yere's his coffin,' a-pintin tu hit.

"George, my 'sperience is that sheriffs, an' lor officers giner'lly, onderstands the bisness ove runnin better nur mos' folks, enyhow, an' durn my shut ef ole Dozier didn't jis' then sustain the kar-acter ove the the tribe mons'ous well.

"He hes pow'ful presence ove mind too, fur I'd scarcely sed 'coffin,' afore he wer at the top ove his speed to'ards the river. Now Maje, like most durn'd white fools, b'leved the sheriff tu be greater nur enybody, an' hed the power tu du enything. So a idear got onder his ho'ns, an' ahine his eyes, that Dozier cud help him sumhow, tu git rid ove the chasin devil, an' he holler'd 'Marster Dozier——' Dozier drap't his quill. 'Marster Sheriff——' Sheriff lef loose a cloud ove flyin papers in the wind. 'Stop dar; I hes a word wid yu.'

"Dozier run outen his hat an' specks wif a jerk, an' I seed his dinner tub a-swingin out each side ove him, like a bag wif a skared dorg intu hit, every lope he made. I galloped caticorner'd across lots, an' got in a paw-paw thicket on the bank ove the river, afore they got roun thar; as Dozier whizz'd by, the sweat flying ofen his head in all direcshuns, like warter ofen a runnin grindstone. I spoke tu him in a mournful way: 'Sheriff, yu're time am cum; *he's got a rope.*'

"Durn ef he didn't sheer outen the road like a skeer'd hoss, an' went ofen the bluff, frog fashun, intu the river— an' dove. The waves washed up on tuther bank, three foot high; a steamboat cudn't hev dun hit better, an' es good a growin rain fell, fur five minnits, as wer ever prayed fur, an' not a cloud tu be seed that day. Yere cum Maje, his eyes an' thar stripes like buggy wheels, wif red lamps in the hubs. Sez I, 'Yere I is, clost tu yu're starn; I *mus'* hev my toll co'n.' Durn ole Paddilford, ef he didn't play skeered hoss better nur Dozier did, fur he lit furder in the river, an' we hed anuther refreshin shower; but I swar, I tho't hit smelt ove whisky. Bof on em wer swimin fur tuther bank, like ole otters. The sheriff's hot head wer smokin like a tub ove bil'd shuts, an' Maje's look'd like black bull yearlin's, jis' a-bilin thru the warter. Es ole Dozier trotted drippin up the bank, I yell'd: 'Rise sheriff, he's a-reachin fur yu wif his rope, *an' hits got a runnin noose'.* He look'd over his shoulder an' seed the bull yearlin's head clost in shore, an' a-cummin. He jis' rained san an' gravil intu the river, frum his heels, an' went outen site in the tall weeds. As Maje went up the bank, I call'd tu him, 'Major, my son, *whar's* Wright's bottil?' I seed him feel on his coattail; the durned nigger hed forgot flingin hit over his head, an' he tuck the sheriff's trail, like ontu a houn. I tuck a good holesum pull outen that bottil, an' tho't what a durn'd discumfortin thing a big skeer is.

"Plenty peopil am redy tu swar that they seed the devil chasin Dozier, plum tu the mountin, an' one ole 'oman, a-givin in her sperience at meetin, sed she seed him ketch him, an' eat him plum up. She tole a durn'd lie, I speck.

"I performed two christshun jutys that night. I stole the coffin, an' buried Seize out in the woods whar I'd hid him, an' his rale grave stans open yet, the bes' frog-trap yu ever seed. See the orful consekenses ove bein skeery when a nigger dies. Hunicutt gone; Seize's corpse los'; *doctor* gone; *passun* gone; *sheriff* gone; an' tu cap the stack ove vexashus things, the *doggery keeper* gone. Why, the county's ruinated, an' hits haunted yet wif all sorts ove orful haunts; yu ken buy land thar fur a dime a acre, on tick at that."

"What became of Mrs. Hunicutt, and Mrs. Loftin, Sut?"

"Oh! Es tu em, Missis Hunicutt is playin widder, in red ribbons, an' Missis Loftin's jin'd meetin.

"I'se furgot sumthin; what am hit? Oh! I minds now; 'twer that tuther christshun juty I performed. I minister'd ontu Wright's doggery, an' run hit till the grass burn't up, when hit went dry. I wish hit mout hev a calf soon."

Rare Ripe Garden-Seed

"I TELL yu now, I minds my fust big skeer jis' es well as rich boys minds thar fust boots, ur seein the fust spotted hoss sirkis. The red top ove them boots am still a rich red stripe in thar minds, an' the burnin red ove my fust skeer hes lef es deep a scar ontu my thinkin works. Mam hed me a standin atwixt her knees. I kin feel the knobs ove her jints a-rattlin a-pas' my ribs yet. She didn't hev much petticoats tu speak ove, an' I hed but one, an' hit wer calliker slit frum the nap ove my naik tu the tail, hilt tugether at the top wif a draw-string, an' at the bottom by the hem; hit wer the handiest close I ever seed, an' wud be pow'ful cumfurtin in summer if hit warn't fur the flies. Ef they was good tu run in, I'd war one yet. They beats pasted shuts, an' britches, es bad es a feather bed beats a bag ove warnut shells fur sleepin on.

"Say, George, wudn't yu like tu see me intu one 'bout haf fadid, slit, an' a-walkin jis' so, up the middil street ove yure city chuch, a-aimin fur yure pew pen, an' hit chock full ove yure fine city gal friends, jis' arter the peopil hed sot down frum the fust prayer, an' the orgin beginin tu groan; what wud yu du in sich a margincy? Say hoss?"

"Why, I'd shoot you dead, Monday morning before eight c'clock," was my reply.

"Well, I speck yu wud; but yu'd take a rale ole maid faint fus, rite amung them ar gals. Lordy! Wudn't yu be shamed ove me! Yit why not ten chuch in sich a suit, when yu hesn't got no store clothes?

"Well, es I wer sayin, mam wer feedin us brats ontu mush an' milk, wifout the milk, an' es I wer the baby then, she hilt me so es tu see that I got my sheer. Whar thar ain't enuf feed, big childer roots littil childer outen the troff, an' gobbils up thar part. Jis' so the yeath over: bishops eats elders, elders eats common peopil, they eats sich cattil es me, I eats possums, possums eats chickins, chickins swallers wums, an' wums am content tu eat dus, an' the dus am the aind ove hit all. Hit am all es regilur es the souns frum the tribil down tu the bull base ove a fiddil in good tchune, an' I speck hit am right, ur hit wudn't be 'lowed.

"*'The sheriff!*' his'd mam in a keen trimblin whisper; hit sounded tu me like the skreech ove a hen when she sez 'hawk,' tu her little roun-sturn'd, fuzzy, bead-eyed, stripid-backs.

"I actid jis' adzacly as they dus; I darted on all fours onder mam's petticoatails, an' thar I met, face tu face, the wooden bowl, an' the mush, an' the spoon what she slid onder frum tuther side. I'se mad at mysef yet, fur rite thar I showd'd the fust flash ove the nat'ral born durn fool what I now is. I orter et hit all up, in jestis tu my stumick an' my growin, while the sheriff wer levyin ontu the bed an' the cheers. Tu this day, ef enybody sez 'sheriff,' I feels skeer, an' ef I hears constabil menshun'd, my laigs goes thru runnin moshuns, even ef I is asleep. Did yu ever watch a dorg dreamin ove rabbit huntin? Thems the moshuns, an' the feelin am the rabbit's.

"Sherifs am orful 'spectabil peopil; everybody looks up tu em. I never adzacly seed the 'spectabil part mysef. I'se too fear'd ove em, I reckon, tu 'zamin fur hit much. One thing I knows, no country atwix yere an' Tophit kin ever 'lect me tu sell out widders' plunder, ur poor men's co'n, an' the tho'ts ove hit gins me a good feelin; hit sorter flashes thru my heart when I thinks ove hit. I axed a passun onst, what hit cud be, an' he pernounced hit tu be *onregenerit pride,* what I orter squelch in prayer, an' in tendin chuch on colleckshun days. I wer in hopes hit mout be 'ligion, ur sence, a-soakin intu me; hit feels good, enyhow, an' I don't keer ef every suckit rider outen jail knows hit. Sheriffs' shuts allers hes nettil dus ur fleas inside ove em when they lies down tu sleep, an' I'se glad ove hit, fur they'se allers discumfortin me, durn em. I scarcely ever git tu drink a ho'n, ur eat a mess in peace. I'll hurt one sum day, see ef I don't. Show me a sheriff, a-steppin softly roun, an' a-sorter sightin at me, an' I'll show yu a far sampil ove the speed ove a express ingine, fired up wif rich, dry, rosiny skeers. They don't ketch me *much,* usin only human laigs es wepuns.

"Ole John Doltin wer a 'spectabil sheriff, monsusly so,

an' hed the bes' scent fur poor fugatif devils, an' wimen, I ever seed; he wer sure fire. Well, he toted a warrun fur this yere skinful ove durn'd fool, 'bout that ar misfortnit nigger meetin bisness, ontil he wore hit intu six seperit squar bits, an' hed wore out much shoe leather a-chasin ove me. I'd foun a doggery in full milk, an' hated pow'ful bad tu leave that settilment while hit suck'd free; so I sot intu sorter try an' wean him off frum botherin me so much. I suckseedid so well that he not only quit racin ove me, an' wimen, but he wer tetotaly spiled es a sheriff, an' los' the 'spectabil seckshun ove his karacter. Tu make yu fool fellers onderstan how hit wer done, I mus' interjuice yure minds tu one Wat Mastin, a bullit-headed yung blacksmith.

"Well, las' year—no hit wer the year afore las'—in struttin an' gobblin time, Wat felt his keepin right warm, so he sot intu bellerin an' pawin up dus in the neighborhood roun the ole widder McKildrin's. The more dus he flung up, the wus he got, ontil at las' he jis cudn't stan the ticklin sensashuns anuther minnit; so he put fur the county court clark's offis, wif his hans sock'd down deep intu his britchis pockets, like he wer fear'd ove pick-pockets, his back roach'd roun, an a-chompin his teef ontil he splotch'd his whiskers wif foam. Oh! he wer yearnis' hot, an' es restless es a cockroach in a hot skillit."

"What was the matter with this Mr. Mastin? I cannot understand you, Mr. Lovingood; had he hydrophobia?" remarked a man in a square-tail coat, and cloth gaiters, who was obtaining subscribers for some forthcoming Encyclopedia of Useful Knowledge, who had quartered at our camp, uninvited, and really unwanted.

"What du yu mean by high-dry-foby?" and Sut looked puzzled.

"A madness produced by being bit by some rabid animal," explained Square-tail, in a pompous manner.

"Yas, hoss, he hed high-dry-foby *orful*, an' Mary McKildrin, the widder McKildrin's only darter, hed gin him the complaint; I don't know whether she bit 'im ur not; he mout a-cotch hit frum her bref, an' he wer now in the roach back, chompin stage ove the sickness, so he wer arter the clark fur a ticket tu the hospital. Well, the clark sole 'im a piece ove paper, part printin an' part ritin, wif a picter ove two pigs' hearts, what sum boy hed shot a arrer thru, an' lef hit stickin, printed at the top. That paper wer a splicin pass—sum calls hit a par ove licins— an' that very nite he tuck Mary, fur better, fur wus, tu hev an' tu hole tu him his heirs, an'——"

"Allow me to interrupt you," said our guest; "you do not quote the marriage ceremony correctly."

"Yu go tu *hell*, mistofer; yu bothers me."

This outrageous rebuff took the stranger all aback, and he sat down.

"Whar wer I? Oh yas, he married Mary tight an' fas', an' nex' day he wer abil tu be about. His coat tho', an' his trousis look'd jis' a skrimshun too big, loose like, an' heavy tu tote. I axed him ef he felt soun. He sed yas, but he'd welded a steamboat shaftez the day afore, an' wer sorter tired like. Thar he tole a durn lie, fur he'd been a-ho'nin up dirt mos' ove the day, roun the widder's garden, an' bellerin in the orchard. Mary an' him sot squar intu hous'-keepin, an' 'mung uther things he bot a lot ove *rar ripe garden-seed,* frum a Yankee peddler. Rar ripe co'n, rar ripe peas, rar ripe taters, rar ripe everything, an' the two yung durn'd fools wer dreadfully exercis'd 'bout hit. Wat sed he ment tu git him a rar ripe hammer an' anvil, an' Mary vowd'd tu grashus, that she'd hev a rar ripe wheel an' loom, ef money wud git em. Purty soon arter he hed made the garden, he tuck a noshun tu work a spell down tu Ataylanty, in the railroad shop, es he sed he hed a sorter ailin in his back, an' he tho't weldin rail car-tire an' ingine axiltrees, wer lighter work nur sharpinin plows, an' puttin lap-links in trace-chains. So down he went, an' foun hit agreed wif him, fur he didn't cum back ontil the middil ove August. The fust thing he seed when he landid intu his cabin-door, wer a shoe-box wif rockers onder hit, an' the nex thing he seed, wer Mary herself, propped up in bed, an' the nex thing he seed arter that, wer a par ove littil rat-eyes a-shinin abuv the aind ove the quilt, ontu Mary's arm, an' the nex an' las' thing he seed wer the two littil rat-eyes aforesed, a-turnin intu two hundred thousand big green stars, an' a-swingin roun an' roun the room, faster an' faster, ontil they mix'd intu one orful green flash. He drap't intu a limber pile on the floor. The durn'd fool what hed weldid the steamboat shaftez hed fainted safe an' soun es a gal skeered at a mad bull. Mary fotch a weak cat-scream, an' kivered her head, an' sot intu work ontu a whifflin dry cry, while littil Rat-eyes gin hitssef up tu suckin. Cryin an' suckin bof at onst ain't far; mus' cum pow'ful strainin on the wet seckshun ove an' 'oman's constitushun; yet hit am ofen dun, an' more too. Ole Missis McKildrin, what wer a-nussin Mary, jis' got up frum knittin, an' flung a big gourd ove warter squar intu Wat's face, then she fotch a glass bottil ove swell-skull whisky outen the three-cornered cupboard, an' stood furnint Wat, a-holdin hit in wun han, an' the tin-cup in tuther, waitin fur Wat tu cum to. She wer the piusses lookin ole 'oman jis' then, yu ever seed outside ove a prayer-meetin. Arter a spell, Wat begun tu move, twitchin his fingers, an' battin his eyes, sorter 'stonished like. That pius lookin statue sed tu him:

"'My son, jis' take a drap ove sperrits, honey. Yu'se very sick, dumplin; don't take on darlin, ef yu kin help hit, ducky, fur poor Margarit Jane am mons'ous ailin, an' the leas' nise ur takin on will kill the poor sufferin dear, an' yu'll loose yure tuckil ducky duv ove a sweet wifey, arter all she's dun gone thru fur yu. My dear son Watty, yu mus' consider her feelins a littil.' Sez Wat, a-turnin up his eyes at that vartus ole relick, sorter sick like—

"'I is a-considerin em a heap, rite now.'

"'Oh that's right, my good kine child.'

"Oh dam ef ole muther-in-lors can't plaster humbug over a feller, jis' es saft an' easy es they spreads a camrick hanketcher over a three hour ole baby's face; yu don't feel hit at all, but hit am thar, a plum inch thick, an' stickin fas es court-plaster. She raised Wat's head, an' sot the aidge ove the tin cup agin his lower teef, an' turned up the bottim slow an' keerful, a-winkin at Mary, hu wer a-peepin over the aidge ove the coverlid, tu see ef Wat *tuck the perskripshun,* fur a heap ove famerly cumfort 'pended on that ar ho'n ove sperrits. *Wun* ho'n allers saftens a man, the yeath over. Wat keep a-battin his eyes, wus nur a owl in daylight; at las' he raised hissef ontu wun elbow, an' rested his head in that han, sorter weak like. Sez he, mons'ous trimblin an' slow: 'Aprile—May—June—July—an' mos'—haf—ove—August,' a-countin the munths ontu the fingers ove tuther han, wif the thumb, a-shakin ove his head, an' lookin at his spread fingers like they warn't his'n, ur they wer nastied wif sumfin. Then he counted em agin, slower, Aprile—May—June—July—an', mos' haf ove August, an' he run his thumb atwixt his fingers, es meanin mos' haf ove August, an' look'd at the pint ove hit, like hit mout be a snake's head. He raised his eyes tu the widder's face, who wer standin jis' es steady es a hitchin pos,' an' still a-warin that pius 'spression ontu her pussonal feturs, an' a flood ove saft luv fur Wat, a-shinin strait frum her eyes intu his'n. Sez he, 'That jis' makes four munths, an' mos' a half, don't hit, Missis McKildrin?' She never sed one word. Wat reached fur the hath, an' got a dead fire-coal; then he made a mark clean acrost a floor-plank. Sez he, 'Aprile,' a-holdin down the coal ontu the aind ove the mark, like he wer fear'd hit mout blow away afore he got hit christened Aprile. Sez he, 'May'—an' he marked across the board agin; then he counted the marks, one, two, a-dottin at em wif the coal. 'June,' an' he marked agin, one, two, three; counted wif the pint over the coal. He scratched his head wif the littil finger ove the han holdin the charcoal, an' he drawed hit slowly acrost the board agin, peepin onder his wrist tu see when hit reached the crack, an' sez he 'July,' es he lifted the coal; 'one, two three, four,' countin frum lef tu right, an' then frum right tu lef. 'That haint but four, no way I kin fix hit. Ole Pike hissef cudn't make hit five, ef he wer tu sifer ontu hit ontil his laigs turned intu figger eights.' Then he made a mark, haf acrost a plank, spit on his finger, an' rubbed off a haf inch ove the aind, an' sez he, 'Mos' haf ove August.' He looked up at the widder, an' thar she wer, same es ever, still a-holdin the flask agin her bussum, an' sez he 'Four months, an' mos' a haf. *Haint enuf, is hit mammy?* Hits jis' 'bout (lackin a littil) *haf enuf,* haint hit, mammy?'

"Missis McKildrin shuck her head sorter onsartin like, an' sez she, 'Take a drap more sperrits, Watty, my dear pet; dus yu mine buyin that ar rar ripe seed, frum the peddler?' Wat nodded his head, an' looked 'what ove hit,' but didn't say hit.

"'This is what cums ove hit, an' four months an' a haf am rar ripe time fur babys, adzackly. Tu be sure, hit lacks a day ur two, but Margarit Jane wer allers a pow'ful interprizin gal, an' a yearly rizer.' Sez Wat,

" 'How about the 'taters?'

" 'Oh, *we* et 'taters es big es goose aigs, afore ole Missis Collinze's blossomed.'

" 'How 'bout co'n?'

" 'Oh, we shaved down roasin years afore hern tassel'd——'

" 'An' peas?'

" 'Yes son, we hed gobs an' lots in three weeks. Everything cums in adzackly half the time that hit takes the ole sort, an' yu *knows*, my darlin son, yu planted hit waseful. I tho't then yu'd rar ripe everything on the place. Yu planted *often,* too, didn't yu luv, fur fear hit wudn't cum up?'

" 'Ye-ye-s-s he—he did,' sed Mary a-cryin. Wat studied pow'ful deep a spell, an' the widder jis' waited. Widders allers wait, an' allers win. At las, sez he, 'Mammy.' She looked at Mary, an' winked these yere words at her, es plain es she cud a-talked em. 'Yu hearn him call me *mammy twiste.* I'se *got him* now. His back-bone's a-limberin fas', he'll own the baby yet, see ef he don't. Jis' hole still my darter, an' let yer mammy knead this dough, then yu may bake hit es brown es yu please.'

" 'Mammy, when I married on the fust day ove Aprile'—— The widder look'd oneasy; she tho't he mout be a-cupplin that day, his weddin, an' the idear, dam fool, tugether. But he warn't, fur he sed, 'That day I gin ole man Collins my note ove han fur a hundred dullars, jew in one year arter date, the balluns on this lan. Dus yu think that ar seed will change the *time* eny, ur will hit alter the *amount?*' An' Wat looked at her powerful ankshus. She raised the whisky bottil way abuv her head, wif her thumb on the mouf, an' fotch the bottim down ontu her han, spat. Sez she, 'Watty, my dear b'lovid son, pripar tu pay *two* hundred dullars 'bout the fust ove October, fur hit'll be jew jis' then, *es* sure es that littil black-eyed angel in the bed thar, am yer darter.'

"Wat drap't his head, an' sed, *'Then hits a dam sure thing.'* Rite yere, the baby fotch a rattlin loud squall (I speck Mary wer sorter figetty jis' then, an' hurt hit). 'Yas,' sez Wat, a-wallin a red eye to'ards the bed; 'my littil she—what wer hit yu called her name, mammy?' 'I called her a sweet littil angel, an' she is wun, es sure es yu're her daddy, my b'loved son.' 'Well,' sez Wat, 'my littil sweet, patent rar ripe she angel, ef yu lives tu marryin time, yu'll 'stonish sum man body outen his shut, ef yu don't rar ripe lose yer vartu arter the fust plantin, that's all.' He rared up on aind, wif his mouf pouch'd out. He had a pow'ful forrid, furreachin, bread funnel, enyhow—cud a-bit the aigs outen a catfish, in two-foot warter, wifout wettin his eyebrows. 'Dod durn rar ripe seed, an' rar ripe peddlers, an' rar ripe notes tu the hottes' corner ove——'

" 'Stop Watty, *darlin*, don't swar; 'member yu belongs tu meetin.'

" 'My blacksmith's fire,' ainded Wat, an' he studied a long spell; sez he,

" 'Did you save eny ove that infunnel doubil-trigger seed?' 'Yas,' sez the widder, 'thar in that bag by the cupboard.' Wat got up ofen the floor, tuck a countin sorter look at the charcoal marks, an' reached down the bag; he went tu the door an' called 'Suke, muley! Suke, Suke, cow, chick, chick, chicky chick.' 'What's yu gwine tu du now, my dear son?' sed Missis McKildrin. 'I'se jis' gwine tu feed this actif *smart* truck tu the cow, an' the hens, that's what I'se gwine tu du. Ole muley haint hed a calf in two years, an' I'll eat sum rar ripe aigs.' Mary now venter'd tu speak: 'Husban, I ain't sure hit'll work on hens; cum an' kiss me my luv.' 'I haint sure hit'll work on hens, either,' sed Wat. 'They's powerful onsartin in thar ways, well es wimen,' an' he flung out a hanful spiteful like. 'Takin the rar ripe invenshun all tugether, frum 'taters an' peas tu notes ove han, an' childer, I can't say I likes hit much,' an' he flung out anuther hanful. 'Yer mam hed thuteen the ole way, an' ef this truck stays 'bout the hous', yu'se good fur twenty-six, maybe thuty, fur yu'se a pow'ful interprizin gal, yer mam sez,' an' he flung out anuther hanful, overhandid, es hard es ef he wer flingin rocks at a stealin sow. 'Make yere mine easy,' sed the widder; 'hit never works on married folks only the fust time.' 'Say them words agin,' sed Wat, 'I'se glad tu hear em. Is hit the same way wif notes ove han?' 'I speck hit am,' answer'd the widder, wif jis' a taste ove strong vinegar in the words, es she sot the flask in the cupboard wif a push.

"Jis' then ole Doltin, the sheriff, rid up, an' started 'stonished when he seed Wat, but he, quick es an 'oman kin hide a strange hat, drawed the puckerin-string ove that legil face ove his'n, an' fotch hit up tu the 'know'd yu wer at home,' sorter look, an' wishin Wat much joy, sed he'd fotch the baby a present, a par ove red shoes, an' a calliker dress, fur the luv he bore hits granmam. Missis McKildrin tole him what the rar ripe hed dun, an' he swore hit allers worked jis' that way, an' wer 'stonished at Wat's not knowin hit; an' they talked so fas', an' so much, that the more Wat listened the less he know'd.

"Arter the sheriff lef, they onrolled the bundil, an' Wat straitched out the calliker in the yard. He step't hit off keerfully, ten yards, an a littil the rise. He puss'd up his mouf, an' blow'd out a whistil seven foot long, lookin up an' down the middil stripe ove the drygoods, frum aind tu aind. Sez he, 'Missis McKildrin, that'll make Rar Ripe a good *full* frock, won't hit?' 'Y-a-s,' sed she, wif her hans laid up along her jaw, like she wer studyin the thing keerfully. 'My son, I thinks hit will, an' I wer jis' a-thinkin ef hit wer cut tu 'vantage, thar *mout* be nuff lef, squeezed out tu make yu a Sunday shutin shut, makin the ruffils an' ban outen sumthin else.' 'Put hit in the bag what the rar ripe wer in, an' by mornin thar'll be nuff fur the ruffils an' bans, an' yu mout make the tail tu drag the yeath, wifout squeezin ur pecin,' sez Wat, an' he put a few small wrinkils in the pint ove his nose, what seemed tu bother the widder tu make out the meanin ove; they look'd mons'ous like the outward signs ove an on-b'lever. Jis' then his eyes sot fas' ontu sumthin a-lyin on the groun whar he'd onrolled the bundil; he walk'd up tu hit slow, sorter like a feller goes up tu a log, arter he thinks he seed a snake run onder. He walk'd clean roun hit twiste, never takin his eyes ofen hit. At las' he lifted hit on his instep, an' hilt out his laig strait at that widdered muther-in-lor ove his'n. Sez he, 'What mout yu call that? Red baby's shoes don't giner'lly hev teeth, dus they?' 'Don't yu *know* hits a tuckin comb, Watty? The store-keeper's made a sorter blunder, I speck,' sed that vartus petticoatful ove widderhood. 'Maybe he hes; I'se durn sure I *hes*,' sed Wat, an' he wrinkil'd his nose agin, mons'ous botherinly tu that watchful widder. He scratched his head a spell; sez he, 'Ten yards an' the rise fur a baby's frock, *an' hit rar ripe at that, gits me;* an' that ar tuckin comb gits me wus.' 'Oh, fiddlesticks an' flusterashun,' sez she. 'Save the comb; baby'll soon want hit.' 'That's so, mammy; I'm dam ef hit don't,' an' he slip't his foot frum onder hit, an' hit scarcely totch the yeath afore he stomp't hit, an' the teeth flew all over the widder. He look'd like he'd been stompin a blowin adder, an' went apas' the 'oman intu the cabin, in a rale Aprile tucky gobbler strut. When he tore the rapper off the sheriff's present, I seed a littil bit ove white paper fall out. Onbenowenst tu enybody, I sot my foot ontu hit, an' when they went in I socked hit deep intu my pocket, an' went over tu the still-'ous. I tuck Jim Dunkin out, an' arter swarin 'im wif a uplifted han', tu keep dark, got him tu read hit tu me, ontil hit wer printed on the mindin seckshun ove my brain. Hit run jis' so:

"MY SWEET MARY:
I mayn't git the chance tu talk eny tu yu, so when Wat gits home, an' axes enything 'bout the *comb* an' *calliker,* yu tell him yer mam foun the bundil in the road. She'll back yu up in that ar statemint, ontil thar's enuf white fros' in hell tu kill snap-beans.

Notey Beney.—I hope Wat'll stay in Atlanty ontil the merlenium, don't yu, my dear duv?

Yures till deth,

DOLTIN.

An' tu that ar las' remark he'd sot a big D. I reckon he ment that fur dam Wat.

"Now, I jis' know'd es long es I hed that paper, I hilt four aces ontu the sheriff, an' I ment tu bet on the han, an' *go halves wif Wat,* fur I wer sorry fur him, he wer so infunely 'posed upon. I went tu school tu Sicily Burns, tu larn 'oman tricks, an' I tuck a dirplomer, I did, an' now I'd jes' like tu see the pussonal feeters ove the she 'oman what cud stock rar ripe kerds on me, durn'd fool es I is. I hed a talk wif Wat, an' soon foun out that his mine hed simmer'd down intu a strong belief that the sheriff an' Mary wer doin thar weavin in the same loom.

"Then I show'd him my four aces, an' that chip made the pot bile over, an' he jis' 'greed tu be led by me, spontanashusly.

"Jis' think on that fac' a minnit boys; a man what hed sense enuf tu turn a hoss shoe, an' then nail hit on toe aind foremos', bein led by me, looks sorter like a plum tree barin tumil bug-balls, but hit wer jis' so, an' durn my pictur, ef I didn't lead him tu victory, strait along.

"What narrated hit, that he b'leved strong in rar ripe, frum beans, thru notes ove han, plum tu babys, an' that his cabin shud never be wifout hit. The widder wer cheerful, Mary wer luvin, an' the sheriff wer told on the sly, by ole Mister McKildrin's remainin, an' mos' pius she half, that Wat wer es plum blind es ef his eyes wer two tuckil aigs. So the wool grow'd over *his* eyes, ontil hit wer fit tu shear, an' *dam ef I warn't at the shearin.*

"Things, tharfore, went smoof, an' es quiet es a greased waggin, runnin in san. Hits allers so, jis' afore a tarin big storm.

"By the time littil Rar Ripe wer ten weeks ole, Doltin begun tu be pow'ful plenty in the neighborhood. Even the brats know'd his hoss's tracks, an' go whar he wud, the road led ni ontu Wat's, ur the widder's, tu git thar. My time tu play my four aces hed 'bout cum."

"And so has orderly bed time. I wish to repose," remarked the man of Useful Knowledge, in the square-tail coat, and cloth gaiters.

Sut opened his eyes in wonder.

"Yu wish tu du what?"

"I wish to go to sleep."

"Then why the h——l didn't yu say so? Yu mus' talk Inglish tu me, ur not git yersef onderstood. I warn't edikated at no Injun or nigger school. Say, bunty, warn't yu standid deep in sum creek, when the taylure man put the string to yu, fur that ar cross atwix a rounabout an' a flour barril, what yu'se got on in place of a coat?"

My self-made guest looked appealingly at me, as he untied his gaiters, evidently deeply insulted. I shook my head at Sut, who was lying on his breast, with his arms crossed for a pillow, but with head elevated like a lizard's, watching the traveler's motions with great interest.

"Say, George, what dus repose mean? That wurd wer used at me jis' now."

"Repose means rest."

"Oh, the devil hit dus! I'se glad tu hear hit, I tho't hit wer pussonal. I kin repose now, mysef. Say, ole Onsightly Peter; repose sum tu, ef yu kin in that flour barril. I ain't gwine tu hunt fur yure har ontil mor——"

and Sut slept. When morning broke, the Encyclopedia, or Onsightly Peter as Sut pronounced it, had

> "Folded his tent like the Arab,
> And as silently stole away."

Contempt of Court—Almost

"OLE Onsightly Peter tuck his squar-tail cackus kiver away frum this yere horspitable camp, wifout axin fur his bill, ur even sayin 'mornin,' tu us. Le's look roun a littil; I bet he'se stole sumfin. Fellers ove his stripe allers dus. They never thinks a night's lodgin cumplete, onless they hooks a bed-quilt, ur a candilstick, ur sum sichlike. I hates ole Onsightly Peter, jis' caze he didn't seem tu like tu hear me narrate las' night; that's human nater the yeath over, an' yere's more univarsal onregenerit human nater: ef ever yu dus enything tu enybody wifout cause, yu hates em allers arterwards, an' sorter wants tu hurt em agin. An' yere's anuther human nater: ef enything happens tu sum feller, I don't keer ef he's yure bes' frien, an' I don't keer how sorry yu is fur him, thar's a streak ove satisfackshun 'bout like a sowin thread a-runnin all thru yer sorrer. Yu may be shamed ove hit, but durn me ef hit ain't thar. Hit will show like the white cottin chain in mean cassinett; brushin hit onder only hides hit. An' yere's a littil more; no odds how good yu is tu yung things, ur how kine yu is in treatin em, when yu sees a littil long laiged lamb a-shakin hits tail, an' a-dancin staggerinly onder hits mam a-huntin fur the tit, ontu hits knees, yer fingers *will* itch tu seize that ar tail, an' fling the littil ankshus son ove a mutton over the fence amung the blackberry briars, not tu hurt hit, but jis' tu disapint hit. Ur say, a littil calf, a-buttin fas' under the cow's fore-laigs, an' then the hine, wif the pint ove hits tung stuck out, makin suckin moshuns, not yet old enuf tu know the bag aind ove hits mam frum the hookin aind, don't yu want tu kick hit on the snout, hard enough tu send hit backwards, say fifteen foot, jis' tu show hit that buttin won't allers fetch milk? Ur a baby even, rubbin hits heels apas' each uther, a-rootin an' a-snifflin arter the breas', an' the mam duin her bes' tu git hit out, over the hem ove her clothes, don't yu feel hungry tu gin hit jis' one 'cussion cap slap, rite ontu the place what sum day'll fit a saddil, ur a sowin cheer, tu show hit what's atwixt hit an' the grave; that hit stans a pow'ful chance not tu be fed every time hits hungry, ur in a hurry? An' agin: ain't thar sum grown up babys what yu meets, that the moment yer eyes takes em in, yer toes itch tu tetch thar starns, jis' 'bout es saftly es a muel kicks in playin; a histin kine ove a tetch, fur the way they wares thar har, hat, ur watch-chain, the shape ove thar nose, the cut ove thar eye, ur sumthin ove a like littil natur. Jis' tu show the idear, a strange fellow onst cum intu a doggery whar I wer buzzy a-raisin steam, an' had got hit a few poun abuv a bladder bustin pint.

"He tuck off his gloves, slow an' keerful, a-lookin at me like I mout smell bad. Then he flattened em ontu the counter, an' laid em in the crown ove his hat, like he wer packin shuts in a trunk. Then sez he—

" 'Baw-keepaw, ole Champaigne Brandy, vintage ove thuty-eight, ef yu please, aw.'

"He smelt hit slow, a-lookin at hissef in the big lookin-glass ahine the counter, shook his head, an' turned up his mustachus, sorter like a goat hists his tail.

"Mustachus am pow'ful holesum things I speck, tu them what hes the stumick tu wear em. Bes' butter-milk strainers on yeath. All the scrimpshuns ove butter lodges in the har, an' rubbed in makes it grow, like chicken dung dus inyuns. Strains whisky powerful good, what hes dead flies in hit, an' then yu kin comb em off ur let em stay, 'cordin tu yer taste. They changes the taste ove a kiss clear over; makes hit tas' an' smell like a mildew'd saddil-blankit, arter hit hed been rid on a sore-back hoss three hundred miles in August, an' increases yer appertite fur sich things 'cordinly. I seed a blue-bird devil a feller onst, all one spring, a-tryin tu git intu his mouf tu bild a nestes, an' the durn'd fool wer proud ove the bird's preferens, but wudn't let hit git in.

"Rite then, I thought, well, durn yure artifishul no-count soul, an' my toes begun tu tingle. He tuck four trials, a-pourin back an' forrid, afore he got his dram the right depth, a-lookin thru the tumbler like he spected tu see a minner, ur a warter-mockasin in hit. Then he drunk hit, like hit wer caster ile, the infunel fool. Lordy crimminy! how bad my toes wer itchin now. He lit a seegar, cocked hit up to'ards one eye, an' looked at me agin thru the smoke, while he shook his hat over ontu one ove his years. Sez I, 'Mornin mister.'

"He never sed a word, but turned an' started fur the door. When he got six foot nine inches distunt (that's my bes' kickin range), the durned agravatin toe itch overcum me, an' I let one ove these yere hoss-hide boots *go arter 'im;* hit imejuntly cotch up wif the fork ove his coatail, an' went outen my sight, mos' up to the straps. He went flyin outen the doggery door, over the hoss-rack. While he wer in the air, he turned plum roun an' lit facin me wif a cock't Derringer, a-starin me squar in the face. I tho't I seed the bullit in hit lookin es big es a hen's aig. Es I dodged, hit plowed a track acrost the door-jam, jis' es high es my eye-brows. I wer one hundred an' nineteen yards deep in the wheat-field when I hearn hits mate bark, an' he wer a pow'rful quick moshun'd man wif shootin irons.

"I wer sorter fooled in the nater ove that feller, that's a fac'. The idear ove Derringers, an' the melt tu use em, bein mix't up wif es much durned finekey fool es he show'd, never struck me at all, but I made my pint on 'im; I cured my toe itch.

"Well, I allers tuck the cumplaint every time I seed ole Jedge Smarty, but I dusn't try tu cure hit on him, an' so hit jis' hed tu run hits course, onless I met sum-thin I cud kick.

"Wirt Staples got him onst, bad; 'stonished the ole bag ove lor amos' outen his dignity, dam ef he didn't, an' es Wirt tuck a skeer in what's tu cum ove my narashun about the consekinses ove foolin wif uther men's wives, I'll tell yu how he 'stonished ole Smarty, an' then yu'll better onderstand me when I cums tu tell yu how he help't tu 'stonish ole Doltin.

"Wirt hed changed his grocery range, an' the sperrits at the new lick-log hed more scrimmage seed an' raise-devil intu hit than the old biled drink he wer used tu, an' three ho'ns histed his tail, an' sot his bristils 'bout es stiff es eight ove the uther doggery juice wud. So when cort sot at nine o'clock, Wirt wer 'bout es fur ahead as cleaving, ur half pas' that.

"The hollerin stage ove the disease now struck him, so he roar'd one good year-quiverin roar, an' riz three foot

CONTEMPT OF COURT—ALMOST 189

inside the doggery door, an' lit nine more out in the mud, sploshin hit all over the winders, tuther side the street. He hed a dried venerson ham in one han, an' a ten-year old he nigger by hits gallus-crossin in tuther. He waved fus' the nigger an' then the venerson over his head, steppin short an' high, like ontu a bline hoss, an lookin squar atwixt his shoe-heels, wif his shoulders hump'd hi up. Sez he,

" 'Hu—wee,' clear an' loud es a tin ho'n; 'run onder the hen, yere's the blue-tail hawk, an' he's a-flyin low. The Devil's grist mill-dam's broke; take tu yer canoes. Then he roared a time ur two, an' look'd up an' down the street, like a bull looks fur tuther one, when he thinks he hearn a beller. He riz ontu his tip-toes, an' finished a good loud 'Hu-wee.' Es he drap't ontu his heels agin, he yelled so hard his head shook an' his long black har quivered agin; he then shook hit outen his eyes, wipin the big draps ove sweat ofen his snout wif his shut-sleeve, still hangin tu the venerson an' the nigger. Sez he,

" 'Look out fur the ingine when yu hears hit whistil; hits a-whistilin rite now. *Nine*teen hundred an' eighty pouns tu the squar scrimpshun by golly, an *eighty*-nine miles in the shake ove a lamb's tail. Purfeckly clear me jis' ten acres tu du my gesterin on, yu durned Jews, tape-sellers, gentiles, an' jackasses; I'se jis' a mossel ove the bes' man what ever laid a shadder ontu this dirt. Hit wilts grass, my breff pizins skeeters, my yell breaks winders, an' my tromp gits yeathquakes. I kin bust the bottom outen a still by blowinin at the wum, I kin addil a room full ove goose aigs by peepin in at the key-hole, an' *I kin spit a blister ontu a washpot, ontil the flies blow hit*. Listen tu me, oh yu dam puney, panady eatin siterzens, an' soujourners in this half-stock't town; I'se in yearnis' now.' Then he reared a few times agin, an' cut the pidgeon-wing three foot high, finished off wif 'bout haf ove a ho'n-pipe, keepin time abuv his head wif the venerson an' the littil son ove midnite. He hilt em straight out at arm's laingth, leaned way back, an' lookin straight up at the sky, sung 'bout es loud es a cow bellers, one vearse ove the sixteen hundred an' ninety-ninth hyme—

> The martins bilds in boxis,
>   The foxis dens in holes.
> The sarpints crawls in rocksis,
>   The yeath's the home ove moles.
> Cock a-doodil-do, hits movin,
>   An' dram time's cum agin.

'*Yere's* what kin jis' sircumstansully flax out that ar court-hous' full tu the chimbly tops, ove bull-dorgs, Bengal tigers, an' pizen bitin things, wif that ar pusley-gutted, leather whisky jug ove a jedge, tu laig fur em. Cum out yere, yu ole false apostil ove lor, yu cussed, termatis-nosed desipil ove supeners, an' let me gin *yu* a charge. I'll bet high hit busts yu plum open, frum fork tu forrid, yu hary, sulky, choliky durn'd son ove a slush-tub. Cum out yere, oh yu coward's skeer, yu widder's night-mar, yu poor man's heart ache, yu constabil's god, yu lawyer's king, yu treasury's tape-wum, yer wife's dam barril ove soap-grease, saften'd wif unbought whisky.'

"Thinks I, *that's hit;* now Wirt yu'se draw'd an ace kerd at las', fur the winders wer histed an' the cort hearn every word.

"Wirt wer bilin hot; nobody tu gainsay him, hed made him piedied all over; he wer plum pizen. So arter finishin his las' narashun, aim'd at Jedge Smarty, he tuck a vigrus look at the yung nigger, what he still hilt squirmin an' twistin his face, what warn't eyes, glazed all over wif tears, an' starch outen his nose, an' sez he, 'Go.' He flung hit up'ards, an' es hit cum down, hit met one ove Wirt's boots. Away hit flew, spread like ontu a flyin squirrel, smash thru a watch-tinker's winder, totin in broken sash, an' glass, an' bull's-eye watches, an' sasser watches, an' spoons, an' doll heads, an' clay pipes, an' fishin reels, an' sum noise. A ole ball-headed cuss wer a-sittin a-peepin intu a ole watch, arter spiders, wif a thing like a big black wart kiverin one eye, when the smashery cum, an' the fus' thing he knowed, he wer flat ove his back, wif a small, pow'fully skeer'd, ash-culler'd nigger, a-straddil his naik, littil brass wheels spinnin on the floor, an' watches singin like rattil-snakes all roun. I wer a-peepin outen the ole doggery door, an' thinks I, thar, by jingo, Wirt, yu'se draw'd *anuther ace,* an' ef yu hilt enything ove a han afore, yu hes got a sure thing now; so better bet fas', ole feller, fur I rather think the jedge'll 'call yu' purty soon. Wirt seed me, an' ove course tho't ove whisky that moment; so he cum over tu lay on a littil more kindlin wood. I'll swar, tu look at him, yu cudn't think fur the life ove yu, that he hed over-bragged a single word. His britches wer buttoned tite roun his loins, an' stuffed 'bout half intu his boots; his shut bagg'd out abuv, an' wer es white es milk; his sleeves wer rolled up tu his arm-pits, an' his collar wer es wide open es a gate; the mussils on his arms moved about like rabbits onder the skin, an' ontu his hips an' thighs they play'd like the swell on the river; his skin wer clear red an' white, an' his eyes a deep, sparklin, wickid blue, while a smile fluttered like a hummin bird roun his mouf all the while. When the State-fair offers a premin fur *men* like they now dus fur jackasses, I means tu enter Wirt Staples, an' I'll git hit, ef thar's five thousand entrys. I seed ole Doltin cumin waddlin outen the court-hous', wif a paper in his han, an' a big stick onder his arm, lookin to'ards the doggery wif his mouf puss'd up, an' his brows draw'd down. Sez I, 'Wirt, look thar, thar's a 'herearter,' a-huntin yu; du yu see hit? Whar's yer hoss?' He tuck one wickid, blazin look, an' slip't intu the street wif his arms folded acrost his venerson laig.

"Now Wirt wer Wat Mastin's cuzzin, *an' know'd all about the rar ripe bisness*, an' tuck sides wif Wat strong. I'd show'd him the sheriff's note tu Mary, an' he hed hit by heart. The crowd wer now follerin Doltin tu see the fun. When he got in about ten steps, sez Wirt:

"'Stop rite thar; ef yu don't, thar's *no calliker ur combs in Herrin's store*, ef I don't make yu fear'd ove lightnin. I'll stay wif yu till *thar's enuf fros' in hell tu kill snap-beans.*'

"When Wirt menshun'd snap-beans, I seed the sheriff sorter start, an git pale ahine the years.

"'Git intu that ar hog-pen, quick (a-pintin at the court-hous' wif the venerson laig), ur I'll split yer head plum tu the swaller wif this yere buck's laig, yu durn'd ole skaley-heel'd, bob-tail old muley bull; I'll spile yer appertite fur the grass in uther men's pasturs.'

"'Don't talk so loud, Mister Staples; hit discomboberates the court. I hes no papers agin yu. Jis' keep quiet,' sez Doitin, aidgin up slow, an' two ur three depertys sorter flankin.

"Wirt seed the signs. He jis' roared, 'the lion's loose! Shet yer doors.' I seed his har a-flyin es he sprung, an' I hearn a soun like smashin a dry gourd. Thar wer a rushin tugether ove depertys an' humans, an' hit look'd like bees a-swarmin. Yere cum Wirt, mowin his way outen the crowd, wif his venerson, an' sprung ontu his hoss. Thar lay Doltin, flat ove his back, his belly pintin up like a big tater-hill, an' eight ur nine more in es many shapes, lyin all about, every durned wun a-holdin his head, 'sceptin Doltin, an' he wer plum limber. Wirt hed a pow'ful fine hoss, an' he rid 'im roun that crowd like a Cumanche Injun, ur a suckis, es fas' es quarter racin, jis' bustin his froat a-hollerin. Then he went fur the court-hous', rid in at one door, an' out at tuther. Es he went, he flung that mortul buck's hine laig at the jedge's head, sayin:

"'Thar's a dried supeaner fur yu, yu dam ole cow's paunch.'

"Es hit cum, hit hit the tabil afore him, an' sent a head ove hit, the broken glass ove a big inkstand, an' a half pint ove ink, intu the face ove the court; then glancin up, hit tuck a par ove specks what hed been rared back ontu his head, outen the winder wif hit. Ole Smarty hes a mity nice idear ove when tu duck his head, even ef a rainstorm ove ink am cumin upwards intu his face. Warn't that mons'ous nigh bein a case ove contempt ove court?"

Trapping a Sheriff

"WHEN Doltin got his hed cooper'd up arter that cavin in hit got frum the venerson laig, so he cud think up sarcumstances a littil, he sent fur me. You see Jim Dunkin, the ornary devil, foreswore hissef, an's now a parjurd man; he tole Doltin that I hilt his note tu Mary, an' he wer arter hit hot. Well, I tuck aboard enuf wood tu run me a few miles, an' over I went; but fus' gin the note tu Wirt Staples, tu keep, fur fear the ole bull-dorg mout *skeer hit outen me.*

"Thar lay Doltin on a low one-hoss bedstid, wif 'bout three wet towils tied roun' his head, an' cabbige leaves a-peepin out all roun' frum onder em. 'Bout half ove a doctor's shop wer sittin ontu a tabil.

"Thar sot the sheriff's wife, in a rocking cheer. She wer boney an' pale. A drunk Injun cud a-red a Dutch almanac thru her nose, and ther wer a new moon ove indigo onder her eyes, away back intu them, fifty foot or so. I seed her tear wells; thar windlass wer broke, the buckits in staves, an' the waters all gone; an' away still furder back, two lights shin'd, saft, like the stars above 'jis 'afore thar settin. Her wais wer flat, an' the finger cords on her han's wer mos' as high, an' look'd es tight, and show'd es clar thru the skin, es the strings ove a fiddil. The han' hitsef wer white, not like snow, but like paint, and the forkid blue veins made hit look like a new map ove the lan' ove death. She wer a coughin wif her han' on her hart, like she hed no more spittil nur she hed tears, an' not much louder nor a crickit chirpin in a flute; yit in spite ove all this, a sweet smile kiver'd her feeters, like a patch ove winter sunshine on the slope ove a mountin, an' hit staid thar es steddy an' bright es the culler dus tu the rose. I 'speck that smile will go back up wif her when she starts home, whar hit mus' a-cum frum. She must onst been mons'us temtin tu men tu look at, an' now she's loved by the angils, fur the seal ove thar king is stamp'd in gold on her forrid. Her shoulder blades, as they show'd thru her dress, made me think they wer wings a sproutin fur her flight tu that cumfort and peace she desarves so well. She's a dealin wif death now. Her shroud's in the house, an' sum ove the nex' grass will grow on her grave, an' she's willin fur the spring tu cum. *She* is ready, an' *I* raly wish she hed started. As' I look fus' at him, an' then at her, I'd swore tu a hereafter. Yes, *two* hereafters, by golly: one way up behint that ar black cloud wif the white bindin fur sich as her; the tuther hereafter needs no wings nor laigs ither tu reach; when you soaks yersef in sin till yer gits heavy enuf, yu jes' draps in. An' way down in the souf corner ove hit thar's a hole, what the devil prides hissef on, fur hit is jis' sixteen thousin times hotter nur a weldin heat, an' plum intu the center ove hit, wifout tetchin wall ur rafter, sum fine arternoon Doltin'll drap head fus' an' dive deeper nur a poun' plum bob kin fall in nine months. Wouldn't you like to be in a safe place to see him when he plouts in, wif a '*whish*' intu that ar orful strong smellin, melted mixtry ove seleck damnashun. He'll sizzil like a wet cat flung intu a kittil ove bilin fat, an' he'll slosh hit up agin the walls so high that hit will be a week tricklin down agin, an' sen' the blazin draps so high, that they'll light on yeath an' be mistakened fur shootin stars.

"Well, he ris up ontu his elber, and sez he, mighty saft like, 'Mister Lovingood, you holes a note ove mine fur *ten dullers*. I wants tu pay hit,' a holding out a bank ove Tennessee X, an' a winkin prudins' an' silence at me frum onder the aidge ove a cabbige leaf monsus strong.

"Sez I, 'Mr. Doltin, I'se powerful sorry, but the fac' is, I'se dun traded yer note.'

"'Oh, dear me! I hopes not; hu did you trade hit tu?'

"I look'd strait intu the center spot ove the eye wif the cabbige leaf curtin, es innersent es a lam, an' sed, slow an' sorry like, 'WIRT STAPLES, Wat Mastin's cuzzin.'

"He jerk'd his elber frum onder him like springin the triggers ove a bar-trap, an fell back, pulled down the cabbige leaf low, and sez he, low atwixt his teef, tu keep his wife frum hearin hit, 'You've play'd hell.'

"'Folks generlly sez that's my trade,' sez I.

"'What did yu say yer trade wer sir?' sed she, es saft

an' sweet es a well-played flute.

"'Tradin notes ove hand mum,' sez I.

"'Oh! I hopes you don't take usury, sir.'

"'No mam,' sez I, 'by no means; I takes *venerson* fur em.'

"'Go tu yure room,' growled the durned ole sore-headed bar; I wants tu talk tu this pusson.'

"Dam 'im, he call'd me a *pusson*.

"Arter she lef, sez he, 'Yu git that paper back, an' fetch hit tu me, an' ef yu don't, I'll put yu in jail, 'bout that nigger meetin business, an' thar yu'll *stay*. Dus yer onderstan' me? I'll gin yer venerson,' a-grittin his teeth, an' shakin his finger at me like a snake's tongue; 'don't yu fool wif me, yu infernel grasshopper ove hell.'

"Sez I, 'I'll try,' a-backing fur the door.

"Sez he 'Stop,' an' I stopt, but wif the door leaf hilt sorter atwixt us, an' all ove my laigs outside.

"'Yu *stole* that paper frum Missis Mastin. Now yu git hit imejuntly, if not sooner, ur yu'll lay in jail till—'

"'Thar's enuf white fros' in hell tu bite snap-beans,' sez I, a-mockin his bull voice.

"He jis' rar'd back agin, an' let his hans fall on the floor each side the cot, es I shot the door ahine me. I hearn a hoss snort sumwhar. He mus' a been sorter flustrated at me, fur the cabbidge leaves wer wilted wif sweat.

"I tole Wirt Staples what hed been sed an' dun over tu the sheriff's hous'. So him an' me an his wife an' Wat Mastin, a few days arter, hilt a rale no-nothin convenshun, tu oursefs, at Wirt's hous'. We bilt a trap, an' baited hit. Now, what du yu reckon we used fur bait? Nuffin but *Mary Mastin herself;* an' by golly we cotch Doltin the fus' pass. Wirt's wife did the planin, an' ef she aint smart fur an' 'oman, I aint a nat'ral born durned fool. She aint one ove yure she-cat wimmin, allers spittin an' groanin, an' swellin thar tails 'bout thar vartu. She never talks a word about hit, no more nor if she didn't hev eny; an' she hes es true a heart es ever beat agin a shiff hem, ur a husban's shut. But she am full ove fun, an' I mout add as purty es a hen canary, an' I swar I don't b'l'eve the 'oman knows hit. She cum intu our boat jis' caze Wirt wer in hit, and she seed lots of fun a-plantin, an' she wanted tu be at the reapin of the crap.

"Well, the fust thing did wer tu make her she-nigger overlay the road fur Doltin, an' tell him that Mary Mastin hed sarch'd my pockits when I wer asleep, an' foun' a note ove his'n, an' that she wanted him tu meet up wif her nex arternoon, jis' arter dark, back ove the blackberry patch, an' he'd *git his note*. The cussed ole billy-goat jis' sot in tu lickin his lips and roachin his back, like he wer a-tas'in the farwell ove ole brandy. He ris in his stirrups an' swore he'd be thar, ef hit rain'd red hot railroad spikes, an' bilin tar.

"Wirt's wife got yearly supper, a rale suckit-rider's supper, whar the 'oman ove the hous' wer a rich b'lever. Thar wer chickens cut up, an' fried in butter, brown; white, flakey, light, hot biskit, made wif cream; scrambil'd aigs; yaller butter; fried ham, in slices es big es yure han; pickil'd beets, an' cowcumbers; roas'in ears, shaved down an' fried; sweet taters, baked; a stack ove buckwheat cakes, as full ove holes es a sifter; an' a bowl ove strained honey, tu fill the holes. I likes tu sock a fork intu the aidge of one of them spongy things 'bout es big es a hat crown, put a spoonful ove honey onder hit, an' a spoonful ove honey atop ove hit, an' roll hit up ontu the fork like a big segar, an' start hit down my froat aind fus', an' then jis' sen' nine more after hit, tu hole hit down. Nex tu speerits, they goes down the bes'. I kin tas'e em es low down es the bottim ove my trowsis pokits. Fur drinks, she hed coffee, hot, clar an' brown, an' sweet milk es cold es a rich man's heart. Ontu the dresser sot a sorter lookin pot-bellied bottil, half full ove peach brandy, watchin a tumbler, a spoon, an' a sugar bowl. Oh! massy, massy, George! Fur the sake ove yure soul's 'tarnil well-far, don't yu es long es yu live ever be temtid by money, ur buty, ur smartness, ur sweet huggin, ur shockin mersheen kisses, tu marry ur cum *ni* marryin eny gal a-top this livin green yeath, onless yu hes seed her yursef cook jis' sich feedin as that wer. Durnashun, I kin tas'e hit now, jis' es plain es I tase's that ar festergut, in that ar jug, an' I swar I tasis *hit* plain. I gets dorg hongry every time I sees Wirt's wife, ur even her side-saddil, ur her frocks a-hangin on the close-line.

"Es we sot down, the las' glimmers ove the sun crep

thru the histed winder, an' flutter'd on the white tabilcloth an' play'd a silver shine on her smoof black har, es she sot at the head ove the tabil, a-pourin out the coffee, wif her sleeves push'd tight back on her white roun' arm; her full throbbin neck wer bar to the swell ove her shoulders, an' the steam ove the coffee made a movin vail afore her face, es she slowly brush'd hit away wif hur lef han', a-smilin an' a-flashin hur talkin eyes lovinly at her hansum husbun. I thot ef I wer a picter-maker, I cud jis' take that ar supper an' that ar 'oman down on clean white paper, an' make more men hongry, an' hot tu marry, a-lookin at hit in one week, nor ever ole Whitfield convarted in his hole life; back-sliders, hippercrits, an' all, I don't keer a durn.

"Well, arter the supper things wer put away, an' the cows milkt, I hilt the calves off by the tail, tu make myself useful; Wirt an' *me* by golly, an' Wirt's wife, an' Wat Mastin went over tu the blackberry patch, tu inishiate ole Doltin intu the seekrit ove home-made durnashun. The moon wer 'bout four days old; yu cud scarcely tell a man frum a stump, sixty yards off han', arter night farly sot in; jis' the kine ove a night fur sly meetins ur stealin, fur the yeath.

"We'd scasely got things fix'd an ourselfs hid seperit when we hearn his ole hosses huffs soundin on the hard road. That soun' stopt, an' torreckly we hearn a low, patridge whistil, *'Whee-chee,' 'Whee-chee,' 'Bob White,'* tuther side ove the patch.

"'Oh! the durn'd ole fool,' said Wirt tu his wife. 'Partridges don't whistil *arter night.'*

"Sez she, 'The whipporwill wud be better,' an' she whistil'd *'whip-poor-will'* in her froat sumhow, so like that I thot I seed the spot onder one's wings.

"Ole Doltin tuck hit up an' answered, cummin nigher *'whippoorwill.'* Purty soon we seed him, loomin big up agin the sky. He'd whistil an' listen, an' cum a littil, steppin saft es a cat. *'Whee-chee,' 'whee-chee,' 'wee-chee,'* whistled Missis Staples, so *low* an' sweet yu jis' cud hear hit. The tone of that whistil sed 'cum lov,' 'cum lov,' so plain I cud scarcely sit still myself. I swear, I thot I hearn *his heart a-beatin.* I jis' know'd mine wud a been a-poundin like the devil a-beatin tanbark, ef I'd been a-spectin what he wer."

"Stop a moment, Mr. Lovingood," said an old batchelor, an old field schoolmaster, who was one of Sut's auditory; "allow me to interrupt you, that I may more clearly comprehend your story. What was this Mr. Dalton in expectation of?"

Sut looked up at the overhanging elm boughs, and said carelessly, "Oh, nuffin but his note, I speck. Say yu thar mister a-b ab; is the fool-killer in the parts yu cum frum, duin his juty, ur is he ded?"

"I never saw such a personage."

"I thot so, by the jinglin Jehosephat."

The old gentleman turned to me and asked in a confidential whiper, "Is not that person slightly deranged?"

"Oh, no, not at all, he is only troubled at times with violent attacks of durn'd fool."

"He is laboring under one *now*, is he not?"

I nodded my head. "Go on, Sut."

"When ole Doltin got wifin ten steps, Missis Staples stept forrid outen the briars, wif her bonnet sorter over her face. He jis' gin a low, gurglin sort ove bray, an' sprung squar at her. He grabbed her in his arms a-dartin his ole pouch'd out mouf at her face, like a blue crane sen's his bill arter minners, she a-dodgin so that every dip hit the bonnet. Sez he, 'My dear Margaret, what makes you so skittish, tu-night. Don't be——'

"Wat Mastin hed closed his paw on tu the knot ove his neck hanketcher, an' comenc'd a-twis'in hit hard.

" 'Yu infurnel ole scoundril, I'se cotch yu at las'. What's yu a-duin wif my wife?'

" 'Nuf—nufin. Yer—yer wife, got her coatail tangled in the briars, an' I wer jis' in a neighborly way *ontanglin her.*'

" 'Yas,' sez Wat, 'an' dam ef I don't ontangle yu, in a neighborly way. Say the shortes' an' mos' sarchin pray'r yu knows, fur yure season's over.'

"Jis' then Missis Staples spoke up, like she wer vishusly mad, 'Don't yu git *too smart,* Wat Mastin, 'bout yer sorril-top wife. I aint her, by a frock full. Jis' go home tu Mary, an' simmer down cool; yu hev no bisniss yere.'

"Wat 'tended tu be stonish'd. Sez he, 'I begs pardon,' an' step'd back frum Doltin. The ole cuss wer pow'fly 'stonish'd hissef, an' glad all over too, fur hit spilt Wat's title tu choke him tu deth.

"Hu in the devil kin she be, an' hu wer she 'spectin tu meet? wer now Doltin's tho'ts, an' he aiged up tu her agin, when Wirt at one spring lit atwix' em.

"'Susan—Doltin, by—— I wants tu know what this means?' Doltin tho't ove the venerson laig, an' he sed in a houn' whimper, 'I never tetched her,' an' broke tu run. In two jumps Wirt cotch 'im and fotch 'im back by his coat collar.

"Sez Missis Staples, 'Han' me the shawl yu promis'd me (she said this sorter low, and pitiful like), afore yu desarts me.'

"'Shawl! shawl!' shouted Wirt. 'Oh! yu preshus pair ove dam furnitur-takers.'

"I now stept forth jis' so, 'bout seving foot. Sez I, 'Mr. Doltin, I hes fotch yu that note yu rit tu Mary Mastin,' in a seckrit sort ove whisper.

"'Never mine hit now, Mister Lovingood, never mine; I'se pow'fl busy jis' now; sum uther time'll du.'

"Sez I, 'Yu mus' take hit now. Yu talked ove jugin me 'bout the durn'd thing. Yere hit is,' an' I reach'd hit forrid, an' Wat grabbed hit. Ole Doltin groan'd.

"Sez Wat, a-rubbin hit onder Doltin's snout, *'that's testermony* ontu yu, yu dam ole raskil.'

"'Yas,' sez Wirt, a-pintin tu Susan, 'an thar stan's one hundred and twenty poun's *more testermony.'*

"She purtended to cry, an' she sed, 'Oh, Mister Doltin, what made yu use me so?'

"'I wish I may drap dead ef ever I used yu at all,' sed Doltin, right quick.

"'Yu hes ruinated me, Mister Doltin.'

"'*I never*,' said Doltin.

"'An' yu never fotch me—no—no—sh-sh-all arter all, hu, hu, hu,' an' she wiped her eyes.

"'I don't owe you no shawl; wish I may drap dead in a minut ef I dus.'

"'Hu, hu, hu,' sez she; 'yu never gin me a thing yet, yu dratted stingy hog, yu.'

"I swar he wer the wust befoozeled man I ever saw; he rub'd his eyes wif his fis', an' batted em a few times; then he looked wide open owl fashun, fus' at wun an then at tuther, like he'd been dreamin a orful night-mar, an' wurn't sure whether he wer awake yet. Susan, still a-cryin, an' a-talkin 'bout hevin his heart's blood, tellin Missis Doltin, killin hersef, an' I dono what all. A gran' tho't now struck im, an' he jis' roar'd, 'I is the high sheriff ove this county, an' I *cumands the peace.*'

"Wurn't that a smashin lick?

"Sez Wirt, 'Strip, high sheriff ove this country; I'se gwine tu hang yu dorg fashun. Wat, han' me that rope.' The blusterin ole bell wether jis' wilted down' an' sot in tu strippin slow, an' a-beggin, an' a-promisin, an' a-makin money offers, we helpin him tu du his shuckin. I foun' a par ove wimin's shoes, his buckskin gloves an' a smellin bottil in his coat pockit. Missis Staples slipt off tu the hous', when the strippin begun, an' I don't blame her.

"Well, when we got all off but his shut an' shoes, Wirt slipp'd the noose in wun aind ove the rope over his head, an' thar wer tied tu tuther aind a ball ove tow soaked in tupentine es big es a half bushel, wifout his seein hit. I'd fotch a par ove wile, vigrus, skeer'd tom-cats in each aind ove a bag, wif leather cullars, an a big fish-hook sowed tu each cullar by a foot ove strap. While Wirt wer fixin the noose, so es not tu choke, I slipp'd up ahine him, an' hooked a cat tu each corner ove his shutail, a-holden em off; he wer so trimblin an' skeered he didn't feel me. While I wer duin this, Wat struck a match an' lit the tupentine, sayin:

"'I means tu toas' yu es yu swings, yu dam maleafactory.' I jis' craned forrid, an' whispered intu his year—

"'Bulge squar fur the briars; they won't foller in thar.'

"By the great golly, when he hearn that sentiment, cuppled es hit wer wif Wat's toastin idear, he jis made a rale hoss lunge, *an' I drap't the cats*. Wun tuck up his bar back, a-haulin up arter him the noth corner ove the shutail onder-handid, an' tuther wun tuck down his thigh, a-haulin the souf corner ove the shutail arter *him.* They pulled agin each uther like ontu two wile steers in a yaller-jackids nes'. The cat-a-gwine up hill, made the ole feller tote that side, an' shoulder sorter ahead ove tuther, like he wer leanin frum a hot fire. The cat gwine down hill, made him lift that laig like a spring-halted hoss, only a heap faster,

while the briars hookin him everywhar, made him dodge
all over, every way at onst. Frum his moshuns, he mout
a-been pussessed wif the devil, pow'fully. Yu never seed
sich lap-sided, high up, low down, windin about, jerkin,
oneven runnin in the world, but every durned step ove hit
wer strait away frum whar we wer, squar thru the briar
patch. The tupentine lit up a bright road ahine him,
kivered wif broke down an' tore up briars, an' his white
shut, an' the cats' eyes 'zembled a flag ove truce, kivered
wif litnin-bugs. I think I never seed es meny cat's-eyes
in es many places afore, tu be no more cats than thar
wer; tails too, wer ruther numerous, an' sorter swelled,
an' claws a plenty. The noise he made soundid jis' like
a two-hoss mowin-mersheen, druv by chain-lightnin,
a-cuttin thru a dry cane brake on a big bet. An' thar wer
wif the noise a ondercurrent ove soun, like tarin starched
muslin; this, I speck wer the briars an' cats a-breakin
holts. 'Ha, ha!' sez Wirt; 'wudn't he be great in a new
country tu open out roads, ur tote news ove the cumin
ove the Injuns? Hell! how he travils! Listen, jis' listen.
Don't he make things roar?' I run tu his hoss, an'
mounted, an' tuck thru tu Wat's afore he got roun that
far. I jump't off in the thicket, an' crept up tu the road,
furnint Wat's door, tu see him tar apas'. Yere he cum;
I seed his lite a-shinin, long afore I seed him, way abuv the
trees; *hit* warn't hid onder no bushel. Wirt wer openin on
his trail, makin the mountains ring wif yells an' dreadful
threats. Doltin toted his lite pow'ful irregular; sumtimes
hit wer trailin on the yeath, an' sumtimes hit warn't, by
'bout fifteen foot. Hit wer a-lightin on, an' a-flyin off the
fence, on bof sides ove the lane, an' yu cud a-seed tu
a-pick'd strawberries, an' hit roar'd like a storm; the
moshuns ove that lite, I speck, wer govern'd by the workin
ove the cats. I seed the activ bulge ove one cat onder his
shut, a-tryin hits durndes tu pull hits corner ove the shutail
up onder the collar, at the back ove his naik; the tuther
cat wer a-dividin hits time, 'bout ekal, a-jumpin at the
weeds, an' a-tryin tu run furder down his big laig, an' they
swap't work now an' then: the down-hill cat wud go up
onder the shut an' a-tarin big fight imejuntly foller'd,
aindin in tuther cat cumin down a spell. While they wer
bof up thar atwixt Doltin an' his shut, he look'd pow'ful

hump-back'd, an' lordamity! how low he'd run then. Sweet Margery! Jis' think ove two agravated, onsantified he cats at yearnis' war, makin yer bar-back thar battil groun, an' pendin *on yer hide fur all thar foot-holts.* I swar hits a rale red-pepper waknin idear, jis' tu think ove, wifout a cat in a mile—jewillekins! The eyes an' tails wer dreadful tu behole, an' thar groanin an' spittin beat cats when they'se courtin, wus nur they dus city folks at the same work.

"Mary hed hearn the noise, an' seed the lite, so she cum tu the gate, jis' es the ole exhited fernomenon tore apas'. She fotch a scream.

" 'Dear bless us! What's all that? Oh, mammy, run out yere quick, an' see the devil a-chasin whippwils.'

"When she sed that, Doltin tho't ove the whipporwill *he'd* hearn at the briar-patch, an' b'leved Mary wer mixed up wif the thing, an' he sobbed out—

" 'Oh yu dam 'saitful b—h, this is yure work.'

" 'Oh, mammy, mammy, that's poor Mister Doltin's voice, as sure as yu ar born'd! The poor dear man's ded, an' that's him. Ole Smutty's arter, wif a torch ove hell-fire. I dus wonder what he's been duin?'

"She sed this sorter whifflin. I put my han roun my mouf, an' bellered thru em in the mos' doleful way yu ever hearn, frum the thicket—

" 'Margarit Mastin, the lawfal wife ove Watson Mastin, the blacksmith, prepar tu go down whar thar's no sly courtin, nur rar ripe garden-seed. Margarit, thar's rath tu cum, yer crap's laid by, prepar,' an' I groaned.

"She arched her naik, an' tuck a wild blazin look over at the thicket, like she wer studyin 'bout sumthin, an' sez she, short an' vigrus—

" 'Durn my soul ef I go a step,' an' jis' busted thru the standin corn like a runaway hoss. Thinks I, that ar blade will never git religun frum a skeer. The ole 'oman got tu the door, jis' in time tu hear the las' words, an' the soun Mary made a-tarin thru the corn. She wer a-pinnin up her frock-bussum. Sez I, doleful—

" 'Peggy Jane, my b'loved wife, I'se in hell, a-sufferin fur robbin the peddler; *yu made me du hit!*' Sez she—

"Sammy, *I didn't;* I only tole yu we needed his truck.' Sez I—

" 'Fetch me sum warter, fur my tung's parch'd wif fervent heat.' Sez she—

" 'Thar's a spring back ove the ridge thar' (that wer a cussed lie). Sez I—

" 'I'm a-cummin fur a gourd.' Sez she—

" 'Thar's nara gourd yere.' Dam ef she didn't hist all her coats, haf a foot abuv her knees, an' tuck thru the co'n too.

"I went intu the cabin, drawed one ove Doltin's gloves ontu littil Rar Ripe's head, fur a night-cap. Hits name wer printed wif ink roun the wris'; this went roun hits forrid; tuther glove I put in Wat's overcoat pockid, a-hangin on the wall, mounted the hoss, an' tuck acrost the ridge tu head off Doltin at the ferry. The ferryman's ole whipporwill wife hear the noise ove his cumin, an' seed the lite shinin fru the winder. So she bounced outen bed in her shiftail, an' run tu the door. Sez she—

" 'Laws a massy! Ole man, git up quick, an' set em over; make haste, ur they'll swim. The big show's a-cumin in a hurry, fur yere's the rhionoserenus aready, an' lots ove monkeys clost ahine him, an' the big Barnum Bengal lite arter them. Good lordy! What tails! Grashus me, what a noise! Marcyful hevings, what a belly! An'——Oh, lord a massy on my poor soul! Sakes alive!'

"She pernounced these las' words like she wer pow'ful shamed, an' I speck the fool wer, fur she pulled up what she tuck tu be her aprun, an' kivered her face, an' shet the door wif a snap, an' lef hersef *on the outside*. I holler'd 'Higher—yer forrid ain't kivered yet.' She run roun the chimley outen sight, still holdin up her aprun.

"Doltin flew apas', shot down the bank, run thru the ferryboat an' plouted off the fur aind head fust intu the river. When he got farly tu swimin, hit wer cumfurtin an' nice tu look at frum a high pint. He swum breas' high fur tuther bank, and the durn'd cats, contrary tu the las', wer swimin fur *this* wif thar tails trait up, an' leanin frum each uther. This straiched his shutail flat ove the warter, an' the lite wer a-bouncin over the waves on Doltin's wake, aidgin em all wif gold. He look'd like a big high preshur snapin turkil, wif a dark head, white shell, an' the cats answered fur a par ove activ, brindil hine laigs. The river wer trubbil'd pow'ful, a-slushin high up the banks, an' a-slappin up agin the rake ove the ferry-boat, fur he wer a-stirrin hit plum tu the mud. Every now an' then he'd snort like a hoss, an' look back over his shoulder; his eyes wer es big es a bull's, an' blazed like ontu two furnace-doors; that mine ove his'n mus' a-been pow'ful active jis 'bout then. Cats—ropes—mad husbuns—an' a orful hell perdominatin amung loose tho'ts ove wimen an' thar onsartinty as he riz tuther bank, wif the limber cats danglin roun his laigs. I holler'd over:

"'Say thar, rar ripe cat 'tachmints am wus in law nur sashararas, ain't they?'

"He never sed a word, but crawled tired like intu the paw-paw thicket, drownded cats, rope, wet tow, an' all. When he got home he tole his wife a doleful tale. How the Democrats, jis' caze he wudn't tell the nonuthings' seckrit, hed tied him tu a wile hoss's tail, an' turned hit loose, an' then started a passenger injine ontu his trail tu skeer the hoss. He knowed they did, fur he seed the head-lite clost arter 'im, the hole way, an' hearn the *tchish, tchish shew!* ove the steam. (Cats, George, by golly! Nuffin but cats.) What a thundrin liar that man mus' be; but lyin's born'd wif sum folks, jis like squint-eyes. While his wife wer ilin ove his torn hide, an' a checkerin his back wif stripes ove court-plarster, she axed him how so much *fur* cum tu be stickin tu his wouns. He sed the hoss run thru a hatter's shop wif 'im. Warn't that right down shifty?

"Then sez she, 'Yer shut an' yu bof smell sorter catty, strong like. When she hinted at cats, he rar'd up on aind, lookin wild round the room; sez he, *'Whar's eny cats?'*

"George, them ar tom-cats mus' a-scratched intu his con-shuns afore they died, fur he jined chuch jis' es soon he got abil tu walk thar. Hits strange, haint hit? In ole times I hearn tell they hed cities whar fellers run tu, an' wer safe arter they'd dun sum pow'ful devilmint."

"Yes, Sut; cities of refuge."

"Well, durn my rags ef gittin ove religun ain't the city ove rayfuge now-a-days; yu jis' let a raskil git hissef cotch, an' maul'd, fur his dam meanness, an' he jines chuch jis' es soon es he kin straitch his face long enuf tu fill the pius standurd, an' that's eighteen inches fur lean peopil, an' fourteen fur fat ones. I hes a city ove rayfuge mysef, what I allers keeps along wif me," and Sut looked down proudly and fondly at his legs.

"I furgot tu menshun a day ur two arter the catrace, I met up wif Wat Mastin at the store. He moshuned me roun back ove the hous'. Sez he—

"'Sut, hell's tu pay at our hous'. Mary's been hid out sumwhar till this mornin. She cum up draggil'd an' hungry, an' won't say a durn'd word. An' ole Missis McKildrin's plum gone.' Sez I—

"'Ain't yu glad?'

"He stretched his mouf intu the wides' smile yu ever seed, an' slappin me on the back, sez he—

"'I *is*, by golly!'

"Then he lookt serious wif his head down. Sez he—

"'Doltin mus' be a pow'ful parseverin man when he sets his head fur enything.' Sez I—

"'Why?'

"'Caze don't yu think, wif them cats, an' that skeer, an' that hurtin, an' us arter 'im, tu hang 'im es he tho't, he tuck time tu stop an' *see Mary!*' Sez I—

"'Oh no!'

"'Yes he did, fur I foun one ove his gloves in my overcoat pockid, an' he'd gin tuther one tu the baby, fur a night-cap.'

"George, Wat Mastin hes a right thick streak ove durn'd fool in him, sure es yu are born'd.

"Bout three days arter seein Wat I meets up wif Mary on the road. She wer swingin her sun-bonnit afore her by the strings, walkin fas' an' lookin down at the groun. Sez I—

"'Mornin! Missis Mastin; I hes lost two pow'ful fine cats; hes yu seed enything ove 'em roun yere?' Sez she, an' her eyes blazed—

"'I hope they ar in hell, whar yu ought tu be yu infunel mischief-maker yu!'

"The 'oman sartinly hes got sumfin agin me. I wonders what hit kin be?"

Dad's Dog-School

I HAD often laughed at an anecdote anent training a puppy to hold fast, and doubtless so has many of my readers, as told by the gifted W. T. Haskill.

I began to tell it one summer night at our camp-fire, when Sut interrupted me:

"Stop, George; yu can't du jestis' tu that ar doleful bisness. Hit happen'd ur ruther tuck place apupus, in our famerly; hit cudn't a-been did by eny uther peopil on this yeath but us, fur hit am plum clarified dam fool, frum aind tu aind. Dad plan'd hit; an' him, an' mam, an' Sall, an' Bent, an' me—oh, yas! an' the pup. I'd like tu forgot him —we did the work, an' ef we didn't make a purfeck finish'd cumplete durn'd momox outen the thing, thar's no use in hevin a genus fur bein infunel nat'ral born fools et all.

"Dad, he's es tetchy about hit tu this day, es a soreback hoss is 'bout green flies. Ef yu want tu see him shed his shut, quick es a fox kin cum outen a bag, an' fall intu getherin rocks, an' then flingin em, jis' dam permiskusly, a-soltin an' a-pepperin the job wif red hot ravenus homeade cussin, yu growl like ontu a dorg a-holdin ontu a hanketcher, ur a rag, an' yu'll mons'ous soon see a bal'-headed man hot enuf tu fry spit. Hits a pow'ful delikit 'speriment tu try an' git out wifout a scab abuv yer years. Be purfeckly redy tu run es soon es yu growl; ef yu don't, hit'll rain on yu bad. Sures' way is tu growl arter yu hes started, an' ef yu's mons'ous fas' on foot yu may venter tu holler, 'Sick 'im Sugar!' But be keerful; I'se seed hit tried.

"Yu see when I wer 'bout sixteen, Steve Crawley gin me a bull pup, the culler ove rich cream, white onder the belly, an' on the lower aind ove the laigs, blue snout, red eyes, wrinkl'd forrid, an' show'd his teef even when he wus sleepin. Ugly as a she ho'net, an' brave es a trap't rat. Dad tuck pow'fully tu 'im, 'caze thar naters wer sorter like, I reckon. He wer the only critter I ever know'd dad tu be good tu, an' narra pusson yet.

"Late one Saturday, we sot in an' kill'd a-tarin big black an' white yearlin bull beastes, an' on Sunday mornin, arter gittin a big bellyful ove fried liver an' chopp't inyuns, dad sot down ontu the cabin steps, in the sun, a-playin wif 'Sugar,' that wer the pup's name. I wer mounted ontu the fence a-shavin seed-ticks ofen my laigs wif a barlow knife, an' mam wer in the yard sittin ontu the half-bushel wif three ur four ove the childers' heads in her lap, bizzy rite in the middil ove a big still hunt arter insex. At las', sez dad—

"'Sut, s'pose yu tote Sugar off wif yu down tu the crick tu keep 'im frum follerin ove me, an' seein what I dus. Yu cum back when yu hears me beller like ontu a yung bull, an' I'll larn yer dorg tu hole on. I'se jis' studied out the bes' way in creashun tu make 'im hold tu enything ontil bunty hens sprouts tails. This yere day's work'll be the making ove the pup.'

"'How on the yeath, dad, will yu du hit?' sez I.

"Dad got up an' cotch a big hanful ove britches ahine, atwixt the wais'bun an' the fork, rayther nigher the fork tho', an' arter ginin hissef a few good holesum scratchin rubs, sed—

"'Jis' so; I'll make yer sis Sall, thar, sow me up in Suggins's hide (that wer the yearlin's name, mine yu), an' I'll play ho'ned cattil rite squar intu Sugar's han, while yu sicks 'im on, an' ef yu dus the sickin part like yu orter, hit'll be the makin ove that ar pup. When he gits a savin holt ontu the hide, yu seize his tail, an' *sorter* pull 'im back, but don't yu break the holt; ef yu dus yu spiles a dorg, an' when I cums outen the hide, dam ef I don't spile yu.'

"Mam cracked a insex vigrusly atwixt her thumbs, an' then wiped her nails ontu her gown along her thighs, an' sez she—

"'Good law sakes! now fur more onanimated foolishness. Hu ever hearn ove the likes bein dun by the daddy ove a famerly, an' him a bal'-headed man et that, a-shedin his har fur the grave. Lovingood, yu'll keep on wif yer devilmint an' nonsense, ontil yu fetch the day ove jedgement ontu our bar heads sum night, kerthrash, afore hits time, ur sum uther ailment—colery—measils—pollygamy, ur sum sich like, jis' see ef yu don't, an' then yu'll *run*, an' leave me tu fight hit out by mysef, yu know yu will. Now jis' quit, an' let that ar blasted roun-headed pup edecate hissef like yer uther childer dus.'

"'Shet up that ar snagy feedin-hole ove yurn, yu durn'd ole she hempbrake; yu'd 'pose my gwine tu heaving, I raley du b'leve,' sez dad.

"'No I won't,' sez mam, shakin her head. 'Yu'll never try tu du that,' an' she peaner'd her fingers down thru the har, along the side ove one ove the childer's heads, clost arter a knowin ole insex, what hed been raced before; he wer aimin fur the wrinkil onder the year-flap, but he never got thar; he got hissef busted like ontu a 'cussion-cap, 'bout a inch an' a 'alf frum his den.

"'Now,' sez dad, a-turnin tu me, still a-rubbin slow wif the hanful ove britches, 'yu see, Sut; he'll git good holts ontu the hide, smell the blood, an' larn the nater ove the varmint he's a-contendin wif. I'll beller an' make b'leve I'se a-tryin tu git loose't, but not ack cow fur enuf tu tar loose't, ur dishartin 'im. Better nur gwine tu school tu a Yankee cuttin-box 'oman, a durn'd site; an' in a month, jis' let ole widder Bradly's cow jump intu the cabbiges agin, ef she's fond ove freezin snouts wif a dorg. He'll stay wif her ontil apas' milkin time nex day, an' not quit then. Oh! I tell yu hit'll be the makin ove the pup.'

"So dad tuck Sall off tu the loom-hous' whar the hide wer a-hangin. I hed soltid hit good, tu keep frum spilin, till dad cud turn hit intu whisky, an' I whistled off Sugar. Arter I hed gone a few steps, I hollered, 'Oh dad!'

"'What?'

"'S'pose Sugar gits that savin holt yu wer speakin ove, ontu yu; what am I tu du then?'

"'Du hell!' sez dad; 'du nuthin but sick 'im on. Hu ever hearn ove a man's bein dorg-bit thru a cow-hide?' Sez I—

"'He's pow'ful fur reachin fur a pup, better mine, dad.'

"I seed 'im begin tu hunt fur a rock, an' I struck a peart shanghi trot fur the crick. Me an' the yung dorg lay down amung the mint, an' listen'd tu the gurglin ove the warter.

"Well, thinks I, my juty's a plain one enyhow. 'Jis' sick 'im on an' du nuthin else,' an' I means tu du hit, fur hit am tu be the makin ove yu, my sweet Sugar, I raley du 'speck.

"Torreckly I hearn dad a-bellerin jis' the bes' sampil ove

a yearlin's nise yu ever hearn, 'sceptin hit wer a scrimpshun too coarse, an' a littil too fas'; dad wer exhited. 'Boor, woo woff—Bohua a huah'—fust rate, by the jinglin Jehosaphat! thinks I, an' Sugar cock't his years an' bark'd.

"Dad hed fool'd the dorg. The only livin thing I ever know'd 'im tu fool, 'sceptin a new doggery-keeper now an' then, an' mam; she sed he fool'd her pow'ful onst; that wer when she swore hersef tu be the mammy ove his brats.

"Well, thar he wer in the yard ontu his all fours, sow'd up body an' soul in the raw hide, hary side out, an' he'd tuck off every durn'd stich ove his close. I tho't pow'fully how my soltin the hide wer gwine tu work arter the show begun tu be exhitin, an' dad begun tu sweat. Sall hed sow'd his hans plum up intu the hide ove the fore laigs, an' the loose huffs wer floppin an' crackin about below em es he walked, ur paw'd up dus'.

"She hed turn'd the head an' ho'ns back, raw side out, es high es dad's eye-brows, an' tied the nose tu the naik, so he cud see the inimy. His face wer smeer'd wif the blood an' fat, the tail trail'd arter him sorter dead like, his sturn wer way up yander, his hine laigs bein longer nur his fore wuns, an' takin the site altugether hit cudn't be beat, fur a big, ruff, skeery, thing outen hell, ur a mad-hous'.

"I seed mam a-pullin up a bean-pole in the garden, an' arter tarin off the vines she sot hit up in the chimbley corner wifout dad's notisin hit. I whispered 'What's yu gwine tu du wif that ar pole? Gwine a-fishin, say mam?' Sez she—

"'I'se gwine tu play 'She hempbrake' wif hit ontu that ar raw-hide, arter a while.' Then she went an' stud in the door, wif her hans ontu her hips, an' the childer mounted the fence.

"'Well dad,' sez I, 'is yu good ready? Shall I sick 'im on?'

"Dad wer fear'd Sugar'd fine out the trick, an' wudn't speak, but jis' nodded his head, an' durn ef he even didn't du hit like ontu a bull.

"I straddled Sugar, patted him ontu the ribs, an' sez I 'Sick 'im boy,' an' the dorg went squar in. Dad sorter horn'd at 'im an' blow'd. Sugar flew roun, an' my dad flew roun; the tail trail'd limber an' lazy, an' tangled sumtimes amung dad's hine laigs. Sugar, a-huntin fur the right spot tu bite, dad 'tendin like he didn't want 'im tu fine hit. The pup made a gran rush, an' got a holt ni ontu the root ove the tail, an' sot hissef back. My dad kick'd wif bof hine laigs es quick an' vigrus es a muel, an' 'stead ove bellerin, es he orter, he shouted out right plain, 'Oh hell-fire!' He hed kicked the pup plum intu the hous', atwixt mam's laigs. Sez I—

" 'Dad, *that* won't du; that warn't *cow*-kickin at all; them's rale stud-hoss licks. Yu'll never be the makin ove the pup, ef yu pouns 'im that ar way.'

" 'Make hell!' sez dad; 'this hide haint es thick bout the tail es hit orter be fur a yearlin's,' an' he tried tu rub hissef back thar, wif his fore laig; but the loose huffs flopp't about so, an' his hans bein sowed up, he didn't du hit tu suit hissef much, so he backed agin the fence, an' rubbed his rump agin the aind ove a rail, hog fashun, up an' down wif a jerk, yu know.

" 'Is Sugar's teef sharp, ole man?' sez mam, sorter keerless like.

" 'How du I know,' growled dad; 'hits none ove yure bisness, nohow, yu durn'd ole par ove warpin-bars; what du yu know 'bout the makin ove pups?'

"Mam sorter glanced at the bean-pole, but sed nuffin. Sugar wer sittin ontu his tail, his head an' fore laigs stuck out frum under mam's frock-hem, whar dad hed sent 'im, lookin sorter like he hedn't made up his mine adzackly what wer bes' tu du.

"I cotch 'im by the nap ove the naik, an' drug 'im out, an' sick'd 'im on agin. Durn my shut ef he hadn't been studyin tu sum pupus while he wer onder mam's coatails, fur he made his rush at *tuther* aind this time. Sez I—

" 'Don't dodge dad, the hide's thicker 'bout the ho'ns then hit am 'bout the tail.' I'd scarcely spoke, when I hearn Sugar's jaws snap. The yearIin's tail warn't draggin lazy now. Hit wer stiff strait out, way high up, an' sweepin the air clar ove insex, all roun the yard. Jis' then I wudn't a-tuck ten dullers fur my dorg.

" '*Baw aw!*' sez dad.

" 'Yearlin fur the yeath, adzackly. Yu mocks thar voice better nur yu dus thar kickin,' sez I.

"I wer disappointed, fur I wer listenin fur sum durn'd plain Inglish frum dad, fur Sugar hed got hissef a steel-trap holt ontu the pint ove his snout, an' his upper-lip. Nose tu nose they wer, an' no yearlin skin atwixt, not a durn'd inch es I cud see. Dad's ole warty snout wer pull'd out tu a pint, like ontu a mad bar's, an' es taper, an' red an' sharp es a beet. The lip wer straiched es fur onder hit, like ontu a shovil-plow, ur a store-keeper's tin coffee-scoop, a-ketchin red gravy frum the snout. Great golly! how sweet hit mus' a-hurt; hit makes *my* snout itch now.

"'Ka-ka-a!' sed Sugar, leanin way back, an' wallin his eye up at me. Dad leaned way forrid, an' they swap't sides ove the yard faster nur folks turns in a dance, an' the tail a-keepin every durn'd fly an' gnat outen the yard fur six foot high. Jis' then I wudn't a-tuck twenty dullars fur my dorg.

"The childer all yell'd, an' sed 'Sick 'im'; they tho't hit wer all gwine jis' es dad wanted, the durn'd littil fools. Sugar wagg'd his tail, an' roun they'd fly agin.

"I hearn a new soun in the thicket, an' hit bein Sunday, I wer sorter 'spectin a retribushun ove sum nater. I look'd that way, an' there I seed the bald aind ove Squire Hanley's ole Sunday hoss, a-pushin hits way thru the chinkepin bushes, the Squire hissef up on daik, a-steerin wif wun hand, an' a-fendin off the lims an' burrs wif tuther. Thinks I, thar, by golly! Yere's a regular two hundred an' twenty-five poun retribushun, arter us, an' our famerly devarshun sure enuf, armed wif a hyme book, an' loaded tu the muzzil wif brimstone, bilin pitch, forkid flames, an' sich uther nicitys es makes up the devil's brekfus'; an' sum ove hit am gwine tu be ladled out tu us, rite now, ef the Squire's face am tu be trusted es a sign. Hit looked jis' like he'd swaller'd a terbacker-wum, dipp'd in aquafortis, an' cudn't vomit. Even his pius ole hoss show'd a grieved spirit frum foretop tu lip. A appertite tu run began tu gnaw my stumick, an' I felt my face a-swellin wif shame. I wer shamed ove dad, shamed ove mam's bar laigs an' open collar, shamed ove mysef, an' dam, ef I minds right, ef I warn't a mossel shamed ove the pup. But when I seed the squar, blazin look mam met him wif, I made up my mine ef she cud stan the storm, I cud, an' so I didn't run that time— nara durn'd step.

"Squire Hanley wer one ove the wonderfulest men in all my knowin. He wore a hat ten years, an' wore a nail in the church wall bright, a-hangin hit on. He wore a holler spot in the side ove his walkin-stick, wif his finger allers tetchin the same place, an' he wore anuther greasy holler in one ove the groanin bainches, ni ontu the noth corner ove the pulpit, jis' like the sittin hole in a shoemaker's stool, only hit warn't lined wif leather. His pea-sticks wer shod wif spikes, his fire wood wer clar ove knots es waggen timber, his hens never laid on a Sunday, an' sot when he told em to. He gin the hole ove Sunday tu the Lord, an' shaved notes two days onder the skin ove weekly days, an' allers made the feller what got shaved, wait an' git prayed fur; an' he throw'd intu the bargin a track ur two, about the vanity ove layin up store goods on yeath, fur the moths et the broadcloths, an' the thieves stole tuther things. He toted the munny-puss ove the chuch, an' histed the tchunes an' the backsliders. He wer secon enjineer ove a mersheen, made outen a mess ove sturgeon-backed, sandy-heeled ole maids, devarsed wives, ur wimen what orter been wun ur tuther; an' uther thin minded pussons, fur the pupus, es they sed, ove squelchin sin in the neighborhood, amung sich domestic heathins es us, but raley fur the mindin giner'lly ove everybody else's bisness. I forgot tu menshun his nose; hit wer his markin feetur; no uther mortil ever hed heart tu tote jis' sich anuther nose. The skin ofen hit wud a-kivered a saddil, an' wer jis' the rite culler fur the job, an' the holes looked like the bow-ports ove a gun-boat. He waded in onst tu stop a big fite at muster, in a Christian way, an' a feller broke a dorg-wood hanspike ur a chesnut fence-rail, I'se forgot which, acrost that nose, an' twenty-seven bats, an' three king-fishers flew outen hit. The lick only made the Squire blow hit tolabil strong, scatterin roun a peck ove cobwebs, an' muddauber's nestes, an' he went on a-stopin ove the fite. He wer on his way tu chuch that mornin, an' hearin orful souns, he struck thru the bushes tu 'zamine intu hit, bein his juty es greaser ove the squelchin s'ciety.

"His hoss wer ove a pius turn ove mine, ur ole Haney wudn't a-keep him a day. Nobody ever seed him kick, gallop, jump a fence, smell uther hosses, ur chaw a bridil. He wer never hearn squeal, belch, ur make eny onsightly soun, an' 'side all them marks, he hed scabs ontu his knees an' mud on his snout. Mine yu, I speaks ove the karacter ove the hoss afore, an' up tu arter breakfus that Sunday mornin, nuffin more, fur I show'd him that day tu be es durn'd a ole hiperkrit es ever toted a saddil, ur a hyme book. His wickid kareer ainded in a tan-vat, an' the buzzards clean'd his bones. That orful Sunday shook even the Squire's b'lief on sum pints ove hereafter. He now thinks, they orter take folks in hell, like they dus intu chuch, six months on trial, an' that the vartue ove the thing be tried imejuntly on me, an' mam. He b'leves we'd bof make 'tarnity members easy.

"He rid up to the fence keerfully, drap't the reins, hilt up his hans, an' sez he—

"'Furgivin Father abuv! What's am yu tormentin them ar two varmints fur, on the Lord's Holy Sabbath? Say, O ye onregenerits, whar' the patriark ove this depraved famerly?'

"'Look a-yere, Squire Haney,' sez mam; 'I'se hits patriark jis' now; mos' ove the time I'se hits tail, I knows, but one thing sure; yu'd bes' trot along tu yer meetin. This am a *privit soshul famerly 'musement* an' hit needs no wallin up ove eyes, nur groanin, nur secon han low-quartered pray'rs tu make hit purfeck; 'sides, we's got no notes tu shave, nur gals ole enuf tu convart, so yu' better jis' go way wif yer four laig'd, bal-faced pulpit, an' preach tu sich es yersef sumwhar else; go 'long Squire, that's a good feller.'

"I'd pull'd a big jimsin burr, an' hilt hit up so mam cud see hit, a-moshunin to'ards ole Ball-eye's tail. Mam nodded her head. So while the Squire wer sarchin a packet ove tracks, fur one against devilmint ove Sundays, I sneak'd up ahine 'im. Sez mam es saft an' sweet es ef I wer a sick baby—

"'Sutty, my darlint, jis' start the Squire's hoss thar fur 'im. I'se fear'd he'll be late fur meetin, speshully ef he stops at *Missis Givinses*.' (Yere he gin mam a look frum onder his hat-brim, what spoke dam yure ole soul, jis' es plain es ef the cussinest man in the county hed hollered hit.) Start him easy my son, so es not tu jostil the ole man's breakfus'; hit mout sour on his stumick; poor ole critter, he's colikey an' ailin enyhow, ef his looks don't lie.' I say ailin; he only pull'd down four greasy fifty-sixes, an' ef yu'd a-twisted his sweaty neck-hankecher intu a rope, hit 'ud burn like a torch.

"I planted the burr high up onder ole Ball-eye's tail, an' he clamp't hit clost instantly. 'Bout the time he'd squeezed hit tu the hurtin pint, I'd dun busted a four foot, white-oak clap-board plum open, atwixt the root ove his tail, an' the Squire's. The shock brot his tail warter-tite atwixt his laigs, an' every sticker on the burr wer buried tu the butt in hoss-meat, ur hoss-tail.

"He kicked one pupendicler kick, es high es the cabin chimly. I seed the hole laingth ove his belly even tu the susingil buckil frum behine, an' sure enuf I hearn the Squire's coffee sloshin his chaw'd chickin an' hard biled aigs 'bout pow'ful.

" 'Wo yu! Sirr,' sez he.

" 'That ar las' observashun am no use, Mister Haney,' sez I. Anuther kick strait up at the sun.

" 'Wo yu orful ole fool.' Sez I—

" 'He *can't* wo, Squire; he's a-gittin happy, an' that's hoss way ove shoutin.'

"Atwixt the kicks, he'd rise all fours frum the yeath, 'bout a foot, bouncin way, an' lite in the same tracks, a-sweatin roun the eyes, wif a snort fur every bounce an' a grunt wif every kick. Then he made a gudgeon ove his fore laigs, an' kicked a plum suckil wif his hine ones. Ef the air cud be printed on, yu'd a-seed a ring ove hoss shoe marks, twenty foot acrost, eleving high, an' jis' 'bout a han an' a half apart, heels all pintin tu the center.

"The Squire got a good pullin holt wif wun han, ontu the crupper, an' a-pushin wun wif tuther, in the mane, while he sot his stirrips 'way forrid apas' Ball-eye's bitts. Hit kep me pow'ful bizzy tu watch the dorg makin an' ole Haney's happy hoss; bof on em wer makin things happin so durnashun fas'.

" 'Trus' freely in heving, Squire, es long es crupper holt lasts. I think hit'll hold a hour ur so yet, fur I see the pint ove his tail laid clost tu his belly a-tetchin the girth,' sez mam.

" 'Then pick a spot bar ove rocks fur yure profile tu strike,' sez I. That wer a pow'ful cumfurtin remark ove mine, an' wer soun doctrin too, warn't hit?

" 'Wo! Wo! Sirr, (a kick) *yu* blasted fool, (a kick) wo! I say, yu in——' (a kick). Thinks I, *thar* that ar kick wer a interpersision, fur hit kep the Squire frum plain cussin. 'Sum ove yu (a kick) ketch hes bitts (a kick).'

" 'Better pray fur a anvil tu cleave ontu his tail, a sockdolagin big anvil,' sez mam. 'Hit'll cum if *yu* ax hit, yea verily.'

"Jis' then Ball-eye findin his inimy tu be kick-proof, his faith gin out. He tuck a skeer, an' sot intu gittin away, in a style no hoss ever used afore. The gait he picked out fur the 'casion, warn't jis' the thing fur leavin wrath, ur tribulashun wif, I don't think; thar warn't enuf strait ahead leavin in hit; hit wer a 'sortmint made up ove dromedary gallop, snake slidin, side windin, an' ole Firginey jig, tetched off wif a sprinkil ove quadrille, step't off infunely fas' fur a pius-minded hoss on a Sunday. 'Bout every thuty yards, he'd mix in a kick, aimed at the back ove the Squire's head. Es soon es he farely started, mam hollered—

" 'Squire, when yu calls fur the anvil, moutent hit be es well tu ax fur a lockchain, an' a interpersition, too. Yu don't know what mout happen; them's orful strange moshuns he's a-makin fur a pius hoss.'

"Ole Haney hed grabbed his bridil fur stoppin ur steerin puposes; his hat wer jam'd fast on the back ove his short fat naik, an' cock'd sharp up ahine his years, red es a cock's comb, sot squar out onder the rim. His elbows an' toes wer wide apart, like his hoss wer red hot, an' durn'd ef I don't b'leve he wer.

"The las' words I hearn the Squire menshun es he went outen site wer, 'Now I lay me down tu sleep.'

"Thinks I, that's a clost shot fur a off-han prayer wif wet powder, but hit am *aimed at the wrong board.* A man mus' a-had a pow'ful soun conshunce tu a-slept on es wide awake a hoss es ole Haney hed atwixt his fat laigs—a clar fall frum grace that hoss wer.

"The engineer ove the sin squelshin mersheen wer foun that arternoon in the lauril, amung the rocks on the krick, an' every way fur thuty foot, the groun wer paper'd wif tracks, an' notes ove han. He wer hauled home ontu a ox slide; Ball-eye wer sole at public outcry nex day at cort fur backslidin an' fallin frum grace, an' fotch one dullar an' eighty cents, on 'count ove his hide an' shoes. The burr wer sole an' delivered wif 'im, still sunk onder his tail.

"The fust words I noticed cumin frum dad, arter Squire Haney lef us in that ar mos' onnatral an' onmanerly way, wer—

"'Oke e 'urn'd 'up 'oose,' sez dad.

"His talk wer changin frum yearlin tu human, an' hed got 'bout half way. He ment hit fur chok the durn'd pup loose, but I jis' minded my orders, 'Sick 'im on an' du nuffin else,' an' I did hit like a man.

"Dad's tail flew frum the door tu the gate; then Sugar's tail flew frum the door tu the gate, then frum the gate roun back agin, a constunt swappin ove places, an' nobody pleas'd; right peart ove dus' too. Jis' then I wudn't a-tuck thuty dullars fur my dorg.

"'Oke 'e 'up 'od 'am yure 'oles.'

"Oh, durnashun! thinks I. I wer mistaken 'bout a-changin ove tungs; that's good plain Inglish, wif the trimmins, wantin nuffin but the use ove the upper lip. I minded my fust order—'Sick 'im Sugar.'

"The snout ove the hide what wer tied back on the naik, worked sorter loose, an' the fold hung down on dad's an' Sugar's snouts, an' my onregenerit dad wer blinefolded. The ho'ns hung dolefully loose at each side ove his head, like *they* were tired ove the dorg.

"Mam kept watchin thar moshuns pow'ful clost. Sez she—

"'Sut, that ar dorg's holt won't break, will hit?'

"'Not,' sez I, 'onless dad's nose's rotten.'

"'Thar is sum onsartinty 'bout hits bein soun, he's soaked hit so much in sperrits,' sed mam, an' she studied a minnit, wif her finger ontu her lip. 'I'll risk hits tarin, enyhow,' sed she. 'I never will furgive myself ef I lets this chance slip.'

"She got the bean-pole, spit in her hans, clar'd the chips frum onder her wif her feet, an' as the two varmints flew roun agin, she riz on her tip-toes, an' fotch down the pole wif bof hans frum *way up* yander, an' laid 'bout four foot ove the aind es strait es a line frum the root ove the hide's tail tu the ho'ns. Hit sounded like bustin open a dry poplar log; raised a stripe ove dus' tu the top ove the har, four inches wide, an' hit smoked all along thar, like hit wer afire. I jis' tho't jewhillikins 'bout twiste.

"Dad squalled low onder hit, like a sore-back hoss when you'se a-mountin, an' es he flew roun agin, sez he—

" '"Ell 'ire an' 'amnashun, 'ot's 'at?' Sez I—

" 'Nuffin; but yu've knock'd down the martin's gourd-pole, an' spilt the yung'uns.'

"He tried tu rise tu the human way ove standin, but the tassil a-hangin tu his smeller were too heavy, an' the holt wer es tender es a sore eye. Jis' then I wudn't a-tuck forty dullars fur my dorg. Sez he—

" '"Am 'e 'artin 'ord 'ole, an' 'e 'unyuns 'oo.'

"Then he tried sum fust rate overhanded knockin wif fus' one fore laig, an' then tuther. He made the loose huffs rattil over Sugar's rump, but he jis' sed 'Ka! a,' an' surged back tu his snout-pullin, an' roun an' roun they fly agin. What the devil they 'spected tu gain by that, I can't fur the life ove me tell, but they seem'd tu be greed 'bout hit enyhow, fur every time Sugar started, dam ef dad didn't start too, so quick yu cudn't say which made the fus' moshun. The solt mix'd wif sweat, wer one ove dad's reasons fur not stayin still much, I sorter think, an' a tender nose made 'im foller Sugar's lead quick. Now, warn't hit a hell ove a fix fur a ill-natered cuss like dad, hu allers *wud* hev his own way, tu be in? Every time that my dad's tail cum to'ards mam, down cum the bean-pole, sure es sunrise, cherow! soundin an' lookin like beatin carpets, an' feelin like splittin a body's back-bone wif a dull axe.

"Dad, bline-folded es he wer, soon larnt the place in his sarkit whar the licks fell, an' by the jumpin Jinny he'd cummence squattin afore he got thar.

"I dunno how hit wer adzacly, but the wind sumhow gethered atwixt the hary side ove dad's hide, an' the raw side ove the yearlin's; an' every lick mam isshood tu 'im wif that ar never-tire bean-pole, hit wud bust out at the sowin, pow'ful suddin, soundin loud an' doleful. Mam smiled every time she hearn hit.

" 'That ar yearlin mus' a-hed the colic afore hit wer kill'd,' sed sis Callimy Jane. She's allers sayin sum durn'd fool thing, hevin no barin on the case.

" 'Oh, hush, yu littil narrer-tail'd tucky hen,' sed brother Benton; 'hits the onexpectedness ove the cumin ove that ar bean-pole.' 'Ur the tetchin sensashun arter hit dus cum,' sed I mysef.

"Mam also tuck time tu spar Bent a fust rate tetch wif her pole, cradlin fashun! He went flyin outen his tracks over the fence, wif his hans flat ontu his starn. Es he lit in the weeds, sez he—

" 'I wer right, by golly! *Hit am the pole* what dus hit.'

"Callimy Jane, who wer a-lookin at Bent while he wer up in the air, like she wer a-listnin, chirped out, 'An so wer I.' I tho't myself I hearn Bent's gallus buttons bust off. Jis' es he started up, he shet his mouth, jis' in time tu ketch his heart.

"Cherow! cum that eternil wollopin pole down agin, along dad. He farely bawl'd—

" "On't 'et up 'at 'artin' ole eny 'ore, yu 'am 'ules.' Sez I—

" 'I haint sot the martin-pole up one time. Hits *mam* what keeps a-settin hit up, an' hit won't stay up.'

" 'Quit, yu 'am 'itch, an' let 'e 'ole lie,' sez dad.

" '*Thar hit lies*,' answered mam, es she fotch hit down along his back anuther rale saftnin swallop. The dus' hed quite risin now, outen that ar skin. Sez I—

" 'Stan hit dad, stan hit like a man; hit may be a littil hurtin tu yu, but dam ef hit ain't the makin ove the pup. Stay wif that hide, Sugar, my boy, yu'se mity ni a deplomer'd dorg.'

"Dad begun tu totter on his hine laigs; his sturn warn't way up yander, like hit wer when he fust open'd the dorg-school. Hit wer down 'bout levil wif his shoulders, an' he wer a-cumin tu his knees pow'ful fas' behine. I seed his tail a-trimblin, a mons'ous bad sign in ho'ned cattil. Dad ax'd ef hit warn't twelve o'clock? Jis' then I wudn't a-tuck fifty dullers fur my dorg. I felt like he wer ni about made.

"When Sall hed got dun sowin up dad, he started her tu the still-hous' arter a jug ove Spanish fly whisky, tu make happy cum arter he let out his dorg-school, an' she jis' now got back, tuck a look at the case es hit stood, an' got mad. Sez she—

" 'Yu durn'd yaller son ove a b—h, *I'll* break yer holt.' She flung down the jug, an' snatched the axe. Sez I—

" 'Mine, Sall, whatever yu du, don't yu cut the dorg. He's 'bout made; be keerful how yu place yer licks.'

"'Aim fur the *ho'ns* my darter,' sed mam.

"Yere she cum, wif a vigrus overhandid splitter, aidge foremos', aimd'd tu fall atwixt Sugar's years; but he yerk'd back a littil es the lick cum, an' hit went thru the dubil ove the hide, skelpin a piece ove skin ofen dad's forrid, 'bout es big es a duller, kept on an' sliced off Sugar's two smellin holes a half inch thick. Then hit tuck a chunk ofen dad's snout, 'bout the size an' culler ove a black hart cherry. Then hit went littil lower an' kerried along a new moon ofen dad's upper lip, an' a littil ove Sugar's lower lip, an dad's fore finger pint, kept on down, tuck one ove Sugar's fore paws clean, a yearlin's huff, an' then pass'd on intu the yeath, up tu the helve, an' thar hit stop't. Sez Sall—

"*'Thar, durn yu!'*

"Sugar keeled over one way, an' dad tuther. One fainted stiff, an' tuther ruinated furever, es a dorg. I'd a-tuck a raggid counterfit dullar on a wile cat-bank fur him now. That wer the liveliest Sunday I ever seed at home.

"I cried rite peart, tho', es I flung a big rock wif a strip ove bark tied roun hit intu the ho'net hole in the crick that night."

"What made you cry, Sut, was it your father's condition?"

"Father's con-durnashun. I furgot tu menshun that Sugar wer fas' tu tuther aind ove that ar strip ove bark. Who wanted a three-footed dorg, wif no smellin holes? I didn't. He wer the mos' pufeckly spiled pup in the makin I ever hearn tell ove. Mout a-lookt fur a gineral durn'd momoxin ove things tho', when dad tuck the job wif Squire Haney tu help.

"Boys, I'se sleepy now; yere's wishin (Sut raised on his elbow and held up his flask to the light) yu all good dreams, an' yu, George, may yu dream ove ownin three never-failin springs, so clost tugether yu kin lay on yure belly an' reach em all—the biggis' wun runnin ole whisky, the middil one strained honey, an' the leas' an' las'—cold warter, wif nara 'natral born durn'd fool' in two miles tu bother yu, an' when yu wake up, may yu fine hit tu be a mortal fac'.

"Es tu me, ef I kin jis' miss dreamin ove hell ur ole Bullin's all I ax. Sum one ove yu move that ar saddil down yander, by the corner ove the camp, further outen the way ove my laigs. Now le's snore sum; blow out the light."

Sut Lovingood's Adventures in New York

"WHAT became of your brass gun man, Sut, after you shot him with the lump of coal?"

"Durned ef I know, George: I hearn them say 'tote him to the Horsespital.' I 'spect he's j'ined the church, ur the perlice. Shootin' ove strange varminty critters ain't his gift; he ain't sly enuff an' he'll git kingdum cum sum day soon ef he dont quit that trade. 'Spose he wer tu undertake tu shoot Ole Beacher, in open day, afore witnessis like he did me, why durn my melt ef the passon's sister didn't have his haslet outen him, an' a dryin' atop of thar church-steepil in a minit; ef thar's enything in looks, she'd be wus on him nor I wer. But I *kin* tell you what becum ove me; I jist relyed on these yere laigs (d'ye see 'em?), and tuck up the steps and started in a monsous fast wiletuckey pace down the road, an' run inter sum man-an'- 'oman's fool explite at making new-fangled invenshuns, an hit flew all tangled up, inter the middil ove the road; while hit wer a sortin an' a strai'tnin' ove hits laigs an' arms, I axed a little larfin boy with a heap ove noosepapers onder his arm, what he call'd the cussed grasshopper-lookin' thing. 'Hay!' says he, 'don't yer know? Why hit's nuthin' but a dandy outen Fifth averner; hit can't bite an' is tu weak an' wuthless to run; so pitch in an' knock Jerusalem outen it. I'll holler fur you.' Now, afore I tells what happened thar, I wants tu talk sum of my noticin' ove things.

"No'th Ca'lina am noted fur pole cats, Georgia fur ground-hogs, an' Tennessee for coons; I knows this frum 'sperience; an' now I kin say that New York am noted in the same line fur dandys (do you know the varmint?), an' I'd a durn'd site rather mix with the stink ove the pole cat, the rascality ove the coon, an' the dirty ways ove the groun' hog, then jest tu see one ove these cussed infunel spider laig'd wuthless fixin's. They haint neither man nur 'oman, 'caze they can't talk good nor fight like wun, or kiss ur scratch feelin'ly like t'uther. They seems sorter like a strange wether what had seed a heap ove tribulashun among an ekal number ove rams an' yews— they's butted about permiskusly by the one, an' is snufft at by t'uther; and as they can't fill or feel the instink ove a man, nur do the juty ove an 'oman, they jest settles on a cross fence atween the two, an' turns inter the wust kind ove fool monkeys despised by wun, an' larft at by t'uther, and the most human view you gits ove 'em, is when they is above you a climbin' up. They haint half es smart as their chatterin' kin folks, fur they can't begin tu du what the monkey kin. I knows monkey nater pow'ful well. I seed one once, an' I studied hits nater and gifts, when I weren't skeared; he were pow'ful peart tu be a ugly litil beast; I seed him a killin' ove insex, an' then I obsarved what he did with 'em. Now, a dandy haint smart enuff fur that; he jist lets his insex run. S'pose a expectashun towards him wer a cumin' from a tarin wild school gal what had seed snow say about sixteen times, an' flowers an' leaves es often; wou'dn't she meet a disappintment? An' then she'd jest kill him with contem't, an' feed the ca'kus tu her daddy's work steer what is yoked with his bull, in the view ove hit bein' suitable feed fur one in his condishun. They skims and flutters roun' fool wimmin, jist like li'tnin' bugs roun' a tuft ove hollyhocks, only the bugs am six tu thar two, an' hes the deal at that on the amount ove fire they kerries, an' whar they kerries hit. I never sees one but what I wants him atween these yere thumb nails—the human way ove killin' all sich insex. Well, arter his laigs were ontangled, hit sed I had insulted hit, and wanted satisfaction. Now, the idear ove me, a natral born durn'd fool, insultin' ove enything what c'u'd talk, sounds sorter like a hog insultin' ove a settin' hen, by tearin' up her nest an' eatin' the aigs; 'twer mons'ous like fool talk. But I tho't I'd gin hit satisfaction, eny how, so I drapp'd ontu my all fours, sorter behind hit, fotch a rale fightin' hoss squeal, an' landed both my hine feet onder the fork ove hits coteail.

"Now, George, whenever I strai'tens out bof ove these yere laigs tugether (d'ye see 'em?), kickin' fashion, whatever they hits am bound tu *go jist then,* so he riz in the ar an flew hed fust inter a door in the hine aind ove a steamboat-cabin on wheels, among a passel ove men readin' noospapers, an' wimmin with babys ur big baskits ove garden truck, dead chickins, an chunks ove meat. You cou'dn't a onmixed all these things, takin' in a few par ove specks, a bird cage or two, an a crock ove flowers, in a week arter he lit among 'em. Oh! sich a mess, an' sich a cussin an' squawkin' in Dutch, an' French, Cherokee, an' other outlandish tongues, you never hearn since the Devil an' the Dutch, an' Tom Dawson fit; the driver—a bald faced, roach maned, wall eyed Irishman—cum down ofen the harycane deck an' cotch mister dandy by the collar an' the slack, an' sent him up a flyin' outen the door ag'in, a loanin' him a holesum kick es he went. While he wer in the ar, I moved so es to let him lite astradil ove my neck; he turned heels up an' hed down ahine me; I tuck a bill holt with my teeth on the inside ove his thigh, an' paw holts ontu his breeches laigs, fotch a bray, an' put towards the ruver, about es fast es a big dog kin go with a tin bucket a chasin' ove him. He opened in a voice weak, sorter like a sick 'oman; fust he call'd 'perlice,' then he sed 'mu'daw,' then he sed sumthin' about 'dwedful vulgaw pussons,' then sum words about doin' ove things he hadn't orter done, an' leavin' ondone things he had orter done. I speck that were sorter prayin' in his durn'd one horse way. He strung out his words over a heap ove ground, fur I wer a travelin' like a fox houn' with a wolf arter him; he kicked out in every course with them pipestem laigs ove hisn, owin' to his skare an' the hurtin' I wer supplyin' him with, fur I hes an orful bill holt when I wants to keep hit. Him and me looked jist like a travelin windmill in full blast, with a cord ove fence rails tied to the arms by thar middils, a swingin' about every way, ur a big crawfish totin' off a bunch ove grasshoppers an' long laiged spiders ag'in thar will—laigs, arms, heads, coatails, an' watch chains wer so mixed an' tangled that hit wer bewilderin tu the eyes tu foller us. He thought ove the grabin' game, an' snatched at everything we passed. I run, unbenowenst, onto an ole feller, whose years hung down like a houn's, an' his cheeks hung down like a ground squirril's jaws when he's a totin' in corn for winter, an he kerried his belly in a sling, an' hed on a white throat latch, an' wer fat enuff tu kill; he jist squatted, an' I straddled him in my stride. Dandy fastened in his har, and I jist wish I may be discriminately durn'd ef he didn't tar off his whole skulp—didn't leave a single har—his head shined like a tin ball atop ove a church. He flung the skin ove ole lard stand's hed away, an' went tu grabin ag'in.

The next he fastened ontu wer a black minner-net an 'oman hed round her shoulders; she turned wrong aind up; but he got most on the net; his watch chain cotch on the hook of her littil umereller, an' hit went along too. A wide-coupeled duck laiged Jew, what had a nose jist the shape an' size ove a goose wing broad-axe, had a string ove about ten histed umerellers tied one below t'uther, an' hung outen a high winder in his loft ontu a pole; well, Mister Squt snatched the handil ove the bottom one an' fotch pole an' all. The follower of Moses an' ole close came out a tarin' an' a chatterin jist in time fur the hind aind ove the pole tu lite on his slick hat—face, nose, black whiskers an' all disappeared inter the hat, an' then the hat struck the groun' an' rolled, with the Hebrew intu the gutter. Now, you had orter seed that pole an them open umerellers clar the road; sumtimes the pole wer on one side of the road, a barkin ove shins an a smashin' hoops, then hit wer on t'uther, a bustin' out winders an' a sweepin ove appils an' gouber peas ofen the tables, an' a crackin the ole wimmin the side over the head; every wun hit totch about the head laid down; an then the umerellers was a scoopin up babies an' go carts, an' littil dogs at wun place and drapin' them at another jist to scoop up more. Thar warn't a pusson on that road that know'd what we wer; an' sum tuck intu the houses, sum down the cross roads, an' sum tried tu outrun me the way I was agwine; but the last durned one what played that game got run over. I was a gwine like a crazy locomotive skeared at a yearthquake—in fac, I *was* skeared by this time, fur I'd got more nor I'd paid fur; I hed suckseedid in raisin hell generally, an' all that road wer either mad ur skeared at me, an I know'd they'd want my pusson monsous bad, so I jist hilt my bill holt on Mister Squt's thigh an' kept on. We met a feller in a slick roun' cap, a sittin' on a par ove wheels (they all believes in wheels), with his feet ontu the shaftez each side ove a fast trottin' hosse's hips, just a leanin' back an' a gwine it: the hoss jist tuck one look, turn'd tail, an' Jehosefat! how he mizzled tother way; the next thing I saw, was slick cap, doubled at his hip-j'ints, with his toes, hands an' years within an inch ove each other, aflying sturn fust, through a big glass winder, among a passel ove doll babys, bonnets, caps, fans, gloves, an' purty wimmen; he j'ined Orful Gardner's church the nex' day; his hoss left his wheels fast ontu a forked cart tail, an' betuck hisse'f to the country, with nothin' on but the collar, and the wust kind of a big skeer fur a hoss. I run through atween the leaders an' the wheel hosses ove one ove them steamboat cabins on wheels (they loves wheels), what wer a cummin' ontu a cross road, an' thar we turn'd our string ove umerellers wrong side out, an' left 'em, pole an' all mixed up with hosses. The perlice, what oughter been arter me, gathered round tu save the umerellers an' arrest the driver, an' one ove 'em toted a little newspaper boy off tu jail onder his arm fur larfin', while another stole his papers, an' a third went along to help guard that orful boy, an' they didn't seem a bit more fear'd tu do hit than I'd be tu take a horn ove tanglelaigs whisky.

Now, all this time Mister Squt kept up his prayin' in his way, mixed in with hollerin', cussin', and cryin', an' when we run inter that team ove hosses, he sweat orful, fur my shoulders wer plum wet. Well, I went a tarin' ag'in' a fence, what's built between the road an' the ruver (they calls hit the Battery), intendin' to bust through hit, drown Squt, and swim for tuther side. I cum ag'n hit ni' ontu as hard as an ole bull c'u'd a done, but hit wer thar, an I like tu a busted myse'f open. All my holts tore loose, an' Mister Squt's eatin aind cum round overhanded, makin' a big cirkil in the ar, an' he lit hed fust, kachug, sixty foot out in the ruver. Arter his boot heels went outen site, I seed a greasy skim on the warter, sorter green an yaller, an' purple, a spreadin' over about half acre. He didn't cum up; but lots of dead fish did. I know'd he wer p'isen. Wonder ef thar's eny law in this yere place fur drowndin' sich reptiles. I wer feard'd thar mout be, they're so durn'd curious, eny how. So I tried tu make myse'f mons'ous sca'se.

"You never will know, George, what a discumfort hit

is tu be a natral born durn'd fool; hit makes ag'in a feller
so, an' allers keeps him onder cow. Why, when I meets
a 'nowin' lookin beast I'se feard ove hit, an' watches to
see that hit don't git me inter sum cussed skeary scrape.
Arter that feller fell in the ruver, I jist biled, tuck down
the lane, an' seein' ove a pair ove stairs gwine strait up
inside a door, I tuck up 'em, aimin' fur the loft, tu hide
in the hay; I busted inter the room an' lit about the
middle, and thar wer about forty gals a cypherin', and a
mons'ous strong minded 'oman a walkin' about teachin'
ove 'em. She squar'd herse'f an' tuck a look at me,
an' then it wer I seed she wer strong minded tu kill; her
foot wer the biggest, saftest piece of meat I ever seed
not to hav guts in hit, an' her anklis wer like untu the
eye ove a mattick, sorter diamunt shape, an' she wer
coupled es wide es a bedste'd; her laigs looked like they
j'ined her cackus like a wheel barrer's handils j'ines hit;
she stamped that ar carpet bag foot ove hern, an'
sqawked, 'Yeou get eout!' *She* took me fur a beast, and
talked dog talk tu me. I seed her eyes a turnin green, an'
she sot in tu sharp'nin ove her nails ontu the back ove a
bench, like she wer hungry for har. I knows the nater
ove cats mons'ous well; Ise studied 'em. Thar I stood a
fixin' of my laigs tu run. She went tu the winder and
made a moshun, an' the fust thing I seed thar wer a perlice,
in the room atween me an' the stairs. I jist swung round
one ove my fistes an' sent hit at him; I split hit onter
his nose, an' two ove my 'nucks went inter each ove his
red eyes; I seed the fire fly myself, an' he turn'd a back
summer set over a bench, an' while he wer a tryin' tu git
up ontu his all fours, I seed run'in every laig he hed—they
wer a makin' the moshuns a ready, so I jist grabbed him
untu the back ove his bar neck with my teeth, an' gin a
good coon dog shake, a sorter growlin'; he made the *no
nothin'* sign, mixed in with a heap ove 'O don'ts,' that
made me wus nur ever; I shook him ag'in, an' mended my
holt. Sez he, 'Hurrar for Buckcannon,' sorter enquirin'
like. I let him go when he sed that, an' swung one ove
these yere laigs (d'ye see 'em?) arter him; hit landed rite
whar he forked, and he lit belly fust and head down atop
ove the fence built down aside ove the stairs; an' don't
you think the durn'd fool warn't a snappin' his fingers an'

a chirpin' with his mouf every chance he got; the 'hole time he tuck me fur a dog, too—durn his ugly perlice cackus! Well, he slid tu the foot ove the stairs like a lizzard a gwine down a fence stake, and made fust rate time down the road, a feelin' the nap ove his neck with wun hand, while he wer a pullin' his britches loose behind with t'uther. I turn'd roun', an thar *she* was a standin', with all her laigs so clost together that a buckit hoop w'u'd a went roun' all ove 'em—above them ar feet o' hern, ove course, an' her back wer like an ox-bow, an' reached up almost tu the ruff ove the house, an' her tale wer made inter the shape ove a goard neck, an' es big es a ka'g, an' es a fence rail—all the har on aind like a bottil brush; in fac' she wer all eyes an' claws an' tail. Oh, she were dre'dful tu behold! An' all the t'uther shes in that are rume wer in the same persishun an' fix, only not over half es big, an' their tails warn't bigger nor a stove pipe. All heads turn'd towards me, an' thar wer groanin' an spittin' enuff tu skeared a team ove bull dogs. I never seed so many green eyes afore, or since, an' thar were little devils a dancin' in all ove 'em, like yaller jackets in a em'ty green whisky bottil. I tuck a skeer—jist made myse'f inter a ball, an' rolled down stars, across the pavement, an' inter the road—a rollin' in among a winein' blades lookin' feller's laigs, what wer a blunderin along in a ole white hat, with a mud dauber's nest built in the crown, a throat latch made outen a piece ove ole sweaty saddilgirth, an a ole dirty white coat, with a small soap factory in full blast in one pocket, and a patent nigger trap in t'uther; he uses his shut to clean stove pipes with, an' he gits his boots by stealin' a par ove leather fire buckets—hes 'em footed, an' then pulls 'em on by the bales, over a par ove britches what he has hed patented es a flea hatchin mershean.

"I tuck fust a look fur runnin room, an' then a look at him, an' I seed he didn't onderstand my nater, an' wer feard ove me; he kep' a tryin' tu look ahine me, like he thought I toted a string. Sez I, 'Mister, ar you agent for a paper mill? Or dus you make soap fur a livin'?' He commenced a backin'. I picked up a little rock, an' whetted my teeth an' finger nails with hit, an' now, says I, 'Hev you eny word to send to your marm, yer gall or the Mare?—Ef you hev anything a weighin' on your mind, jist unbuzzom yerse'f tu that bladder lip'ed nigger, an' gin him all yer loose change tu carry the word, fur, *dam me if yer time haint come!*' He jist never said a word, but rounded too and put in a lumberin sort of cow gallop. I never seed so many different moshuns gone through, an' so many tracks made in a minit, to get no further off then he did; he distributed 'em all over the road, a pi'ntin' every way; frum the work an' the number ove tracks, I'd a dun been outen the city while he wer still in reach ove a pound rock. 'Tis a pity runnin' aint one of his gifts, fur he's a mons'rous skeery man tu be as dirty es he is. He printed sumthin', nex' day, in his paper about 'Free Love an' Human Progress'; sed he believed that crosses yet would be made atween animals an' varmints, an' sutin mersheans, what would perjuce s'thin' tu answer in place of humans (Dad tride that explite once, durn his potheaded soul! An' Ise a kerrien the consekenses)—that he hed seed the day afore, the projuce ove a cross atween a broken laiged kangaroo and a fust class mowin' mershean; that it tuck mostly arter the mershean; that hit hed a sting the size an' shape ove a reap hook (what a h-l ove a lie!), but in the laigs hit wer all kangaroo; he hed never obsarved jist sich laigs (what did I alers tell you, George?—thar haint sich anuther par on yearth, d'ye see 'em?); that I'd be wuf a great deal, tu tote expresses an' steal niggers, ef I only wer tamed ('speck I would, but *who's in New York tu tame me?*); sed he wer onable to get a satisfying inspeckshun ove me, owin' to my vicious natur; that he'd tu withdraw cautiously, for the wild beast perdominated tu much in my cross; but take me all tugether, I wer a livin' sample ove human progress an' free love atween a kangaroo an' a mowin' mershean, an' he thought much mout be done in that way; calls on Misses Branch tu try a few small 'speriments with a steam rock drill, while he practises a while on a thirty ton locomotive, an' specks the consekenses will 'stonish the world. I speck hit will; he'll keep on till thunder strike him yet, see ef hit don't. He's the only man in New York what kin hold a candil for me tu act durn'd fool by, an' he works onder a disadvantige, fur I'm told he won't tetch a drap ove sperits. Oh! he's a mons'ous promisin' ole durn'd fool, ef he don't get sot back, ur thunderstruck!"

Nashville *Union and American*, August 15, 1858.

[Editor's note: As this edition went to press, Ben Harris McClary published his discovery of the issues of the New York *Atlas* containing the original printings of both installments of "Sut Lovingood's Adventures in New York." Only the second installment is included here as it was reprinted in the Nashville *Union and American*. See *The Lovingood Papers 1964* (Knoxville: University of Tennessee Press), pp. 10-21.]

Sut Lovingood at Bull's Gap

I HAINT never gin you the account ove my travels in the regin ove Bull's Gap, last winter. I hev kep hit back, case I wer feard while I wer mad I mout do the cussed branch of hell injestis. But now I've got over hit, an am prepared, bad as hit is, to gin hit far play. Ef ever a yearthquake cums round en dus the same, you'd never see Bull's Gap agin, that's all.

I means to tell jist what I seed, hearn and felt, an don't speck enybody what haint been thar'll believe a word ove hit; but I don't keer a durn, for I aint spected to act ur talk like human, no how.

Well, Bull's Gap am a bottomless mud hole, twenty odd miles long, mixed with rocks, logs, brush, creeks, broken stages, dead hosses, mean whisky, cold vittils, an cross dogs. Me an about forty other travelers wer making a trip amongst all this mixtry, while hit would fust rain the best six outen eleven; then hit would snow awhile tu rest hitself, then sleet a littil jist to show what hit could do, freeze awhile an begin another rainin match, an a doin wun ur tuther all the time es hard es a shoemaker workin by the job ur the devil a splittin fat pine tu lite up a new comer, and him a Congrisman ur a suckit rider.

When we got in sight ove whar we wer tu eat supper, I loped ofen the stage waggin an put out at a peart lick towards the supper bell; an I hearn a feller say, "I'd gin a hundred dollars fur them laigs (speakin ove mine); they'se the only par what'll git thru this piece of saft country, tu tuther railroad, caze they kin touch bottom sometimes; an, darnation! how they reaches forward towards better things—jist watch him measure the yeath with em. Why, he looks like a cussed ole winder mop with two handils, dam ef he don't. He's split from the yeath to his haslet, an is still a splittin. Jist watch him wade thru that pile ove rocks an cross ties," an a heap more sich talk about me what I'se forgot. Wonder what he'd said if he'd seed me a workin em onder a orful tarin big skeer? Durned ef I don't speck he'd a tuck one hissef, an turned tuther way. George, never wer es proud ove these yere laigs afore (d'ye see em), only when I outrun ole Burns' houns. I'se tuck tu ilin ove em every day with frog ile; hit helps em powful, an they'se my only pendence on this yeath; an I thinks I onderstands how to use em. I'm gwine to be more keerful ove em, an not run fur nothin, but jist tu save to use em onder big skeers.

Well, the wimmin travelers went intu one room an the ballance ove us intu another, whar thar stood a littil meetin house lookin stove what had been tryin to git hot; an as hit couldn't, hit tuck the studs an wer a smokin like ontu a Noth Calina tar kiln, en smelt like burnt har. The warter an slush stood in the room more nor half way up hits laigs (that's what comes ove havin common laigs), but we all waded in an stood round that littil cussed cold sulky nigger-lookin cast-iron-smoke-box, sum a cussin hit, sum a cussin tharsefs, sum a cussin Bull's Gap, sum a cussin wun another, sum a cussin the lake they stood in, sum a cussin that are shanty tavrin, sum a cussin fur supper, sum a cussin the strike nine snake whisky, an all a cussin thar levil best. One monsous clever little feller frum Nashville endorsed all the cussin, an then sot in an cussed the world; sed hit wer all vanity an vexashun ove spirit—a dam onmitigated humbug frum the center all round tu the sea—an then run the neck over the bottil up tu the bulge down atween his shoulders and hilt hit thar es long es he had breth ur hit hed mixture; flung hit agin the stove, an then cussed the bottle fur being the strongest ever he wanted tu smash.

I axed the tavrinkeeper how he liked that cussin es a specimint ove the gift in perfecshun. Oh, he sed, hit were ornary, not third rate in quality, an wan't powerful in quantity; hardly listened tu hit; in fac, hit didn't even warm him up; wouldn't do as a sampil ove the art at all; an axed me ef I hadn't been fotched up by monsous pius pussons ni untu a church, fur hit wer clar I wer a poor judge ove cussin. Sed he had a crowd the nite afore what understood the business—Sixty-seven ove em; an they wer so well trained that hit sounded like one man only sixty-seven times louder. Sed they cussed him pussonely, till his jackit buttons flew off an the ainds ove his har cotched fire; then they turned in ontu a stage agent an cussed him into a three week's spell ove fits an diarrear, but he hadn't much ove a constitushun no how; an then finished off by cussin wun ove the stage waggins ontil hit run off inter the woods without eny hosses tu hit. "In fac, mister laigs," sez he, "I got the best nites sleep arter they got throu, what I've had in six months; never felt the fust durned bug, an would gin a duller ef your crowd could jist cuss half es purfectly. Hits a monsous holesum quietin thing fur a man tu get a tip top cussin jist afore he goes tu bed, perticulerly if the wimmin ove the crowd jines in with that ar 'nasty hog,' and 'aint you shamed ove yersef, you stinkin brute you!' chorus ove theirn. I tell you, mister, hits all I keeps tavrin fur." An I believed him; fur, bein a natral-born durned fool, I never onct thought ove the half dullers he got arter the cussin wer over. They mout a kep him from feelin his bugs, moutent they?

Well, when that bottil smashed agin the stove hit skared out from onder hit the all-firedest, biggest, spottedest, long laigedest bull frog I ever seed. He hed a iron teaspoon crosswise in his mouf, an he struck out an swum to an injun rubber over shoe what wer floatin about boat-fashun loose. He climbed aboard, an sot in tu paddlin hissef with his spoon, injun way, fust one side ove the keel and then tuther, across that ar pond. The cussin hed stopped by this time, an I never seed as menny big eyes afore; they were es round an big es ef their leds hed been stretched over martingil rings an durn the word were spoke. He steered fur the bluff bank ove a old har trunk, an clomb tu the top of hit with his spoon in his mouf agin, an then tuck hits bowl in his paws, stood up on his laigs, an scratched his back over-handed with the handil. Arter he satisfied hissef at that devarshun, he tuck aim at me (he'd been a watchin me afore), an fired his durned ole rusty spoon at my hed. I hearn hit whiz apast my year. Then he squatted ontu the har trunk, spread his fore laigs wide like ontu a bench laiged fice, a facin the crowd, an in the most human-like way yu ever hearn in allyer born days, begun in a orful hoarse voice a croakin, "Bull's Gap"— "Bull's Gap"—"Bull's Gap"—an as the tail aind ove the word gap lef his mouf he'd snap his lips together like shettin ove a par ove woffil irons in a hurry, and his countenance looked like he wer powerfully discumforted about sumthin. The thought got throu my har that hit were the ghostes ove some Frenchman what had got pizened with sumthin he'd et thar, ur got hissef drownded in the mud. The whole performance wer too human like tu suit me; so a fust rate big skeer begun in the middil ove my laigs; I jist loped outen the door inter the slush in the middil ove the road. The ballance ove the crowd seemed to be waitin for a hint ove that sort, fur durn my gizzard ef they didn't pour outen that ar door in a solid sluice into the dark and mud, an every now an then sum feller more skeered an active wud cum out a flyin over the heads ove the ballance; an thar warnt a mossel ove cussin done, nor a single pussin lef in that ar warter tight room. The frog had hit all tu hisself, durn his spotted soul; I reckon he wer satisfied now.

Well, don't you think, George, nex mornin every cussed infunel lyin raskil ov em didn't deny the whole thing, and swore thar warn't ara frog seed at all, an hit were nothin but the strike nine whisky I hed drunk, what hed hatched a frog in my hed. But I'm durned ef hit warnt just es I tell hit; fur, es I cum back, a week arterwards, I seed his skin stretched up again the house, an hit were es big es a old he coon's, an the tavrin keeper wer a rubbin in ole butter intu the fleshy side. I axed him what he were agwine tu do with hit. He sed he ment tu make a night cap outen hit fur the President ove the Railroad, es a compliment. I wish he wud. Now won't he dream skary dreams when he socks his hed inter that frog-skin cap? A durned fust rate idear, warn't hit? an hit will look so becomin on him, spotted side out. How I'd like tu bounce a brick bat ofen hit yearly sum frostly mornin, jist tu see ef hit wud do to risk in a big fight.

Well, arter a while the secon bell rattilled, an we all sneaked roun the house an went in at the back door, fur that orful frog sot monsous heavy ontu our minds. Thar wer a big-thunderin Duchman along, the wust Duchman I ever seed fur fat an unonderstandable lingo; he looked like he'd been moulded in a elefant's paunch, an his laigs in a big crooked holler log, an stuck on arterwards. His britches wer es big es a bedtick, with two meal-bags sowed tu hit fur laigs, an his head wer as round es a ball; an his har—well, hit mout a been a sandy boar's skin tuck ofen the beastez when he wer mad an had all bristils sot, an then fitted without eny combin ur cleanin tu his skull. His face looked like sum stout pusson hed busted a ripe tomato ontu hit, an seeds an innards an skin hed all stuck an dried thar. He talked like he hed a jewsharp in his throat; an when he sot in tu cussin, he did hit in Dutch mostly, an hit sounded like sawin a loose sheet ove iron with a dull hansaw. I tell you, he wer fearful tu look at, an dredful to hear, an overpowerin tu smell. Well, he planted hissef at the tabil forninst a two year old chicken cock biled whole, an a big tin pan ove sourcrout what smelt sorter like a pile ove raw hides in August, an a bullit ladil wer socked inter hit. He jist fotch a snort an socked his fork up tu the hilt in the rump bone ove that misfortinate ole cock an started him down his throat head fust, and then begun tu hump hissef an grunt. Every yerk he gin the chicken went an inch, an he'd crook his neck sorter sidewise like a hen does with a lump ove dough stuck in her throat. When he'd swallered hit apast the rump, the laigs stuck out at each corner ove his mouf es wide apart as the prongs ove a pitchfork, an then he sot intu ladlin in the crout atween em. At last the toes ove the rooster went outen site, an he sent the ballance ove the crout arter him, now an then pitchin in, lef handed, a chunk ove bull-steak es sorter mile stones tu separate the ladles ove crout. He rubbed his belly an pernounced hit "tam goot," an axed ef they had eny more "lettle schickins." The tavrin keeper jist shuck his head; he wer too full tu speak. I wer feared that his feelins would overcum him entirely. Dutchy then axed fur lager bier, an Noel fotch him a yeathen crock ove dish water with a teacupful ove red pepper an a pint ove tanglelaig whisky mixed in. He tasted hit, smacked his lips, an said hit wer "tam goot too"; then he jist dried the bottom ove the crock afore he sot hit down, an then rubbed his belly agin.

Right forninst whar I sot thar wer a sumthin onto hits butained in a plate, ni onto the bigness an shape ove a beef's heart, an carved like ontu a pine burr, an mout (mine I dont say hit wer) been made outer flour mush with a scrimpshun ove indigo in hit, an hit cudent keep still—jist sot thar an trimbled an quivered every time every body totcht the tabil, like hit wer skared durned ni ontu death, an knowin hit hed no laigs tu run with, jist tuck hit out in shakin. I begin tu skeer myself at hits human like kerriens on, for I made hit out tu be a infunel mershean, the invenshun ove sum cussed infunel murderin know nothin, calculatin frum my nater that I'd swaller hit whole when he ment hit tu go off an scatter my meat over a squar acre ove that black mountain, an make a breakfus for the tucky buzzards what waited roun thar fur stage hosses an misfortinat passengers. Them ar buzzards got so sassy at last, that ef a hoss or man stumbled an fell, they'd kiver him all over afore he cud get up. Why, they hilt a lection every month, an hed meetin every Sunday, same es humans. They'se monsous nowin critters, them ar Bull's Gap buzzards is, as they wer the best fed fowels I ever seed. Rite here, George, I'l tell you why I thought that ar tremblin thing wer invented an sot thar to turn me inside out. When I wer a boy, an my laigs not longer nor John Wentworth's, dad fotch home a durnd wuthless, mangy, flea bitten, grey old fox houn, good fur nothin but tu swaller up what orter lined the bowels ove us brats. Well, I natrally tuck a distaste to him, an hed a sorter hankerin arter hurtin his feelins an discumfortin ove him every time dad's back wer turnd. This sorter kep a big skeer allers afore his eyes, an a orful yell ready in his throat tu pour out the fust moshun he seed me make. So he learnt tu swaller things es he run an alers kep his laigs well onder hisself, fur he never knowd how soon he mout want tu use em in totin his infunal cacus beyant the reach ove a flyin rock. He knowd the whiz ove a rock in moshun jist as well, an he never stoped tu see who flung hit, but jist let his head fly open tu gin a howl room tu cum, an sot his laigs a gwine the way his nose happened tu be a pintin. He'd shy roun every pound rock he seed in the road, fur he looked on hit as a calamity tu cum after him sum day. Ef he lef home, sum neibor's dog tanned his hide, an ef he staid at home, I was allers arter hit tu tan hit, so he dident see much more peace ove mind nur a suckit rider dus in a baptis neiborhood at sacramint time when the ruver am up in good dippin order. And in all my born days I never seed him a gwine the same way I wer; he made that an onbreakabil rule. I think I got my fust

noledge ove gittin away frum imijut trubbil an cummin
tribulashun frum him; an with the vantage ove a holsum
par ove laigs an the power ove usein em quick, I allers
found his plan tu werk well. I tell you, George, that running
am the greatest invenshun on yearth when used keerfully.

Whar'd I a been by this time, ef I hadn't relyed ontu
these yere laigs? D'ye see em? Don't they mind you ove
a par ove cumpusses made tu devide a mile inter quarters?
They'l do, I'l be circumstanshaly durned ef they don't?
Well, one day I tuck a pig's bladder ni ontu the size ove a
duck aig an filled hit with powder an corked hit up with
a piece ove spunk, rolled hit up in a thin skulp ove meat,
sot the spunk afire, an flung hit out; he swallered hit at one
yerk, an then sot in tu gittin away fur doin hit. I hearn
a noise like bustin sumthin, and his tail lit atop ove my
hat. His head wer way down the hill an hed tuck a death
holt onter a root. His fore laigs wer fifty feet up the road,
a makin runnin moshuns an his hine ones a straddil ove
the fence. His innerds wer hangin in links onter the cabin
chimley, sept about a yard in mam's bussum, an his paunch
cum down permiscusly like rain. Es tu the dog hisself,
es a dog, I never seed him agin. Well, Dad, durn his
onsanctified soul! flung five or six hundred onder my shut
with the dried skin ofen a bull's tail, an gin me the remainder
nex day with a waggin whip what he borrered frum a feller
while he wer a waterin his hosses; the waggoner got sorry
fur me, an hollered tu me tu turn my beggin un squallin
inter d—d fust-rate runnin, which I imejutly did, an the
last lick missed me about ten feet. Well, now, ye see I
minded all this, an I thot that shakin new-fangled fixin
were the dog's retribushun (I believes in retribushuns, I
duz) an the biggest kind ove a one at that, an hit were
morally intended fur me tu swaller, an ef I had, I'd a been
jist about as easy tu bury as the dog were. But I didn't
happen tu swaller hit, not that time. I gin Dutchy a punch
an pinted tu hit, jist ater the chicken cock's toes went outen
site, in the hopes that if he seed hit he'd send hit ater the
fowel. Suppose—he—had? I wanted orfully tu see the
roof cum offen the house, and tu larn whether tucky
buzzards will eat dutch meat tore up fine an mixed with
chicken cock, bull beef, crout an linsey breeches. But he
jist gin hit one spisious look an shuck his head—too durned

smart for the no nuthins ef he wer a thunderin Dutchman. So thar hit sot and trembled, and they lost all thar trubbil and powder, fur thar haint a pusson bornd durnd fool enuf tu ondertake tu eat enything while hit trimbled as hit did, an run the risk ove kingdom come fur doin hit. Durn thar souls, they's been tryin to kill me ever since I dreamd about old Buck a beatin Fillmore and Freemount at a game ove old sledge fur the Presidency.

I wer monsus hungry misef, so I levied ontu a chunk ove beef fried in cake taller, about the size an shape ove an iron wedge that had been cut outen the back ove sum misfortunate ole bull's neck, jist ahine his hons. I socked my fork thru one aind an ondertuck tu bite off tuther; but I dident. I hilt on with fork an teeth, an tried tu saw off a bite with a case knife. Couldn't do that. Tried tuther aidge, an hit wur es dull es the fust. So I made up my mind tu cum slutch over hit an swaller hit whole. I hed like tu let the fork go arter it, twer so hard tu pull out. Hit hed rusted intu the meat. Now, jist like a durned onthinkin, onmitigated, cussed, natral born fool es I is, I hed swallered hit with the grain the wrong way; an like crawlin grass a gwine up yer britches laigs, hit started up agin an felt like ontu a terbacker wum a crawlin up my breakfus pipe. But I hilt hit down by sendin anuther hunk arter hit with the grain the right way. Then I drunk a bowl of coffee made outen an ole chopped wool hat, an a stage driver's ole boot laig. The grease, sweat, glue, leather, blackin, an wool in the ole hats an boots, makes a fust rate biled drink, when hit am sweetened with a mixtry of Orleans sugar, pissants an cock roaches; hit jist does that hoss; durned ef it dont—that's so.

Well, arter we had et up most everything but the cook and skillet, they went off in bunches tu bed. I dasent ax fur a bed, least they mout take me fur a beastes and send me tu the stabil; so I sneaked inter the room whar Dutchy wer, made a piller outen my bag ove duds, an lay down ontu the floor, an sot intu the darndest, hardest sleepin now in fashion, an dreamin the durndest, skeriest dreams now in use—dreamed that two hundred head ove horned cattle wer arter me, with thar tails up an thar heads down, follered by an ole sick bull with a chunk ove meat es big es a boot jack, cut outen the back ove his neck; an they looked

like they thought I had hit inside ove me. Ole hats with
wings like ontu bat's wings flew round, not makin a bit
of noise, an ole boots ontu wheels trundled over the floor.
I don't know what would hev becum ove me (for in dreams
yer laigs wont go off—yer can't use em a bit) ef I hadn't
been wakened with the durndest doleful soun I ever heard.
En thar wer that infernal bag ove soap-fat, the Dutchman,
in his shuttail, mounted up ontu the foot board ove his
bedstead, a flappin his wings an a crowin like ontu a durned
ole shanghi cock with a June bug in its craw.

Hit sounded like a mule colt a brayin in a empty barrel,
and hit farly shuck the tavrin, wakin up everybody, an a
settin the cussin agwine agin; then he loped down ontu his
all-fours on the floor, an his shuttail looked shorter nur
ever, an sot in tu rakin up dirt with his huffs, an a honin
ove the bedstead with his hed, and a bellerin orful.
Bo-wo-wo-woof-bo-wo-a woah a woah, a woah-woof. I sot
up on aind, an, thinks I, well, I bedurned! You never
hearn bull acted es perfectly in yer life. His voice suited
the job he'd ondertuck adzactly, only ef eny thing, hit wer
too loud fur a common mountain bull. The passengers
were fool'd with hit, an got all thar wimmin huddled inter
one room, an they drug a bedstead agin the door, an all
ove em got ontu hit, fur they wer morrally durnd sertin
that thar wer a rusty ole bull up stairs, en mad at that.
I seed that the infernel ole crout barrel wer fast asleep,
an I fell on a plan to wake him. So I tuck a crockery war
vessil from onder his bed an socked hit onto his hed, a
snappin hit over his years an snout, nite-cap fashun. He
seem'd tu take hit es a challenge tu mortal combat, fur he
fotch a loud whoof outen his snout, gin a short beller, an
tuck a runnin butt at me by guess on his all-fours. I tell
you he cum a tarin. I jist histed one of these yere laigs, so,
gin a crow hop with tuther, and let him charge atween em;
an es he went throu I cum down ontu his but aind with a
fire shovil, an hit cracked like ontu a pistil, an, I think, added
sumthin tu the force of his rush. He cum again the board
wall so hard that his shuttail flew over his head, an he
smashed the crockery night cap intu a thousand bits; hit
flew all over the room, and sounded like sum feller hed flung
in a shovelful ove gravil. He himself bounced back from the
lik inter the middil ove the floor, an lit on his sturn with

his laigs doubled onder him, an looked monsous like the snake an picter tent what goes with a suckus. Some ove the sharp scraps ove the delf war wer stuck in the wall, an some in his head. Thar he sot, plumb wide awake. His greasy-lookin eyes wer wide open, an sorter like the butt ainds ove two green bottils. He sot em on me, an then he shot em up rite slow, an opened em with a jirk and anuther whoof outen his snout; an es he did hit, he sed "Cott am." The cussin by this time wer a gwine on all over the house at an orful rate, an like thar hearts were in their work, the wimmen were a chatterin es bad es a campmeetin ove crazy monkeys with a bulldog amung em. Sez I, what the hell mistopher dus you mean by actin the bull in a bed-room, at midnite an makin yer self a durnd fool generally for, kin ye tell me? He jist went throu his moshuns with his eyes an sed "Cott am," agin. Is that all ye kin say? Has ye busted all ye Dutch talk outen you but that fool "cotam"? The idear now seemed tu strike him fur the fust time that he could talk Dutch, fur he jist sot intu a long job ove cussin in good Dutch. Hit run outen him in a solid sluice es thick es a hoe-handil. I listened ontil hit guv me the tooth-ache, an I had a sour taste in my mouf. When he stopped tu take breff, I axed him how does that chicken cock rest on yer bowels what yer cum the boarconstructor over. The thought on hit seemed tu tickle him, fur he spread out his mouf into a greasey grin an sed, "Tam goot, all put de does an de spurs, dey schraches shum mine pelly," an he rubbed hit onder his shut with his paw an made a face orful tu behold. "Put shune I trinks von bitcher ove viskey vot vill eat de points of de sphurs an does an ten all coshe goot—tam goot;" an he put his paw under his shut tu rub his belly agin, but fotch hit out with a jerk an anuther cotam. An now, George, I jist wish I may be infunely durned tu scrimshuns ef he warnt busted open for more nur a foot. Hit hed happened when he smashed the delf agin the wall. I tell you, hoss, that wer a orful jolt he got—that's so. I jist laid him ontu his back, tuck a nife fur a needil, an a ole bridil rein fur a thread, an sowed him up adzactly like ye sows up the mouf ove a par ove saddil bags with the strap, an then tied a knot on bof ainds ove the rein. While I wer makin the holes in the aidges ove the tare, he axed me to look inside fur the spurs of "tat tam schicken cock an gut tem off," but all I could see were his paunch, an hit looked adzackly like the flesh side ove a raw hide. Arter I got done, I axed him how he prospered, an he said "tam goot," and that he wouldn't keer a cuss fur the whole scrape, only he knowd that ontil he growd up he wer bound to *leak his lager bier*—knowd that with my long stitches he would loose "te las tam trop." Jist at this minit a big Shanghi bellered out a big crowd ni ontu the house. Dutchy widened his mouf ontil hit opened onder his years, an his eyes shined, an he sed: "Gut off hish spursh an pring him to me." I wer feard tu do hit, least the old bridil rein mout break, ur the knots pull out. The last I hearn ove Bull Dutchy, he had got well an war at Bristol, whar he hed bet a feller his trunk agin a barrel ove sourcrout that he could drink lager bier faster and longer nur a big muley cow could salted meal slop, an durnd ef he didn't win on bof pints. The bridel rein had hilt hits holt. That's so!

Nashville *Union and American,* December 5, 1858.

Sut Lovingood Travels With Old Abe as His Confidential Friend and Advisor

WHEN I told you, George, that I wer agwine tu travel with ole Abe Link-Horn, you thought I wer a lyin; but now ye see I'm here, aint I? I jis struck across the country and kotch'd up with him at Harrisburg (durn sich a place, I say), and I hev stuck clost to the old Windin Blades til I got him safe intu this heer tavrin, they calls hit "Willard's," an I'm durn ef the ole hoss ove the house aint a jedge ove liker. I've tasted hit I has, an I'll tell ye anuther thing, old Windin Blades am sleepin in the same rum what I dreamed ove in one thousand eight hundrd an fifty-six, whar Ole Buck played that orful game of kerds with Fill an Freemount fur the President's cheer, an won hit too, an he prides hisself in sittin in hit more by a durnd site nor them dus what set him thar.

But cs I wer agwine tu tell you, es I wer a gittin thru Bald-timore I seed a feller a sittin ontu a barrel a filin at the lock ove a durned ole revoltin pistil. Sez I, "Mister, are ye gwine tu war?" "Yes," sez he; "I'm gwine tu bore old Abe's years fur him es he cums along."

I went a piece furder an seed another fat ole tub a cuttin a cheese with a nife a foot long. "That's a monsous nife, Mister," sez I. "Y-a-w," sez he; "I means tu feel old Abe's haslet with hit," sez he.

I rocked along, an seed another feller a rubbin brite a orful cannon; hit wer es big es a pump log. "Gwine tu shute?" sez I. "Not jist yet," sez he, a measurin my hite an heft with his eye. "When are ye gwine tu shute, ef I moute be so bold?" "Day arter tumorrow," sez he; "I'm jist gwine tu take Ole Abe in the place what fust tetches a hoss, an dam ef he don't lite beyant Washintun, hit 'il be that this yere powder aint good"; an he dipped up a tin cup full outen a barrell and poured hit back like hit wer whisky. Jist about this time the ideur got onder my

241

har that Bald-timore warn't much tu speak ove, fur ole Windin Blades, and that they ment tu hev a funeral outen him when he got thar. So I put out tu meet him an tell ove the imedjut rath tu cum, an the orful tribulashun barrelled up fur his widder an that promisin sun, Bob, ove his'n. Now, George, Bob may make a monsous fine man, I don't say he won't; but es a boy—mind, I say *es a boy*— I'm d—d ef I fancy him a bit. Sum feller will turn him inside out sum of these days, see ef he dont (an who knows but hit would improve the little critter). He can't live es he is, that's surtain.

Well, when I told old Windin Blades what I had seed an hearn, his eyes sorter bulged and sorter spread, an his mouf swelled out, an sez he, "I hain't perpared tu die, Sutty, my Sun"—he calls me Sutty when he wants help, an Mister Lovingood when he's got his dignity on, an a passel of flat backs roun him an he feels good an safe—"I hes dun the things I hadn't orter, an lef ondun the things I had orter," an here he hung down his hed an studied a long time, while I sot still an tuk a gineral observation ove a President, an if he aint a long wun an a narrow wun, I'm durned. His mouf, his paw, an his footzes am the principal feeters, an his strikin pint is the way them ar laigs ove hizen gets inter his body. They goes in at each aidge sorter like the prongs goes intu a pitch fork. Ove all the durned skeery lookin ole cusses fur a president ever I seed, he am decidedly the durndest. He looks like a yaller ladder with half the rungs knocked out.

I kotch a ole bull frog once an druv a nail thru his lips inter a post, tied two rocks tu his hine toes an stuck a darnin needil inter his tail tu let out the misture, an left him there tu dry. I seed him two weeks arter wurds, an when I seed ole Abe I thot hit were an orful retribution cum ontu me, an that hit were the same frog, only stretched a little longer, an had tuck tu warin ove close tu keep me from knowin him an ketchin him an nailin him up agin; an natral born durn'd fool es I is, I swar I seed the same watry, skeery look in the eyes, an the same sorter knots on the "back-bone." I'm feard, George, sumthin's tu cum ove my nailin up that ar frog. I swar I am, ever since I seed ole Abe, same shape, same color, same feel (cold as ice), an d—d I'm ef hit aint the same smell. Sumthin orful es tu happen tu me in spite ove these yere laigs, much as I 'pends on 'em, see ef hit don't.

Well, arter he had studied an sighed, an sorta groaned a long time, he ris his head up an sez he, "Sutty, what had I best do in this orful emergincy? The party can't spare me now; besides I ain't fit tu die, an my wiskers hev just begin tu grow an I want tu try the vittils in Washintun City; hit won't du tu let me be made a sifter by these seseshun bullits just at this time. Will it, Sutty, my son?"

Sez I, "Mister Linkhorn, Ise called a natral born durn'd fool in Tennessee, but I think I ken averidge in these parts purty well, an ef you will jist put yesef in onder my keer; an ef ole Scott cums a cluckin about with his wings a trailin, or ole Sea-Ward cums a whinin an a smellin an a scrachin onder the door, jist gin the tavrin keeper the hint to hist thur cotails with his boot an that you'l pay fur toein one of em ef he busts em. I'l be constitutionally, sirkumstantially, an indiscriminately durned, ef I don't put you safe tu bed with Missis Linkhorn at Willard's Tavrin. I'l *du* hit; d'ye see these yere laigs?" an I hilt one straite out abuv the lamp what sot ontu the tabil.

He looked at me mournfully fur a minit, an his eyes run over, and sez he, "Sutty, my son, I'l du hit, an ole Abe won't lie, so gin yer orders an fix things; now I feel like I will be President yit," an he pulled out a pint bottle frum onder the piller ove the bed, an he measured hit with his thumbs, one over the other from the bottom tu the top ove the whisky, an thar wer jist seven thumbs; he then mesured back four an hilt the last thumb fast an run the neck ove the bottel in onder his nose about four inches; when he turned hit up again thar wer a half inch clar day lite onder the thumb, an he sot hit ontu the table. When he cotch his breff, says he, "I never incourages eny wun tu drink, but thars the bottel an *hit hes your whisky in hit.*" I tuck abourd the ballance. I did, an we went tu bed. Now how I got him tu Washingtun Il tell yu the next time we meet. Good bye. Say, George, ye never seed old Abe, did ye? Well, youve missed a site; nur seed Bob?—No, nur the ole 'oman? No. Well, Ise sorry, fur you aint yet ready tu die.

Nashville *Union and American,* February 28, 1861.

Sut Lovingood With Old Abe on His Journey

WELL, es I told you, we went tu bed arter that onekally divided horn and I sot in tu sleepin in yurnest, when I hearn "kerdiff, kerdiff"—an thar stood the old par ove Windin' Blades, jis as he cum inter the world, his shut hung on top ove the bed postez, an he had his red flannin drawers in his hand by the laigs, a thrashin ove em agin the wash stan; then he peeped down wun laig and then down tother; then he turned em inside out an zamined onder the seams from aind to aind.

Sez I, "Whats rong? Ar you huntin fur a seseshunist in as narrer a place as them ar drawer laigs?"

He shook his hed, and still zamined the seams. At last sez he, "Sutty, my sun, are you troubled *much* with flees down South?"

"Not es I no's ove; our dogs are sumtimes," sez I, "an we allers kicks em out when they scratches."

"Well," sez he, "I've allers had more ur less vexashun ove spirit with em, and the nier I gets tu Washintun city the wus they ar; ef thar number an enterprize encreases es they hev dun, afore I am thar a week, I'll be a dead man," an then he reached down both hands and scratched both laigs, frum his ankles up to his short ribs, an hit sounded like rakin' ove a dry hide with a curry comb, an then he cum tu bed agin, but kep on a rakin' ove hissef an sorter a cussin onder his breff.

Sez I, "holler up a nigger an git sum more tangle-laig."

"What's tangle-laig, Sutty?"

"Sum truck like what you hed in that ar lonesome lookin feller a standin on the tabil *by hissef*."

"Do you want sum more?" sez he.

"I dus that, onless you'll go tu sleep."

He got up an drug a ole har trunk from onder the bed. When he turned back the led, thar the bottils stood jis like sogers ove a muster day ur a Doctur's Medicin chist. We divided wun tolerable far atwixt us an wur a fixin fur sleep an a talkin ove fleas an how I would git him safe tu Washintun, when a thunderin knockin cum ontu the door. Ole Windin Blades jumped outen bed an agin the lock at one pop an keerfully opened the door, a holdin tu the handil with boff hands. Ater he seed an knowd em, he opened, when in popped two fellers in store close an a Sorrel irish-mun with flax mane an tail; an he had a letter. Ole Abe sot up cross laiged in a cheer in his shirt-tail an read hit a long time, fust wun side up an then tuther, an ater talkin an whisperin a spell they left.

Sez he, "Sutty, my sun, this ar a dis-patch from Gineral Scott, an hit proves what you sed about Bald-timore tu be true, an a tarnal sit wus. He sez that Alek Stevens am thar with a twelve-pounder strapped ontu his back an a lit rich pine torch in his hand awaitin fur me, an that hit is loaded with a quart ove escopet (old Scott calls everything escopet thats round) balls, three smoothin irons, four par ove butt hinges, an a gross ove shoe tacks, an the ole Gineral thinks frum his nolidge ove perjectils that ef it wer turned loose ontu me that my hide would be es well opened out es a fish net, an my close made redy tu stop cracks in a rain barril."

I jumped plumb outen bed an lit afore him an looked him stedy in the eye fur a minit, an I felt that I wer a standin fur the fust time afore a man I warnt feared ove, an hu, I knowd wer scaser ove sence then I wer, an I wer glad I had found him, fur you know, George, that I thot I wer the king fool ove the world, an allers felt shamed an onder cow about hit. *Aleck Stephens totin a twelve pounder*. I stood stonished, fust et him an then et old Scott, two bigger fools in the world than me, an boff on em able tu read an rite an a holdin high places in the naseun. Sut's got a chance yet, thinks I.

Sez I, "Mister Link-Horn (an I were skeered at the boldness ove my own voice), du you onderstand southern law!"

"No," sez he, "only es hit tetches niggers."

"Well," sez I, "I'll tell ye sum nolidge ove hit hes saved my life fur the last twenty years, twiest a year, an hit may save yourn once a month ef ever ye cum out thar, not tu speak of hits imedjut use in this imargincy. When

we lects our Governers we lects a fool-killer fur every
county an furnishes him with a gun, sum asnic, stricknine,
an a big steel trap, an hit is his juty to travel, say about
wun day ahine the Suckit Rider. You see, the Suckit
Rider gethers the people tugether an hit makes hit more
convenient, an he kills off the stock ove fools tu a consider-
abil extent every round he takes. Our fool-killers hev dun
thar juty, an consekently the South hev seceded. Ise been a
dodgen em sence I wer able tu run, and I now tell you,
Mister Link-Horn—"

"Stop, stop, *Sutty, my sun,*" sez he; "I wants tu ax you
a questun; why don't you stop the breed in a more humane
way by emaxulation an still let em live? The decleration
ove independence, you no, sez—"

"Stop," sez I, fur I found I war on risin groun, "An I'l
tell yu why emaxulashen wont kiver the case, no more nor
freein or stealin a nigger il make him a white man. Fools
break out like measils. They cums from the best familys.
An agin, a neighborhood ove fools will sumtimes breed a
smart fellow. Just look at Sea-Ward as a sampil, or
yerself. Yu cum from Kaintuck. An hit perjused Hart,
a feller hu makes people outen stone, till they kin du
everything but drink, talk an propugate thar speeches; an
caze they can't du that he's an onmitigated durned fool for
makin em stead ove rale livin folks. Spose the fool killer
wer tu kill (as in juty bound he orter) every 'bolitionist
now livin; woudent the same sile an climit, an feedin what
perjused the d—d ole cusses what burnt ole, palsied
wimen as witches; an perjused Jo Smith, an ole Miller, en
Miss Fox, an Wendil Phillips, an Missess Bloomer, with
her breeches an shut, nex year perjuse just such another
crop, say? Ove course hit would, an yet the rich strikes in
that ar country ove cod fish an mullen stalks, perjuced a
Hancock an the *Day Book,* so emaxulashen wont du; yu
must kill em jist es yu ketch em, es yu du your fleas, an
rely (es I dus on my laigs) on hard work in follerin arter
em frum generashun tu generashun. They onderstand this
ere thing in Texas adzactly; give em a black jack an a pece
ove bed cord, an that ar all they ax."

He studied a long time an scrached, an sez he, "Sutty,
atween the flees an your talkin, Ise sorty got tu wool
gatherin; I swar I hes; when I stopt you tu ax that ar

questin, what wer you gwine tu say about the fool killer in connecshun with my case?"

"Oh, nuthin," sez I. "Do you ever speck tu cum down souf, Mr. Linkhorn?"

"No, Sir," sez he.

"Well, then, hit dont signify," sez I, an we sot in tu plannin how tu get thru Bald-timore, an save his hide hole, an hit were done, an done well, tu, ef not wisely. Me an *Ethredge,* an ole John, am the only fellers from the souf, what am in the raffle at all. Nex time I see you, George, Il tell you how we eucherd all Bald-timore.

Nashville *Union and American,* March 2, 1861.

Sut Lovingood Lands Old Abe Safe at Last

ARTER the flees, and the tanglelaig, an my talk about the juty ove the fool-killer an hits effecks, we couldn't sleep any more, so we konkluded tu start on the fust train. I hed told a tayleur man—with a white face, a big foot turned out, a long measurin string, an a piece ove chalk—yearly in the nite, tu measure a a terbacker hogshead fur the body, an a par ove telegraph poles fur the laigs, an make a jackit an a par ove britches, outen cross-barred truck, an to let them bars run cati-cornered, that is, one what started on the shoulder should aind among the ribs on tother side, an bring along a pot ove red paint, an a small bale ove hay. Well, he did hit, an I run the ole Windin' Blades inter the breeches, an tied a string roun the ankles; then stuffed in a mixtry ove hay an the contents ove the har trunk; I did likewise with the jackit, an perjuced the biggest cross-barred man you ever seed; tu judge by site, he weighed seven hundred pounds, his hed didn't look bigger nur a apple. I painted the yaller off his face with the red truck, an hit tuck three coats to kiver hit; an I swar, when I wer dun with him he looked like he'd been on a big drunk fur three weeks. When we got outer the train the tavrin keeper didn't know him, an he got off without payin ove his bill; he winked et me es the kers started, an sez he, "thar am two dullars saved, sartin." He hes muney sence, ef haint eny uther kind.

We hadnt gone fur, when a littil, mild, husband lookin feller in gole specks an a pencil, cum up to me an sez he, "whars yer agent?" Sez I, "what agent?" "The agent fur yer show." I tuck the hint, and sez I, "Ise the agent." "Ah," sez he, "I thought you were the long half ove the show." "So I is; an Ise the smart half too, an em celebrated fur the use of these yere laigs," an I onfolded one an reached hit thru the winder on tuther side ove the ker; sez I, "aint that some laig fur reachin?"

He run his eye twist along hit frum aind to aind, an sez he, "Mister, you hes run powerfully to laigs; didn't a tellergraff pole fall across yer mom afore you wus bornd?" "No," sez I, "but we kep a pet sand hill crane, an mom an him hed a differculty, an he chased her onder the bed."

He sot that down with his pencil, an then he tuck a measurin sorter look et ole Abe who tended tu be sleep. Sez he, shakin his hed, "that am a monsous man, I mout say an orful man. What dus he weigh?" "Seven hundred an ninety even." He sot that down. "Hes he a family?" "Yes, he had thirty-four children, but a sorter diseas hes tuck off seven ove em, an he's spectin more tu die every day." "The ole man mus be in powful trubbil?" Sez he. "Not much," sez I; "he don't onderstan his loss." "Is he smart tu speak ove?" "Nun tu hurt," sez I; he sot that down an started.

Ole Abe opened his eyes an reached over an whispered in my year atwixt his sot teeth, "that ar las observashun ove yourn, Mr. Lovingood, am a durn lie," an he straitened up an hunted amung the straw onder his close, till he foun wun ove the bottils, an he gin his sef sum comfort, an never ofered me a durn mossel, but hilt the bottil up to the lite, an sez he, "on thinkin over hit you wer right tu tell him that I warn't smart, ur I woudent be here in sich imedjut danger, jis fur my party an a pack ove durned niggers," an he sot in tu thinkin an I went tu sleep, an when I waked he wer a kickin my shins.

Sez he, "Sutty, my son, we am in Bald-timore," an sure enouff, thar wer lites along boff sides the road as far as you cud see, jis like a string ove litnin bugs; an fellers a standin about with clubs onder thar arms an a revoltin pistil fur a brest pin. I seed ole Abe had obsarved hit, an he wer skared, fur the ash culler showd thru the three coats ove red lead ontu his face, an he scrached his hed an tried tu scrach his stern thru about a foot an a half ove straw an bottils. Then he looked out the winder a minit an fotch in his hed with a jerk an a ketchin me by boff hans, sez he, "great hevings, Sutty, es thar em an orful hell, thar em Aleck Stephens now with his drefull canyun."

I tuck a look an thar stud a pale Ytalian with a dubbil barrelled trumpet strapped acrost his back. Hit did glitter sorter skeary like, that am a fac. They calls hit a tom-bone an sez that hit makes musick.

"Now don't show yerself tu be a fool," sez I. "That feller am in a durned site more danger ove blowin out his own brains with that thing than you am. Sit still an keep yer shut on, will yer," but a big skeer wer on him all over, an I seed that nuthin but a runnin spell would help the old cowardly cuss. Well, I relyed on these year laigs; I knowd I cud ketch him ef he did break; sez he, a tremblin all over, "Sutty, my sun, ef Alex Stephens kills me I want you tu go tu illinoi an tell em that I died in the line ove my juty, like a man orter, an mine, tell em I died game an that my las wurds wer the Declerashun ove Independence sez—," an here he tuck a squint et the Ytalian; he hed outstraped his long twisted brass horn an hed hit in his hand sorter shutin fashion, thats a fac—an durn ef he dident go outer that keer like a cat outen a cellar when a broom am follerin; the straw made a monsous swishin sorter soun es he went thru the door an I hearn the bottils a clunkin es he run—I took arter him a hollerin, "Ketch him—dont hurt him, Ise a takin him tu an asslum; hes crazy es a bed bug but am not dangerous."

Well, a hevy sot yung feller with his shurt collor open an his briches in his boots an a black se-gar pinted up towards his eye, jist squate ontu his all fours afore the ole durnd crazy cuss, an he flung him two summersets over him, an windin Blades lit on his sturn an bounced an the bottils rattild agin; es I cum up the feller what throwd him sez tu me, "Be Gawd, that fat feller hes et a glass works fur supper, hesent he?" "Es like es not," sez I; "hes durnd fool enuff tu du eny thing." "I thot he hed frum the jinglin in his inards when he lit thar," sez he, an then he tuck a look et me fur a long spell; sez he, "Mister, let me gin you sum ad-vice; when you takes fatty tu the ass-lum du you stay out side the gate." Sez I, "Il du hit fur I nos you am a frien ove mine." Sez he, "is thar a tax ontu laigs wher you cum frum?" "Why?" sez I. "Caze," sez he, "ef thar am you am the poorest man in Maryland, thats all. How did the ole hay stack go crazy?" Sez I, "he et hissef outen his sences." "Be Jethero, I thot so," sez he; "I no that he never went mad a thinkin." Sez I, "Mister, you am right."

An then Ole Abe sot ontu his hine aind all this time

either scared or hurt tu bad tu move. I went up an whispered tu him tu git up an git inter the ker, an sez I, "hit won't hurt tu gin 'em a little crazy speech ofen the platform; hit won't cost you much trubile tu du that, an hit will convince 'em you am addled; jist talk nateral," sez I, "that's all yu hev to do."

Well, he groaned, an got ontu his all fours, an I swar jist then he minded me ove an orful elephant, called Hanibald what I wonst seed at a sarcus—now jist tu think ove this crossbarr'd great beastes bein ole Abe, President ove the United States ove North Ameriky. I swar, natral born durn'd fool es I no's I is, I felt shamed, an sorter humbled, an I sorter felt like cuttin ove his throat an a sellin the hay tu pay fur my shame, an drink all the whisky on his carcuss tu make miself feel good agin, but I shook him up, an got him tu the kers an thar he made a sorter talk.

Bout his wiskers an puttin his foot down on the Declerashun ove Independence an so on—Swish—apat—pop cum about a peck ove aigs, an they smelt powful. I jerked him inter the ker an hearn a feller holler, "we wer a savin ove em fur ole Abe tomorrer, but durn ef you aint entitled tu a few, fur being es big a fool es he is." The kers started fur Washinton an I wer glad.

"Now," sez I, "ef you'll keep yer mouf shut, Il git yu throu, an hit wouldn't be bad ef yu kep hit shut fur the nex four years." He sot still a while, an at last sez he, "Sutty, my son, what becum ove Aleck Stevens an his on yearthly canyun? Did hit go off?" "No," sez I, "but you did; you moved yerself." Sez he, "Sutty, we orter not be hilt sponsibil, when we are onder a big skeer." "That's a fac," sez I, "an that orter be norated tu the pepil, an get em tu endorse hit for hits all that'll save you, Mister Linkhorn, jurin yer stay es President. Jis take the persishion that you haint sponsibil while onder a skeer an hit will kiver your hole admistrashun."

"Sutty, my son, you am great," sez he, an we trundled on, nobody knowin the ole feller, an got inter the rume at Willard's; an afore I hed time tu git the hay an bottils an cross-barred truck ofan him, I hearn a noise in the passige like the rollin ove a wheel barrer mixed up with a heavy trampin soun; I thot hit wer a Irishman a fetchin coals, when the door flew wide open an in cum a peacock's feather, six foot long, with all the fuzz stripped off sept the eye at the pint; then cum a hat, shaped like ontu a funnil an kivered with gold, an then har an whiskers enuff to stuff a bed, an then more gold leaf an shiney buttons an then the forrard aind ove a swo-rarard, with ole Marcy's hed on top the handil; then a par ove boots what mout a been fire buckets footed, an then the hind aind ove that orful sworard, cum supported frume the floor by a wheel es big es a wash pan, to keep the scabbard from warin out a trailin on the ground, an when hit all got intu the rume an wer tuck together hit proved to be Lieut. General Winfield Scott, commander in chief ove all the yearth, an the whole afar, when straitened up, reached ontu the ceilin about fourteen feet, an that orful swo-rard nearly crossed the rume. Ise too dry to talk eny more now, but will tell you agin what that orful mixtry ove gold feathers, iron, noise, gass, an leather did, an how I wer skeered. Ain't a gineral an orful thing tu meet an contimplate, George, perticularly when they am a struttin an a gobblin.

Nashville *Union and American,* March 5, 1861.

Sut Lovingood's Hog Ride

HEARING an unusual noise on the road one morning, I looked for the cause. Ducktown was all alive, shouting, cheering, laughing.

Here came an "Israelite, in whom there was *much* guile," hatless, breathless, coatless, as fast as his abridged legs would allow, protesting most vociferously that he "vash *not* Levi Shacobs." Sut was in hot pursuit, with a table knife in his mouth and a clothes line in his hands. He would throw the coils over the Jew's head, lariat fashion, with great precision of aim, and he, with equal dexterity, would shed them off again, increasing his speed and his protestations against the "Shacobs" charge.

Sut would shout furiously in reply, "Yes you am Jacobs. Whar's my breetches, yeu durned close clipt, Ch—st killin, hog hatin, bainch laiged son of a clothes hoss? I means tu fust circumsize yer snout, and then hang yer arterwards. *Yeres* the tools," brandishing the knife and rope.

The vender of raiment made his shoulder-blades and elbows fairly flutter with his terrible efforts to "get on more steam." When Sut failed in his efforts to lasso his victim, he would bring the coil with whistling force across the Israelitish hips, fairly raising him from the ground, accompanying it with *"Thar,* that's wus nor yer bed bugs, an fleas, haint hit? *Whar's* them breetches?" The individual who "vash not name Shacobs" darted into the mouth of a mining tunnel, and I detained Sut.

"What's the matter, Sut?"

"Nuff's the matter, by golly. If old Job himself wer inside this yere shut, he'd shed hit an wade into that dumpy cuss afore you cud say drink. That ar cussed one story varmint in the tunnel thar, stole my breetches, my cross bar'd breetches; he stole em from a ole sow in Nashville, he did, an I'se arter em."

"But he says he is not Jacobs."

"Yes he am Jacobs. Haint he got a white face, a goose

wing snout, rat eyes, black har, bainch legs, slick hat, an a breaspin, and dont he sell shuts, and jackits, an coats, and fishin lines? Oh you cant fool me. I know a chesnut hoss from a hoss chesnut."

"Yes, but your description is general; it is adapted to most of his race."

"Well, it mayn't be him, but ef you'd a let me alone, I'd soon skeer'd im outen a par ov breeches in the dark ove that tunnel thar. His skeer was commin to a head pow'f'l fas. Jacobs, Jerusalem or Jehosaphat, hits all the same tu me. I'se arter britches hot; sum britches mus' cum now."

"Tell us about your breeches, Sut, and let that poor frightened fellow alone."

Sut thrust his head into the tunnel and shouted, "Say, old tabernickil, Ise got you now whar Alexander had the pole cat, an I'm gwine to watch the hole. A par ove breeches or a jackit for intrus', ur rite thar you'l lay yer bones."

"Well, I speck I mout es well tell hit my self, fur hits boun to leak out anyhow: Everybody in Nashville knows hit, and my karacter's made thar fur life, es bein the durndest plum fool ever in Davidson, not sceptin my own Dad.

"I hed foller'd a whisky waggin wifout a halter, plum inter town, and were slungin along a narrer lane name Union street. My eyes swelled es big es aigs at the bran new sights and sounds, and me just plum ready to ketch the runninist kine of a skeer. In wun of my sudden jerks a dodgin somethin, I felt boff ove my hine gallus buttons loose holt, an my cross bar'd britches war beginnin to wrinkil round my ankils bad, and a gittin lower every move. Tu make hit wus, thar wer a pint flask of swell hed whisky in wun pockit, and a pone of corn braid in tuther.

"The infunel street wer sock full of rale fine sunflower wimin, smelin ove bargamint, and a smilin kingdum cum all roun em. The men folks ove that ar town mus be a ornary set ove cusses, not to gin the wimin sumthin else tu do besides huddlin tugether in that street, jis like a drove ove red comb'd hens. Hits a durnd shame.

"I cudn't strip tu fix things thar, es I orter dun. I wus so monsous shame faced it has made agin me in gittin along mos es bad es my unyealthy looks and my durnd fool nater; but sumthin hed tu be dun, and that durnd soon. Spose them trousis hed fell jus thar, why I'd a follerd em tu the pavement in a twinklin ded es a stone hammer. I begun tu sarch fur a hole, and seed a narrer path, they calls hit a alley, guine out from the corner ov a gingercake and gouber pea factory. I took a 'zaminin look up hit, and seed nobody, so I gits me a savin holt with bof hans ontu the waisbun, and I shot in thar tu fix things. I felt sorter like a rabbit dus jus arter he's got inter a holler tree, and hears the dorg tar a mouful ov bark off clost ahine his tail. I tuk me a double ho'n the fust thing on the strainth ov findin a safe spot.

"I hed on a notail coat, sum calls it a rounabout, an a bobtail shut. In a jineral way I likes bobtail shuts; they dusent ketch dust es bad es long fan tails, an ef yu hes deep wadin tu du, they dusent git wet. A dry shutail is a comfortin thing tu go tu sleep wif, arter a holesome ho'n. Did you ever try hit?

"Well, arter I'd traveled up a piece, I turnd my face toards the street, an I cud see ef eny ove the wimin follerd me tu watch me. Theys powful curious things enyhow, bout men folks' doins. I let my britches drap tu the groun, so es tu see what had cum ove the hine buttons. They wer thar; hed jis got tharsefs onbuttind. I cotch my trousis by the front tu hist them agin, and had got my han holt es high es my knees, the starn part yet lyin on the yeath, and I war stoopin *low* forrid, when a cussed, medlesum New Founlan dorg, es big es a yearlin, an es black es the devil, cum a tarin outen sumbody's gate way up the alley ahine me, clost arter a thundin big spotted sow. He wer jis a movin her from haste, head down, bristils all sot, an a sayin booh, woof, goosh, every jump. I wer a lookin at em cum from atwixt my laigs, an a wonderin ef he'd ketch her. Thars a nuther 'vantage in bobtail shuts—I cud see good wifout risin up or turnin roun. The sow's eyes wer wallid back at the dorg, fust wun side and then tuther, an she never seed me, but dam ef the dorg didnt. Instuntly he hung out signs all over im ove big skeer. He wer the wust surprised, wust 'stonished, and the wust trimblin dorg I ever seed. He sot all his laigs and his tail ahead tu stop hissef, and he slid fifteen feet, whinin pitiful, and lookin monsous wishful

back up the alley, the way his hart wer gwin. He hadn't
the melt tu venter a secon' look—the fust wun hed run him
crazy, an ef he ever sees the likes agin, which I doubts
much, I'l bet high he jis gins up the ghost, not wantin tu
headway sorter stopt, he whirld roun, sez he, 'meew ra
harrowed wif sich orful, onnatr'l, onuseful, an tarifine
sights. He's right, dam ef he aint. When he got his
headway sorter stopt, he whirld roun, sez he, 'meew ra
a ap,' an ove all the durnd wholesale runnin—the pint ove
that ar bushy tail ove hisn wer glued clost tu his belly
atwixt his fore laigs, an wer drippin wet wif sweat. He
flung his hine laigs onder him like he wer tryin tu send
em home fust atwixt his fore ones, and his backbone
seemed es limber es a string. Oh Jerusalim, what a site
he mus a seed, to a throwd im intu sich spasms. I'll bet
a hoss you cant hawl im down that ar alley agin wif a
pair of mules an a log chain. Ef dorgs hes churches he's
jined wun sure. Well, he orter be surcumspeck in his ways
arter sich a warnin. I wish frum my heart the sow hed
seed me tu, an preshiated me half es well es the dorg did;
hit wud a saved my feelins, my cross bard breeches, an
pervented an undue exhitement amung the sunflower
wimin. But yere she cum jis a tarin, big black dorg
weighin pow'f'l heavy ontu her mine, run her snout atwixt
my laigs *over* the hine waisbun, and sock *intu* the fork on
the inside ove my trousis, jerked my heels frum onder me,
an sot me squar and bar sturn'd ontu her rump, my laigs
nakid frum my shutail mos tu my nees, up my britches
in tu hundred short wrinkils frum thar to my feet, an she
flindfolded in the seat ove em; rather discumfortin to a
sow ove delicate feelin's, warn't hit? I rid her outer the
mouth ove that ar alley intu the street es fas es a bird
kin fly. I hear'n the hem ove my bobtail shut snapin in
the wind way up level wif my years; jis then misfortunately, very misfortunately, a big red faced 'oman 'bout
the size ove a stack of oats, dressed in black silk, wif a fan
in wun han, and a half grown umbrella in tuther, wer
crossin the mouf ove the alley ontu the stepin stones. I
know'd what were cummin now, so I duck'd down my head
low ontu the sow's withers, and shot up my eyes fas' fur
manners sake. She run her durn'd ole britches kiverd
snout ahine the 'omans formos' gaiter, and afore the

hinemos' gaiter, and underminded her; hit were dark es midnight in the devil's tatter cellar in a moment, an staid so jis long enuf fur the sow to say "booh, woof, goosh," and we busted intu daylight agin, way up the midil ove the street. I looked back at a big black pile of sumthing in the gutter, wif a white stockin stickin out as big as a chun. I hed the young umbreller ontu my hed, an half ove a red flannel petticoat acros afore me, like a suckis rider toats his overcoat on his saddil ove hot days. The 'oman mus a bin sorter flustrated, fur she tole her husban' the steam fire ingine wif four hosses in a full blast hed run over her, an he, like a durn fool, believed her, an tuck a shot at the ingine wif a hoss pistil nex day.

"We tuck down towards Collige street, makin things happen every jump; you orter seed the slick niggers in gole hat ban's atop ove shiney carriages, a tryin to rein thar fool hosses outer store doors; every durned hoss wanted to hide hissef, an were a dancin the "Devils dream" in quick time. Down Collige we flu. "Booh, woof, gooosh," everybody dartin hither, and yan, an ove all the durned laughin you ever hearn, cum frum the folks what were outer our way.

"Wun big fat feller, plenty fat tu kill, standin in a tavern porch, scz he, 'Ha-ha-ha, say, shutail, he's arter yu; what'l yu take fur yer spotted mar?'

"Lord geminy, how bad I wanted a bridil jis then. 'Gallus up them britches, ur yu'l sun burn yer starn,' sed one. He were a pusson ove clost observashun, he wer.

"'Lainthen yer stirrups,' squeked a smutty faced boy. 'Hole hard, gingercakes, yer gwine down hill,' shouted a feller outer a packin box. 'Hole h-a-r-d.'

"Jis then we upsot a feller, wif a big pocket book under his arm; he wer a bank president. Sez he: 'Shoot that durnd fool, afore he kills sumbody,' like I cud help hit. I wernt thar apurpus by a durnd long site.

"'Say, hog express, what's happened in Cincinnaty?' sed sum one.

"'The loonatic asslum's burnt down,' sed sum one else—that feller mus a knowd me pussonally.

"I her'n the words 'dam fool' cum frum sum whar; thinks I, mister, yuse hit hit tu a dot, whether yu mean me ur this yer infernel sow. Wer eny body else roun yer?

" 'Hits nuffin gentlemen, but a lard oil advertisement got drunk an runnin outer time,' surjested a red nosed youf wife a patch over his eye. I wanted sum body tu say 'dam fool' jis then agin, but they didn't an I hadn't the time.

" 'The devil's in that swine, and she's makin for the river; better roll off yer yaller laigs,' sed a pale man wif a han saw under his arm. I ventured tu surjest tu him tu go tu hell, but hadn't time tu see if he minded me.

"Thar wer a big shiney bed stid a standin acrost the pavemint, whar they sells sich plunder, an a feller in a paper cap and bedtick aporn, wer a whitewashin hit wif varnish; we went atwix him an the yeath frum ahine, his brush lay in the store door, his pot tother side ove the street, an him flat ove his back, wif his arms spread like he wer crusified dead fur the time es Nebucadnesar's off-ox.

"I rekon, he thot hit mus' abeen lightnin.

"The sow shot onder the bed stid, a skinnin me plum outer my britches, still totin em entu her snout, wrong side out, an lef me sittin on the very pint ove my tail bone ontu the pavemint; by golly, the stones felt powrful hard an cold.

" 'Ha, ha, ha,' sed a nigger; 'sumbody ketch dat crazy man's hoss.'

"Thar I war, wif my long har, yaller laigs, socked into a par ove short hoss hide boots, not fillin em up much more nur the dasher dus the chun. I swar they lookt tu me jis then tu be es long es a par ove stack poles; a bob tail shut, a rounabout, and a little flimsey umereller, made up the picter, an ef it warn't purty, I'm durnd, an sooted tu a nicity, a street full ove wimmin folks. I jis wanted sumthin wif a big mouf an strong stumack tu swaller me. I thot if I jis hed my britches, I cud stan it, so I riz an tuck arter the cussed sow. The ole rase hoss fool. She'd tuck down Broad street, and when I got thar, she wer outer site; tuck the rever, sure enuf I rekon, but I seed that feller in the tunnil thar, ur his twin bruther, a brushin my cross bard britches; an agin I got tu him, he'd hung em up tu a nail at his door, wif 'Fur Sale' in chock on the stern; sez he, 'O mien frent, yu vants shum pants vera mosh; zey feets yu goat, zo vera long in ze laig.'

" 'Yas,' says I; 'gin em up, theyse mine, you durn raskil; you stole em,' an I made a grab fur em. But he dodged atwix us sayin 'yu steal my goots, I puts yu in shail.' Jis then two perlease grabbed me, flung a blankit roun me and hauld me tu the work'us, ontu a forkid tail coat, charged wif an ondecint showin ove my pussin, 'soltin an 'oman, killin a painter, bustin a bank, an raisin hell ginerly an never sed the fust durn word agin the sow, ur the Jew; that's jistis haint hit? Now Ise yere, an arter my britches; they mus cum. Say yu in thar, Moses, Levi, Solomon, Samuel, Jacob or Pontshus Pilit, cum out yer an 'goshitate like a human, ur I mus cum in thar arter yu, wif my rope."

Sut got a pair of breeches, and the "follower of Moses" went his way.

Nashville *Daily Press and Times,* September 14, 1865.

Sut Lovingood's Big Dinner Story

I'L agree to be doddrabited, if my bristils ain't sot this morning. I has a right sharp appetite to fight sumfin, I has. Don't you believe, that bald faced, check apron'd, calicker cap'd, ole she pot ove purgatif intment, Misses *Jarrold,* on Willow Creek, hain't sot in to writin' about *me,* in Ivinszes' noospaper, a-belitilin, an' a-bemeanin me, wus nor if I wer a suck aig dorg—yes, wus nor if I wer even a radical, an' all for nuffin. Now, by golly, no body can't tramp on *me,* wifout gittin thar foot bit. I means to let a cat outen the bag, an' if she quiles up her snout about hit, I'l print the cat, all along a noospaper. She'l find hit heavier to bare, than the tiltin' hoop disease, what she says she has a ragin' so bad in her famerly, or that cross she has to tote, weighin' a ton, or bofe ove em together.

You know, *George,* that thar is some folks powerful feard ove low things, low ways, an' low pepil, an' everlastinly a-tryin' their durndest, to show that they ain't low. Always on a fiddil string strain, a-lookin' up for a higher limb to roost on, an' wringin' in every chance far or onfar, what a h—l ove a feller thar granmamey was, never seed a louse—smelt a bed bug, or hearn tell ove the eatch, in thar lives, no sir, never. They ginerily has a pedigree wif one aind tied to thar sturn, an' tother one a-soakin' in *Noah's* flood, an' they'l trace hit back for you, round the jails, onder the galluses, apast the soap works, an' over the kitchens, ove four thousin years, an' if you'l notice clost, hit makes some ove the shortest kind ove dodges, to miss 'em all; but by golly, hit does miss 'em, an' hits every durn castil, an' throne, on the whole road.

I likes that pattern ove pepil, most wonderfully I does, an I think, *George,* if ever I could jist git to sleep wif one a night or so—a *he* one I means, durn you; what are you grinnin at? I sees nuffin to laff at myself—hit mout fix *me* for mixin decent society, roostin high—eatin peas wif a fork, an play h—l wif my insex forevermore; but durn em, I never hev yet got nigh enuff to one, even to larn his smell,—thars a gulf atwixt them an me, an I speck hits well for me that thar is. Well! Old Misses *Jarrold* is one ove that brand ove cattil; her big pints ove gentility is kiverin the looking glass wife bobinett, quilin up her snout at "low trash," scourin the door sill, havin a red cushion stuffed wif hen feathers on her banch at church, makin old *Jarrold* tote a hot rock arter her when she goes thar, scoldin neighbor wimmen for sucklin thar brats afore folks. hangin paper nets up to the ceilin to ketch flies, larnin her gals to play the "Flowers of Edinburgh," on an accordeon with the rattles, growin a row of hollyhawks from the door to the gate, an back agin, marryin her gals to a pedigree, whitewashin the—springhouse, keepin the *Pilgrim's Progress* on the candle-stan, an' a par ove plarster ove paris pigeons on the mantle-shelf,—an' thinks callin dung—dung, bad grammer. *Her* granmamy wer a h—l ove a feller, I reckon. Now, a hongry lookin' young lawyer, wif black freckils an' mink eyes, one ove the kind ove varmints that wud hide onder a bed to listen—peep through the key-hole ove a gal's bedroom, or break open other folks' letters, had settled on the crick, offerin' to practize law, an' while he wer breedin' a few suits amung the old neighbors, Misses *Jarrold* was a breedin a weddin' atwix him and her darter *Susanah Jane* (her "bud ove promice," as she calls her). Very well! Her fust move wer to make a big dinner, an' invite all the ugliest gals round thar what cum up to her idears ove decent standin', so as to set off the "bud ove promice" in the eye ove this legal fickshun, named *Gripes*. Amung them was *Violet Watson*, not a purty gal, I know, but smart, neat an' as full ove mischief as a turtil is ove aigs in May. She had no sort ove fancy for Misses *Jarrold's* fool ways, an' valued Mister *Gripes* about as she would any other peckerwood or pole cat; so you see she woudent stand back a minit to devil 'em any time. I warn't invited, in course I warn't; Misses *Jarrold* would as soon tho't ove invitin' old *Barkley's* big bull.

The arternoon afore the big *Gripes'* dinner, *Violet Watson* an' me hilt a convention, sorter barin on the subjec. I wer to follow her to *Jarrold's*, an' then she wer to tell the old quilt that I had toted her across the crick dry-shod, an' for her to please let me slunge round the kitchin, an' give me some dinner in a tin pan, or skillet, provided I kep outen sight ove her cumpany, an' behaved mysef. I kep my contrack; I never behaved myself better in my life, an' *Violet Watson* will say so, any day. As soon as she got farly in the house, she pinned up her frock, an' tucked up her sleeves, an' sot in to helpin the old jade get dinner ready. What wif her neat ankils, plump, white arms, an' the coming mischief a sparklin in her brown eyes, she looked rale holsum—sorter eatable like, I swar she did. Hit warnt long afore she coaxed old climb-a-pole outen the kitchen, an' got her to go to the big room whar the cumpany was, when she imejuntly sot in to lecterin on pedigrees, an' spreadin herself generally. Now this give *Violet* full swing in the kitchen, an' me helpin in my rough, fool way, we sorter *did* fix things. If anybody had been a noticin right clost that mornin, they mout a seed me a hidin three or four little pokes full ove sumfin in the jimson weeds ahine the smoke'ous—them ar pokes, George, contained venemous rep-tiles, too numerus an' horrid to menshun. Well! *Violet,* she cut two holes in a sheet, socked my arms through them, pinned hit clost roun' my naik, tucked hit in an' pinned hit roun' my wais', and hit reached to my heels—the all-firedest, long, graveyard lookin apron you ever seed. I tell you, hoss, I looked like the ghost ove a dead rope-walk. I were bof sickly, an' skeery to look at, I swar I wer. Then she sot me to totein in the kivered dishes ove vittils an' things, an' a settin em on the table in the dinin room. I had filled some ove them for her, she bein feared to handle the vittils, if hit could be called vittils at all, what wer in em.

Ole Misses *Jarrold* had gin up the dinner bisness to *Violet,* out an' out. She know'd she couldent be beat—her mind was easy, an' so she jist lumbered on the needsecity ove pedigrees to her company, to her heart's content. Oh geminey! What a misplaced confidence that wer. I tell you, hoss, I wouldent trus' myself outer my own sight a minit to save my life. Well! while I wer a totin in the last dish, *Violet* sent word to Misses *Jarrold* that dinner wer ready, tuck her bonnet, slipped out the back way, an' cut for home, by-golly—onbenowenst to me or any body, leaven me thar among inemys, shrouded up in a durned old sheet, onable to make the first bulge towards a run, an' a h—ll ove ove a big storm about to bust. But thinkin I had good backin in the kitchen, I wer carlm enuff to watch things as they happened, plum through the whole rumpus. Down they all sot, Misses *Jarrold* at the head, an' her ole corn-stalk ove a man at the foot ove the table, *Gripes* on her right, the "bud ove promice" on her left, an' the ugliest, cross-grained gall in the house next to the "bud." Passun *Bussum* sed grace: sed "make us thankful for what we are about to reseive," an' so forth, an so on, an' so along. Thinks I, old hoss, if these folks *am* thankful, you may consider yourself *a whale*. She had her boys an' galls, an' five or six young free niggers, standin in rows behind the chairs, drill'd, and waitin for the word to lift the kivers. That wer another climb-a-pole idea she'd picked up some whar. She 'spected hit to hev a perfoun' effect—an I'm dam if it dident. She looked as solemn as a Tuesday night arter a funeral, or a snowstorm, an' ses she, a tappin the table wif her finger, "one-two-three, *onkiver*." All at onst they did hit, and all at onst, an durnd quick, too, they drapt the kivers smashin onto the floor, an' jist went sliucein out ove the doors, a climbin one another, an' a screamin—boys, galls an' young niggers—they hustled, by golly. You see they wer a standin, an' got the first good peep into the dishes. Now, doleful things begin to happen all along the table, an' all at onst; but as I can't tell hit all at onst, not bein a 'oman, I'l take a dish at a time, an go slow.

A big, brindil tom cat, in a state ove hot agravation, with his tail swell'd as big as a rollin-pin, ris outen a dish; as he flew he gin a surjestif hiss, an' lit on Passun *Bussum's* head, whar he jist staid long enuff to gether nail holts, when he went agin for the lookin-glass; stickin, spreadeagle fashion, to the bobinett, an' wavin that orful tail, he looked green-eyed over his shoulder down at us, an' issoed a long, fightin groan. Sez I, "skat," an' he skated instuntly. This time he made a bee-line for Misses *Jarrold's* cap crown, but havin' in a leetle too much powder, his belly jist brushed her top bow of red ribbon, an' he lit a tip top ove the "bud ove promice," scratchin up a shower ove rose leaves from among her har. He jist staid long enough for me to "skat," him to hiss, an' her to screech, when outen the door he flew breast-high, his swell'd tail flyin round an' round like the crank ove a grindstone, an' him lookin as big as a fox, closely chased by a 'vengeful dish kiver, what I tried my durndest to kill him wif, for not stayin amung us longer. I sorter liked his company, an' his performance—he wer jist four secon's in the house arter the kivers wer lifted. Outen another dish cum a half peck or so ove striped garden frogs, an' one big bull feller—every cussed one had an idear ove his own as to the course home. The bull, about as big as a smoothin' iron, made a lubberly lunge at random, an' lit, flat ove his belly, spat on top ove a big mound ove butter, an' thar he stuck, with his laigs mired up in it to his body. He contented his sef by sorter grittin his teeth, an' sayin somfin like "jugsrum." One long laiged, acktif little cuss made a vig'rous lope at old *Jarrold's* snout, an' shot into his mouth up to his hamstrings. The old feller gin a vomitin sort ove a jerk, an' blowed him half the length ove the table. He lit on his back, but flirted over like a flash, lookin knowingly roun' for another hole to jump at. He seed Passun *Bussum's* hary breast through the crack in his shut bussum, jist sed "chouk," an' in he went a flyin. The old fat rip ris from there; a holdin out his shut wif bof hands, like hit wer red hot, an' sot into dancin Killacrankey, in double sole hoss-hide boots, powerful thankful fur what *he'd* received, I speck. Another ove the interprizin little devils, mistakin hit for a hole in a stump, went head fust into a fat, sweaty, sour lookin gall's bussum, an' set in to scramblin down the valley. She did the durndest, slickest, slight ove hand trick I ever seed any 'oman do. She jist jump'd with her feet up in the chair, an' cotch hold ove her shut back ove her naik wif bof han's, an' commenced a haulin hit up overhanded, from onder her dress, until she got hit all out from behine, an' over her head; then she jerked the front tail out ove her bussum, as slick as you could draw a handkercher. I seed the frog jist then, fall between her feet on the chair, and lope into the fire place; he looked powerfully out ove countenance, an' stonished. Seein a baby-faced feller a sittin opposite wif his pop eyes sot, a starein impudently at her, she flung the ruffle tail thing over his head, an' then busted a full soup tureen on hit. I speck he thought the infunel shif' had exploded. Then she broke for home, a durnin old

Misses *Jarrold* an' all her crowd, orfully. I thot she wer a little hostil like, from the way she behaved herself. As she walked off, I 'zamined her general 'ppearance, an' you couldent tell to save yer life that she had no ruffle tail thing on. She shook her hips tho', powerful as she walked—mad, by golly, mad as a hornet.

George, you never did see a matter of half a peck or so ove frogs show as much anxiety to distribute tharsefs abroad as they did, an now comes the reason for thar hurry. When the kiver come off the dish next *Misses Jarrold* (she wer a lookin for roast venison), *Gripes*, he peeped in, an says he, "dear me, madam, what a remarkable sassenger." "Law, *Mamey*," sez the bud ove promice, "if it haint got eyes." Jist then, the purtiest, slickest, shiniest four and a half foot black snake, what wer quiled in the dish, begin to pour out over the aidge ove hit, onto the white table cloth, like a stream ove ink, as big as a broom handle, runnin slowly towards madam *Jarrold;* he wer a whippin out his blue steel spring lookin tongue, first towards a pile ove sassers on one side, an then towards a milk pitcher on tother. Now, hoss, I reckon you know what hit wer that skeered the frogs so. Misses *Jarrold* aimed to scream, but dident draw the puckerin string in her throat tight enuff, an hit cum out a pitiful blate, like onto a calf, when you is a crowdin him. She tried to shove her chair back wif a jerk, but hits hind laigs cotch agin the aidge ove a puncheon, and over hit tilted. She flung a summerset backwards, showin her shoe soles to everybody at the table. She had on gray garters, bein the salvidge tore off a piece ove white flanin. Now, she had tuck about two yards ove black ribbon, an' had pin'd one aind to her back, then fotch hit round her, to mark the huggin line, and made tuther end into a big bow behine, fastenin hit wif a pin. The jerk of her tumble backwords lost out this last pin, an' the ribbon trailed arter her, as she run, sorter ratlin over the chips in the yard; she look'd over her shoulder, an coch a glimpse ove hit cummin. *"Snake arter me,"* shot through her head like a hot knittin needle. She jist tuck up her coats, mos' to her knees in bof han's—its a habit she's got any how. Old *Jarrold* is a mitey slow, rumatick, keerless, forgetful sort ove body—she hates draggild skirts—an' has a rale purty laig, so for these three reasons she shows hit.

By the ghost ove old *Flyin* Childers, she jist tore through the orchard, like an old doe; her white stockins flashed apast each other so fas', you couldent begin to count. Old Jarrold, in runnin outen the door, saw what he tuck to be the black snake a *climbing his wife's back*; this made him as hot as a ho'net, so he grabb'd up a hoe, an' tuck arter her, to kill hit. Ketch the comit—kill the devil, the durnd old rumatick fool, why she tuck four steps to his one. Old Squire *Ball,* wer jist ridin up, sorter belated to the dinner, an' seein old *Simon Jarrold* hot arter his wife, wif a drawn corn hoe, he thought theyd been a scrimagin, so he jist reign'd round his mule—went home, an' issooed a warran' for im, chargin salt, an' batter, wif intent to kill, an' hit tuck the durndest, hardest swarin, you ever hearn, to keep the old cuss outen jail.

Now the rale snake hisself jist glided clost roun the bottom ove the milk pitcher, an' started to pour hisself over the aidge ove the table, but he couldn't get good scale holt on the hangin' cloth, so he fell and lit in *Gripes*' hat, what he had sot by his chair, an' forted hisself onder some law papers in the crown. *Gripes* seed 'im fall, but couldent see what become ove him, an' tharfore took the skeery fool idear into his head that the snake wer in *both* ove his boots. You jist orter a seed him shell them boots; they jist shot ofen his feet. He socked on his hat an' broke to run in his stockin' feet, an' the fust thing I seed wer the snake a comin' out from onder the hat behine, an' a gwine in atwix *Gripes*' shut collar an' his yaller naik, strait down his nakid back. Sez I, "*Gripes,* he's a cold one, ain't he?—powerful pizen, too." He fotch a snort an' a shiver, an' knocked off his hat wif a back-handed lick, jist in time to fasten bof han's on blackey's tail. Now, hoss, believe me, hit wer pull *Dick,* pull devil; he couldent haul the snake up, and the snake wouldent come up, but mind you, George, that reptile wer four foot an' a half long, an' he wer obleged to strenthen his purchase against the pullin at his tail some how, so he straightened out some ove his kinks, down the dark, greasey, pimply holler, along that legul back-bone, ontil he cum to the forks ove the road; then he would roun' the turn, a leavin' a laig on his right an' a laig on his left, an' started up hill agin, along the legul belly, aimin' for a little sink-hole, jist onder the waisbun buttons ove the crazy, frighten'd cuss, but afore he got thar he seed a streak ove day light, an poked out ni onto a foot ove hissef to 'zamine the open country a little; this wer as fur as he could git, for the holt onto his tail, so he made the most ove hissef, an commenced a reachin' round, an about, in all directions, now an then makin letter S's, an whippin out his tongue, the madest, sassiest kind. He looked sorter curious, durned if he dident. *Gripes* had gin his hole sole up to the lively bisnis ove bouncin, from the moment he found hissef to be astradle ove a snake—stradlin bounces, two feet high bounces, nervous bounces, and a heap ove em, by golly, keepin his socks fur enuff apart to have rolled a whiskey barrel atwixt em, wifout barkin his laigs. I tell you, hoss, a bull cockroach, in a hot skillet, would a been thought sorter lazy. Snakes, you know, George, *do* feel dreadful cold—then thar scales, a scrapin the dander off yer skin—then the sarchin idear hitself, *snake* atwixt you an yer trowsis behine, an before, wif no yeathly hope left, that it mout only be a wet rope arter all; for thar a starin you in the face you sees a libral seckshun ove the bitein aind ove the shiney, vengeful lookin reptile, jis a cavortin, an a sloshin, and you have nuffin atwixt you an imejut death an durnation, but a few slick inches ove onsartin, live, taperin tail holt—bounce! Hu the *h—l wouldent* bounce? *George,* jist look at my forrid. See how I am a sweatin; let me res a minit.

Well, I'll try hit agin. *Gripes* had been a doin his bouncin purty much at random, until he seed the snake, then he reversed the engine, an' sot in to bouncin backwards. I tell you he retrograded over everything, hands still fast at the back of his naik, ontu that life or death tail, an' his eyes jist *hanging down,* by golly, sot an' glassy, onto tother aind ove the snake. I'd bout as leaf been well rubbed wif gunpowder an' in the devil's buzzum, on a hot arternoon, as to had his thoughts an' feelins for a minit.

Says I, "risk one han', and yamp him by the naik, you durned fool."

(Advice, you know, *George*, feels *so* good when you is skeered out ove all idears ove yer own.)

Says he, still a bouncin, "Han' me some san' to mend tail hold wif."

"San' be d—d," sez I, "risk one han' dry so."

He ventered hit, and made a wipeing grab at the snake's naik; hit dodged like a weazel, an' come back wif an open jawed lick at his han'.

Sez I, "Oh, by gravy, he'll fight hoss, but snakes don't know anything about left hands; try hit."

He changed han's, and made a *long* wipe, sorter like you would at a fly on yer hoss. The snake struck this time afore he dodged, an' the wipe turned into a dodge. *Gripes* fell back on double-handed tail holt an' bouncin agin. I could think of nothin else to tell the poor devil, an' hit grieved me. When I comes to be hung, I don't think I'll hev any hard feelins at the lawyer what pleads agin me, unless I forget *Gripes*.

The mos' ove the boys an' galls wer in the yard, or on the fence, an' the sight ove *Gripes* ridin' an onbroke, cavortin', four year old snake, made them forgit all about thar own skeer, so when his terrible hoss druv him crazy, an' he tho't he wer in open Sarkit Court, an' holler'd beggin' like, givin' a backward bounce atwix every word, "May hit please yer honor, he's a sawin' me in two; I feels the hot links ove my intrals down bof laigs ove my britches —a injunction, Jedge,—a injunction—quick, lord, Jedge," —I tho't in my heart, they'd all die, sich yellin,' screamin, an' laffin', was never hearn before. One stutterin', onthinkin', durn'd fool, blind ove one eye, arter two or three hurtin' lookin' trials, to git his mouf on a full cock, said "W-w-wo, Alborax!" The words warn't cold, afore *Passun Bussum* sprawl'd him on the wood pile, wif an old ax helve. Passuns, you know, are always a-watchin' for some chance to repruve pepil, an' I think old *Bussum* took the slimest chance, that time, I ever seed; what yearthly harm was there in, "Wo, Alborax?" I had been tryin' my durndest to think up some more advice for *Gripes*, an' at las, the ginuine idear come, an' I belched hit out. Sez I, "Tail holt be durn'd, hit'l break some time anyhow; let hit go, an *run* by golly, run plum outen yer close, that's yer ticket, hit never fails." The infernel fool had wasted bouncin' enuff already, to hev put him three miles beyant the last snake in the world.

He tuck me at my word, an' bulged; he run jist adzackly like you'd take steps wif an open par ove compuses, a side at a time, but faster nor a flutter-mill, the snake's head swayin fust apast one hip an' then apast tother, so quick I thot thar must be two ove em. Thinks I, solemnly: "Hoss, the 'bud ove promice' wudent have you now to save yer durn'd life." He tuck through a co'nfield, whar hit was higher than his head, makin hit roar. I watch'd his cource by the fluttern ove the co'n tassils. Torreckly I seed his coat an' jackit fly way up in the air; still furder away I seed a sheet sail up an' fall, lodgin on the tassils; still furder, an' up went his brecches, galluses an'—a snake. Follered my council to a dot, dident he. I haint met up wif that snake, as I knows on, an' durn'd ef I dont fear I never will. *He* knows a few sumfins. As to Gripes, I haint seed him; hes you? I *has* hearn that he's in Texas, tendin sheep for *George Kendall,* an' day an' night totes a snake-pole.

When *"One-Eye"* cum too, he sot up on aind on the wood-pile, and sez he, sorter weak like, "L-l-lets go—d-d-dinners o-o-over."

You haint axed me how I got out ove the grave-yard aprun; you forgot hit, *George*, dident you?

Nashville *Union and American,* August 10 1866.

The Rome Egg Affair

A MAN in Rome, Georgia, sucked six dozen raw eggs at a sitting. "Sut Lovingood" is living in that neighborhood.

When the above was read to "Sut" he thus "onbuzzum'd hisef":

"Say, George, I dusent much like the soun' ove that ar ho'n; I smell a slur in hit—Ise pow'f'ly feard some ornry cuss am a tryin to pin that ar freak ove genus to my cotail on the sly. I never *et em,* by golly! I haint ownd six dozen aigs, since Sherman come yere, an' biled the hens, an' smash'd the delf war. (Wonder if he don't consider hisef a hoss—a hell hoss by geminy! His wife mus' be pow'ful feard ove him, spechuly when he's in one ove his ways; our wimmen all am; they prays some for im too, they dus.) I 'spects some houn' year'd radicul, for wantin to raise anuther mob by cripplin me wif that breckfus of aigs —wants to construct me, may be. Now, I perposes to advise wif him a little. If he has pressed anybodys spoons, he'd better go back arter the ladle—if any body has busted thar boot, a stumpin thar toe agin his later aind, he'd better hev hit half soled for em, an' sorter squar up his bisness ginerly, for if I don't mean to administer on his estate, three secon's arter sight, damee. Mus' think I is fon' ove aigs, the durn'd raskil.

"But, George, the kaig ove aigs *were et* at one meal, an' I knows hu did hit; hit were a Georgia delicate to the poor white trash convenshun, whats a threatnin to spread a epademic ove lice in Quakerdelphia; his wife made im do hit, an' twenty-one days arterwards to a dot, he vomited up forty-one chirpin chickens, a little soft-shell turkle, a hens nes' made outen cotten stalks, an' thirty addil'd aigs what smelt like sour'd gunpowder. The las' I hearn from the reptile, he had a six foot buck nigger swaller'd to the kidneys; the nigger bein wide coupl'd, he wer a waitin for sum more grease. That job, when finish'd, is intended to give a extra weight in the convocation of pole cats. I'l swar eny time to his eatin the aigs, for his wife *show'd me the shells*. She calls 'em a dead loss—flung away on him entirely, an' seems ruther down-hearted.

Nashville *Union and American*, September 2, 1866.

Sut Lovingood, on the Puritan Yankee

"POWERFUL ornary stock, George, powerful ornary."

The rale, pure puritan, yankee baby, has a naik like a gourd, a foot like a glut, an a belly like a mildew'd drum head. He gits his eyes open at five days, while uther purps hev to wait nine, an' long afore that time he learns to listen ove a night, for his mam's snorin, when he sneaks in to suck on the sly, not that he's hongry for he's got the usual yankee mess ove biled starch, but becaze stolen meat is sweet even this yearly, to the blue, bline, scrawny young trap maker. He hes cheated his mam, wifout eyes—so I guess he'l make a average yankee, able to keep up the famerly name, an' perhaps invent a cod hook, or a clothes pin. From that night on the varmints whole life is a string ove cheats—straight along, never restin, never missin ontil the clock's wore out an the cords broke. As the dorg vomits, as the mink sucks blood, as the snail shines, as the possum sham's death, so dus the yankee cheat, *for every varmint hes hits gif'*.

He believes in schools an' colleges, as a barber dus in strops, an hones, as bein good tools to sharpen razors on. He'l sing hymes, an' pray prayers for you, an' maybe gin you a dime, but if you don't soon fine out yersef sot back five miles on yer road to heaven, an' ninety cents loser by his zeal, an' charity, you may shoot my eyes out, wif a buck load of cow——slop, an' I wont even say "Phew!" His long, cold, flat back is the color ove a merlatter-gall's head, jis arter hit has been close shaved, an' hits stuck all over from the scrag to the tail, wif his sins like revenoo stamps on a law suit, an' if you'l zamine em clost, you'l fine a cheat of sum sort in the las' durn'd one. If he sins amung the she's, thar's a cheat either in money ur expectashuns. If he sins a cussin, thar's a cheat in the words; he'l try to smuggle in G-d d—n, onder the whinin sham ove "gaud darn." If he sins a stealin chickens, he'l steal back at day break, an' crow jis' to cheat the poor devil inter believin that the ole cock is still on the roost. If he sells you an apple for a cent, arter smellin the copper he'l try to slip a peach ontu you, even if hit is ove the same price, jis' for the sake ove stick'n a cheat intu the trade. If he scalds his leather snout a dippin hit intu your soup, he'll offer you a wooden nutmaig for enuff of the skeemins to grease the burn. He'll eat a codfish, and try to cheat hissef intu believin hits beef, an' he'll listen tu the chirpin ove the cricket in his fire jamb, tellin his childer that it says, "cheat," "cheat," "cheat." His big, limber foot is a cheat, for hits size and shape makes you think hit *mus'* have guts in hit, when hit haint got one. If you cut his throat, you'll find a cheat, for instead of warm red blood, a stream sky blue will run so cold that hit'l freeze the black ants what gits overtuck by the flood, and when the devil gits 'im, *he'll* be cheated, for he wont burn as good as a salted raw hide. What he wer ever made for is what's a pesterin' me, onless hit were to make us hev a better 'pinion ove pole cats, possums, an' cotton-mouths, or as livin sampils to skeer us out ove the road to hell. I reckon it wud be a tolerable safe rule to do nuffin the yankee does, an' do mos' enny thing what he lets alone.

I kin sorter bar the idear ove my bein a natral born'd durn'd fool, my dad a playin h——l actin hoss, the sody bisness, sister Sall's onlawful baby—everything—everything, even the las' war an' Thad Stevens—but for the life ove me, I can't reconstruck mysef on the idear ove the landin ove the *Mayflower*. What cud our Maker be thinkin about that he forgot to lay his finger on her rotten old snout, an' turn her down in the middil ove the soft sea, wif her pestiferus load of cantin cheats an' moril diseases. The wust that cud a happen'd wud a been the pisinin ove a shoal or two ove sharks, an' killin the coral whar the old tub lay.

I is mad at the injuns too, for they dident begin to do thar juty to 'em arter they did lan'. If they had carcumsized the head ove the las' durn'd one, burnt thar clos, pack'd thar carkuses heads-an-tails, herrin fashun, in thar old ship, sot the sails, an' pinted her snout the way Ward's ducks went, they'd desarved tobacker an' whisky, while wood grows or water runs. 'Spose they had a strung three hundred an' one scalps on a willerswitch for bait, an' went a mackril fishin. We'd hev mackril now a days I reckon, but what a gineral blessin hit wud a been to the hole yeath—the isles ove the sea, the witches, an' the niggers. Wudent them injuns had a savory smell in my snout, in spite ove thar grubwurm oder, an' wudent I rise ove a midnight, or any other night to call 'em blessed, in spite ove thar roastin my grandady. No wooden clocks, horn gun flints, nur higher law. No Millerism, mormonism, nor free love. No abolishunism, spirit rappins, nor crowin hens. No Bloomer bit—britches I meant to say, no Greeley, no Sumner. Oh! My grashus, hits too good to think about. Durn them leather injuns; they let the bes' chance slip ever injuns had to give everlastin comfort to a continent and to set hell back at leas' five hundred year. I is powerful feard I aint reconstruktid on the injun question ither.

George, pass the jug; the subjick is overpowerin me, an I aint quite dun onbuzzumin mysef yet. That's powerful fur reachin whisky ove yourn.

Well! Everything the yankee does am a cheat in sum way. The word cheat kivers his hole character as pufeckly as the ball ove dirt kivers the young tumil bug, an' like the bug, he lives on hit, wallers in hit, rolls hit, an' at las' is buried in hit. Thar may be a iron coffin, an' silver tassils; thar may be a grave stone from Italy; the side ove his face may be cut outen rock, an' stuck up agin the wall inside his chu'ch; an' they may call thar trottin' hoss's, cod boats, an' blue babys arter 'im; yet still onder that black velvit kivirlid, inside that iron coffin, atwix the fine linnen an' that shrivil'd hide ove his'n, *is that ball ove dirt*. He cudent live wifout hit, he cudent die wifout hit, he cudent lie still in his grave wifout hit, an' he never will be wifout hit ontill the sheriff angel at the door ove the last supreme court shells him outen hit with a kick, afore he slings 'im naked into the prisoner's box, whar for the *fust* time frum his fust squall, at the cold air in his snout, up to that orful kickin out, on judgmint day, he'l stan' only on his rale merits—A YANKEE nakid—wif a winder in his breast, like one ove his own hemlock clocks, showin all his inside, springs, traps, an' triggers. Then we'l see what he raley is for the fust time, an' perhaps we'l find out then what he wer made for, if he wer made at all, or only jis happin'd like Sall Simpson's baby did. *Now* we jist knows that he is a cuss to the yeath, an' a pest to every human on hit, like fleas, an' lice, an' eatch, made as a cuss, kep' alive as a cuss, an' should be doctor'd as a cuss. *Then* we'l know it all, but whether hit'l pay then to know hit is mightly mix'd wif the doubts. I hopes we'l hev sumfin better to do than to pester our brains 'bout fleas, lice, eatch, yankees or spreadin adders iether. Powerful ornary stock, George, powerful ornary.

Nashville *Union and American*, October 16, 1866.

Sut Lovingood Reports What Bob Dawson Said, After Marrying a Substitute

"I ASKED Sut one day, why he had never married."

Becaze I ain't fond ove them kine ove inves'mints. If you has observed me clost, you never cotch me foolin with ile stock, patunt rights, lottery tickets, cheap jewelry, ur marriage licunses. Sum how, my turn runs more intu the substanshuls ove life. Whisky an' sich. In fac' I won't trade fur eny thing that I can't 'zamine, at leas' as clost es I ken a hoss.

I'l tell you another thing George, I wish I may be substanshualy durn'd if I don't b'leve the breed ove wimmen am run out enyhow.

Hits true the hen tailors, an' sich cattil, hev invented a substitute, but hits sorter like rye for coffee—hit may look like coffee, an' smell like coffee, but durn my swaller if hit tastes like coffee, I don't keer how hot you make hit nor how much sugar you put in.

Bob Dawson, the sharpest trader I ever saw—jist outsmarted 'em all at tradin'. He bit at a substitute wonst, an' hit like tu a put him in the asylum. If you will listen tu me, I will norate in his own words as nigh as I kin the case; hit may be a warnin' tu you by golly. I know hit hes been tu me. I sleeps in a one hoss bed the ballunce ove my nights, aymen!

Sed Bob tu me. "Sut, I never mind ove gittin fool'd in a trade in my life but wonst. I wer over in Tennessee buying up stock, an' met up with es, I thought, the nicest material tu make Missis Dawson out of, I had seed. I cudent git tu 'zamine her pints much tho' for she wer as skittish as a colt, but I ballunced that by thinkin that she warn't spiled in breakin, an' bein' onbroke I cud break her in tu suit mysef; thar wer sumfin tho' in her gait, an' was that made me think she had been broke to the saddle, if not in harness, an' I spisioned her too for bein' older than she claim'd, so I tried mitey hard to git to look in her mouth, but not a bit ove hit wud she hev—didn't kick nor bite, nor show vishusness, only shyness—jis' adzactly the shyness ove a three year old, what had never looked through a bridil.

"Well, she nibbled grass daintily, an' trotted roun' me circumspeckly ontil at las' I bid on her an' I be cussed if ever I closed a trade quicker in my life. Me, a fool, thinkin' I had her dog cheap.

"The weddin' cum off soon, rather onusualy soon, but you see I was expectunt, an' anxious, she wer feard of a back down, or a rue bargine, an' what the devil was to hinder hit coming off soon.

"Arter we wer hitched in, an' an hour or so spent in passin round vittils—dancin—playin a peaner with dropsy in its laigs, an' a whezin ailment in its chest—pomgranatin' up an' down the porch, giglin, amung the galls, an' winkin amung the men, she whispered to me to slip off to bed, that she would foller in my footsteps in a half hour. I plead to have it a quarter. But no, she must have it a half 'jist for delicacy's sake you know dear.' We compromised at last on twenty-five minutes, arter whisperin about it ten. An' Sut, if it was to do over again I should sujes' twenty-five years, an' never fall a single dam snake. 'Jist for delicacy's sake'—the allfired old umbreller frame ove durnashun.

"I, Robert B. Dawson, the fresh married stock trader, went up them stair steps four at a bounce, an' heard old 'Squire Mankham remark, as I did so, 'That's faster than Bob will ever go up again.' Miss Squills, an old maid of the steel trap persuashun, replied, 'I wouldn't be astonished tho' to see him come down faster.' If it hadn't been for prolongin' that dismal gulf of half an hour atwixt me an' paradise, I'd a cum back and kill'd both of them. I did cuss the old 'Squire to myself, for his want ove confidence in me, an' Miss Squills for her want ove it in my wife.

"But when I went in atwix sheets that smelt ove dried rose leaves, an' found myself bouncin' on a steel spring mattras, I freely forgive him and all the ballance of the world. I could see floatin' in the air wreaths of honey-suckles, an' sich, with humminbirds flashin' among 'em, until I thought I was a humminbird, or would be one, as soon as that doleful half hour devoted to delicacys, should drag its slow sled away.

"'Delicacy,' Sut Lovingood, there never was a durnder humbug on earth than it is, except the delicates themselves, an' their appurtinances. Oh! it's jist so.

"Well of course the half hour ainded, you know, sometime, and with it went all my confidence in old Hymen, and the left hand half of his worshippers—a whole skinfull ove hopes and expectashuns, an' leavin' me about as doubtin' a Thomas as ever you heard ove. *But* one of the durndest knowin' men you ever seed out ove Utah. When I hearn her turn the door knob, my heart was poundin' so hard that I hearn the echo again the head board. I felt like I wer floatin' atwix the mattrass and the ceilin' like Mahomet's coffin, an' the mountin' a mile off. I'd a give fifty dollars to have had a bar of railroad iron in my hands, to hold me down to the bed.

"She glode into the room like the embodiment of a Haleluigah, or a vision of unspeakable joy. She had a candle in her hand; its flame looked (to me, that is) like a boquet ove a thousand shades, an' as big as a half bushel. It was the effort ove my life to keep from snortin', but I *didn't* snort, nor hev I yet, perhaps never will, at a substitute for a woman, I'm sure I won't.

"She set down the light, smiled towards the wooden run on the middle ove the head board, and commenced drawin' her pins, an' slingin' them right an' left as cool as if I, Robert B. Dawson, had been only anuther gall, or a bolster or sich. I was astonished to the frontiers ove elysiun, an' could almost see the rough crags of the common world.

"Says I, 'Julianner, my dear, hadent you better blow out the light? Jist for delicacy's sake, you know.'

"She replied in a firm voice, 'Robert, my true love, delicacy is one ove the fanciful atributes ove unmarried wimmen, an' jist as useless avterward, as their peaner or paint. You an' I are one now, so there must be no secrets or flummey atwix us; you will see me strip, sooner or later, and I might as well begin tonight. I hes my fate to meet, and I wont do eny useless dogin'; I'll meet my crosses like a man.'

"'But, my—my dear,' ventured I, 'hadent you better administer the comin' effulgince to me in broken doses. I— I think I can't stand—that is, I mean it will last the longer.'

" 'Never mind,' said she, 'if you are afraid ove effulgences, shut your eyes,' and she stepped out ove a huge pile ove hoops, an' countles square yards ove starched muslin, standin' revealed a darn bean pole, in one layer of linnen, more like the ghost ove Jezable's mother, than Robert B. Dawson, the stock trader's bride.

"Mister Lovingood, a cold horror swept over me like a huge wet wing.

"That self-poised, deliberate swindler, now Misses Robert B. Dawson, ontied a garter, an' drew from between her stockin', an' her laig, the counterpart of a big dried codfish, made of muslin stuff't with something—bran suggested itself to me at the moment—and as she did so, her stocking fell limp, in a pile around her shoe mouth, and her laig looked like the pint aind ove a buggy shaft, with nearly the same crook to it, an' be d——d.

"I swallered a time or two, an I sed 'Julianner, dear, I never knew before that you had a wooden laig.'

" 'Neither hev I,' she replied, rather tart-like. 'But I is ove a delicate organisation. That adjunk,' pointin' to the imitation, 'now goes with delicacy.'

"She looked at me, feelin' in her bussum the while, an' said, 'Robert, my love, when I come to look at you clost, your eyes seems larger, an' rounder than I thought for, an' more bulgin—they bulge as much as these palpitators,' drawin' forth a pair ove somethings like sugar bowl leds, knobs an' all. When she flung 'em on the table, they bounced a time or two. Mister Lovingood, I was speechless, but I thought to myself, 'I jist wish I may be d——d, with all my power ove thought, and will twice or three times, at least.'

"Deliberate-cool-slow, she stuck a thumb in each corner of her mouth, an' brought forth a full set ove bottom upper an' lower teeth, fastened together behine with a spring, an' laid *them* on the table, gapin' open an' facin' me. They looked like a saw tooth'd rat trap, ready set to ketch another dam fool.

"Said she, lookin' at me again, 'Robert, my love, I do declare, you are real pop eyed; I hope you are not habitualy so; it would be *so* disapointin' to me.' I jist had brains enough to think one word emphaticaly, an' that word was 'He——.' She, with her fore finger, bounced out one of her eyes, and put it in her mouth, while she lifted her whole head of hair, leavin' her skull, white an' glossy as a billiard ball. When she laid these down, she looked one eyed at me, an' then at the candle, a time or two as if undeterminded. I busy all the while recapitulatin'. 'False calves, false breasts, false teeth, false eye, false hair,' what next? The most horrible idear that ever burnt an blazed in the brain of man, was now fast resolving itself into its dreadful shape in mine, an' her remark, 'Don't be impatient, Robert love; I is most through.' Flashed it into its fiendish maturity, without darin' even a glance at her, I was up *out-gone;* I went down them stair steps six at a bounce in my shirt tail through that festive throng in my shirt tail out of that house, out of that lot, out of that town, in my shirt tail. States separate us now, an' I wish they were oceans."

Now George, arter hearin' that 'sperience ove poor Bob Dawson's, I puts hit to you, as a man ove gumshun, if I orter add another word only to forewarn you not tu menshun marryin' tu me agin, unless you wants that durn'd shriveled little snout ove your'n scabb'd. Ketch me rockin' cradles, or totin meal home for a palpititytator toter, or buyin' stockin's for a par ove bran bags, or givin' an 'oman a legal right tu bite me, with teeth made out ove delf. *No sir,* I'd marry the figgerhead ove a steamboat first. I jis' can't sit still, an' think 'bout thar menyfold shams an' traps an' gewolly-tockery, speshuly the palpititytators. Why don't you believe, that even Ratsnes' hes got her a par, a homemade par.

"Who the dickens is Ratsnest, Sut?"

Why sister Sall, an' be durnd to you, she saw'd a round dry gourd in two, a gourd as big as my head, an' then made a hole in the middil ove each half, an' stuff'd in white oak acorns, butt first, an' dad shave me if she dident hist the whole contrapshun intu her buzzum. I wish I may be dam if you cudent see the bulge ove the acorns acrross a field. Then she went on a rale turky gobbler strut to church, a leanin' back from 'em like a littil boy totin a big drum. She looked like a dairy, by geminy. I sware I jist wanted tu kill the dam-fool, that's what ail'd me.

My stars, George, 'spose an' 'oman *wer* tu stock a par ove palpititytators ontu me, what has no more stimulus in em than the buffers over a freight car, on a cold frosty night; wudent I be in a devil ove a fix, say? Why dam if I hadent rather swim the Tennessee with a powerful interprizin fourteen foot alligator arter me when the mush ice is runnin. I jist woudent be half as feard tu face an' 'oman with a peck measure ove sanke in her buzzum, as a palpititytator toter. Now jis' answer me one questin; what in the thunder an durnashun do you recon the comein generashun ove babies am to do for milk? That's what's a pesterin' me. Oh, the devil! I wont think about it any more—le'ss go to sleep—George—George, say, George, am you awake?

"Yes, partly."

Well then lisson tu my las' words. If ever I interjuces, insinuates, or socks ary one ove these paws in atwix the silk callicker or gingham an' the bustez ove one ove the tother sort ove cats, onless I hes had a purfeckly fur sight afore han', I jis' wish hit may get bit off at the wrist.

No, by giminy hoss, *that* appertite's dead, an' the ballance of 'em scept for sperrits ara sinkin fas', thanks to the hen-tailors, an' dam fools.

> "The galls am all a made up show,
> For fools delusion given,
> With pads above, an' hoops below,
> An' gizzards cold as mountain snow
> Thars not one soun' in seven."

Dident I sing that verse in a way tu bring tears intu the eyes ove a brick kiln? Say.

Chattanooga *Daily American Union*, November 27 and 28, 1867.

Sut Lovingood's Big Music Box Story

"MUSIC hath charms to soothe the savage breast."

George, stop readin', a minit, an' look at that ar substantial lookin' dorg, a sittin' on his sturin over yander; see his crap years, an' watery eyes, an' that countinance; would you trus' *him* in a meat hous'?

I tell you, he minds me a power ove dad's ole Boze, a half bull, half raskil ove a dorg, what dad had stole from a Noth Caliney movin' famerly. He soon proved hisse'f to be the bes' match for that h—l fired ole cuss, what had the misfortin to call me "Son, Sut," when he dident call me "Pot head," that I ever seed or hearn tell ove.

He wer jis' as ugly in pusonel bild, an' feeters—Jis' as cross, an' mean in temper—Jis' as lazy, an' jis' as durnd a fool. The only vantages Boze had over dad wer, he coudent drink whisky, an' woudent whip the dorgs. But then agin, dad woudent eat mutton with the wool on, nor suck aigs. At leas' I never cotch him at hit. He mout tho', for I never yet seed eny thing walkin' on aind, as hard to 'count for, as my onregenerit dad. Why he jis' cud beat a pinch back watch, a hen, or the devil at bein' onsartin.

Well, one day I wer sittin on the fence in the sunshine, with my trousis rolled up mos' to my pockids, a saftenin' the holts of the dorgticks on my laigs with spittil, so I cud pull 'em off without leavin' thar heads in the hide.

Did you ever pull a dorgtick, an' leave his head in yer meat, George?

"No Sut, I do not think I ever did."

Oh! You be dadrabbited; you is tryin' tu be finneky. Well, any how, tick bites am curious; they makes the sweetest scratchin' spots, for about a day, I ever had the scratchin' ove, an' arter that the sorest bump, an' the blackest scab outside ove the small pox.

While I wer at this delicate job, an' jis' beginin' tu make hit inturestin' tu the littil blood suckin' cusses, what shou'd

I see a coming along the road but a hongry lookin' varmint, in a slouch hat with a twine band, an' linsey briches with a big casinett patch on the sturin. He had strapp'd ontu his back a squar passel, kivered in ile cloth, about the size ove a faro dealer's chist ove tools, or a rezin box. I happind to cast my eye up towards our cabin, an' seed Boze a cummin' in a squatin sneak strait for slouch hat. Thinks I, yere is a chance for a race, an' by golly I'll be the jedge.

Sez I—"Hello thar mistopher; if you hes eny superfine runnin' amung yer mussils, now is the bes' time in the worild tu be a usein' some ove hit durnd profitably strait up this road. That is, if you sits much valuer on that ar sampil ove blue casinett what you sits on. For thar cums a regular onintermittunt calamity, wropped in dorghide arter you. Don't you see him sightin' at the patch on yer latter aind? He means sumfin, ole hoss." The cussed fool cuss looked roun', an' instid ove follerin this holsum savin' advice, he aim'd for a sour apple tree; as he made his bulge, Boze changed his sneak intu a rush, sot his bristils, an' sed "wouff! wouff!" Thinks I, blue patch, or appil tree, which will hit be, an' I hilt my breff, anxiously.

Slouch hat, as soon (or perhaps a scrimpshun sooner) as he reached the tree, started up the body by yerks, like a cat goes up a saplin, when sumfin exhitin' am a crowden her; *jis* as he got han' holt on the fust lim', Boze reached the casinett, an' secured hise'f thar to, an' thar he dangled.

Sez he, "g-i-t o-u-t," loud enough for dad to hear hit in the cabin, whar he wer half solin his shoes. As Boze dident git out, I put up the game at about six an' six, an' Boze's deal, an' sorter hope that he mout turn Jack.

Sez I, "Stranger, listin tu me. You now hes a hangin' tu your sturin, about as parsevarin', vengeful, an' interprizin' a dorg, as ever froze tu a casinett patch, or 'et up a man." I sed this yearnestly.

Sez he, "Call him off, you dam san' hill crane, why don't you?"

"Jis' becaze I dident sick 'im on," sez I. "I never interferes in fights amung kin, an' hit seems about a even thing enyhow, stranger, only you can't eat the dorg, an he can eat you. Don't you hope that ar patch sowin' may be rotten?"

Sez he, "go tu——then, I ken hold on as long as yer dorg."

I now tho't ove the gallus buttons, for the fust time, an' so I tho't I'd help the poor devil tu a idear, that mout *sorter* set Boze back a littil.

So I sez.

"Onbutton yer galluses; thars no wimmen about."

"You mus' be a dam fool," sez he; "how ken I? Don't you see I'm usein' my han's."

"Oh! I had forgot that" sez I, an' I wonder'd who'd told him my nater. Jist then, yere cum dad a runnin, with a poplar fence rail in bof ban's, an' I knowin' his onsartinty wer studyin' which ove us three wer tu ketch the rail, when I hearn crack-pop. Hit wer the gallus buttons by golly. An' the britches cum off inside out, afore you cud bat yer eye, Boze a shakin the fleas out ove 'em rather vigrusly, an' vishusly as I thought.

Dad wer now amung us, smakin' an' snortin', an' when I seed him draw back for his lick, I foun' hit wer intended for the back ove my naik, an' if I'd a been jis' a mossel too slow, he'd a onjinted hit as sure as shootin'. But I warn't; I duck'd my head, like drakes a courtin, an' slouch hat cotch hit all along his jowl. I swar hit sounded like smashin' a fat gourd, an' han' holts broke imejuntly, lettin' him drop, bar laiged atop ove Boze. Dad flung down the rail, an' kivered *him*. Thinks I, by golly, yere is a fust rate chance for me too tu be the upper dorg in the fite, one time in my life, so by the jumpin jinney, I lit astradil ove dad. Jis' think ove *that,* a minit, George, while I takes a ho'n.

Well, the instunt I lit across the small ove his back, he grunted, an' so did barlaigs, an' Boze he did too, whilest I sot intu maulin' dad, on fust one side ove the head, an' then on tother—left, an' right, a sayin', "Oh, you cussed, barlaiged raskil; dad, an' Boze, an' me'l give you h—l; we'l show you how to climb our sour appil tree, without axin' my dad's leave."

Sez dad, aidgin in a word, atwix' every one ove my licks, "Bar laiged — bedam — you — durn'd — fool, — hits — *me* — youre—givin—h—l."

You see, George, dad wer pufickly awar that I allways had been the biggest fool in the worild, an' that's why he call'd my attention tu the fac' that hit wer him I wer a poundin', an' not bar laigs.

Well, while this wer agwine on, poor Boze wer fightin'

tu a powerful disadvantage, he bein' the ondermos' dorg ove all, but, he wer a doin' the best he cud in the dark, bitin' roun', an' about whar the casinett orter been, yes by golly, whar a dry hoss hide orter been. Dad wer counter bitin' above, so atwix' 'em, bar laigs mus' a had a very happy time; at leas' I jedged so; from the way he kicked an' hollered, durn if I don't expect he tho't the merleanyum had cum.

But misfortinatly every rashnel enjoymint hes tu cum tu an aind. Jis' about now, I hearn sumfin below me somwhar begin tu play, "Billy in the low groun's," jis es plain. Thinks I, my soul, which ove 'em is hit? Dad, bar laigs, or Boze, that is a havin' the music mauled out ove 'im in that style, I don't keer a durn which hit is, he'l be a dead dorg in five minits, hits beyant natur, tu stan' hurtin' long, that fetches music instid ove gruntin' ur squawkin'.

Then I calkilated how, if hit were Boze, an' he *did* live, that I'd git plum rich, by holdin' him by the tail, an' cowhidin' him ove court, an' muster days, at a dime a tchune. I tho't the same about dad, but then who the devil wer tu hole *him* by the tail while he wer bein' cowhided! I hearn "click-whizz" an' the musick changed to, "Oh! She wouldent, an' she couldent, an' she dident cum at all," louder, an' faster than ever. By golly, this fotch forth Boze; he cum from onder, tarin', an' whinin' as pitiful as a purp.

Now George, when Boze begun that rumpus, he wer as compack, an' chunky a bilt dorg, as you ever seed. Hits true, I had but a moment tu 'zamine him that mornin' atwix that appil tree, an' the back fence, eighty yards off, but he looked more tu me like the wooden axle-tree ove a two hoss waggin flyin' aind foremos' than eny dorg; he jist *sailed* over that fence, without tetchin', his tail clost atwix his laigs, an' givin' only one short bark, while he wer in the air above the rails. He disapeared in the woods purhaps the worst skeer'd dorg that ever wagg'd a tail.

Talk tu me, 'bout "music soothin' savidge beastes"—durnashun!

A skeer about the music had been workin' powerful on bof dad, an' me, but hit broke out tho' on him furst, when jis' arter Boze lightened across the lot, the music changed to, "Hark from the tombs a doleful soun," with the deepest bass you ever hearn rumblin' seeminly *in* bar laigs. Dad, he jis' made a mustang lunge, on his all fours, an flung me, as slick as if he'd been a mule. Then, Lord you ought tu hearn him whizz, an' seed his bald head glimmer down the road. *Ho'nets!*—why all the ho'nets in Georgy, cudent a made him hum, like that tchune did. He never looked over his shoulder but wonst, an' then he seed *me,* instid ove *hit* arter him, for the durn'd supernatral cuss wer then playin' "The devils dream," an' I jis' know'd that meant me.

Well, Boze never cum up ontil nex' arternoon, draggiled, gaunt, an' sneakin'; the sight ove the dorg sot me to hummin' sorter onthoughtedly, "Oh! She woudent." He jis' looked at me wild, half a moment—whined, an' axletreed hisse'f intu the woods agin, like a injun arrer arter a groun' squirrill. A few days arterwards, about a mile frum our cabin, I finds Boze, layin' straiched out flat on his belly, tail still clost onder him, an' *his years shut up with his paws,* dead, dead, by golly, as a stone hammer.

"Well, Sut, did you ever ascertain how the music was made?"

No, an' dod rabbit me, if ever I try.

"Might it not have been a large music box, under that oil cloth?"

Dam if *I* know.

"Well what caused your dad to run when he heard 'Hark from the tombs'?"

Feard ove his herearter bein' clost about, by geminey.

Sceptin' ove Sumner, Wade, Ashley, an' Stevens, four sich d——d fools wer never together before as Boze, Barlaigs, dad, an' me. Mam allowed the last durn'd one ove us orter be hung.

Chattanooga *Daily American Union,* December 11 and 12, 1867.

Sut Lovingood, a Chapter from His Autobiography

HIT takes a feller a long time, George, to fine out what his gif' am, his bes' pint, what game he's stronges' on. I knows hit tuck me a mortul while, but a las' I got hit narrer'd down to two things. Gittin' intu trubbil wer one, an' then runnin' out ove hit wer tuther. I wavered a good while which ove 'em I'd bes' foller fur a livin', an' I studied, an' studied, an' sum how I cud see no way ove siperatin' 'em, so at las' I made up my mine to run the dubbil ingine, that is, take 'em together, an' I finds 'em to suit together jis ad-zackly, an' better nor all that, they bof suits me. "Man am born'd to *see* trubbil," you know, an' natural born'd durnd fools to *feel* hit. Well, to go back a littil, so as to show you how yearnisly I hunted fur my gif', mam sot me up as a merchint (I wer about thuteen year ole I recon) wif a willer basket ove red ginger cakes an' sour apples; that wer the fust thing I tried, an' hit wer a splendid failur. I et up the las' durn'd one, apples an' all, an' los' the baskit a playin' mumble-the-peg afore dinner. Mam jis' got hostile, an' soaked hickory ile intu my back, ontil hit greazed my shut buzzum. The effeck ove this kine ove linamint wer to take all ove the merchint, an' mos' ove the ginger cakes outen me right then an' thar. Mam orter felt powerful sham'd ove hersef, but she dident. She druv me into the crick, roll'd a big rock on my shuttail to keep me frum floatin' off, an' scour'd me wif a scrub broom an' san' ontil I shin'd; an' what wer mos' 'stonishin' to me, arter she'd finish'd the job, she then purnounc'd me to be "a nasty stinkin' littil devil." I still thinks I wer *sorter* clean at leas'. In 'bout a half hour, yere cum ole Missis Simmons, what lived a mile below, a axin mam what had mudied the crick so, "that she'd spiled a washin' ove clothes, an' she b'leved thar wer a ded hoss in hit." Thar wer an ole grudge atwix 'em enyhow, sumfin 'bout dad, I think, so mam, sez she, "the warter's good enuff fur the clothes madim," an' she bow'd her naik. Missis Simmons sot her han's on her hips, an' stood so strait that she lean'd back, an' sez she "the clothes *you* war, you means I recon, you dirty, drabbil-tail, slop eatin', ole louse pasture." "I dusent suckil cum by chance childer, an' hev no latch to my door, nur *greaze the hinges* either," sez mam. Missis Simmons jis' squeal'd like a hoss, an' mixed wif my mam afore you cud bat yer eye. Thar wer a purty levil san' bank on the crick, whar they cum tugether; I look'd at hit, an' thinks I, a proverdenshuly perpard fitein groun', no loose rocks to take an onfar lick wif, good foot holts, an' *no body to show foul play.* What more cud a body ax for. So I clomb a dogwood wif a chip in my mouth, an' sot astradil in the fork, to watch the fust fight I ever seed, whar I had no choise ove sides, so I meant to holler for bof ove 'em. To be pufeckly far atwix 'em, I flung up "wet or dry," to see who I should holler fur fust. I spit on the chip fur mam, lef' the dry side fur Sall Simmons, an' toss'd hit up in the air. I watch'd hit lite in the san', dry side up, an' sez I as loud as I cud "Hurray *Sall*"; mam, wall'd up one monstus blazin' eye at me (Sall wer a gougin tuther one) an' sez she, "Dad like, fur the yeath." Sez I "Hurray mam," "Hurray Sall," "Hurray mam," strait along. Well, they fit, an' they fout, they scratch'd, an' they claw'd, they grab'd, an' they snatch'd, they knock'd, an' they hit, they grunted, an' they groaned all over every durn'd foot ove that san' bank, ontil hit wer tore up wus nor hogs sarves a tater patch, then intu the crick knee deep, an' thar they tried the drownin' dodge. If they flung one another once, they did twenty far falls, time about by golly, an' jis' as I wer hollerin' fur 'em. If they'd a quit right then, they'd abeen the cleanis' wimmen in the county. I never did see warter slosh'd about so, an' the eddy below 'em wer kiver'd wif bubbils as big as tea cups; thar har wer down thar backs, an' over thar faces in five hundred littil dripping strings, an' sum ove 'em tangl'd the wus' kine. Thar pins, an' strings in thar onder geer wer failin', fur every now an' then a petticoat wud pop up an' float down the crick. They fit thar plumb acrost an' out on tother bank. I tho't they had the whites' laigs I ever seed onder wimmen. Jis' then I hearn dad cummin' bellerin', "you Betts, you Sall, *stop that, stop that."* He kick'd off his shoes, an' commenc'd rollin' up his britches laigs to wade over to 'em. Sez he, "What's the cussed fools a fightin' about?" Sez I, "Better not go over thar Dad, fur I thinks they'se fightin' 'bout *you*." "Oh! no, I recon not," sez he; pickin' up his shoes, he jis' stuck his feet in 'em slipshod, an' started up the crick to the stillers, mumblin' as he went, "I think, durn 'em, they 'mout live in peace; thar aint so many ove 'em." They still fightin' away, at las' mam broke about a foot off ove a dead knotty lim', as big as yer finger, an' run hit in amung Sall's har, an' commenc'd a twistin' roun', an' roun'. As soon as she foun' hit had good holt, she jump'd behine Sall, an' kep on a twistin'. Thinks I, oh shaw! That's a gwine to spile the fight; thar's no use in my hollerin' for you Sall, eny more, so I jis' hollered for mam, hopin' to make far weather fur my ownsef. Well, when the stick begin to tighten to her head, she begin to lean back to hit, mam still a twistin' away. "Let me go, Betts Lovingood, durn you," sez Sall. *Thar*, by golly, thinks I she's caved. Mam stood 'way back frum her, wif her laigs sot wide, holdin' on still to the stick, an' sez she, "If you hes eny reques' to make ove me, you merlatter lookin' strumpit, you mus' put hit in perlite words," an' she gin the stick a littil more twis'. "Oh! Outch, please Missis Lovingood, let me go, that's a lady." Sez mam, "them words sound sorter decent; now *aint* I a natral born'd lady, every inch ove me, say?" An' she jis' threaten'd more twis' wif her wris'. "Oh! Yes you am, *indeed* you am," whimper'd Sall. "An' aint *you* a dirty, drabbil-tail, slop eatin', ole louse pasture?" Sall farly busted out a crying, an' sez she, "ye-yes, I rec-recon *I is*." Sez I, thar mam; let her go; don't be gluttunus. Mam let go the stick, an' waded across, an' I swar I never seed a frock fit an oman as clost as hern did. I cud count her ribs thru hit. Arter they rested a spell, they bof went down the crick, one on one side, an' one on tuther, to hunt up thar petticoats, not sayin' a durn'd word. I clomb down outen the dogwood, thinkin' what a blessed thing hit wer that mam hadent et the apples an' ginger cakes, an' then went a huttin' huckelberrys.

The nex' trial I made to fine my gif', wer trappin' fur varminty things, musrats an' sich like, an' I thar larnt one thing, an' that is, that a steel trap am a powerful smart thing, not to be able to talk, fur durn me if the very fus' varmint I cotch warn't name Sut. I los' all confidence in steel traps right thar; they know too durn'd much. When I tuck hit to a feller to git him to onlock the durn'd bull dorg thing off ove my han', dont you believe he hinted as much, as that I had foun' hit in sum mans co'n crib. Trappin' warnt my gif'; I wer plum sure ove that. Nex', I tried rail maulin', an' I hadent been at hit two hours, ontil I foun' the crack in a log shet up on my fingers; thar I staid ontil I durn'd ni starv'd, even arter I'd et all the bark off ove the log. While I wer fas' thar, if I tho't once ove the baskit ove apples an red ginger cakes, I did five hundr'd times, an' the whippin' I got fur eatin' 'em never enter'd my head 'onst—strange that, warnt hit?

Tryin' tu maul them rails tho' hes saved my life I think at leas' fifteen thousin times since then. You see hit wer a chesnut oak, an' the bark I et tann'd my pauch into upper leather, an' hits been pisen proof ever since. I'd like tu see a sampil ove the whisky what cud gnaw a hole in hit, ur even make hit yerk. Ole Pike his sef never made a drap what cud singe the fuzz on hit, an' he made spirits mean enuff to set a passun tu stealin', an' pisen enuff tu kill a alligator, if he jis' sun'd his sef on a barril. Nex' a cute ole devil coax'd me tu the idear that trimmin' shade trees wer a trade tu git rich at, an' that seein' hit wer me, he'd let me larn on his'n fur nuffin. Thinks I, thars a chance to git up in the world, so I clomb one ove his tall white oaks, wif a han' saw in my mouf, got astradil ove a big lim', an' saw'd hit off atwix my belly an' the tree. I never cotch the idear ontil I hearn the saw hit the ground clost by my year. I think I beat hit down ni onto three feet; that wer sum comfort. Don't you b'lieve the durn'd ole raskil dident threaten tu snatch me bald-headed, fur duin' hit apupus, tu break his han' saw. Sum men am durn'd fools, thats a fac'. Well, trimmin' shade trees warn't my gif'. I cudent afford tu take a fall fur every lim' I saw'd off. I never trim'd but two arter that, an' yeres how hit happen'd. Thar wer a feller what everlastinly kep a devilin me 'bout sawin' my sef out ove ole Bell's white oak, ontil I got sorter tired ove hearin' hit. You know folks kin keep a tellin' you the same thing, ontil hit will smell sorter mouldy like. Well, he had a par ove the purtiest big oaks afore his door I ever seed, an' he tuck a notion to hev 'em trim'd. Sez he tu me, "Sut, do you think you kin trim these trees, wifout fallin' ara time?" I tole 'im I'd bet a hoss on hit. Well, he call'd up witnesses, an' pinted out the lim's he wanted tuck off, an' if I fell ara time, I warnt tu hev any pay, an' the money wer put in Holt McClellun's han's to hold stakes. He started off tu town, an' I wer tu hev the job dun by the time he got back. Now, he tho't he'd git my work fur nuffin, ur I'd kill mysef, which wer all the same tu him, so he went off sniggerin' at a good trade. Holt wer buisy plowin', so he sed he'd take my word 'bout fallin', an' when I got dun to cum by an' git my money. Well, I trim'd bof trees, tuck off adzackly the lim's he tole me too, an' piled the brush, went to Holt an' got my pay. As I wer a puttin' hit in my pockit, sez Holt, "How did you manage, Sut, so as not to fall?" Sez I, "I never clomb, by golly." "Why, how did you trim the trees then?" Thar wer a monstrus wide fool grin a strait-chin' my mouf (fur I felt hit thar) as I anser'd Holt, "*I cut 'em down, an' trim'd 'em a lyin, by golly!*" Now strange tu tell, this gin me more standin' as a durn'd fool than sawin' mysef outen old Bell's white-oak dun, an' I swar I don't see why, fur I got my pay, an' nara fall. Well, this bisniss rais'd the devil, as mos' everything I onder-takes dus. That ar feller what hired me wer name Poulter; he'd lived in sum town afore he bought the farm whar I trim'd the trees. He wer a high-headed, stuck up, whelp, an' tho't hissef better nur *eny* body. His wife wer ove the high-falutin perswashun too, an' I tell you how I knows—she toted a parasol, an' kep' her shoes black'd. Him an' her talk'd a power 'bout me, all over the settilment; I cud hear frum 'em mos' every day, bemeanin' me the wust kine; at las' I hearn ove 'em callin' me a "*nusance.*" This made me hos-tile as be durn'd; hit wer the meanis' soundin' name eny body had ever gin me, an' I jis' know'd hit meant sumfin wus nur hoss thief, so I makes up my mine tu purswade 'em tu change the subjeck—"nusance," durn the nasty word; I hates hit tu this day. Doctors oughter call pukes "nusance"; hit wud make 'em cum up a heap quicker.

I foun' a log in the woods, wif a nes' ove big black ants in hit; so one night when they wer all in thar den, I sets one aind ove the log afire, an' fix'd me a bag over the rotten heart hole in tother; hit warnt long afore the heat an' smoke druv 'em intu my bag, an' when I cum to tie hit, I foun' I had at leas' a quart. Hit wer a purty moonlight night in July; the Katydids wer jis' makin' the leaves trimbil wif thar fuss, an' hit wer powf'l warm. Poulter an' his wife wer gone tu bed, an' lyin' onder a sheet. I tuck off my shoes, an' clomb in at a winder in the passage. I crawl'd keerfully on my han's an' knees, wif my bag ove ants in my mouf, ontil I got tu the foot ove thar bed. I hearn him snorin', an' her a mumblin' in her sleep. Jis' as easy as ever you seed an' 'oman lift a blister plaster, I turn'd up that sheet, laid the ontied poke atwix' 'em 'bout knee high, an' put the kiver as I foun' hit; then I got outen that house soon, monstrus soon, an' squatted amung the mornin' glorys, onder the winder at thar head. He grunted, an' she ansered wif a moan, bof on 'em begin to scratch an' roll, an' that sot the ants to hurryin' roun', an' wharever they crowded one, he bit. By golly, sez he, "Evangeline my darlin', are you awake?" (He tuck a power ove pains wif his words, an' allers spoke 'em slow.) Sez she, sorter spiteful, "Tobesure I am; the fleas is eatin' me up. Oh! Grashus me." Sez he, "That is what I wished to speak to you about; they are annoyin' me prodid——." "Dear bless me," sez she jumpin up on her sturn, an' lookin' roun'; "thars ten million ove 'em." By this time, he wer standin' on *his* sturn, in the bed. Now, mine you, all this time they wer bof buisy, slappin', scratchin', an' rubbin' thar sefs, fust one place, an' then another. Sez she, "Good lord! I can't stand this," an' out ove bed she plouted, over the foot board, a shakin' her shiftail, the savagest kine. Out he bounced; sez he, "Evangeline my darlin', what *shall* we do?" Sez she, "don't bother me with your nonsense; don't you see I am buisy?" "Evangeline my darlin' I——" "Don't talk to me, but get the broom an' sweep me, sweep me quick, dunce head." The full moon wer a pourin' lots o' light thru the winders tother side ove the house, makin' 'em look tu me like a par ove ghostes a dancin' an' sloshin', an' slappin' roun'; they sorter skeer'd me by golly. The flutterin' shiff, an' the bouncin' shut, look'd too durnd white tu suit me adzackly. "Evangeline, my darlin', this is intol——."

"The broom, the broom, you idiot," she sed as she whipp'd her shiff' over her head, an' hit cum whizzin' apas' my years, crumpl'd up in a ball an' stuck fas' amung the mornin' glorys. Poulter stagger'd back agin the wall, an' while he scratch'd savagely onder one armpit, sez he, "Why, Evangeline, my darlin'; shame honey wrap the sheet roun' you, do dear." Sez she, "No time this fur finickey feelin's; if you are *much* ashamed leave here." I swar she minded me ove the shadder ove a par ove scissors, a openin' an' shuttin' powful fas'. 'Bout now hit got a heap too hot fur him, modes' as he wer, an' his shut cum flyin' thru the winder, arter the shiff', an' sez he, "Evangeline, my darlin', pardon me, I am druv crazy." Down he drap'd on the floor, an' roll'd frum one side the room tu tuther, fas' as a barril gwine down hill; she wer dancin' in the middil ove the room, a rale Firginy break down, when he went onder her, trippin' her tu her all fours. Yere he cum back again, an' she had tu loose a step or two ove the dance, tu jump over 'im as he cum. Sez she, as she lit, "Mister Poulter, don't be a fool." Sez he, as he cum agin, "Evangeline, my darlin', clear the road." As she danc'd roun' his head, she wer so mad she kick'd at 'im. He ainded hissef up in the corner, a rubbin' his shoulders agin the wall, an' sez he, "Evangeline, my darlin', it cannot be possible that these are fleas." Sez she, "How can I tell, they won't give me time to 'zamine 'em." "Oh! My grashus goodness, they'l kill me." Out he cum, on his all fours, frum the corner, sayin', "Evangeline, we must retreat." "Whar to?" sez she, "for my sake say whar to?" Says he, "Evangeline, my darlin', I have been thinkin' ove the crick." Sez she, slappin' fust a hip, an' then a shoulder, "Why dident you think ove that afore I got to sweatin', but go I mus', sweat, or no sweat." Intu the passige she darted, an' out at the back door, he arter her. I tho't she wer the longes', slimes', whites' 'oman I ever seed by moon shine. She went in a stretchin' lope an' every jump she slapp'd her sef sum whar, an' him, I think he hit hissef five hundred licks, atween the house an' the crick; a twix 'em they kep up a wus poppin' than a big skillet ove parchin' co'n. I listen'd, an' hearn 'em slunge in. Thinks I, that's the fus' smart thing you hes dun since the ants awaken'd you, an' as I dident want tu bring trubbil on myself, I tho't I'd slip intu the house, git holt ove my littil bag, an' git frum thar. I seed 'em sittin' at church nex Sunday, finely fix'd up, an' lookin' so quiet, an' innercent, an' pius that I cudent to save my life make myself feel that they were the same par I had seed nakid, by moon light, jis the Wensday night afore, rarin' an' scutterin' roun', like two crazy kangaroos. Folks in public don't look much like folks in private, no how, dus they, George?

Now mine you hoss, he's the feller what call'd me a "nusance," the durn'd stuck up, ant killin', perpondrus raskil. If he thinks me a "nusance," I'd like powful well to hear what name he calls black ants, so I cud use hit on him, durn 'im. Folks do say, that him an' her dont agree very well, since they danced that Firginey reel naked, by moon light. But then folks do lie so, you know, George.

Chattanooga *Daily American Union,* March 31 and April 2, 1868.

Correspondence Extraordinary.
The Forthcoming Early Life of Sut Lovingood, By His Dad.
Negotiations Completed

MESSRS. Editors:

Gentlemen—It affords me pleasure to inform you that I have accomplished the important mission which you entrusted to my management. I have closed a contract with the venerable father of Sut Lovingood, for "the early life" of that distinguished person, to be written *con amore*, and expressly for your paper. The triumphant close of this important negotiation, should be a cause of gratulation among your personal friends, and will be hailed with joy by the admirers of genius throughout the world. The early and inner life of the greatest living man, *in his way,* will be sought after, and read, from the shadows of Cape Coast Castle, to the gleaming ice spires at the pole, and the day of its publication will be a white stone on the roadway of time, a pointer, and a warning, to the coming generations, as they file past, on their way to the end. This thought cheered me, as I struggled against the many obstacles thrown in my way during the negotiation, and doubtless assisted in impelling me forward to a successful result, not the least of which was a vile emissary of Bonner's, amply supplied with means, and openly my competitor for the prize. I am not sure but he would have succeeded, had not the fact leaked out, that Bonner was the means of inflicting on the reading public, that matchless production, "The early life of Gen'l Grant, by his father." When old Mr. Lovingood became convinced of this, he turned a cold shoulder to all propositions from that quarter, declaring, in his own peculiar manner, "That he never roosted on the pole where another damfool did any of the crowing." This, and other utterances of "Hoss" Lovingood (as he is familiarly termed, by his acquaintances) leads me to the belief that his feelings towards the progenitor of Sut's rival are none of the kindest; it is natural too, that this bitterness should be most cordially reciprocated by Grant, *pere*, when the sons are so palpably and unmistakably pitted against each other for the same prize. Such hostility, backed as it is, by the obstinacy, prejudice and partiality of a second childhood, is sure to culminate in a personal collision, unless Mr. Bonner and yourself can rise to the level of the occasion, by joining in keeping the peace between these patriarchs of the flock. When such a man as "Hoss" Lovingood openly avows his willingness and ability to "maul the benzine out of Grant, *pere*," "To sweat out his lard at his ears," "To sun his moccasins"—and to "snatch all sich, bald headed," it is high time for the interference of thoughtful friends. As Mr. Bonner and yourself have been the means of placing the jealous old gentlemen in a belligerant attitude, you owe it to society that they be kept apart, for we have every reason to believe that the finale of the fight among the cats of Kilkenny would be a wild and bloodless ending, as compared to a meeting between these sturdy old Aries', of the respective flocks of Lovingood and Grant.

I am satisfied that if Grant, *pere*, has shown the whole strength of his hand (and I incline strongly to that belief, from the twenty-five foot jumping anecdote, the photographic prophecy touching the Presidency, &c.), that Sut Lovingood, will make a respectable race for the crown. Let no one hug the delusion to his heart that "Ulyssus" will walk over the track unmarked by whip or spur, to be proclaimed the durn'd fool of his day. Neither will his earnest biographer find in "Hoss" Lovingood a foeman altogether unworthy of *his* steel. Grant a fair field, and no favor, with the honest wish from all parties that, "the best man may win," and I have a hope for "Sut" yet.

In closing, I may remark, that in addition to your offer of $10,000, I was compelled to add a forty-four gallon barrel, full of Pike's unrectified whisky, a bunch of fiddle strings, and a promise of the postmastership at the village of Soaptail. I further stipulated and agreed that no daguerreotypes of himself, his wife, or their cabin, are to be "mixed in" with his letters, and that his utterances are not to be "tinkered up," or mended, by the compositor, particularly his poetry if he indulges in any, and he rather thinks he *will* "try it a jump or two," if it comes easy. I was forced to these concessions, and hope they will meet your approval, as without them (to use his own emphatic language), he wouldn't "budge a single durn'd inch," and the world thereby would have been left in ignorance of "the early life" of another great man "by his father." If the reading public will make as much allowance for the partiality and zeal of the "dad," in Sut's case, as they have been compelled to grant to "the father of Ulysses," I shall ask no more, only that all stand back, and watch the fur fly—for two more earnest souls, never entered the lists for their respective "boys" than Grant *pere* and "Hoss" Lovingood. Very Respectfully, Agent.

Knoxville *Press and Messenger,* April 30, 1868.

The Early Life of Sut Lovingood, Written by His Dad

MISTER Ramige,

Dear Sir:—You sent me word, that you wanted to print sumthin about the yearly life ove my most notorious son "Sut," and as how I bein' his dad (so far as eny body knows), you tho't I wer most knowin' ove his littil tricks, an' tharfoar the very feller to rite 'em down for you to print frum. Well, jist you count me I-double-en in. I ruther like hit, havin' a strong honein arter a pen enyhow; hevin been ofen called on in my yearly days, to tally bushels at corn measurin's, to keep count at shootin' matches, or games ove "old Sledge," witnessin' notes ove han', an' articles for a hoss race, or a rastilin mach. In fac', almos' all short jobs ove writin' done off han'. In this way I becum eggspert with a pen. I'd jist as lief as not butted agin the schoolmaster hissef. Ove late years, I hev writ so much, that hit has affected the sinnews, an' puckerin strings ove my coteail, to sich a egstent, that I can't sit on hit, onless I hole hit down clost to my hams as I squat. The fac' is, my coteails quirls up like a pine shavin, but then even this is sometimes both handy an' timely.

You say, that you want me to go behine Sut's bornin' a generashun or two, an' partickulerly, to dwell on mysef, an' my doin's right smartly. Well, "My Son" Sut, comes of as good, and as pure durn'd fool stock, as most public caracters now figurin' on top ove the pot. His great gran'dad, arter a long life spent doin' the durndes fool things done in them durn'd fool days, killed hissef a jumpin down a bluff, two hundred feet into a rocky dry branch, jist to save a half a mile gwine to the stillhouse.

"My son" Sut's gran' mamey's cousin, on the she side, must a been a hell ove a feller, in his way; he fit the very best men, in all Noth Caliney, an' Firginey, an' never foun' one that he was abil to whop. He also fit a nigger, name

Prince or Jupiter, a pitch battil, for a gallun ove appil brandy, an' a barlow knife. That barlow, war foun' in the pockit ove a dead nigger, on the day arter the race from Belmont to the gunboats; I think from this, that Prince or Jupiter must a flax'd out our ancestor. I hev in my persession, the written agreement ove this pitch battil, signed with Crassis, only the niggers Crass is a fish hook. I menshun this to show, what they tho't ove niggers, one hundred and twelve years ago.

Sugartail Lovingood, was a son ove his daddy, and bein' my daddy is tharfoar gran' daddy to "my son" Sut—That is if thar was no stockin' ove kerds, or sich. He did'nt git killed often, doin' any thing, nor never got whipp'd, as I knows ove, becaze he never did eny fightin'. He jist sloshed along lazily, an' this sort ove life spiled him for finanshul business, all except multiplyin' childer, ove which I am one. My mamy was an 'oman hard to beat, or forget; she had the quickest lick with a hickory, or a clapboard, ove eny 'oman I ever seed, except my Betts, "my son" Sut's own mam; she also had a sharp eye for insex. A sunshiney, Sunday mornin', was a day ove doom, to all creepin' things, an' we all had sore heads on Monday, an' scratchin' scasely ever begun afore Wensday.

Down to this point, the Lovingood blood hadn't a single bad crass—Durn'd fools, the last cussed one, that toted the name. Now as to me, myself. I wer hatch'd in Ole Noth Caliney, clost to Firginney line, an' tuck my fust drink ove warter, outen Tar River, whar herrins, gourd martin boxes, an' tupemtime did mos' abound. When I wer about so years old, Dad packed plunder, an' we got a three year old bull, to haul hit, while we follered in the cart ruts to Bunkum county. I led two houn dogs, mam toted twins, an' the chances, with a dinner pot on her back, while dad, Sugartail Lovingood, rid the bull, a toatin' a rifle gun; the rest ove the childer follered durn'd permiskusly, pickin' huckilberys, an' fightin' the hole way. I never will forget that bull (we eat him the nex' winter), for through his sagacity we foun' Bunkum at last.

When I wer a littil *more,* so year old, dad moved agin to Bertie, whar I boun' myself out, to the trade ove varmint huntin', corn shuckin', an sich. Arter I had sarved out my time faithfully, I sot up for myself, an' staid sot up ever since, except when I git knocked down, or lie down apupos. Along about now, I suffered a sevear, an' perlonged attack ove onintermitunt durn'd fool, jurin' which I got married. Folks talked a good deal, said Betts wer too good for me, an' they say so yet. I tho't hit a good thing, an' don't think so yet. I married Betts Leatherlaigs, daughter ove old man Leatherlaigs, an' we imejuntly sot in to house keepin' in a bark camp, wher, sooner nor you would expeck, I foun' mysef the daddy (so called) ove "my son" Sut, the prominent subjeck ove a heap ove talk now-a-days, an' sartinly a most remarkabil son in his way. I must be allowed, as his daddy, however, to remark, confidensially—dam such a way as his'n. If the camp whar he fotch his fust squall in is standin' yet, I knows nottin ove hit—I speck hit is rotted down. Seventeen other brats wer cotch in my net, an' strung on my string. I hes retired from business, with a compitancy ove brats, an' I keep a retirin' from hit—you bet.

I has allways had a heap ove reputashun, so much in fac, that if I dident now an' then spree away the surplus, I'd be smothered with reputashun. I never owned a nigger, an' never tried, arter I foun' out how much one cost, an' the danger ove mixin'.

I hev voted for Gin'l Jacksin, sum, that is as often as three times ove a morning; I vote for Jacksin, yet—I never wer much ove a politishiner, owside ove the whisky part. I never wer "technically" term'd a abolisionist (that means durn'd fool), but hit has been insinuated to the childer, an' charged purty strong on "My son" Sut. I am proud ove mysef; I hev a constitution like a daug. I am a hoss, in fac' hoss rather perdominates amung the Lovingoods. "My son" Sut was fust engineer to one, for a long spell—we dream hoss, we talk hoss, we act hoss, we smeel hossey—in fac' Lovingood an' hoss am now, an' forever one an' inseperable. I may add, that I think nex' arter the nigger, that hosses orter vote, an' thar hides be exempt frum the tan vat.

You reques' ove me my dogratype; now Mister Ramige, I aint down bad (jist at this time) with a spell ove durn'd fool, so you gits no dogratype from me; a man is powerful low with the disease, when he manages to git his picter into the noospapers. I will tho' give you a small mess ove dogril, jist to put a good taste in your mouth. I ken rite poetrie; in fac' I ken do eny thing I want to, except tannin dorg hides, with saw dust, or sellin' hoss hides with cows tails to 'em; try who will they'll find hit a failur. I mus' repeat afore I put in the dogril so as to impress the great fac' on your mine, that *I am a hoss,* an' if I aint a hoss, I'm nothin', an' *if* I'm nothin', I haint foun' hit out yet— you bet.

> "Mister Ramige, my good kind friend,
> I'd see you durn'd afore I'd send
> A picter, profile or pot-o-graff,
> To give durn'd fools a chance to laff.
> Or bust the box, an' break the glass,
> Strainin' to picter out an ass.
> As for Betts, she'd take a skare,
> A log chain coudent hold her there
> While a feller sighted her. Through
> A fixin', shiney, bright an' new,
> That shows the hide, throu' shift an' dress,
> She'd *never* stand such wicked-ness.
> My whiskers, too, Ise shear'd 'em off—
> A hen's nest now, in the stable troff.
> So now to you, I'd look all wrong,
> A dam poor tune, to a sleepy song.
> But if you're dry, an' whisky want,
> Jis' come to me, an' hit I'l Grant,
> I'l rise, an' shine ————————"

Thar—if I haint crack'd my skull two inches right in the crown, thar's narra devil. I think I'l stick to plain ritein, strait acrost the paper; hits safest—ain't so strainin'. In my next I will come squar up to "my son" Sut, an' his wonderous doin's, not forgittin' the hoss part, nor how he rid 'em. Don't forgit, always afore the word Sut, to put in the words "my son." An' bar in mine strait along, that I am his daddy; the time has come, the worild mus' be kept in mine ove that great fac', that "my son" Sut has a daddy, an' that daddy is a hoss, an' I am HE.

Yours Respectively,
HOSS LOVINGOOD,
Sire of the renowned Sut.

NOTEY BENEY—Never another durn'd line ove poe*trie* do *you* git—mine that.

Knoxville *Press and Messenger,* May 7, 1868.

The Early Life of Sut Lovingood, Written by His Dad

(Continued)

MISTER Ramige,

Dear Sir:—It is said, that every man thinks his own wife, the best woman in the world. But if all men think as I dus—a durnder lie never wer told. When I fasten'd onto Betts Leatherlaigs, for a mate, she wer a rale slide easey, smilin', saft footed gall, but she soon spread, an' hardened into the durndest, scaley heel'd, rule-a-roast 'oman, atwix h—l, an' breakfast time. She stomp'd a heap ove her caracter onto her brats; in fac', I don't think eny ove 'em takes arter me to a suspisious egstent. I have studied a power about this. The leadin' passions uv "my son" Sut, from the time he could go alone, wer skeers—whisky—obstinacy, an' hosses. The fust hoss he ever druv wer a muel, an' him he druv crazy, in two secon's an' a half, by comin' at him, sturn formos' on his all fours, an' in his shut tail. That ar animule wer never worth a cuss arterwards—*His hart was broke*. Folks sed then, that if "my son" Sut met with no bad luck, or accident, to stunt him, or set him back, he'd make a beautiful damfool some day. Hit don't become me, his dad, to speak. He is before the world, but I mus' be allow'd to remark, that I do believe in perdicshuns. If a suckis, or eny show comes along—an' got away without a slit canvass, a lost dorg, or a hamstrung hoss, "my son" Sut wer sick—absint—or drunk. Wonst there come a suckis, with a little cuss ove a muil, an' they call'd hit Lee. The ring marster, name Abe, call'd aloud for some able bodied boy, to ride this vishus cuss. Well boy arter boy tried hit, an' got flung right, an' left. One hit head fust on the candy stand; then Abe mos' incontintly kick'd him out. Another, name John Pope, lit sturn fust amung the "nashun's wards," an' Abe, in bootin' his rear, misfortinately stove out his brains. I hes watch'd the kareer ove that boy, an' he haint been worth a dam since. Another got flung clean into the Rapahanock. Abe dident stun his sturin (stun means benumb), for he never drown-did, an' aint fish'd out yet. In stepp'd "my son" Sut, an' offered to ride—got mountid, an' the performince begun. Roun', an' roun', an' roun', they went—Lee's tail gwine roun', an' roun', too, like the crank ove a grindstone. Every now, an' then, the muel would send "my son" Sut, spreadeagle fashion, clean acrost the ring, an' then stan' still, an' wait for him to come agin. The people sot up a great shout, some few for the muel, an' a heap for "my son." So many hollered for him, that the ringmaster wer feard to boot him out, although he wer a smashin' things bad, every fall he got; an' besides all that, go as hit would, the performince wer *payin'*. Arter a while, yere cum a great, ugly, chatterin' monkey, name Washburne, an' up he jump'd ahine "my son" Sut's shoulders, cotch him by the har, an'—*thar he sticks to this day.* Jurin all this tryin' time, an' up till now, "my son" Sut has never moved a muscle ove his face. Queer, aint it? One time, a poor blind cuss come along, callin' hissef a freenolegist, an' a tellin people thar caracter by feelin' ove thar heads. The neighbors, hevin a lively idear ove "my son" Sut's proness to cussedness, an' damfool, immejuntly sent for him. I haven't yet remarked, that at this time ove his life, he was as fat as a butterball, it bein' a great season for 'simmons, an' punkins. Jist as soon as the blind man toch "my son" Sut's face, he shrunk back, an' said—"Gentlemen, it is unmanly and a shame, to play tricks on one blind." They all dident onderstan' him, an' swore if thar was a trick, they dident know ove it. "Well! well!" sez he, "It *might* a been a mistake, your puttin' the boy at me wrong aind foremos'—fetch him up agin." This time he touch'd "my son" Sut, first on the snout, an' after feelin' ove hit, for a good spell doubtfully, he went for the bumps, an' give in the verdick, that if he escaped bein' a suckis rider, or a stage driver, thar was no knowin' what he mout come too—hit all depended on luck *entirely,* for his was the best ballanced head, to make a damfool, he'd ever felt, an' that he wouldent be surprised to hear of his goin' to the peniten-tiary, hell, or Congriss, any day—that he was equal to the imergency. I think I have remarked before, that I believe in perdickshun.

Somewhere about this time, a well-to-do neighbor, after

trying' to school several boys, an' all ove 'em turnin' out miserabil, *miserabil* failures, concluded, as public opinion had fixed "my son" Sut's fate, that he'd give him a chance to dodge hit; so, by a sartin slight ove han', not at all necessary to mention here, he got smuggled into school. The marster give him the first five letters ove the alfibat, to git by hart. Ove course, to this good day, "my son" Sut haint recited—he's very taciturn. A powerful sharp boy (as *he* thought) wonst offered to bet "my son" Sut a dozin marvils, that he ("my son" Sut) couldent jump foar feet, an' let him (the smart boy) pick the groun', an' the course to jump. Ove course "my son" Sut tuck him up (he woudent a tuck a dare from the devil). Well! Smarty tuck "my son" within three feat ove a frame house, an' told him to jump toards the house, an' at hit he went—you bet. The licks could be hearn a mile, but, arter a while, the weatherboards give way; so did the laths, an' plarster— "my son" Sut *won them marvils*. When he come home, his head was as big as a bushell, an' his brains wer churned as thin as water, an' when he shook his head, they sloshed. They slosh yet.

In consequence ove the above norated great feat, the boys roun' thar concluded that "my son" Sut, warn't fit to live, so they "went for him." He come home arter a shot gun to defend hissef, an' never went back again. "My son Sut" was slow to wrath but generally fast *from* hit. He was born a beautiful child, but some how, didn't git purtier as he grow'd up, like tother childer. I shall always think that bustin' head fust throu' that ar weather boarded house had sumthin to do with hit. That is his beefey egspression ove head, an' face.

Yours Respectively,
HOSS LOVINGOOD,
Sire of the renowned Sut.

Knoxville *Press and Messenger*, May 14, 1868.

The Early Life of Sut Lovingood, Written by His Dad

TO OUR Readers.

We are truly sorry to announce that the last letter from our old friend, "Hoss," closed the series of his letters on the early life of his son *Sut*. This truly to be deplored fact is owing to the imprudence of a friend. It seems that this friend called on *Mr. Hoss Lovingood* and informed him that the public looked with anxiety and interest for *his* version of that "playing hoss business," and also the reasons why he had always treated *Sut* as the black sheep of his flock, until he obtained for himself a national distinction. This palpable prying into private affairs insulted the old man— he took what is commonly termed "the sulks," and swore that "he wouldn't budge another durn'd inch," and he won't. We think, too, that some unfriendly criticism has reached his ears touching his poetry and egotism, be this as it may. We fear that this is "his last appearance on any stage," and we in our heart can not much blame the old man, for really he has been very cavalierly treated, simply for thinking his very black crow was a very white one; and, no one else volunteering, he blew his own cracked horn to that note, not dreaming that he would become the laughing stock of the continent.

Knoxville *Press and Messenger*, May 21, 1868.

Bill Ainsworth's Quarter Race.
A Story of the Old Times (1833)
in East Tennessee

A STORY of the long ago, when "William the fourth was King."

Thar now, does that fire suit you, George. If this camp wer bilt facin the south, a little more, hit wud be better, on account ove smoke. The win sets plumb from the no'th. Hoy! Yander comes Hyram, with the jug. Hush, say George, Hyram don't drink you know; now jist 'zamine that jug, when he comes, an' see if thar ain't a tear track, down over the bulge. I rubb'd hit all dry, with flour, on a rag, afore he started.

"Well! Sut, what if the poor fellow has taken a drink; he is welcome to it." Oh! Sing sam's to a dead mule, an' then watch if his years move, will you! I warnt begrudgin hit to him. You pays for hit, an' hits only a mile to the still house. But, I is studyin' caracter. I wanted to see, if he aint a hypocrite, that's all.

"What if he is!"

Nuffin, only I'l pizen the jug.

"Why?" Becaze, whisky warn't made to be drunk on the sly. Hit warn't intended no how for wimmen, passuns, nor hypocrits.

"Sut."

What?

"I have heard several accounts, of your difficulty, at Bill Ainsworth's horse race, something about catching a flea, or a bug, off a young lady."

'Twarnt neither; hit wer a *tick*—that is, I tho't hit wer. But, wait till the jug comes. I ken allways talk better, when I see a jug with a wet corn cob in hits mouth, leanin' up amung the saddles, an' hoss geer, like hit wer a listenin' to me. A feller feels sorter like he has backin. Pour out a morsel for me, while yer han's in. Thar. Thar.

Well! You minds the time (hits "long ago" now) Bill

307

Ainsworth had Ariel, "the little one eyed grey." The fastes' quarter hoss with a ketch on 'im that ever mark'd the yeath, by golly!

Hit was the day that he run aginst "Kate," the fas' Alabam mar', for a thousin dollars. Thar was swarms ove people, from all parts, to see, an' share in the joys, an' sorrers, ove what every body expected to be the fastes' quarter race ever run. "Kate" wer a powerful mar', almos' sixteen han's high, an' every inch a race hoss, from her iron up, an' as yet, she had never foun' enything wearin' shoes that straighten'd her out. She walked with a limber, sassy step, that look'd like she cud step as fur agin, if she wanted too, and she actid as if that was jist what she was thinkin'. She look'd right at every body an' thing roun' her as a human would. But Ariel, she never even seem'd to see him at all. I has seed wimmen in my time adzackly like Kate, both in looks an' manners, an' every one ove 'em wer oncommon people, either for good or bad, jist as the toss up chip fell, when thar lot wer chalk'd out. 'Oman like too, she cud show her temper, an' heels, like gun flashin', an' had tharfoar, a rather wide circle ove acquaintances. I has spoke ove Kate afore Ariel, becaze she wer a shemail. That's manners, haint hit? I tho't so, by gravy!—I ken guess right now an' then, if I is let alone, an' not flustrated. Ariel wer from Kaintuck, onder fourteen han's high, but adzackly as long as a fence rail. His mussils moved onder his glossy grey hide, like cats crawlin' onder a carpet, an' the shape ove his short head minded you ove a fox sqirril's. His eye (he had but one you mind) was a lazy, sullen one, an' his brows wer jackass, to a dot; his years wer short, an' seem'd as stiff as boards; study the littil hoss as long as you wud, all you cud think was, *danger,* an' *he* notised nothin'. When they pass'd in exercisin', they actid like humans in a huff—never seed one another at all, that was the way.

Standin' side by side, they 'minded me ove a locomotive, with steam up, all brass, polish an' power. An' a lathe, for making sich things, squat-long-heavy-an' still. No more alike than a bullit an' a bird, yet you jist *know'd* that both could fly. Now, who the devil wer to judge atwix 'em, an' pick the right one; the one you look'd at las' was the one you tho't *mout* beat, an' you never tho't eny thing more positive than "mout." Kate wer a splendid, rich, bloody-brown, changeable-in-the-sun; while Ariel, as I sed before, wer a gray, almos' white. Kate wer the "dark hoss." So people, the evenin' before, was wonderin' what kind ove a day tomorrow wud be.* Out, tharfore, wer every body, by day-break, smokin' cob pipes, in bunches, in pars, an' alone, watchin' for the first streak. *It was a dark day*. Now the bettin' begun, an' Kate had the call. The race warn't expected to run ontil late. So kerds, in the stable lof's by the sly ones, an' kerds under the trees by the "don't keer" ones, wer plenty—"three up," "seven up" an' "twenty deck poker," for from a dime to fifty dollars. Ox carts (with the oxes tuck loose, an' hitch'd in the shade) full ove har trunks an' kaigs, an' them full ove cider, an' ginger cakes. While fat ole wimmen sot on top, in brass speks, an' frilled cap borders, kep busy a drappin' fourpence ha'pennys into a black, press'd snuff box, with a red face an' cock'd hat, call'd the juke of Wellington, painted on the lid. While a favorit dater sot on the tail board, keepin' off the flies with a green bush, lookin' soft an' sweet. Little boys, with clean, homeade shirts, an' wool hats, with a rose under the band, look'd up, open mouth'd, into men's faces, an' listen'd, wonderin' if ever they could rise high enough to be a rale hoss-racer. Young men, in their shirt sleeves, with the collar unbotton'd,** an' a fresh cut hickory club in their han's, slung'd roun', winkin' at the red daters ove the cake wimmen, or listen'd to Claib Nance, sittin' in the porch, playin' "Billy in the low groun's," like no other man ever has, or ever will, play that tchune.

Settled men stood facin', in pairs, with thar hats down over thar eyes, whittlin sticks as they talk'd, thinkin' more than they sed, an' wonderin' if they'd bet on the right hoss. Or sot, or lay roun in the shades talkin' of other races, an' other days. Old men, tottered aimless about on long smooth sticks, so stoop shoulder'd that they had to throw thar heads back to see levil, from onder thar faded, flopped hats, with a white string ban', an' a pipe twistin' in hit, mumblin tobacco, or bark on thar toothless gums—fast, like a sheep dus fodder. Trimblin', an' dartin' quick looks from face to face, like they wer huntin' some one, that they warn't sure they wud know, if they did meet 'em. These wer the men that fit Furguson, at Kings Mountain, or Rawdon, at the Eutaw Springs, an' run quarter races, fifty years before Kate or Ariel fust staggered to their feet. Two actif, red cheek'd fellers, with thar galluses tied roun' 'em, jumpin' thirty-six feet at three jumps, here. Thar, a par ove slick, laughin' niggers, wrastlin "briches holts," with the hems above thar knees. Yonder, a mess ove boys stonein a sqirril, up a tree, an' everywhar fun in some shape. Roun' the low log stables, folks peepin' thru the cracks, at the hosses, an' boys rubbin 'em. Back ove the barn, two fellers, one in grey an' tother in brown jeans, swappin poneys, while a dozen more squatted on thar hunkers, agin the wall, listenin' to 'em, an' chawin a dimes worth ove cold chicken laig an' biscuit. The Sheriff too with saddil-bags, hangin' over his arms, an' his arms cross'd afore im, while a loaded whip, mounted with big ivory rings, stuck out from onder the left one, stood well back an' wide on his laigs, with his hat cock'd before, tellin' an open mouth'd dozen, "to a dead moril sutenty," which hoss wud win. Jis' to look at him, you'd a bet yer shirt on his judgemint, an' then went home bar back'd.

Down at the spring another crowd. The grey hair'd tax collector, sittin' on the roots ove the big sicamore, with a quill pen in his mouth, turnin' the leaves ove the tax book, for the name ove the straw hatted man, in ragged linnen coat, standin' stoopin' before 'im, with his han's on his knee caps, lookin' at the book upside down, like he cud read hit, or pay his taxes either. Not knowin', that the red headed young devil, behine him, was hookin' the water gourd to his tail. A fat, clean, holsum lookin', old nigger 'oman, with her grey head, tied up in a white hankecher, comes with pitcher, an' plate, arter milk, an' butter for dinner, from the cold spring hous', an' has to anser half a dozen "dat she *don't* want tu marry,"—"dats what." Crowds, an single ones, begin from every direction, to move towards the field, the judges hev gone, an' got up the white, startin', an' out cum stakes. The boys ar chasin out the hogs with dorgs, an' the hosses hitch'd near the paths, am now led furder away, out ove sight. Men ar walkin' along the tracks, kickin' out, or pickin' up, everything bigger than a grain ove corn. While sum boys foot racin down nigh the start, or climbin' into trees, near the outcum. Hunter,

Kate's owner, axes Ainsworth, "if they moutent as well hev hit over, that his mar is frettin' a little, in the stable, at the crowd, an' the noise." Bill pulls out his watch, looks fust at hit, an' then up, whar the sun orter be, with his one eye, an' sed, "Well! I'm easey; I recon the bettin's 'bout done; fetch out yer nag." "I'l bet my pony on the 'little grey,'" said a quick, lispin, gall like voice. It wer Wash Morgan, a boy then, but es a man, the fastes' foot racer livin', 'sceptin' Beverly Brown Pryor. "My son," sed the game Hunter, layin' his han' on Wash's cap. "I won't win a boy's pony from him." "Oh! Yes, ma sez, you may, *if you ken.*" The pony was staked agin forty dollars.

"Stop, Sut. Say! Did Hunter win the pony?" asked Hyram, whom we all thought asleep.

George, don't that durn'd fool need stampin'? That question seems more like speakin' out in meetin', than any thing I has ever hearn. That ar cuss wud break an aig, to see how fas' the chicken wer hatchin', an' then be fool enuff to poke hit onder the hen agin. Go to sleep, you cussed goat with no beard.

"They're fetchin out the nags," flew from mouth to mouth, every whar in a moment, an' that great mass ove people settled in two black acres, one at the start, an' one at the outcum, lookin' like bee swarms, an', like the bees, hummin' an' buzzin'.

"If you'd a been thar, to a seen them run roun',
You'd a tho't in yer soul they'd ne'er touch the groun."
This, an' t'other song,
"Bet your money on the bob tail-hoss,
I bets mine on the grey,"
floated up, here an' thar, from the swarms, with, now an' then, a laff, or some one hollerin for some one else to "come thar." Watch the centre ove that black acre, at the outcum, how hit's a swayin' about, like high rye in a wind. See hats an' coats fly up in the air. Look at them sticks, circlin' roun' above thar heads—crack, crack, "Hurray, Blount!" "Hurray, Monroe!" "Far play!" "Stan' back!" "That's hit, Jo!" "Close in, Tom" an' in a moment or so you sees two fellers led out from each side ove the crowd, with bloody heads an' no shirts. Jis a fis' fight, with sticks; that's all.

"Look, look, yander she comes," "Why don't they take

her blanket off," "Geminey! Watch her, how she jerks that big nigger at her bits," "Look at her plates a shinin'," "Oh! But she's a beauty," "Ten dollars on Kate, ove Alabam'." This, an' more too, you cud hear twenty times at once. A bald-headed man, in his shirt sleeves, cut the pidgeon wing, an' hollerd "Hurray for Alabam'. I was with Jackson, at Talladega, an' the Hoss Shoe." This wer answer'd by "Hurray for Kaintuck an' the one-eyed grey. I wer at Orleans, whar we whipp'd British, an' not Injuns." "See, see, yander comes the little grey." Sure enuff, about eighty yards behine the mar, here come Ariel. Ainsworth, barheaded an' in his shirt sleeves,, with a red hankecher, tied like a sling, hung roun' his neck, leadin' by the bitts, with little Bob Maddy, a purty, blue eyed child, weighin' seventy-two pounds, switchin' the weeds with his whip, whistlin' an' follerin close behind the hoss. In the toss up, Hunter had won both the word an' choise ove track; so he put Kate *on Ariel's blind side.*

"Clar the track; the riders is up," was shouted along the line. I look'd, an' seed a white spot, circlin' roun' over the crowd; at the start it was the shirt ove the little nigger on Kate; in a moment more I seed another, but hit wer rather still. "Maddy's up, that's Maddy," somebody said low. "Gentlemen," said John McGhee, with hat off, "stand back, and don't shout, if you please, or wave any hats, as they come." "All right, Colonel," an' all was still.

They both turn'd into the tracks, even; Ainsworth watchin' the mar, over Ariel's naik, clost as a hawk. Little Maddy, with both han's in the bridle, was watchin' Ainsworth's anxious face, an' smilin'. They both come in a tremblin' squat—"Are you ready?" sed Ainsworth, from between his set teeth. "No!" shouted Hunter, as Kate plunged towards the hoss lash'd out behine like a very devil an' shook Hunter like he wer only a rag hung to her bitts. Ainsworth, with his hand pattin' Ariels nose, an' him playfully nippin' at the han', as they both swung roun' agin. Kate this time, cum powerful *low.* Hunter look'd up at the nigger, an' he nodded back the look. "Are you ready." "Go," thundered Hunter, an' he struck at Kate with his whip—a clear miss behine. When Ariel heard the word he jerk'd Ainsworth to his han's an' knees, in lettin' loose. "I've got you, Bill," sed Hunter, smilin', and wipin' his face. "I have a fifty left," answered Bill. "I take it," sed Hunter, an' they cum walkin' up the track together.

At our aind, every body was still, an' spoke low, as they wer turnin'. "Now they're off"—no,—yes,—by—, "here they come." I seed Maddy raise his little arms once, an' bring hit down quick. The nigger was whippin' over the withers, by a turn ove his wrist, strait along. I noticed one thing I dident like; the niggers head was levil with Maddys, an' Kate, two han's the highes'. *She was runnin' as low as a greyhoun'.* I tho't too, that I seed her plainer, than I did the hoss, tharfoar she mus' be nearer—my heart wer fairly poundin'.—"The mars got 'im." "No she aint"—"Don't you see, Maddy aint whippin'?" "My soul! They're flyin."—I run two steps, to get opposite the poles, an' I cud see twenty poles an' all ove 'em a dancin'. A noise, like a low fast roll on a kittle drum—a flash—It was the lainth ove Ariel's grey hide, from his bitts to his heels, before Kate's nose. The matchless beauty was *beaten*, an' North Alabama broke.

For about two or three common heart beats, that is, if they beat at all,—the very leaves wer still. Nothin' but a muffled sort ove dry swallerin', like children does jist before cryin'. Then a note like a dove cooin', swell'd an' swell'd into a roar, that run on the mountains again, again an' again.

As the riders walk'd them back, the little nigger's tears wer fallin' in Kate's mane, while Maddy look'd jaded, an' sober, his whip danglin' loose from his wrist. The hoss, as usual slungin along lazily, with scasely a hair turn'd. Kate had a few streaks ove sweat, that look'd like ink on her glitterin' gown ove brown. But with head up yet, an' a purple fire blazin in her eye.—Beat, but beautiful still. * * * * * * * * "What was thar time?" "Who hilt a watch?" "John McGhee did." "Oh! yes," "an' so did Tom Upton, an' Tom Callaway." I seed the three git together, with open watches in thar han's, an' talk a moment. Then Col. McGhee turn'd to the crowd, an' sed, in his quiet way, "Nineteen seccons, gentlemen," an' he wiped the sweat off his brow, like he'd been at hard work. The fastes' quarter race, ever run, was over. An' the dark hoss, "hadent won." * * * * * * * * * "Now Sut, tell us about that 'tick' business; you have dodged it hansomly."

Oh! no, Ise sleepy.

"You never intended to tell that story; you are *ashamed* of it."

No, I aint sham'd—you be durn'd, I'l swear I'l tell hit—some time.

NOTES.— * A popular belief, that on a dark day, the darkest colored animal would win.

** In those good old days, of homespun, and honesty. The buttons on shirt collars, were often as large as a dime, and sewed on with flax thread. It was precautionary therefore to unbutton the collar in joining social gatherings for in the event of a fight. A twisting grasp on the throat, secured by such buttons, and thread, was sure strangulation.

Knoxville *Press and Messenger*, June 4, 1868.

Sut Lovingood's Allegory

THOSE of us who have not yet reached that ferry, so dreaded by many, yet anxiously looked forward to by the footsore and weary ones, who have passed but few cool fountains, or hospitable shelters, along their bleak road, must well remember the good old days of camp meetings, battalion musters, tax gatherings, and shooting matches. Well! There was the house raising too, and the quiltings, and the corn shuckings, where the darkey's happy song was heard for the last time. And then, the moonlight dance in the yard—"Yas by geminey!" interrupted Sut, "an' the ridin home ahine the he fellers, on the same hoss, arter the dancin was done, an' the moon gone down. When, if hit hadent been for the well balanced gall, you couldn't a staid on yer critter, but would a bin foun' nex' morning, with yer hed in the branch, holdin a death holt to a willer root with yer teeth, whilst some feller rode like h—l arter the coroner, afore any body would venter to haul you out."—

I was just thinking boys, while Sut was speaking, whether we are the gainer by the discoveries—inventions—innovations, and prayers, of the last forty years. Whether the railway—telegraph—chloroform—moral reform, and other advancements, as they are termed, have really advanced us any, in the right direction or—

"Stop right thar, George, an' take my idear ove the thing, fresh from water. I know powerful well that I is a durn'd fool, an' all that—but I can *see,* by golly! Don't the Bible tell about them seekin' out many strange inventions? Well! Thars the tex', now. An' if I wer a practiced hard shell, with ontax'd whisky in me deep enuff to swim a rat, I could make these woods quake, an' that ar mountain roar. But bein' as hit is, I mus' just talk, bein' content if ara one ove you boys will stay awake an' listen. Some ove you minds the boy that started to school one sleety mornin', an' slipp'd two steps backward for one forrid. He only got thar, you mine, by turnin' roun', an' gwine tother way. Well! That's the world's fix to-day, an' if heaven is the hotel that they is aimin' to sleep in, if they don't turn an' go tother way, I'm dad-drabitted if they don't 'lie out.'

"Nater, George, teaches the cow not to eat laurel or nightshade, an' the dorg to hunt grass, when he has gorged too much 'turkey with ister stuffin' (dorgs do eat sich things right often, you know). So, as we grow old, nater makes some ove their instinck grow an' brighten in us, showin' one, now an' then, that we is on the wrong road, an' might eat nightshade, for hit's plenty. That's what makes you compar the days ove the fiddle, loom an' cradle with the peaner, ball-room an' wetnurse, ove these days. In comparin' 'em, you may take one person, a family, or a county, at a time, an' you'll find that we haint gain'd a step on the right road, an' if the fog would clear up we'd find heaven behine us, an' not strength enuff left to reach hit alone, if we wer to turn back. No, boys, we aint as *good* as we wer forty years ago. We am too dam artifichul, interprizin an' *sharp*—we know too much. We ought to be sarved like Old Brakebill sarved his black billy goat. We desarve hit, mos' all ove us.

"Old Brakebill was a Dutchman, a rale silver dollar Dutchman. *He* wer fool enuff to think that both parties to a trade ought to hev the best ove hit. That is, somehow in this way: If you had wheat, an' to spare, an' wanted corn, an' I had corn, an' to spare, an' wanted wheat, an' two bushels ove one was worth one bushel of t'other, all the neighborhood over, then we ought to swap. On that sort ove principle he'd trade, an' on no other. As to 'out smartin'' anybody, he know'd no more about hit than the rulin' politicians ove our day know ove statesmanship, or the doctors ove mullygrubs in the brain. He dident attrack much notice then, for he wer jist like most everybody else. But now, if he wer alive, he'd git his broad sturn kick'd out ove church, an' be shot for a damfool, afore he could git out ove the graveyard. 'Behine the age,' an' all that, you know.

"Well! Jist wish I wer behine the age mise'f, say some forty or fifty years."

Well! Sut if you will not let me talk, suppose you tell

us how Brakebill served his black billy goat. And let us draw no comparisons between the lost past and the present, which we must endure.

"Oh! I dont know much about hit. Only hearsay, from the old folks, you know. Hit seems that he had, what would be call'd now a days, a progressive billy goat—a regular, walkin insult to man, an' beast; he strutted, with his hine laigs, and munched, like a fool gall with hir fore ones. An' then his tail—hit said, 'you-be-dam,' all day long, an' him as black as a coal cellar, at midnight at that. He would a suited our day to a dot tho', an' our day would a suited him. He could a hilt his own, even agin the 'busines men' (they am all the go now, you know), an' durn my buttons, if he dident look an' act adzackley like 'em—beard, eyes, forred, dress, tail, and chewin, ways, an' voice. He did, by geminey!

"But, he wer altogether too dam smart for Brakebill, or Brakebill's day, an' generashun beyant all sort of doubt. That ar meterfistickal, free will, billy goat wer forty years ahead ove *his* day. As they say in praise ove some cussed raskil, when he gets a million in a week, when at the gineril rate ove fortin makin, hit had orter took him sixty days. He had been showin many marks ove progress, an' higher law, for a good while, without attractin much notice anyway. Sich as buttin old misses Brakebill, bucket an' all, belly down, clean thru onder the cow, as she stoop'd to milk her. An' then buttin the cow herself out ove her slop tub, so that he could wet his own beard in her supper. That wer "higher law," warnt hit? Or he'd watch for the old man to go from the crib to the hog pen, with thirty big ears of corn, piled on his arm. When he'd make a de-monstrashun in the rear, that would send the old feller, spread eagle fashion, plowin gravel with his snout, while he impudently munch'd the hog's corn. That were financeerin, I s'pose. Or, he'd jump up an' but the under side ove the scaffol, whar the peaches wer spred to sun dry, an' then 'appropriate' all that he jar'd over the aidge. That mus' a been what they now call 'strategy,' don't you recon?

"Old Misses Tardiff, a two hundred pound mother in the church, wer once out in the thicket alone, near the camp groun', durin the fall meetin, at secret prayer, an' hit wer away deep into a tolerable dark night. Benny (that wer the goat's name) were in the thicket too, an' seein her on her knees, bobbin her head up an' down, he tuck hit for a buttin challenge, or purtended that he did. So immejeretly he went for the 'bull curl' in her forred, turnin her numerous summersets, down hill, into the branch, an' then runnin over her, with a 'B-Bu-Bub-Baa-a,' by golly. Geminey cricket! Don't you recon that ole 'oman tho't that the hill had blow'd up? Well, when she got able, an' her cloths sorter wrung dry—she went into camp, an' give in her 'sperience: That she had jist had a pussonel, breeches holt, wrastle, with the devil hissef, an' had come off conquerer, an' ment tharfore to wear the crown, but, that his smell ove brimstone an' hartshorn come mitey near chokin' her dead. Thar was ni onto eighty come up at the next call for mourners. But when they tried old man Brakebill, to git him up, he only smiled an' shook his head, sayin', 'Vait dill I shees if my Benny ishent in der dicket shum var.'

"Now, as I said afore, all this dident give the goat much ove a name, or attract much attenshun. He was look'd on as a raskil, that's a fact. But bein' a *beast*, he warn't dealt with like he would a been had he been a human, by them old time people. If he'd a lived now adays, I'l jist be durn'd if they hadent a made him President ove a college or the passun ove Plymouth Church, an' bilt him a harim or a corectory, which is hit? Them old fogy folks had a mitey poor idear ove progress, that's a fac'.

"But at last Mister Benny overdid the thing; he got to be a little too durn'd progressive for old Brakebill and his times. His sin foun' him out, an' he wer made to simmer down to a level surface with the loss ove all, that makes life wholesome to a goat. The fac' is, like mos' ove these yere human progress humbugs, he jis' played h—l with hissef.

"Old Brakebill got to noticin that thar was something wrong with his sheep. The ewes butted at the ram, spiteful like, butted one another an' behaved powerful bad ginerally. Arter a while, on 'zaminin he foun' that some ove the lambs had patches ove coarse har in their wool, an' wer sproutin' beards. Nex' he found' his young pigs behavin' curious to be dutch hog's children. Rarin' up strait on thar hine laigs, clost fornint one another. Walkin' on top ove the fences—climbin' onto the shed roof ove the milk house, an' then buttin' one another off agin. An' every now an' then, one would hist his tail as strait up as a stack pole, an' put on a stiff strut. Venuses pups, too, seem'd to hev the very devil in 'em. While one ove 'em lived on the goose grass in the yard, another one butted the house cat blind, to pussey's astonishment, wrath, an' hissin' disgust. Then another sprouted periwinkle shells above his ears, an' smelt like a bottle ove hartshorn, with a mouse in hit. An old, one-eyed goose laid aigs with har on, an' then give milk. A jinny's colt walked half hit's time on aind, an' on a par ove split huffs, chawin' a cud made ove an old shoe sole. The hempbrake even rared on *hit's* hine laigs, threatnin the cuttin' box. Misses Brakebill left the plantation, an' the very devil was to pay generally. If you had a wanted to a bought the farm, you would a axed that dam goat the price ove hit, from his airs an' impudent ways, while the owner looked like a scared dorg, or a stepchild on the out aidge ove sufferance. Now, all this troubled the poor old Dutchman a power. He know'd that at the rate things were gwine on, his stock, very soon, wouldent be worth a tinker's durn. He had a hankerin' to believe in witches an' things, anyhow; so he tho't purty strong that some ove 'em must be arter his welfar. He toted a hoss shoe in his pocket, an' got rale serious. He often axed, 'how long it wer to camp meetin' time?' Jist like little children, sittin' round the fire ove a night, axin the knittin' mother, for the fiftieth time, 'how long will hit be till Christmas?' You must bar in mind that the poor feller dident know the fust durn'd thing about 'progress.' At last, by the livin' jingo! the *true* idear struck him, as hit mus *us* some time. So one mornin' arter drams, he come acrost a bran new, curious, little cuss, lookin' like a cross atwixt the devil an' a cookin' stove, standin' on hit's hine laigs, a suckin' the muley cow. Arter brainin' hit with a wagon standard, he jist sot down, an' whetted his knife, ontil it would shave the har off his arm. Now, boys, that's about all that anybody now livin' knows ove the matter. Only this much was noticed thararter: That Mister Benny, billy goat, instid ove chawin his cud, with a short, quick, sassey nip, nip, nip, arter that mornin', an' plum on, ontil he dried up, an' died in a sink-hole, he chaw'd hit arter the fashion ove an old, lazy cow, when she is standin' onder the shade ove the willers, bellyfull, an' bellydeep in the creek. His tail never agin flaunted the sky, surjestin 'youbedam.' He wer the very last one that you'd a thought ove axin about the price ove the farm. An *he dident raise any more family*.

"For the sake ove this an' the nex generashun, I would like to know how Old Brakebill managed to straiten things out. If I only could find out, I'd tell Frank Blair, I would, by golly! He wouldent be afeard to surjest the idear, if he tho't hit a wholesome one. Would he?"

Knoxville *Press and Messenger,* September 17, 1868.

"Well! Dad's Dead"

THAR never wer a man yet, so mean, but what some time, or other, done at least one good thing. Now, my Dad put off doin his good thing for an awful long time, but at last he did hit, like a white man. He died, by golly! Perfeckly squar—strait out, an' for keep. Aint you glad? Don't be fear'd to say so on my account, boys, for hit's so reasonable. Mam declar's that Gineril Washington never did a better thing in his whole life. She only grumbles that he dident ketch the idear twenty years sooner, for then, she mout "a done sumthin." But no, he hilt on, jist to spite her, ontil she broke off her last tooth, crackin' a corn bread crust, an' then he immegintly went. Why, the very las' reques' he ever made ove her wer to "let him look in her mouth." Good people, an' passuns, make a heap ove fuss over what they call the onnatralness ove folks towards the sick. Now, hits all a dad-rabbited lie, for the neighbors acted jist as natral to dad as could be. Nara durn'd one ove 'em ever come a nigh the old cuss, to fool 'im into believin' that he stood a chance to live, or even that they wanted him to stay a minit longer than he wer obleeged to, by givin him sups of warter, fannin' off the flies—axin him if he wer hongry, or any other meddlesome interfarances with nater—not them. I tell you, boys, if ever a man did git a fair launch, every way, into the river sticks, that man wer my dad; he went on time to a seccon', an' no body a holdin on to his coattail. They acted natral clean thru, too, for when he wer a kickin' his last kicks, old Muddleg's wife come to the fence an' call'd mam out, to know if she cudent spar the frock she had on, in pay for sixty cents that dad owed her husbun', for three drinks ove "hoss botts." "That she thought mam mout afford to run in her petticoattail a while, as the weather wer good, an' hit bein' black, would pass for fust rate mournin." Hit's a wonder that las' idear hadent cotch mam, for she's great on style an' bein' in fashun, but hit dident; hit did git her back up tho' for she jist bleated like an old ewe, an' jump'd the fence to her. An' don't you believe! mam kicked her bustle clean off ove her, the passun, an' his wife a ridin' apast at that. Her nose bled, an' mam cried, an sich a snortin' as they had. The las' words dad ever spoke, wer, "which whip'd?" I meant to tell 'im that mam had nearly turned the old crane inside out with her foot, but he cud hear nothin' then for the roar ove the river.

Well, as I wer saying, the neighbors acted natral, an' that's the right way—do as you wants to, by golly! Dad shave the hipocracy ove fixin' a dead man away nice, arter lettin' him starve. Many, many a time, has people spent enough in plantin' a corpse, that if they had ever a loan'd the half ove hit to the mortul a livin', hit would a put off a funeral. But then the cuss wudent a went, when his time had come. Thars the devil ove hit—flustratin' doctrines so bad, you know.

Well, when dad got cool, an' stiff enuff to handle, we cudent raise ara coffin, without diggin' one up, an' totein hit a long mile. We had an old accoutrement box, hit's true, but then mam wanted hit to ketch rain water in. So, we just sot in, an' made a regular mummy out ove him, by sowin' him up, body an' soul, in an old, black bed spraid. Who knows, boys, but what he'l git dug up, some three thousan' years arter this, an' be sot up in a glass case, for a King Pharaoo, an' a devil ove a fuss raised, about the bed spraid bein' a royal mantle? Aint that a future for a Lovingood, arter him actin' hoss, an' bein' daddy to sich a varminty fixin' as me? But thar's plenty durn'd fools, ready to do hit for him, if they only happen to find him. Arter we got done, I swar that I wondered to see how much like a rich man's iron corpse case he look'd, an' hit sorter made me proud, hit did. I look'd roun', an' thar stood sister Sall, a blubberin'. I ax'd her what wer the matter, for the gal 'stonish'd me. Sed she, "Sowin' on that bed spraid 'minds me so much ove the time he made me sow him up in a raw hide, when he opened his dorg school. Bo! hoo! hoo!" I told her to shet right up least he mout hear her, an' want to go at hit agin, an' then we'd loose all our trouble, besides hit's bein' so disap'intin' to mam, for she had comb'd her har an' flour'd her face.

I know'd whar Old Stump Snodgrasses' steers wer a

grazin', with the yoke on. So I goes an' gits 'em, an' hitch'd on to a big shingle sled, what somebody had left on the chestnut ridge, an' we loaded dad up. Mam an' the childer wer strung along on each side, a holdin' on by the standards. "Now," sez mam, a fixin' on her sun bonnet, "hit's the rule to go *slow*." I sot in front an' was driver, an' a feelin' come over me, like I think a durn'd, starvin,' one-hoss lawyer mus' a had, when he fust foun' hissef Captain ove Company A, at the beginnin' ove the war. I'd a cuss'd a man in a minit, but fortinatly for any man, he warnt about just then. So, when I promised mam that I would "go slow," I did hit, with dignerty and 'sponsibility. I'd liked durn'd well to a hearn *any*body venter to order me to go fast, or to go at all, for that matter. I meant to make the most out ove that persession, an' my persition in hit, you understan'.

Now, durn'd fool like, in my big strut, I never tho't wonst about the smell ove the corpse a skeerin' the steers— hit always does, you know. So, jist as soon as they cotch the first whiff ove hit, they snorted—bawl'd—histed their tails up strait, an' with one mind, run away, hoss fashion. I be dam, if they dident git from thar, like they tho't that dad wud be too late for the boat. When I look'd up in the air at the wavin' tails, with the tassels hangin' the wrong way, I tho't ove the plumes ove a hearse, an' their bellerin' minded me ove the brass horns, blowin' some ove the Dead March in Saul; an' dad shave me, if I dident feel proud agin. Thar was *some* style about us, if we wer nothin' but Lovingoods. Hit's strange, I know, but I swar the tho't come over me ove the time dad acted hoss, an' instid ove hollerin "Wo, Buck!" I bawled "Wo, dad!" jist as I had done fifteen years before, in the saidge field, an' it seem'd to me I cud hear ho'nets a hummin' somehow.

You orter a seed that old sled waltz, an' dad an' the rest ove 'em bounce, him a buttin' the childer off, one side an' then t'other. Mam sez, "Consarnd him, he's at his old tricks agin. Roll 'im overboard." But, dadrabbit me, if I hadent a died fust; I meant to steer them cattil *thru* the graveyard anyhow, jist for the name ove the thing. So, I jist sot a foot against each steer's bar sturn, for a pur- chase, clampin' the roots ove thar histed tails atwix' my big toes an' the nex' ones, an' I froze fast to the ropes with both han's. One aind ove my back-bone (an' I scasely know which aind) wud bounce from the sled floor, fur enuff to almost skin my snout on the yoke. Then I'd balance back agin on the ropes, ontil I'd meet the sled somewhar in the air, on hits jumps—yere I'd come, over-handed, for the yoke agin. Dad shame me, if I dident think hit would jar my heart out at the top ove my head. To a look'd at me, you'd a thought I wer a tryin' to butt the oxe's brains out, but I warnt. My toes hilt like vices, an' I kept on a freezin' to the ropes; an' jist sich a game ove over-handed, high see-saw, you never seed—sorter like a walkin'-beam steamboat, you know. You see, I hilt on in the hope that mam wud hev sence enuff to roll 'im overboard, herself, somewhar nigh the hole, but she wer entirely too busy a fendin' off his butts to think ove enything. I generley look'd over my shoulder, as I'd be a balancin' back, towards that cussed, hard sled, to form some idear how hard the next lick wud be onto my lacerated sturn, an' to see how the rest ove 'em wer a makin' hit. When I seed his head take mam a rale goat butt in the ribs, thinks, I, "now we'l hear from her." Arter gruntin' a time or two, an' makin' a face like a burnt saddle seat, she sed, "I'd like to know when the devil *will* go out ove *him*." An' then she cried, dryin' her tears on the tail ove her bonnet. I wer right glad to see her show some feelin' for the old hoss, now he had started to be gone so long.

When we struck the aidge ove the graveyard, I look'd back agin, an' foun' mysef alone with dad. Mam war left behine, about a hundred yards, tryin' her levil best to git out ove the jaws ove a tall, forked stump, that had her fast by the waist. I never did see jist sich a glimmer ove arms and laigs a reachin' for ground. I tho't about an alligator, an' my chances for bein' a full orphan, an' how flustrated mam must be.

I found that the dad rabbited steers wer aimin' to run plum astradle ove the grave. So, I tho't I'd improve the occasion, to save some liftin'. Jist as the sled flew over hit, with a slider on each side, I turned roun'—sot my foot agin dad's head, an' done jist *so*. Hit shot him out, like an arrow, an' he chug'd in, as plum and strait as an 'oman lays a baby in the cradle. Bomp: I never hearn sich a jolt; he wer yearnist dead, or that fall wud a sot him to kicken'. One thing I sorter hated; he fell with his head to the east, an' I'm feared that will make him a little late a risein'. But, by golly! I cudent help hit, for we come in from the west, an' the dad burn'd steers, wer jist a flyin'. Thar's one little comfort in hit tho'—he'l rise with his back to the danger, an' I'l bet he hooves it frum thar. I made my lope from the vehikil, as soon as I could, but had to light on my head among prickly pars, an' slate. When I got the stickers pull'd out ove my eye leds, the steers wer out ove sight, gone glimmerin'. But I dident care, for I consider'd the procesion over, any how. That night, when we wer all hunker'd round the hearth, sayin' nothin', an' waitin for the taters to roast, mam, she spoke up—"oughtent we to a scratch'd in a little dirt on him, say?" "No need, man," sed Sall, "hits loose yeath, an' will soon cave in enuff." "But, I want to plant a 'simmon sprout at his head," sed mam, "on account ove the puckery taste he has left in my mouth. Law sakes alive! Haint hit so pervokin, that we never ken do enything like eny body else? Did you notice, how yer dad kerried on as we wer sleddin' him along?" "An' us a tryin' our best to be sorry, an' solemn," added Sall "An' then them steers, too," mam went on to say. "Blast thar flecked souls! Did you *ever* see the like?" "Well! well!" sez I, "never mind, mam; charms broke at last." "Hand me the fat goard. I wants to grease atwix my toes, dad shave thar rough tails."

Now, boys, say what you will about hit, thar's one thing you all must admit. That considerin' the family gittin' hit up, it wer a allfired, expidishus, imitation ove a funerel.

Knoxville *Daily Press and Herald*, November 15, 1868.

On Young Gals and Old Ones

IF you happens to be the fortinit possessor ove one ove them interestin, an' mos' unfathomabil mackinisms, called a darter (Matilda Japonica Jane, for instance), an' she is old enuff tu cultivate a peck poke ove hoss har, on the back ove her head, an' properly 'preshiate the vartue an' purvailin power ove cinament draps, an' dime photographs; an' then eny vile cuss in tight britches, an' a biled shut, a totin a cow catcher, or a cattipillar mustach, commences a consultin ove you, an' then keeps on a consultin ove you, on the feezability ove his 'stablishing a seventy-five thousin spindle cotton factory, with a hoop skirt and paper collar attachmint some whar in your back calf pastur—jist you summins morril courige tu your aid, an' tell him in deep base english to go to h—l. An' then, by golly, du yu see tu hit, that he immejuntly obeys yu.

On secon' tho'ts, I b'leve I'd advise, say, somewhar about thirty grains ove the same perscripshun, tu be 'ministered "sub linen ah" tu that aforesed mackinism ove yourn, distributed atwixt the hoss har honets nes' an' the groun', on the same side ove the questin—neither favorin' the upper or lower regins, but sorter bunchin' hit on the neutral groun', you know, a kind o' splittin' the difference atwixt the naik an' the heel strings, whar thar's room. Then, p'raps hit mout be as well to foller hit up with a sprinkle ove keean pepper, as a 'mollient. Yes, I think I would, jist for the benefit ove posterity, if nuthin else; not that I keers much about posterity, no way, for hit bids powerful fair to be rale ornary, the way the present is runnin' the thing. It's rather feard that the comin' crop ove brains aint in perporshun tu the tremenjus efforts now bein' made, in all sorts of sile, to grow skulls. Hit won't do eny harm tu set back Matilda Japonica Jane a year or so, eny how. Thar's more babys now than thar's plows.

("Sut" must have been scalded, scratched or scolded, by some worthy spinster. Just hear how the "durn'd fool" goes on to rail—to "onbuzzum hisse'f," as he calls it. He must already be bald-headed, or he would never venture so recklessly. We tremble for him).

Haint hit strange that a gall (when hit's so ordered for her) can't jist run on to old maidenhood smilen, an' smooth, as they dus intu the popular rut ove cradle rocken an' callimus tea bilen. But they can't. Scarcely one ove 'em ken ever take up the crosses ove a one legged fireplace, whar the tongs has no shovel, or the privashuns ove a one hoss bedstid, eny ways gently. They soon gits nervous and skeery, 'maginin vain things, an' givin' tharsefs up tu a fightin' virtue, an' a ghostly prudery, that's tarryfyin' tu behold in one so knowin', and with sich a tenduncy to ever sot bristles, an' sich a apetite for bitein or scratchin' sumfin he.

Them they firmly believes in, an o' nights dreams ove a great big, hairy man, with a mane like a lion, an' tushes like a hog, a constanly lyin' in wait, ahine the ash hopper, ahine the chimley, ahine everything, watchin' for them—them individooly by-golly! to grab 'em, an' tote 'em "viney eat armies," in spite ove bar darnin needle, bodkin, an' rectitude, strait fornint an onrelentin passun, who with holybook, an' sober look, hands 'em over 'cordin tu law, to the wrath tu cum, an' double geers. In the dim distance, too, they dreams that they see shaddowy high posters, with drawn curtains, floating cradles, fleecy, cloud like caticornered napkins, an' smokin pap porringers, while the ghost ove a barfooted, bald headed man sits a rockin, rockin, still a rockin—sumfin, she knows what. She sees too, his empty britches, like a banner of doom, a swingin in the wind, from a nail drove in the distant sky, an' *that,* by golly! wakes her, tu find herself a huggin one aind ove the bolster, while her locked feet purvents t'other aind ove hit from kickin or cuttin up.

I tell you now, that when a gall is alowed to run to seed, thar is jis' no knowin what they can't 'madgine, or won't do, except tu go strait along, like they didn't mind hit. I mus' say tho', in justice to them unfortunits, what haint faced a perposal, or a passun, that the very bes' 'oman that I ever know'd, in my whole life, was a old maid, but then, you mus' bar in mine, she were my own mammy. But then, on tother han', the very worst one I ever seed, wer a old maid too; she warn't anybody's mammy, but she pizened a widders spring—run a two hundred poun' bachelor, intu the fastest kine, ove a gallopin consumpshun, an' then play'd hyena at his grave.

Dad shave me, if I ain't sorter skeery ove the las' one ove 'em, prim, trim, an proper, as they looks. Yea hoss, verily I watches 'em; a body don't know—you know.

Knoxville *Daily Press and Herald*, May 13, 1869.

Sut Lovingood Sets Up with a Gal—
One Pop Baily

By the light of the campfire, after a hunter's supper, enjoyed with a hunter's appetite, I am reading aloud Elizabeth Barret's description of a kiss.

> ——— "A ring of amethyst
> I could not wear, were plainer to my sight
> Than that first kiss. The second passed in height
> The first, and sought the forehead; and half missed,
> Falling upon my hair."

"Stop, stop, George. Duz you happen to know what was the matter thar?"
No, Sut, do you?
"By gravy, I duz. *She dodged.* They'l all do it, an' its a powerful pestersome trick ove theirn, it is. A poor feller is bad enough off, at sich times eny how, without the 'saitful pests, a movin his target, arter he's done pull'd trigger. Dad shave 'em all, I say.

"Let *me* tell you somethin a barin on the pint. You all know—everybody duz—that besides bein a nat'ral bornd fool, clean in to the peth, I is as awkward as a left-handed foot adze, with an injun rubber helve, when I is amung the wimmen folks. Thar's kissin ove 'em, for instance, as you has jist read about. Hits a juty that must be gone through with, if you likes peace better nor you does a freshly grub'd bald head; yet somehow I allways manages to make a momox ove the juty—the kiss, an' now an' then the gal, every time I goes for hit. I reccon its becauze I don't set much store by the article nohow. Hit's sorter like hot soup, not very fattenin—jist a forerunnin shadder ove vittils, that's all. But the wimmen folks seems to think its somethin worth fightin for—so we must sorter "let on," you know, or thar'd never be a mouthful ove sweet milk about the house. They'd "thunder-slay" it afore it was strain'd.

"I hearn 'Tilda Hood, a store clothse gal, with high heels, an' a fringed fan, say that when Doctor Boggis kiss'd *her*, hit felt like as tho' a hummin bird, as big as a speckled hen, wer playin a stream ove wild honey down her throat, about the size ove a woosted bell cord, while he fan'd her cheeks with wings scented with bargamot an' sparklin with spangles, ontil she seed a rouzin big hoop skirt in the sky, made ove rainbows, an' hearn a mockin bird a whistlin Fisher's hornpipe in her nose, an' that she woudent a holler'd, if she could. Well, maybe she woudent. These store clothse folks has some mighty curious ways, any how. But thars Denizade Snodgrass, a home made, nat'ral gal, built out ove live meat an' blood, an' har, an' sich, arter fust fightin me all over the yard, went an' told it,—that I kissed 'like flingin a poor, flanky, slab ove raw beef again a stone chimley. Hit stuck fas' an' *smelt fraish*.' That ar Snodgrass gal is too durned smart to be rale healthy anyhow, an' her kissin's no better than any other gals, what keeps thar mouths wiped. I kin kiss an' fly loose as slick as she ken, dad rabbit 'er!

"Now, jist to show you what a pervokin, great lummox I is, I'l tell you all what happened to a right peart gal named Pop Baily. I wer a settin up with 'er, one night at her house, an' she wer in a rale expectunt frame ove mind, from the way she kept on a sighin, an' a lookin in the fire. Her fat, wholesome old mammy had knit herse'f asleep, leanin back again the chimley jamb; her pipe had fell in her buzzum an' the stem stuck out like the handle ove a stew pan, while the cat play'd with her yarn ball on the hath.

"Thinks I, I'd best indulge right now. So I begin to take an off han' sight at Pop's mouth, as well as I could, by the light ove the embers. Jist as soon as she seed me a bowin my naik, up she got an' sot a pot ove lye hominey, that were a gurglin an' a simmerin in the corner, squar in front ove the pile ove embers, sayin, 'Thar, now, I reccon maybe *you'l* bile.' Then she sot herse'f back in her chair, cross'd her han's, an' set up my target again, pufeckly fair for me to shoot, she purtendin to be in a doze. *Bile*, the devil! The 'saitful huzzy. She'd sot the hominy pot so as to cast a big shadder all over her face, an' that's what spiled my shootin.

"Ah! lordy, boys, how they all does love a *show* ove

shyness. Well, when I tho't that I had a rale fine sight, jist about a short inch below her snout, I pull'd trigger. I mus' do her the jestice to say that *she* dident dodge a bit, for she wer a dozin, you know, but still, I hit her in a thicket ove curls, atwix the eye and the year, greazin my snout slick with old hogs fat. I wiped off the scent ove hit, as well as I could, on my sleeve, an' listened to hear if the old 'oman still snored. I wer feared to look round, least Pop mout wake up, you know, an' *move my board*. I foun' when I got my buzzin years sorter quieted that she *wer* a snorein—that is, if you'd call a hoss snortin in a copper still, snorein. So I fixes up for another shot, an' don't you believe? I hit her on the throat this time, an' her sleepin calm an' still as a baby—an' hit sounded like drappin ove an oven led *flat* into a tub ove cow slop. Dad shave me, boys! If I warnt stone bline for a moment, an' when I did come to see, the room wer full of lightenin bugs, a hummin like bees, an' my laigs wer asleep. Pop fairly flounced out ove the chair, an' tuck up the ladder to bed, so *mad* that she smoked. Jist afore her head got into the loft, she turn'd round on the rungs, with her years flat on her naik, an' her eyes as green as a bottle, an' sez she, in a rale cat hiss, 'If I had a blind male that cudent fine its own stable door at *two* trials, I'd jist cut its dad blasted throat, so I would.' Then her stockins flash'd out ove sight, an' about the time I hearn her empty shoes drap hard on the loft floor, I found out that I was 'settin up' with a hominy pot. I studied a power to find out next who I was, an' what wer the matter with whoever I mout be. The old 'oman's laig, that hung down on my side ove the chair, were seemingly spinnin round so fast that her foot looked like a wheel, an' I'l swar I hearn hit hum.

"Presently, in comes the old man from huntin, with a yearlin deer slung on his back, an' a rifle gun on his shoulder that I thought had about twenty-nine barrels. His stompin the snow off ove his feet waked the old 'oman up. So drawin her pipe out ove her buzzum, like hit was a bowie knife, she ax'd him, 'Dident—you—*shoot*, wonst or twise't awhile ago, old man?' He never answered her, but takin a 'stonished sort ove look at me, sed, Why, you blasted, hongry lookin galiniper, what have you been doin? Been a spoonin in Moll's hominy, haint you?'

"Pop hollered down, 'Oh! no pap, if you wer to take the led off, an' hold a torch, *that thing* haint sence enuff to git the spoon into the pot, atwix this and Chrismus, an' if he did, he'd fetch it out empty—I wish if you aint *too* tired, pap, that you'd jist kick 'im out.' I sorter come to myse'f at this, an' midnight as it wer, I walked two miles to git to a still house. I wer powerfully tuck down, I tell you—I gin the matter a whole Sunday's study, an' at last the idear struck me how to make a centre shot, every pop, an' I haint made ara gal mad since—*that* I haint."

How do you manage, Sut—sneak up on your target, as you call it?

"N—o, not adzackly. I jist makes a target out ove myse'f, an' then lets 'em do all the shootin. I tell you boys, I likes the plan, for besides thar bein all dead sure aim, I think the flimsy truck tastes better than when you go arter hit yourse'f. You see them jist keep a comein a lettle closter, an' a lettle closter—thar eyes half shut, with a 'you stan' still now, sir,' sort ove a look, an' as they fastens to you, they finishes shettin 'em. Then, when they hears the report, they blares 'em wide open, makin 'em ax you the question as plain as thar tongue cood, 'Why, what upon the face ove the yeath was *that?*' Then, hoss, is the tickilish time *with you,* for if you aint *very* keerful how you kerries yersef, they'l fall into spittin an' scratchin immejuntly, an' they'l cross bar yer snout with their nails, a heap quicker nor a cat could, with a wooden clothse pin sprung on her tail. Powerful provokin critters am wimmen, powerful provokin in*deed*. I can't raley hate 'em tho', for they do leave a good taste in a body's mouth, sometimes. Don't they? Ha! ha! Now watch me cut the 'pigeon wing' in these yere ashes."

Knoxville *Press and Messenger*, September 29, 1869.

Glossary

admistration, administration.
adzactly, adzacly, exactly.
ager, ague, or malaria.
aind, end.
allers, always.
apupos, apupus, on purpose.
aquafortis, aquafotis, aka-fortis, aqua fortis, or nitric acid.
ara, any (conventionally spelled *ary*).
arrer, arrow.
arter, ater, after.
arterards, afterwards.
asnick, arsenic.
Ataylanty, Atlanty, Atlanta.
ax, axes, ask, asks.

bainch, banch, bench.
balluns, balance.
bar, bare.
bargamint, bargamot, bergamot.
barlm, balm.
beyant, beyond.
bizzy, buzzy, busy.
'bolitionist, abolitionist.
'bominabil, abominable.
breff, breath.
bunnit, bonnet.
buty, beauty.
buzzim, buzzum, bosom.

cackus, carcass.
calliker, calico.
camfir, camphor.
canyun, cannon.
cashuns, occasions.
casiron, cast-iron.
casteel, Castile (Spanish).
caze, because.
ceroon, seroon, a bale or package covered with hide.
cheer, chair.
childer, children.
chinkepin, chinquapin.
chock, chalk.
claws, clause.
cloff, cloth.
close, clothes.

compus, compass.
co'n, corn.
consekinses, consequences.
crap, crop.
crassis, crosses.
critters, creatures.
cullar, collar.
cumpasmint, cumpassin, encompassment, encompassing.

daik, deck.
delicate, delegate.
Delishus Tremenjus, delerium tremens.
deserlashun, desolation.
devarsed, divorced.
devarshun, diversion.
diamunt, dimunt, diamond.
diarrear, diarrhea.
discomboberate, to confuse, upset, put out of order.
dogratipe, dogratype, daguerreotype.
dost, dose.
drofful, dreadful.
dulcimore, dulcimer.
duller, dollar.
'dult'rs, adulterers.

eatch, itch.
edicated, educated.
eshenshully, essentially.
et, ate, eaten.
eucher, euchre, to defeat at euchre (a card game), hence, to defeat in any scheme.
"Exelcider," "Excelsior," a poem by Henry Wadsworth Longfellow.
exhite, excite.
explites, exploits.

feeters, features.
fice, feist.
Firginny, Firginey, "Virginny," or Virginia.
flanin, flannen, dialect for flannel.
flummey, flummery.
flure, floor.

flusterashun, flustration.
fokis, focus.
fornint, furnint, fornent, opposite to or facing.
forred, forehead.
fortin, fortune.
fotch, brought.
froat, throat.
fus', first.

geminey, geminy, jeminy, a mild oath or expletive, as in Jiminy Cricket!; alteration of *gemini,* third sign of the zodiac.
genus, genius.
gesters, gestures.
gin, give.
glut, a block of wood or metal, often tapered, used as a wedge or lever fulcrum.
'goshiate, negotiate.
grashus, gracious.

hame, ham.
hamon, probably the treacherous Haman in the Book of Esther.
har, hair.
hath, hearth.
hed, head; had.
heving, heaven.
hit, it.
hole, whole.
ho'n, horn.
hone (for or after), desire, want, yearn.
hoss, horse.
hossler, hostler.
huffs, hooves.
huzzy, hussy.

ilin, oiling.
imedjut, imijut, immediate.
immegintly, immejeretly, imejuntly, immediately.
imperdint, impudent.
infunel, infurnel, infernal.
ingine, injine, engine.
injurance, endurance.
insex, insects.
interjuice, introduce.
intermitly, intermittently.
interpersision, interposition.

inyin, onion.
iseter, ister, oyster.
isoo, issue.

Jamakey, Jamaica.
jestis, justice.
jis', just.
jise, jist, joist.
juty, duty.

ken, can.
kerds, cards.
kerrin, carrying.
kers, cars.
kin, can.
kitchen, catching.
kiver, cover.
konsekenses, consequences.

lecterin, lecturing.
licins, license.
lor, law.

maladickshun, malediction.
mar, mare.
martingil, martingale.
marvils, marbles.
melt, milt.
menyfeld, manifold.
mercheen, mershean, machine.
merlatter, mulatto.
merlennium, merleanyum, millenium.
merlignerty, malignity.
meterfistickal, metaphysical.
mine, mind.
minners, minnows.
miserlanus, miscellaneous.
momox, mommix, a mess.
mons'ous, mons'us, mouns'us, monstrous.
morril, moral.
mossel, morsel.
mouf, mouth.
mout, might.
mucement, amusement.
mullygrubs, mulligrubs, a melancholy, despondent mood, dejection, the "blues."
munny, muny, money.
mustachus, moustaches.

naseun, nation.
nater, nature.

GLOSSARY

ni ontu, nearly.
nise, nice; noise.
no, know.
Noth Caliny, North Carolina.
nuffin, nothing.

oaf, oath.
'oman, woman.
on, of.
onekeled, unequaled.
onintemitant, onintermittunt, unintermittent.
onkimon, uncommon.
onst, once.
onvartus, unvirtuous.
orfully, awfully.
orter, ought to, ought to have.
orthur, author.
ossifers, officers.
ove, ov, of.

panady, panada, a bread dish.
par, pair.
passun, parson.
pattrin, pattern.
patren, patron.
payrint, an exclamation, meaning uncertain.
peanor, piano.
pepil, people.
perjuce, produce.
permiskusly, promiscuously.
perporshun, proportion.
perpryiter, proprietor.
peth, pith.
Pherlistshuns, Philistines.
picter, picture.
piedied, pied-eyed.
pint, point.
p'isen, pizen, poison.
pissant, pisant, dialect word for the ant.
pius, pious.
pomgranatin', promenading.
'pose, oppose.
poshole, posthole.
preferens, preference.
proverdensally, providentially.
pufeck, perfect.
pupus, purpose.
puss, purse.
pusson, person.

Qbrute, cube root.
quile, coil.
quirl, curl.

rale, real.
rar, rear.
rase, race.
rastil, wrestle.
rayshure, raysure, razor.
red, read.
redicule, reticule.
regin, region.
rezin, resin.
rosim, rosin.
ruff, roof.
ruinate, ruin.

'saitful, deceitful.
salt, assault.
sarcus, sarkis, circus.
sarmints, sermons.
sashararer mitimurs, certioraris mittimus (Latin legal terminology).
sassengers, sausages.
sasser, saucer.
scase, scarce.
scrimpshun, scrimption.
seck, sect.
seckshun, section.
shears, shares.
shiff, shift.
shuck, shook.
shut, shirt.
sile, soil.
sirsingle, susingil, surcingle.
site, sight.
skeer, scare.
skringe, cringe.
skulp, scalp.
skyance, science.
slunge, slounge (alteration of slouch, under influence of lounge).
slutch, slouch.
smoof, smooth.
snaffil, snaffle.
snaix, snakes.
soger, sojer, soljer, soldier.
solemcoly, solemncholy, or dejection, melancholy.
solt, salt.
sorrer, sorrow.

sot, set.
sow, sew.
speck, expect.
'sperence, experience.
spontanashusly, spontaneously.
squ't, squirt.
statoot, statue.
stomp, stamp.
straich, stretch.
strike-nine, strychnine (whisky, a very inferior type).
stud, stood.
suah, sure.
suckil, circle; suckle.
suckit, surkit, circuit.
'sult, insult.
sumerset, summerset, somersault.
supener, supeaner, subpoena.
surgistshun, suggestion.
surjestif, suggestive.
suvig, savage.
swingltress, swingletrees, or whiffletrees.

taller, tallow.
tangerbil, tangible.
tarifick, terrific.
'tarnil, eternal.
tavrin, tavern.
terbacker, tobacco.
termatis, tomato.
tetchus, touchy.
torreckly, directly.
trowsis, trousers.
truff, truth.
tu, to; too.
tuckil, turkle, turtle.

tumil, tumble.
twist, twiste, twiest, twice.

umeraller, umereller, umbrella.
unick, eunuch.

vagerbone, vagabond.
valerabil, valuable.
valuer, value.
vardic, verdict.
vartu, virtue.
venter, venture.
vide, divide.
vise, voice.

waisbun, waistband.
wallid, walled (past participle of verb wall, to roll one's eyes in expression of emotion).
warin, wearing.
warnut, walnut.
warrun, warrant.
wifin, within.
woffil, waffle.
wuf, worth.
wum, wurim, worm.
wun, one.
wus, worse.

yamp, steal, "swipe."
yearly, early.
yearnis, earnest.
years, ears.
yeath, earth.
yere, here.
yerk, dialect for jerk, or to cause to move abruptly or suddenly.